Dack Meyers

W9-BXN-543

INSTRUCTIONAL
MATERIALS CENTERS

Selected Readings

by

Neville P. Pearson
Associate Professor
University of Minnesota
College of Education

and

Lucius Butler
Assistant Professor
University of Hawaii
College of Education

Burgess Publishing Company

426 South Sixth Street • Minneapolis, Minn. 55415

Copyright © 1969 by Burgess Publishing Company
All rights reserved. Printed in the United States of America
Library of Congress Catalog Number 76-91287
Standard Book Number 8087-1627-1

Second Printing 1970
Third Printing 1970

FOREWORD

Any confrontation with the changes being recommended or implemented in today's schools appears to produce conflicting responses and emotions. Whether the information about these changes is acquired by observation, through the reading of professional literature, or by hearsay, it is obvious that education does not lack for ideas or for a variety of responses to them. All facets of the educational program are being examined, discussed, evaluated, and the results are apparent in everything from the structure of the building to the schedule of classes.

Unfortunately, the number of schools being spurred to action, or even to careful study of innovative proposals, does not appear to be large, nor is it growing with any speed, deliberate or otherwise. This is critical, unless we do not believe that education has a major responsibility for helping to find solutions for society's problems. It also has special meaning for all media specialists. At some point in the schools' successful utilization of any innovations, there is a demand for the resources and the services of an instructional materials center, or in the terminology of the new national standards, a media center. Secondly, as professionals in these centers we have access to all the sources of information - the books, the films, the periodicals, the recordings that carry the ideas and the information needed to stimulate both thought and action. In addition, we also have greater daily access to all of the teachers than anyone else in the school.

Are we then, as media specialists, as media educators, not challenged to put these factors together to speed the development of media centers in all schools? Can we not assume an active role in bringing about desirable change by doing a better job of buying and promoting the use of professional materials? Dr. Pearson's collection provides a welcome convenient source of articles dealing with the materials center concept and should make it easier for all of us to become change agents now.

The recommendations in the recent publication, *Standards for School Media Programs,* prepared by a joint committee of the Department of Audio-visual Instruction and the American Association of School Librarians, also make this compilation a timely one. The inclusion of articles from periodicals covering a period of about ten years makes it possible to trace the growth of the media center concept, and to select those ideas most pertinent to a particular situation. The compilation will also help to interpret the materials center at both the preservice and the inservice training levels.

Ruth M. Erstad
Supervisor
School Libraries
State of Minnesota

PREFACE

The School Library has changed. The silence and austerity of the room housing the book collection has given way to the hum of exciting activity. Students are listening to stored sound, looking at films or television, and generally learning much more than they did in the traditional library of the past. The room itself is apt to be carpeted and colorful. Individual study carrels/wet (with multi-media facilities) and dry (private work/study stations) are available. The librarian has assistants who help the students locate materials. These assistants serve as extensions of the classroom teacher in helping the students learn. This room or suite of rooms, this learning center, may still be labeled a library. More likely it is called the Instructional Materials Center, or the Resources or Materials Center, or the Learning Center — but it is not the old library.

Because many schools are still in the transitional stage between the library and the expanded services of an IMC, and because media people, now being trained, need the wise advice of people who have experienced the development of the IMC, this book of readings was developed.

In selecting these articles we have tried to present the how and the why; articles about problems; articles about budget; articles on the IMC, from the elementary school, the junior high school, the senior high school, the total school district, the junior college and the four-year college and university. Articles from the past decade were considered and some ten years old are included in the collection. Because different magazines have used different authors, we have selected articles from 31 periodicals. *AUDIOVISUAL INSTRUCTION* has contributed most, but the *LIBRARY JOURNAL* and other periodicals have contributed several articles. More than 50 periodicals were studied in our search for these articles. From the magazines the 83 articles in the collection representing the work of 87 authors were selected. Because of publication limitations many articles originally considered had to be eliminated. A list of additional references is included.

This collection of readings may be used as a basis for a course for media people and directors of instructional materials centers. The collection should be useful to school administrators who want to understand the thinking behind the IMC. The collection should also assist librarians or audio-visual material people who are seeking information about other types of media and solutions to the problems brought about by unification of two departments.

Dr. Butler and I express our thanks to the authors and to the original publishers for permission to use their articles. We appreciate the gracious assistance of the Burgess Publishing Company and especially their representative, Mrs. Julie Paulson. Appreciation is also expressed to Dr. Jan Fusaro and Emma Storsteen for assistance in the selection of articles, to Lorna Borman who served as the proof editor, and to Ruth Ersted for her valuable introduction. To all others who have assisted in making this collection of readings possible we also say "thank you".

Neville Pearson, Ph.D.
Associate Professor
Education
University of Minnesota
August 1969

TABLE OF CONTENTS

Section One

THE PHILOSOPHY
OF THE IMC

THE INSTRUCTIONAL SERVICE CENTER: A NEW CONCEPT?

Jerry J. Herman

The concept of an instructional service center developed from some grass-roots questions such as: Can we make use of our personnel? Is there not a lot of overlap in situations where a teacher would like help in science? For example, the helping teacher would be asked for assistance by the classroom teacher. In turn, the science consultant would be contacted for demonstration purposes; the audio-visual director would be contacted for films, filmstrips, etc., and the librarian would be contacted for supplementary reading materials.

Such questions promoted a year's study by a committee of principals, all specialized personnel involved, and the assistant superintendent for instruction. The results of their efforts are presented in the novel concept discussed in the remainder of this paper.

What is the instructional service center?

The title, instructional service center, is descriptive of the underlying philo-sophic basis for the rather unorthodox combination of the services of academic consultants, elementary librarians, audio-visual personnel, and helping teachers. An elaboration of the specific title words will add some depth to the implica-tions of such an organization:

1. **Instructional** — this word is to be interpreted in the broadest sense of the term. All aspects of the instructional program can be enriched by the active involvement of the Center's personnel.

2. **Service** — this term truly implies the necessary dedication of personnel in-cluded in the Center. The services provided by members of the Center to the students and teachers of the school district will proportionately determine the degree of success achieved. Displaying a personality which permits harmonious relations with lay helpers, students, and teachers is a prerequisite, upon which specific skills are built.

3. **Center** — This is a paradoxical term. It implies, justifiably, the coordina-tion of numerous enrichment materials, supplies, and equipment. Contrary to this, it implies an auxiliary service — one which exists solely for the purpose of enriching the educational environment of children.

Reprinted with permission from: Herman, Jerry J., "The Instructional Service Center," SCHOOL BOARD JOURNAL, February, 1964.

Finally, through the media and services available in the Instructional Service Center. It is firmly believed that maximum coordinated services will be offered to a degree which would be impossible to provide by a segmented organization of such services.

What are the specific purposes of the center?

The major specific purposes of the Center are eight in number:

1. To combine a variety of specialized services in such a way that teachers are given maximum assistance in the enrichment of the educational environment of the individual student.

2. To organize the mechanical aspects of the specialized services in such a way that maximum information is given and motivation promoted, while a high degree of efficiency is maintained and the cost of such service is minimized.

3. To provide such materials, supplies, demonstrations, and assistance as are deemed necessary for the continuous enrichment of curricular offerings, while giving foremost consideration to the varied interests, abilities, achievements, and maturities of the students to be served.

4. To provide a single clearinghouse wherein teachers and students are provided speedy and easy access to the variety of instructional materials, equipments, and supplies which are not readily housed or controlled at the local building level.

5. To locate, collect, arrange, catalog, and distribute materials, informations, and supplies which are pertinent to and amplify upon the curricular offerings.

6. To assist teachers to help children grow in knowledge and skill by generating and understanding of and a desire for expanded learnings.

7. To provide advisory services in the procurement, preparation, distribution, uses, evaluation, storage, and maintenance of supplies and equipment.

8. To promote, through the media of planned in-service education programs, such understandings as are necessary to motivate maximum teacher and student use of the variety of enrichment services available.

Is there a need for specific job descriptions which eliminate overlap but provide for built-in coordination?

Yes, specific job descriptions are absolutely necessary to provide for a smooth-running organization. The job descriptions for the Center's personnel are provided in outline form:

Functions and duties of academic consultants:

1. Serves as a consultant, in his area of specialty, to the educational staff and works under the supervision of the assistant superintendent for instruction or an assigned administrator.

2. Exercises leadership in the construction and implementation of a K-12 curriculum program in his area of specialty.

3. Promotes, through leadership ability, top-quality education in his area of specialty by assisting and carrying out projects, developmental units, display, exhibits, etc.

4. Holds in-service workshops dealing with his area of specialty where needed and requested.

5. Provides lectures and demonstrations upon request for classes or staff members. These services are designed as supplements to the regular work done by the classroom teacher.

6. Works with individual teachers upon request of the teacher or principal in in order to aid the teacher in unit planning or program evaluation.

7. Assists teachers in locating resource materials in his area of specialty.

8. Keeps abreast of current research and developments in his area of specialty, and helps teachers to integrate these findings into the curriculum.

9. Prepares manuals, bulletins, catalogs, and lesson units related to the teachers of his area of specialization.

10. Assists in maintaining a subject field library of professional materials to be used by teachers when needed as resource materials or for background information.

11. Serves as a budgetary advisor and purchasing advisor in the area of his specialty.

12. Assists the Instructional Service Center staff in the production and distribution of locally created supplies and materials.

13. Supervises the Instructional Service Center staff in the maintenance of materials in his area of specialization.

14. Makes periodic reports to the assistant superintendent for instruction and to the public.

15. Services community and school groups with programs and information regarding the curriculum in his area of specialization.

16. Acts as a resource person in such areas as outdoor education.

17. Contributes to the curriculum bulletin.

18. Keeps an inventory of all major supplies and equipment.

19. Maintains a continuous program of evaluation.

20. Conducts an annual inventory of materials and equipment.

Functions and duties of helping teachers:

1. To serve all members of the professional staff and to work under the supervision of the assistant superintendent for instruction or an assigned administrator.

2. To originate and maintain a community resource file of speakers available to the instructional staff, and to maintain an up-to-date field-trip file.

3. To oversee the professional library which shall be cataloged by the elementary library consultant.

4. To assist any teacher at any grade level, K-12, who requests aid in whichever area a felt need exists. A principal may also request such assistance for specific teachers. Special attention shall be given to teachers new to the system.

5. To augment administration by interpreting policies and procedures to individual staff members.

6. To promulgate and disseminate the best ideas for most effective instruction.

7. To provide displays of students' work in such a way as to inform the administration of the level of student achievement.

8. To participate in in-service and curricular programs.

9. To assist with the testing program in unique situations.

10. To act as a resource person in classroom situations and in the outdoor education program.

11. To maintain files of materials and records that will prove useful to the instructional staff.

12. To assist individuals and groups in unit planning.

13. To contribute to the curriculum bulletin.

Functions and duties of the instructional materials consultants:

1. Serves as a consultant to the educational staff and works under the supervision of the assistant superintendent for instruction or an assigned administrator.

2. Contributes to the curriculum bulletin.

3. Prepares catalogs, coded cards, bulletins, and units on the use of audio-visual materials.

4. Promotes understanding of audio-visual equipment and materials by conducting workshops and demonstrations.

5. Coordinates instructional aids with the curricular programs.

6. Previews, examines, and evaluates instructional aids and audio-visual equipment.

7. Visits individual teachers and school buildings in order to determine uses and needs in the area of instructional materials and equipment.

8. Supervises the clerical staff in the control of the film rental program by seeing that the clerks:

   a. Keep an account of each individual building's film budget

   b. Order films

   c. Keep record of film confirmations

   d. Notify schools when films are confirmed

   e. Distribute films to the proper school upon arrival

   f. Return films to the proper source.

9. Notifies the building principals of the free films which are available, and those which can be ordered directly by the school principal.

10. Assists in the selection and ordering of instructional aids and equipment.

11. Orders the day-to-day equipment and office supplies necessary for the operation of the Instructional Materials Center.

12. Maintains a file of repair orders, and sees to it that the equipment is repaired by the proper source.

13. Develops the forms which are necessary for the smooth operation of the Instructional Materials Center.

14. Distributes, to all schools, information on free aids, catalogs, etc.

15. Keeps an inventory of all supplies, equipment, and accessories.

16. Promotes and supervises local production work.

17. Supervises the clerical staff in the processing, inspecting, and repairing of 16mm. films and filmstrips.

18. Provides materials which blend into and enrich the school curriculum.

19. Assists in planning basic audio-visual collections for the individual schools and for the Instructional Materials Center.

20. Maintains a continuous program of evaluation.

21. Conducts an annual inventory of all materials and equipment.

Functions and duties of the elementary library consultants:

1. Serves as a consultant to the educational staff and works under the supervision of the assistant superintendent for instruction or an assigned administrator.

2. Contributes to the curriculum bulletin.

3. Assists in the in-service program of lay persons who are assisting in the individual elementary libraries, and supervises the classification of all books by the Dewey Decimal system.

4. Develops and instructs library classes for students.

5. Assists in planning basic library collections for the individual schools.

6. Catalogs and maintains a professional library.

7. Assists in the planning of library budgets.

8. Develops organizational procedures for library materials.

9. Acquaints teachers with the availability and uses of library resource materials.

10. Assists in the total curriculum programs by providing library enrichment materials.

11. Maintains an inventory, shelf cards, etc., in the individual building's libraries.

12. Coordinates the programs of library service and instruction among the several elementary schools.

13. Assists the professional staff in evaluating and selecting of library materials.

14. Directs the processing of all library materials.

15. Interprets the functions and needs of the elementary libraries.

16. Maintains a continuous program of evaluation.

17. Supervises the clerical staff assigned to the library section of the Instructional Service Center.

18. Conducts an annual inventory of library books and materials.

What is the scope of such an operation?

The broadened scope of the Center's operation necessitated a delineation of the divided responsibility involved between an individual building and the central operation. A brief delineation of responsibility, in outline form, is presented on the following page:

DESCRIPTIVE SCOPE OF OPERATION BY MATERIAL TYPE

Type	Individual Buildings	Comments	Central Operation
1. Library books	All	Basic minimum collection at each building; cataloguing	None
2. Supplementary texts	All	No cataloguing	None
3. Professional library books	None	Catalogued	All
4. Films	None	Basic policy rental; limited purchase – set up listing of needs on priorities	All
5. Filmstrips	Limited	Basic minimum collection of each building. Make up listing	Majority
6. Transparencies	. . . .	Catalogue central collection	Production
7. Pictures	. . . .	No cataloguing	Location and distribution
8. Tapes	None	Catalogued	All
9. Record disks	Yes	Catalogue only central collection	Yes
10. Slides	None	Catalogued	All
11. Pamphlets, bulletins, etc.	All	No cataloguing	None
12. Models	Both	Major items catalogued; complete inventory	Both
13. Felt, etc., materials	All	No records	None
14. Kits	None	Catalogued	All
15. Free and inexpensive materials	All	No cataloguing	Information
16. Curriculum library	None	No cataloguing	All
17. Encyclopedias and dictionaries	All	Inventory, but no cataloguing	None
18. Maps, globes, charts	All	Inventory, but no cataloguing	None
19. Field trips	Control	. . . .	Information
20. Community lecturers, etc.	Control	. . . .	Information
21. Books that list free and inexpensive materials	. . . .	Each building and central have one complete set. No cataloguing	. . . .
22. Paintings and reproductions	None	Catalogued	All

Why is this organizational scheme reported?

The sole reason for writing of this organizational pattern is so that other districts might wish to attempt a novel approach to services which they already provide. Certainly educators have a dual obligation: (1) to make the most efficient use of all services and personnel in order to improve the educational environment of each student and, (2) to practice financial economy to the extent that valuable services are not curtailed.

It is believed, by the writer, that such a novel organization provides a very economical approach to maximum services for school districts. Further, curriculum which is the heart of any educational institution, will be enhanced immensely by the organization of an instructional service center.

ROLE AND FUNCTION OF THE INSTRUCTIONAL MATERIALS CENTER

William C. Miller

An educator's life is never dull and our lives have been filled of late with more than the usual number of explosions. The population explosion has filled our classrooms, and the explosion of knowledge has filled our waking hours. There has also been an explosive-like revolution in teaching methods and in the amount of material created for instructional purposes.

Aiding teachers and students in dealing with the flood of knowledge, assisting them in using the wealth of instructional aids now available, and helping them to employ effectively the methods and "hardware" of the new teaching technology is the function of an *instructional materials center.* The concept of a unified service including both library and audio-visual materials is receiving rapid acceptance among educators. Whether it is called "materials center," "curriculum laboratory," or "learning resources library," its purpose is to help create a richer learning environment through providing appropriate learning materials, experiences and resources.

What is a materials center?

In materials centers all learning materials have equal status and receive consideration. The collection may contain the whole range of materials used in teaching. Printed matter such as books, pamphlets, periodicals — audio-visual material such as slides, filmstrips, recordings and the equipment needed to use them are equally available to teachers and students. Free and inexpensive materials, charts, clippings, globes and maps are also included, as are the less common but useful items such as models, specimens, dioramas.

Some centers have equipment which may seem unusual but which makes sense because of the school's instructional program. Production of simple school-made instructional materials using photographic equipment and lettering devices often takes place in the center. Some materials centers in elementary schools have a sewing machine for use in making costumes for dramatizations and others have simple woodworking tools. Art supplies beyond those which are kept in each classroom are often a part of the center's collection.

Ideas, too, are part of the center. Bulletin board materials and suggestions, exhibit and display ideas, scripts, field trip and community resources files, and

Reprinted with permission from: Miller, William C., "Role and Function of the Instructional Materials Center," EDUCATIONAL LEADERSHIP, March, 1961.

all manner of things which will make instruction more effective are housed in the center. Professional books and periodicals as well as units of work and demonstration suggestions are also available.

The most important characteristic of an effective instructional materials center is its skilled staff. A mature, experienced, and creative professional person who enjoys helping teachers and students is the keystone of an effective program. Skill and knowledge in the total field of instructional materials are a necessity, as is a good understanding of child growth and development and principles of learning. Given adequate clerical help and funds, such a person can markedly influence teaching practices.

What a center contains and what services it offers depends on the type of school curriculum it serves. What is appropriate for one school may not be logical for a school of the same size in a nearby district. The purpose of a center is to improve instruction through service to teachers and pupils. Since each teacher, each building staff, and the needs of youngsters in each school are different, there should be variation in the program of service.

How is a materials center used?

Varied activites take place in a center. Teachers inquire about, order, preview or make the materials they need to do an effective teaching job. The materials specialist gives guidance in securing and using materials. Resource units and good ideas employed by other teachers are shared. Students ask for data for research purposes or for a practical project such as making a model. They secure information about resource people or field trips they might take. Administrators and curriculum people receive help in planning effective teachers' meetings or preparing booklets or posters for public relations purposes.

At times a total class will come with a teacher to learn about research tools or to use the center's other resources. Often individuals and small groups will be at work finding information by examining printed or audio-visual materials. Materials and equipment are also taken from the center for classroom use.

In general two major types of activity go on in the center: (a) reading, listening to, and viewing of materials by teachers and students individually and in small groups; (b) teacher and pupil preparation of teaching aids such as graphs, charts and slides.

In the materials center the specialist is concerned with acquiring, organizing, housing and distributing the whole range of possible learning resources so as to enrich the learning environment of the school. Servicing and repair of materials and equipment are also the specialist's responsibility.

What are the advantages?

In order to do the kind of teaching job expected by the community, a teacher must utilize a wide variety of materials and approaches. Administrators and curriculum people can help teachers by providing a climate which enables them to be creative and to bring to bear all possible resources for the solution of an instructional problem. It is in the classroom where the effect of the "explosions" is felt. Teachers have always been busy people but now with the rapid increase in the numbers of children we must educate, an increasing emphasis on quality education, and the deluge of new knowledge and teaching materials, a comprehensive learning resources program is a necessity. It is more efficient and helpful for teachers to have one place to go for teaching materials rather than to visit separate library and audio-visual departments. The unified collection encourages better and more frequent use of the learning materials available.

It is widely recognized that each learner has a pattern and rhythm of growth which are unique. Providing the wide variety of learning experiences necessary to satisfy the different levels, abilities and interests is a challenge. A properly staffed and equipped materials center can have real impact on the problem of differing learning rates. Easy access by teachers and pupils to a wide variety of instructional materials and skilled guidance in the selection and use of these tools is necessary if we are to have the type of education required by today's demands.

We talk about teaching the whole child. We know that the most effective learning experience is a natural and integrated one. Yet many schools have an artificial division of materials. When audio-visual services are separate from those in which teachers and students secure printed materials, it is more difficult to have a unified approach to satisfying an educational need. For example, a chart which could make a valuable contribution is printed, but it cannot be shelved like a book. Since it is not projected material or primarily pictorial in nature the audio-visual person does not feel it is his responsibility. The same may be said of free and inexpensive materials, flat pictures, realia and many other types of learning aids. Because of an artificial division of materials the purposes of education may not be served. A "no man's land" of materials for which no one feels responsible is often created. This cannot happen when a school is served by a unified collection under the direction of a skilled materials specialist.

A building or system center?

Materials should, of course, be as close to the consumer — the pupil or the teacher — as is practically possible. It would be best to have all materials in the classroom immediately at hand. Certainly as many as possible of the commonly used tools for learning should be kept in the classroom. Many maps, globes, and reference books should be always available. Materials and equipment not likely to be used continuously or on the spur of the moment, such as filmstrips, slides, and the necessary projection equipment, can be kept in the building instructional materials center. Other items, less often used and too expensive to be placed in each school, can be stored in a system or area materials center. Such items as motion pictures, cased exhibits, and expensive models could be shared among several schools from a central location. Regardless of location, proper records of all equipment and materials owned by the district will assure that any teacher in the school system can obtain a needed item wherever it is housed.

How can a center be established?

Enthusiastic and skillful teachers have always collected materials to vitalize instruction. Students who have such teachers are fortunate. Not all teachers, however, are so dedicated. Many find the demands of their assignments so great that they have little energy left to collect necessary resources.

Every school has the beginning of an instructional materials center, because every school and most teachers have some library books and audio-visual resources. Usually there is no policy or plan to facilitate the sharing and use of these learning aids. Even a few materials and resources centrally located and under the direction of a service-minded person can serve the instructional program better than the same amount of material when it is scattered and uncoordinated. Once the idea of sharing learning resources is accepted by a faculty, many steps can be taken without a great expenditure of funds. Compilation of a picture file or list of community resources can enrich greatly the learning environment at little cost. Some of the most comprehensive instructional materials programs now in existence started with such a simple pooling of materials and ideas.

One school system which had self-contained elementary classrooms wished to establish and staff a materials center. When the staff members found it was not financially possible to hire a person to do this, they were willing to have the number of children in their classrooms increased so as to free one of their skilled teachers to provide this service. Some formal and much on-the-job training prepared this teacher to implement the program they had envisioned. If the contribution of such a center can be understood, such services can be established even against great odds.

Most schools now have some separate and usually uncoordinated method of providing for audio-visual and library needs. Integrating these two services, while desirable, sometimes can be difficult because of the vested interests of individuals involved. Some librarians may be fearful of the rapidly growing audio-visual field. They may not feel comfortable with the new equipment and materials. In schools where the library is a teaching station or used to some degree as a study hall, it is difficult to take on a broader responsibility. Many audio-visual people do not wish to surrender their area of responsibility to librarians, nor do they wish to be under the librarian's direction.

As with all ideas which call for people to change their ways of working, skilled guidance and attention to the interpersonal aspects of the problem are necessary. Curriculum people have the responsibility and the skill to stimulate new methods of organizing curriculum services to assist teachers and thus improve instruction. An amalgamation of library and audio-visual services, when approached with skill and understanding, is such a step.

INSTRUCTIONAL MATERIALS CENTER

Kenneth I. Taylor

The instructional materials center begins when traditionally regarded library and audio-visual departments are combined. From this union should come not only the sum of what previously was available in two separate areas of the school, but also distinctly *new* services that result from the centralization itself.

Current experiments in class size, in independent student research, and in more effective utilization of professional staff members already are providing implications concerning changes in the use of instructional materials. More audio-visual materials undoubtedly will be used; schools will create many of their own instructional materials, and students will need additional guidance in finding information. Centralization of materials and services into a single department may be the answer for most schools. Facilities that are designed around such services — but still adaptable to future changes — will be necessary.

Not only services and materials, but also instruction in the use of these materials should be provided by the instructional materials center. Of course, economic advantages result from centralization, but better services and more effective utilization of materials already owned by the school are necessary.

This article answers questions pertaining to the philosophy and organization of an instructional materials center.

Is there a trend today toward instructional materials centers in schools?

There is an accelerating trend at present. The philosophy is almost universal in library literature. The American Library Association in its new standards supports the centralization of all materials. Some colleges and universities are experimenting with materials centers for their students and faculties. Certain states, such as California and Florida, are showing major leadership in this direction.

What principles distinguish a school instructional materials "service" center?

Central administration of all instructional materials and services; professionally prepared catalogs to facilitate use, equipment and space to use all materials within the premises of the center; equal emphasis upon student and faculty guidance in the use of materials; direct contact of the entire staff with students and faculty.

Reprinted, with permission from: Taylor, Kenneth I., "Instructional Materials Center," THE NATION'S SCHOOLS, December, 1960. Copyright 1960, The Modern Hospital Publishing Co., Inc., Chicago. All rights reserved.

Is an instructional materials center more than a combination of traditional library and A-V departments?

Yes. When well planned and effectively administered, the materials center offers kinds and quantities of services that cannot result from divided departments.

What are some of these additional services?

A staff of consultants familiar with the content of every type of instructional material owned by the school; organization of materials and records enabling all school personnel to recognize relationships among different types of materials; greater emphasis upon student use of traditionally regarded teacher materials for individual and group study; school-prepared guides that coordinate materials for more efficient use by students and teachers.

Are economic advantages gained?

There should be less duplication of professional and clerical duties, fewer examples of needless duplication when purchasing instructional materials, more efficient handling of rentals of outside materials, and a saving of student and faculty time when searching for materials.

What types of instructional materials are found in a materials center?

All types that are valuable to a school. This includes books, periodicals, pamphlets, charts, posters, graphs, maps, models, portable bulletin boards, felt boards, globes, slides, filmstrips, motion pictures, phonograph records, and others.

Must all instructional materials be filed or shelved in the materials center?

No. Materials often used in departments may be kept on *permanent* loan in the departments. The location of these materials should, however, be indicated clearly in central records that are accessible to all school personnel. Short-term loans of materials to departments also should be made, the materials being returned after the departments no longer need them.

What is the difference between materials centers and libraries?

In many instances, libraries have indicated an exclusive interest in *printed* materials. If a library, however, assumes responsibility for all types of instructional materials, treats them in a uniform manner, and offers service in their use, there may be little difference. There is no magic in the name alone.

What is the difference between materials centers and audio-visual departments?

Usually the absence of printed materials in the audio-visual departments. One of the basic features of the materials center is the coordination of print with audio-visual materials.

Can separate library and audio-visual departments operate as effectively as a materials center?

No, not when consultants in instructional materials (library and audio-visual staff) are in different parts of the school and have no opportunity to become familiar with the content of all instructional materials either owned by the school or under consideration for purchase.

Are there different kinds of materials centers?

Yes, because there is lack of agreement in many instances on the definition of a materials center. Some schools report that they have materials centers in each classroom. They mean that they have classroom collections that contain many types of materials. Some cities, school districts, and counties have multi-school materials centers. Frequently these are no more than central *storage* centers that distribute and collect materials. They are not the same as the centers discussed in this article.

What is the primary difference in materials centers as discussed in educational circles?

Whether they are primarily "storage" or "service" materials centers. The objective of the first is largely economic. The second, while frequently realizing economic advantages is primarily educational.

When is a materials center primarily "educational" in its function?

When it centralizes and organizes materials to promote their more effective use, when it has facilities within its premises for student and faculty use of all materials, and when it has a staff that works with students and teachers.

Why should all consultants in instructional materials have a knowledge of all types of materials?

When the content of printed, graphic, projected and transmission materials is coordinated, better teaching and learning may result. If the consultants themselves cannot relate the content of all types of materials, the burden of correlation falls upon the teacher.

What is meant by "coordinating" instructional materials?

Using various types of instructional materials together. It means learning what is available, recognizing when one type of material will be more effective than another, adapting materials for a particular classroom situation, and using them together to reinforce the content of each.

What economic advantages result when the staff of the materials center knows the content of all types of materials?

Better selection and purchase of materials. There is less frequent purchase of one type of material on a particular subject, when there is sufficient information already available within the school in another form.

How can better selection result?

The advantages to a school might be weighed, for instance, concerning the purchase of a 300 page book, a 50 frame filmstrip, or a 10 minute motion picture on the heart. Although a school might need all three, each type of material should be selected on the basis of how its particular form best presents the subject.

Can a more specific illustration be given?

Yes. If a school is considering the rental or purchase of a motion picture on a country such as Australia, for example, knowledge of what is already available within the school in magazines and reference books would assist in better selection. If one knows that the school already has much statistical information pertaining to agricultural, economic and industrial development, maps pertaining to natural resources, and still pictures that can be projected, a film that places major emphasis upon this information would not be selected. In its place, a film that stresses those aspects of Australia — such as regional dialects and aerial views of ports and terrain — that are best shown through sound and motion would then be selected for our instructional materials center.

What other advantages in service result in addition to better selection?

More attention to the needs of all school personnel. Libraries, by reason of their stress on seating capacity, have emphasized service to students and study without the presence of the classroom teacher, and have given primary attention to print. Audio-visual staff members have tended to work as teacher-consultants, with little direct relation to students themselves.

What kind of personnel is needed in a materials center?

Consultants who are trained and experienced in using all types of materials. They should have a knowledge of the curriculum of the school, knowledge that comes only from experience within the school itself. They should know how to teach, and should understand the needs and interests of young people.

Isn't it difficult to find personnel trained in all areas of instructional materials?

Yes, just as it is difficult to find librarians and audio-visual personnel. What is needed, principally, are consultants who have a desire to continue to understand and use all types of materials and who wish to work with young people. The principles of selection, cataloging, utilization and guidance for all types of materials have more points of similarity than difference.

Does this mean that consultants should not have specialized duties?

No. Staff members may have primary responsibilities for certain types of materials, but they should have or acquire a knowledge of other types, in addition. All staff members should work part of each day with students. They should know how to obtain materials of any type from outside sources. They should also be willing to explore methods by which materials may be prepared within the school by staff, teachers and students.

What major responsibilities should be given to consultants in instructional materials?

Responsibilities that are primarily consultative in nature. Clerical duties should be minimized and should be the responsibility of clerical workers. Whenever possible, repair and maintenance of equipment should be the responsibility of the maintenance department.

What responsibilities may be given student assistants?

Responsibilities with educational value. Their duties should be rotated. Instruction should be given them in the use of all types of equipment and materials. Their work in the materials center should follow a planned course of study, with credit given.

What instruction and assistance should be given classroom teachers?

Schools should train teachers in the use of equipment and materials owned by the school. They should be shown how to find materials with a minimum expenditure of time. They also should be taught when one type of material may be used to better advantage than another.

What instruction and assistance should be given the student body?

How to care for and use all materials effectively. Students should receive an initial introduction to the center by the staff. They should be taught by their teachers in classroom situations, and by the staff of the center when they are working alone.

What services are provided by the staff?

Direct services when staff members work with students and teachers. Indirect services when they provide guides by which school personnel can find materials alone.

What form do these prepared guides take?

Basic to any materials center is the professionally prepared card catalog. In this catalog, in an alphabetical arrangement, are indexed the materials owned by the school. In some schools, outside community resources are also indicated. The subject headings used in this catalog are based on a standard list so that all materials on one subject are found together.

Are other prepared guides available?

In many schools special lists (bibliographies) are provided. They may be lists of filmstrips or of phonograph records available. As these collections grow in size, however, the value of the lists decreases. They grow cumbersome and difficult to use, and the frequent revision needed is expensive. When this is the case, the staff often provides manuals on the use of the various types of materials instead.

Can a school use its existing facilities in order to develop a materials center?

Yes, in most cases. The program of a materials center is based, first of all, upon service. Physical facilities are important only to the degree that they improve the services provided to students and teachers.

What is the first consideration when developing a materials center in an established school?

Usually whether present facilities are large enough, or if expansion is necessary to provide for additional services.

How can present quarters be adapted to provide a materials center?

Some schools utilize adjacent classrooms or study halls. Study halls are frequently converted into reading room areas, and other areas in the school are then used for study halls. Centralized records frequently are developed to allow storage of materials in departments, thus expanding shelf space.

THE PHILOSOPHY OF SCHOOL LIBRARIES AS INSTRUCTIONAL MATERIALS CENTERS

The American Association of School Librarians believes that the school library, in addition to doing its vital work of individual reading guidance and development of the school curriculum, should serve the school as a center for instructional materials. Instructional materials include books — the literature of children, young people, and adults — other printed materials, films, recordings, and newer media developed to aid learning.

Reprinted by permission of the National Association of Secondary School Principals from: "Philosophy of School Libraries as IMC's," BULLETIN OF NATIONAL ASSOCIATION OF SECONDARY SCHOOL PRINCIPALS, November, 1959. Copyright 1959 by the National Association of Secondary School Principals.

Teaching methods advocated by leaders in the field of curriculum development and now used in elementary and secondary education call for extensive and frequently combined use of traditional along with many new and different kinds of materials. Since these methods depend for their success upon a cross-media approach to learning, a convenient way of approaching instructional materials on a subject or problem basis must be immediately at hand in each school. Historically, libraries of all types have been established to provide convenient centers for books and reading and for locating ideas and information important to the communities they serve. The interest a modern school now has in finding and using good motion pictures, sound recordings, filmstrips, and other newer materials simply challenges and gives increased dimension to established library roles.

The school librarian has always encouraged development of appreciation and ability to make good and continuing use of printed materials and library services. Taking into account individual differences of children and young people, the school library stimulates and guides each pupil in the selection and use of materials for the building of taste on appropriate levels of maturity. Now in good library practice, the school library also helps both pupils and teachers to discover new materials of interest and to determine their values. It may provide these materials and the equipment needed for their use for both individual and classroom study and teaching.

The function of an instructional materials center is to locate, gather, provide, and coordinate a school's materials for learning and the equipment required for use of these materials. Primary responsibility for administering such a center, producing new instructional materials, and supervising regular programs of in-service training for use of materials may be the province of librarians, or, it may be shared. In any case, trained school librarians must be ready to cooperate with others and themselves serve as coordinators, consultants, and supervisors of instructional materials service on each level of school administration — in the individual school building, for the city or county unit, and for the state.

School librarians are normally educated as teachers and meet state requirements for regular teaching certificates. They must also receive special training in analysis, educational evaluation, selection, organization, and systematic distribution and use of instructional materials. The professional education of school librarians should contribute this basic knowledge as well as provide understanding of fundamental learning processes, teaching methods, and the psychology of children and adolescents. Also, school librarians must be familiar with the history and current trends in development of school curricula.

In summary, the well-trained professional school librarian should anticipate service as both a teacher and as an instructional materials specialist. Where adequate funds and staff are available, the school library can serve as an efficient and economical means of coordinating the instructional materials and equipment needed for a given school program. It should always stand ready to provide informed guidance concerning selection and use of both printed and newer media.

This statement was passed by unanimous vote at the business meeting of the American Association of School Librarians during the American Library Association Conference, Miami Beach, June 21, 1956. It is therefore, an official statement of the American Association of School Librarians.

INSTRUCTIONAL MATERIALS CENTERS —THE RATIONALE

Murray G. Phillips

While much has been written on the subject of instructional materials centers, no consistent viewpoint has emerged on what a materials center is, or should be. This is not surprising, for each writer tends to view the problem from within his particular frame of reference. Librarians, audiovisual directors, curriculum directors, and teachers all express their points of view – often without unanimity within their groups. Descriptions of college, university, county, school-system and building centers frequently reveal a variety in aims and practice.

Commonality can only be achieved through a discussion of some theoretical aspects of instructional materials centers, but before engaging in such a discussion, it is necessary to describe some of the varying viewpoints which have been put forth over the years. Only in this way can their relative merits be assessed in light of theoretical concepts. Most persons will agree that a basic theory is needed if materials centers are to achieve their maximum potential.

For the purposes of this discussion, an instructional materials center is defined in terms of its several functions – circulation, coordination, inservice education, consultation, and local production – which must be carried on in a vital program. All types of audiovisual materials, not only the printed materials classically associated with libraries, are circulated from and used within the center. The use and selection of these materials are coordinated with the use and selection of of radio and televised programs, both broadcast and closed circuit. A formal and informal inservice program is constantly in operation to improve usage of materials. Consultation service is at hand for students, teachers, and administrators concerning the best resources available to help solve particular learning and teaching problems. A wide variety of materials is locally produced to supplement commercially produced materials.

The above definition is limited to instructional materials centers which are a part of formal education and excludes public libraries.

An instructional materials center is more than a library plus an audiovisual center. Its collection of printed materials includes publications not ordinarily found in the libraries: curriculum guides, courses of study, specimen standardized tests, catalogs of all types of commercial instructional materials and equipment, and sample textbooks from many publishers. Conversely an audiovisual center is not necessarily an instructional materials center without printed ma-

Reprinted with permission from: Phillips, Murray G., "Instructional Materials Center–The Rationale," AUDIOVISUAL INSTRUCTION, December, 1960.

terials. At its best it may be so, provided it offers all the services of an instructional materials center as enumerated above. At its worst, it offers none of the services except storage and circulation of 'the projector.'

An examination of the literature reveals that opinion about the instructional materials center as defined in the preceding paragraphs can generally be classified in one of three ways: absolutely in favor of the idea, in favor of the idea but doubtful that it can be implemented, and firmly opposed.

The rationale for an instructional materials center is based upon the obvious fact that we live in an age whose complexity grows ever greater. No one medium of communication is adequate to the task of providing information and concepts which are unambiguous to students. Each medium — books, films, recordings, filmstrips, TV, radio, and so on — has particular strengths and weaknesses. Only the use of a wide variety of materials — the multi-media approach — can help insure that the weaknesses of any given type of material will be compensated for by the strengths of one or more other materials. Since the multi-media approach to teaching and learning is so necessarily a part of modern education, the problem of how best to make this wide range of materials convenient to teachers and students presents itself . . .

The simplest answer is to make all the media available through a single facility: an instructional materials center. It is the simplest answer because it makes possible the most efficient use of the students' and teachers' time. Only one place need be visited, only one catalog consulted. All necessary help is available from one source. It is commonplace that the extent to which materials are used is directly affected by their accessibility and the availability of materials and consultants. The location of materials and consultants in more than one place, for example in a library and AV center, is less convenient to the user than concentration in a single center.

It is important to note the emphasis on the phrase 'to the user.' Most of the writings favoring instructional materials centers do so in terms of the users. Most of the arguments against the materials centers subordinate or completely ignore the only reason for their existence: to be of service to students and their teachers. Interestingly enough, no group claims that one type of material is clearly superior to all the others and therefore deserving of a separate facility. Opposition to the idea is based on other grounds. One line of reasoning is that there is not enough help, financial support, and physical space available to do the job. Barely able to keep up with the demands of a normal library program, where will the librarian find time to handle all the non-book materials? Funds are inadequate to cover both the purchase of books and other instructional materials, space is already limited, and so on. These are the principal reasons advanced by those who claim to be in favor of the principle of an instructional materials center but doubtful that it can be implemented.

The proponents of distinctly separate library and audiovisual quarters usually present one or a combination of different reasons. One favored by librarians is that libraries have a unique function to perform because they are book centered and the addition of non-book materials will detract from this function. Implicit in this reasoning seems to be the idea that books represent a consistently superior instructional material that can only be degraded by intermixture with othe materials.

It is also claimed by some librarians and AV personnel that the problem associated with handling book and non-book materials are so different that the can successfully be coped with only in separate facilities. This argument seem to neglect the fact that there is no reason why all materials in one center shoul or must be handled in the same way or by a single person.

An extension of this logic would seem to demand separate facilities for audi materials, for projected materials, for each different type of materials, each wit its own director. This is patently absurd. What is needed is a team of specialists the librarian, the audiovisual director, the television director — all workin cooperatively within the instructional materials center. Should self-instruction; materials increase sufficiently in importance, as many writers envision, it may b necessary to add the services of a person skilled in programming. It is in respons to this 'team' proposal that a familiar bugaboo is raised. Who will be in charge the librarian, the AV director, the television director, or some other emergin specialist? Each fears that the other will be biased in favor of his own specialt to the detriment of the one. A solution to this supposed problem will b presented as part of the theoretical discussion which follows.

Acceptance of the materials center concept is dependent upon prior accep tance of three propositions. Two of these are taken for granted wheneve mentioned but nevertheless tend to be forgotten in the stress of daily schoc life. The third is for many reasons not yet widely accepted. The three take together call for instructional materials centers.

We tend to forget that schools and all their component parts have only on purpose: the education of youth. Libraries do not exist to organize and circulat collections of printed materials, but to help educate students by means of thei collections. Similarly, audiovisual centers do not exist to organize and circula collections of a wide variety of materials and associated equipment. Their reaso for existence is to benefit education by circulating this material and equipmen to students and teachers as needed. In like manner, the only valid reason for a instructional materials center's existence is to help educate children and youth.

Secondly, the task of the schools is to help develop each student to the lim of his ability. This is best provided for in an educational environment rich in wide variety of materials and, as previously pointed out, these materials are mos readily available through the instructional materials center.

The third premise, the one not as yet widely accepted, is that all instruction: materials should be as available to students as to their teachers. Common practic is to limit certain types to teachers. The teachers then typically present the cor tent of these materials to their classes as a group. This represents an anomalou situation. All teachers want their students to read extensively and are proud o of those who range far and wide in the library. Most of these same teachers fee that students would be stealing their thunder if they should make individual us of audiovisual materials outside the classroom. If we truly believe that each stu dent should be free to learn all that he is capable of learning, then we canno deny him access to every type of instructional material. There should be as fev restrictions on the use of audiovisual materials as on books.

Granting of these three premises demands the acceptance of the concept of an instructional materials center as the facility whose organized collection, including books and other materials, is made available on call to individual students as well as to teachers. The direction of this facility must be delegated to a person with an understanding of curriculum development and improvement. He may be librarian, AV, TV or curriculum director. The important consideration is that he must be in favor of materials as a totality and impartial as to their type — book or non-book. His professional education must have made him expert in at least one of the center's specialties and familiar with the others. His prime responsibility must be to coordinate the efforts of each specialist on the instructional materials team toward the goal of an optimum educational program.

He can truly achieve this only if he sits on the highest councils which determine curriculum development within his institution.

An important additional consideration is that the instructional materials center, if located within a school building, must provide facilities within the center itself for the use of materials as well as circulating them to the classrooms.

All that has been said about instructional materials centers is applicable at all grade levels from kindergarten through graduate school. There will, of course, be differences between the various kinds of centers, but the difference will be in the type of collections, not of purpose. At the kindergarten level the center will to a great extent be right in the classroom.

At higher grade levels with their increasingly complex subject-matter requirements, the center will first move predominantly out of the classroom into a single location and then at still higher levels break up into several centers, based not upon type of materials but upon specialized subject matter.

Instructional materials centers have a vast potential for augmenting the educational programs of our schools and colleges. This potential can only be realized if the function of centers now in existence and yet to be established is based upon a common theory. The essence of this theory must be service to the student. *Murray G. Phillips, Coordinator of Instruction Materials for the Garden City Public Schools, Garden City, New York. This article first appeared in Audiovisual Instruction for December, 1960.*

IMPROVING INSTRUCTION THROUGH MATERIALS CENTERS

Reynold A. Swanson

Education, like industry, has developed new tools. It has learned much about the type of facilities needed for effective teaching and learning. Today, schools should have ready access to an adequate supply of efficient teaching resources. If teachers are to be expected to do their best work, they must be supplied with up-to-date and efficient tools, materials, and resources.

In fact, "most frequently teachers do not use audio-visual materials because they are not available or not readily accessible." Many of the teachers of the Wauwatosa, Wis., schools, in planning learning experiences with their students, recognize and attempt to provide the variety of materials and resources needed. Sometimes it becomes a frustrating and time-consuming task. It requires the searching out of materials located here and there in the building and conferring with an already busy teacher in charge of maps, globes, and charts. The experience of these teachers pointed up rather forcefully the need for the coordination of instructional materials in a school building as well as in a school system.

It was decided to use the committee approach in the solution of the problem. This eventually involved the entire administrative staff who in turn sought out suggestions from their respective faculties. The outcome has been the development of a central Instructional Materials Center which services all of the Wauwatosa schools. In addition, each school is in the process of developing its own center.

DEFINITION AND FUNCTION

An instructional materials center is a well-planned area housing materials and equipment for instructional use under the supervision of a competent person well versed in general education and available materials. It should provide services, facilities, materials, and equipment to improve the instructional program of the school or system for the benefit of the pupils, teachers, and adults of the community.

The center serves as a depository for special materials which will aid the teacher to present better his subject area and to take care of the wide range of individual differences that exists in classes. The educational aids adaptable to further the professional growth of the teaching staff are also considered a part of this type of organization.

Reprinted with permission from: Swanson, Reynold A., "Improving Instruction Through Materials Centers," SCHOOL BOARD JOURNAL, October, 1959.

This is a place, also, where new or experimental types of instructional materials may be developed, produced, and evaluated for possible future use or adoption.

ORGANIZATION AND SERVICE

More important than specific and limiting directions for organization is the providing for an individual responsible for administering it. Whether a single individual, a committee, or a rotating system of responsibility is best, will depend upon the size of the school, the degree of departmental organization, and the physical plant. However, the principal should assume dynamic leadership in the organization, development, and promotion of the materials center.

What can be done within the existing framework of the school to help develop better materials services and classroom facilities? Here are a few suggestions for providing teachers with needed resources:

1. Encourage teachers to actively participate.

2. Co-ordinate staff efforts through a central committee composed of one qualified staff member from each school with the administrative staff available as consultants.

3. Provide essential information about existing resources and be constantly alert to discover new materials.

4. Utilize the area of student-produced instructional materials. Every school has a potential for producing teaching tools which is rarely tapped — the students themselves. This is especially true at the secondary and adult levels. Classes in art, photography, printing, creative writing, and radio and TV programs can assist in providing many needed classroom materials. Excellent sets of slides, picture sets, tape recordings, and some motion pictures have been produced by student groups. The art class and the shop class can contribute effective dioramas and exhibits; science students can prepare specimens and collections. This program has the further advantage of providing valuable educational experiences for the student himself.

MATERIALS AND EQUIPMENT

Each center should be organized to handle many types of equipment, materials, and services such as the following:

1. Curriculum materials and professional literature for teachers.

2. Bulletin boards, chalkboard, display center, a card index, and an evaluation index should be included. A check-out system should be devised using cards or forms — something which is simple.

3. Preview and laboratory facilties should be provided even though they be in the same room.

4. Equipment for conditioning, rewinding, inspecting, and splicing films should be located here Also provision for simple repair of audio-visual equipment and materials.

5. Materials and equipment should be provided so that pupils and teachers can make maps, charts, graphs, models, mock-ups, objects, specimens, puppets, posters, dioramas, flannel boards, exhibits, slides, and items needed for demonstrations and experiments.

6. Provide tape transcriptions for use in classrooms. Arrangements should be made to record radio programs on tape, particularly those programs which come outside of school time. Tape recordings are also available from central distributing centers such as Minnesota Department of Education.

In general, consideration should be given to the handling of the following types of equipment and materials through the instructional materials center organization: 16mm. sound projector, speed-i-o-scope, reading accelerator, controlled reader, overhead projector, telebinocular, record player, microscope, art objects, teaching aids (puzzles, toys, etc.), printed materials (literature, reference books, pamphlets, magazines), opaque projector, filmstrip projector, slide projector, television, tape recorder, radio, micro projector, terrariums, maps, globes, tapes, specimens, and pictures.

HOUSING FACILITIES

The housing facilities should provide for: (1) the storage and handling, repair and distribution of audio-visual materials and equipment, (2) production of materials, and (3) preview of materials.

Each physical plant and school program should provide adequate storage and functional work space. Two possibilities might be: a central location near the library or administrative suite — a location which is not "out-of-the-way" for teachers, or a small central location plus assignment of materials to specific subject areas; e.g., social studies, English or language arts, science and mathematics, music, art.

The amount of space available and the extent to which each school will develop these operations will, of course, depend upon the individual building involved.

IMPLEMENTATION

The Instructional Materials Center should be so organized that it provides the greatest service for each individual school. In the development of this center the following should be given serious consideration at all times:

1. Annual budgetary allowances for the staff; purchase and rental of materials and equipment, maintenance of equipment and materials and a planned program of equipping building properly.

2. Orientation of teachers to the instructional materials center.

3. An in-service training program as to the use and availability of materials in the instructional materials center.

THE INSTRUCTIONAL RESOURCE CENTER

Florence Simmons

If a survey conducted a few years ago to determine the use of the school library by teachers were repeated today, what changes would it show? There have been such advances in the variety of materials now offered schools as aids in learning that librarians may be pressed to keep up with the demands.

In an effort to prepare teachers to use the many instructional materials available, school systems have expanded their professional libraries to include materials other than books and periodicals, and have organized central resource centers where teachers may become acquainted with or borrow materials for use in the classroom. The scope of the collection is limited only by what is available this week. Next week, never fear, some producer will have devised something new. No teacher wishes to remain ignorant of methods that will make learning more effective. Neither does he wish to waste money on gadgets that will serve no real purpose. He may wish to examine various types of programmed materials as well as research regarding their use. He may examine different types of projectors as well as projected materials, and to these he relates textbooks and other printed materials that will be used with his class.

The ultimate goal of this collection is to improve instruction. In addition to the printed professional materials that keep teachers informed about developments in learning resources, the resource center provides the actual materials and devices so that teachers may examine and become familiar with them. Other dimensions include facilities for preparing materials to be used in the classroom, such as transparencies, mounted pictures, and other aids. Not only are courses of study from other systems included, but also those of the teachers in the system. Work of students is sometimes displayed to interpret successful units of study. Instruction is improved by having materials available, by encouraging their use in the classroom, and by sharing ideas and resources within the system.

Such a resource center will be located in the administrative building in close proximity to the offices of those in charge of the instructional program. It will, of course, be used also by instructional personnel throughout the system, and materials from it will circulate to the schools upon occasion.

The space occupied by the center will be determined by its program of activities and resources. A reading room, conference rooms (which may be used also for previewing and auditioning), and storage and work rooms will be necessary. The staff will also be determined by the program, but a professionally trained librarian with imagination and initiative will be an asset. Imagination and initiative should be emphasized because procedures and programs should be tailored

Reprinted with permission from: Simmons, Florence, "The Instructional Resource Center," A.L.A. BULLETIN, February, 1963.

to the school system's needs, and for this there is no printed guide. While teachers may know the instructional program in certain areas and the audio-visual expert knows the intricacies of equipment and photography, it is the person who administers the total program, directed toward its purpose of the effective use of all materials in the instructional program, who will make the greatest contribution.

Few reports of such centers give any indication of the amount of the budget. Book collections range from less than 1000 to 20,000 or more volumes, depending upon resources and the size of the system. Professional periodicals, memberships in associations, and educational service publications are expensive. A minimum estimate for a budget for the professional library alone would probably be not less than $1500. Collections of instructional materials, such as films, filmstrips, recordings, etc., would be additional and depend upon the degree of centralization of materials in the supervisory headquarters.

PROFESSIONAL BOOKS

Professional books will be a necessary part of any instructional resource center. Since it is a working collection for a system interested in developing its instructional program, the collection will consist primarily of recent and some historical publications of a general nature, depending upon interlibrary loans from colleges and universities for highly specialized or less frequently used materials. Needs of nonteaching staff members will not be neglected, and departments of food service, building planning, etc., will have their professional materials included. Recommendations for purchase will come from staff members, but the librarian will endeavor to see that all areas are represented.

In planning the collection, the article "Bibliographic Sources" in the *Encyclopedia of Educational Research*[1] should be reviewed, since it contains suggestions not only for reference tools for the education library but also recommendations regarding classification and subject headings.

Publications from the National Education Association[2] and its departments should be examined, and recent yearbooks, particularly of the Department of Elementary School Principals, the Association for Supervision and Curriculum Development, and the American Association of School Administrators, should be secured. Yearbooks of the National Society for the Study of Education[3] will, of course, be included. The list of publications from the U.S. Office of Education[4] should also be examined for appropriate titles to add to the collection.

Members of the staff of the division of instruction will be the most important group from whom to seek recommendations for materials needed in the collection. Lists for this staff to check regularly for titles to be included in the

---

[1] *Encyclopedia of Educational Research, 3d edition (Macmillan, 1960).*
[2] *National Education Association, 1201 16th Street, N.W., Washington 6, D.C.*
[3] *University of Chicago Press.*
[4] *Education, price list 31, 50th edition (Superintendent of Documents, Washington 25, D.C.).*

the library will facilitate cooperation in selection of materials. The *NEA Journal* includes a list of "Outstanding Education Books," compiled by the members of the education department of the Enoch Pratt Free Library in Baltimore, in its May issue each year, and the lists from the past few years should be examined. A recent *Curriculum Bulletin*[5] from the University of Oregon is devoted to a list of professional books that may provide a starting point. The *Education Index,* under "Education − Bibliography," provides clues to other current lists. State departments of education often publish lists of professional books added to their collections, and these are helpful guides. Current periodicals will provide recommendations of new books. Pertinent articles often provide bibliographies which are guides to materials on the same subject.

When study in a particular area is undertaken, and particularly when a number of persons may be involved, added copies of a title are usually necessary. Failure to provide sufficient duplicates of a much used title is usually foolish economy.

Rules for circulating books should be as flexible as possible. When teachers have been assigned to a study, it is expected that they will need to use materials over a long period of time. Staff members in the central office may sometimes need books in their offices. This may require extra copies, even of some reference books. Since users are always available by telephone, limitation of the circulation period should not be necessary. Reminders of materials charged out may be sent two or three times a year.

PERIODICALS AND PAMPHLETS

Since the purpose of the professional library is to stimulate teachers to better teaching, knowledge of current research, current practices, and proposals of change will be in demand. Periodicals and serials are some of the best sources. There are over 1000 educational periodicals published in the United States, and the center's purpose and budget will determine the selection.

The general educational periodicals and services should be included as well as important specialized publications in each subject area and on each instructional level. Those included in the *Education Index* of course will be most valuable for reference use. Comprehensive memberships in the departments of NEA and other organizations will bring not only the journals but other publications of the current year. This assures their arrival as soon as published and obviates extra orders.

Staff members may be invited each year to recommend titles to be continued or dropped and new ones to be added. Interests and needs may change from year to year as well as the budget. A list of titles to which the library subscribes should be provided for each staff member and be available in each school.

Some libraries may bind periodicals. However, since their value is primarily for current information and they are useful to more individuals if available as separate issues, the expense of binding should be considered carefully. Back is-

---

[5] *"A Bibliography for the Professional Bookshelf in School Libraries,"Curriculum Bulletin, No. 205 (University of Oregon, Eugene, 1960, 25¢).*

sues seldom need be held beyond five years. Articles of continuing interest may be clipped for the information file.

Much information comes to the library in pamphlet form, only some of which is of considerable importance and timeliness. What will be cataloged and what placed in the information file is a matter of decision for the librarian. In a collection where current information is frequently sought, the cataloging of pamphlets on topics of much interest will probably pay dividends. Some libraries maintain separate files of NEA and government publications. There should be a file of the state department of education's bulletins. Reports from school systems may also prove helpful.

For the information file, the *Education Index* is an excellent guide for subject headings and thus also serves as a cross-reference guide to subjects.

COURSES OF STUDY AND TEXTBOOKS

Courses of study and resource units in specific areas, whether from the local system or from other schools, are invaluable to teachers as they make their own plans. Scope and sequence, teacher references, enrichment materials for the student, and appropriate learning activities are useful as new courses of study are planned or revisions made. Teachers with gifted or slow learners may want ideas of activities and materials to use with these students or they may only want to try something a little different. Valuable as written aids may be, teachers also find help from each other as they use the materials in the center. They should be encouraged to place copies of their own successful resource units there for the use of other teachers. These are particularly helpful when they are concerned with subjects of local interest.

Some school systems maintain an exchange arrangement for courses of study. Others have established prices for all items available for outside use. Knowing what is available and appropriate for the system's needs will require vigilance on the librarian's part and assistance from the instructional staff.[6]

The Association for Supervision and Curriculum Development's annual publication, *Curriculum Materials,* is a good source. If staff members attend the annual ASCD conference, they may be encouraged to examine those on display and inform the librarian of guides that should be ordered. Educational *Leadership* often lists courses of study available. Other listings may be found in *Education Index* under "Courses of Study" and under the specific subject area. *Social Education* and some other journals may, from time to time, include information about curriculum materials. In collecting courses of study, it should be remembered that this type of material is rapidly outdated and superseded.

Staff and teachers evaluating courses of study from other systems as well as those they have prepared will find helpful "Criteria for Evaluating Curriculum Materials"[7] prepared by faculty members of Teachers College at Columbia University.

[6]*Harold F. Smith, "Acquisition of Courses of Study," Wilson Library Bulletin, 31:262+, November 1956.*
[7]*"Curriculum Bulletins," Educational Leadership, 6:188-89, December 1958.*

There is frequent need to examine textbooks from various publishers. Should a class or certain pupils need a text with simpler presentation, copies of different titles may be desired. A collection of as many current texts as possible is a necessary part of the resource center. With the texts will be samples of workbooks, the teacher's guides that accompany the texts, and any other materials developed for the teacher's use.

Teachers look for courses of study and texts grouped by the subject areas included in the course of study. For texts, the authors matter little, since many texts are prepared by a group of authors, and in a series, one name may appear first on one book and last on the next. Most teachers are familiar with the publisher's name, however. Therefore, the most appropriate arrangement for the user's needs is by curriculum area and publisher or issuing school system. Code letters or letters and numbers are most readily interpreted and these make up the "call number." If possible, the grade level for which the item is designed should be added. Courses of study are seldom bound and, if placed in pamphlet boxes by subject area using the same code, they are easily accessible. Some libraries prefer to place these in a vertical file.

OTHER MEDIA

Mention should be made of the recordings and tapes which will enhance the collection. Both music and speech records should be available where necessary. Speeches at professional meetings are now frequently available on tape or phonorecordings. These are timely and relatively inexpensive. Staff members who have attended meetings will know which speeches will be valuable for their uses and can recommend purchase. Individual teachers may wish to borrow them and principals will find them useful for faculty meetings.

Carefully selected films and filmstrips should also be a part of the collection.

PRINCIPLES OF SELECTION AND USE

The evaluation and selection of different types of materials for use by teachers necessitates a well-selected collection of books and periodicals to study the research in the field of learning possibilities and characteristics of the various devices. How satisfactory is the use of films in teaching physics? How are language laboratories used with the greatest success? Questions such as these must be answered.

Indexes will provide references to research and reports of use. Pamphlets from various sources, reports from foundations which are interested in educational research, and many other guides will need to be examined and filed for reference. Before they are filed, however, there is the responsibility to get these to the person or persons who might be concerned. All too frequently, a teacher or supervisor will discover some item filed away that would have been invaluable earlier had he known of its existence.

The librarian must keep in close touch with all facets of the school program so that he can make appropriate materials available. Sometimes it is only a sentence in an article that will give him a clue to the source of materials that will be most useful to a teacher or staff member.

It is not inappropriate to wonder how the librarian is to perform his own functions and also keep alert to the interest of all his co-workers. The development of close working relations with central office staff and interested principals and teachers will be his solution.

One of the important functions an instructional resources center can perform is setting up mechanics for the evaluation of all types of instructional materials. Criteria, policies, and procedures governing evaluation of printed, audio-visual, and other materials should be formulated. This is a cooperative effort of supervisors, consultants, and librarians.

Permanent reviewing committees should be set up. Groups concerned in evaluation should include persons with broad knowledge and discriminating tastes, so that judgments are not biased and special interests do not influence decisions. Some committee members should be experienced, but the committee may well include those who will learn from the experience and thus enlarge the number of knowledgeable reviewers. Time should be allowed for thorough examination and discussion by the members of the committee. The exchange of opinions in the process of making a choice provides worthwhile possibilities for growth of those involved. Teachers frequently discover values in materials of of which they had been unaware, and experiences of others in the use of materials make the evaluation procedure a real opportunity for in-service growth. Periodicals reviewing the different media should be identified and the evaluations made available to the committee. The cooperation of teachers in the evaluation of materials will make them aware of what is available and assist them in being more intelligent users of the selected materials.

Some method of reporting decisions of the groups to the system as a whole must be provided. It may take the form of a recommended book list published annually or semiannually, or more frequent and timely bulletins. Special instructional areas or interests may stimulate the preparation of lists on specific subjects. The reading specialists may work with a group preparing lists of books with vocabulary suited to slow readers of various ages, or one science supervisor may help with preparation of appropriate lists to accompany TV science lessons.

Evaluations should result in written reports for permanent record at the center. These are useful should decisions be questioned and will prevent repetition of evaluation at a later date or by other groups.

OTHER CONTRIBUTIONS OF THE CENTER

Regardless of whether the service is directed toward a teacher reading for personal interest or a group working under the direction of the division of instruction, an instructional resource center can contribute much to the in-service growth of the personnel of the school system. Some systems have found such a center particularly useful in the orientation of new teachers. An atmosphere of freedom and friendliness where teachers and principals can find stimulation and information where they can discuss their problems and successes or exhibit the results of their effort will add much to the development of the instructional program.

One materials center invites its retired teachers to visit and use its lounge in their leisure time, another is opened to teachers in training. Thus the center can serve the teacher throughout his years of service and later provide him with a pleasant place where he can continue his interest in professional matters.

All of the activities described here may not take place in all resource centers, but as more are established, as more teachers and librarians work together, better ways will be found to define and enlarge the role of the resource center in improving instruction. It is to be hoped that such centers will be available not only as a central place in the system, but also on a smaller scale in each individual school.

AUTOMATED INSTRUCTIONAL MATERIALS CENTERS?

Sister Mary Alma

Team Teaching .... Flexible Scheduling .... Ungraded Classes .... Track System .... Schools Without Walls .... Education Parks .... Satellite Libraries .... Independent Study .... these phases evoke concepts of movements in education attempting to cope with the rapidity of change in our society. The effect of these forces on the school library is atomic in its impact.

Within a few years the Instructional Materials Center of a new school probably will be as Edith Meyer envisions it in her book, *Meet the Future: People and Ideas in the Libraries of Today and Tomorrow.* By 1980 (in the Education Parks of tomorrow), here is the way a high school student probably will carry on his research.

He will walk down a vivid, mural-decorated corridor and through the automatically opened glass doors labeled *Instructional Materials Center,* drop two books he is returning into a convenient slot and then complete an information request card. He seeks material on practical methods of desalting ocean water, his current chemistry project.

Moments after putting his request into the electronic information-storage computer, a typed card drops out of the big machine. It lists all the books, pam-

Reprinted with permission from: Alma, Sister Mary, "Automated Instructional Materials Centers?" SCHOOL BOARD JOURNAL, December, 1966.

phlets, magazines, recordings, films and tapes the library has on water desalting. Looking over the column headed *Books,* our student checks with a graphite pencil the titles he thinks sound most promising. Glancing down the study-room corridor, he spots an empty cubicle and writes down the number of the cubicle at the top of the *Books* column, detaches that section and slips it into a slot. Next he goes to the periodical room to pick up some of the magazines listed on the next column of the computer card. Later he will get out of the library's vertical files the pamphlets mentioned, then go to the audio-visual room to select the nonprinted materials listed on the third section of the card. He can either look at them there or arrange to use one of the carrels equipped with audio-visual receiving apparatus. Each of these has a small screen for use with visual materials and earphones for listening to records and audio tapes. Machines also are available to magnify any microfilms or microtapes he wants to read and to photo-print any page desired.

He sits in a well-lighted carrel and his books slide onto his desk from a conveyor belt which noiselessly carries books to the cubicle occupants. Other books he had checked will soon follow.

For two hours he works, reading books and magazines and making notes with the aid of a noiseless typewriter. When it is time to leave, he reverses the cubicle number tag attached to each book and puts books and magazines on the conveyor belt. Collecting his notes, he heads for the relaxation area. Fantastic? . . . not a bit . . . every device mentioned has already been developed and is in use in some information retrieval center. They have not been brought together into one library at the present time — but they *will* be!

A July 25, 1966 article in *Newsweek* describing *The New Librarian* provides an interesting account of the latest developments in the automation of facilities at The National Library of Medicine in Bethesda, Md. In producing the *Index Medicus,* a computerized reference to medical literature, each year the library prepares abstracts of more than 175,000 articles published in 2,500 of the world's leading biomedical journals. The abstracts are indexed and transferred to magnetic tapes. From the tapes computers print a monthly index and answer requests for specialized articles. A mobile camera can select specific pages of material upon request. By 1975, Martin M. Cummings, director of NLM, predicts that complete texts and articles eventually will be stored in computers and be made available through a national network of retrieval devices. Envision the possibilities in education with a national network of retrieval devices!

Another example of automation, mentioned in the same article, eventually might affect the physical design of the Instructional Materials Center of tomorrow. The NASA two-story library in College Park, Maryland, has one section containing 50,000 square feet of stacks with all the NASA reports. Upstairs, the same information is condensed onto microfiche cards stored in a space smaller than a single bowling alley. And in the computer area 18 reels of tape hold all available NASA information!

In addition to providing quick access to materials, through the SDI system (Selective Dissemination of Information), NASA is able to send to some 900 scientists lists of reports published in their fields. If a scientist wants to read an article called to his attention by SDI, he sends back a punched card which tells the machine to send him a copy. This is happening now — this is part of your world today!

In the IBM plant at Los Gatos, California, where projections for the next 20 years in information retrieval and computerized learning devices are being created and developed, the library is completely automated. The system automatically prints:

1. Orders to vendors.
2. Claims for periodicals.
3. The Daily News, medium for communicating all input into the library to the laboratory personnel.
4. Lists of recent accessions to match an employee's interest profile.
5. Bindery information.
6. Index terms for documents from title and text input.
7. Union lists of periodicals.
8. Routing slips for periodicals.
9. Check-in card for each periodical issue.
10. Call number labels for book spines and card pockets.
11. Circulation cards.
12. Book catalogs: author and title catalogs as well as subject catalogs.
13. Overdue or inventory notices.
14. Records of circulation transactions.[1]

Just think what this could mean to your library. At least 40 libraries, some more than 400 miles away, use the same computer in Los Gatos. Many school districts are acquiring computers. How many school libraries are making use of them?

The explosion of knowledge has made necessary different methods and materials for instruction, all of which require additional services from the school library. In an article on *"How Trends in Education Affect Libraries,"* Thomas Kissell points out that the premise for change is based on a complex of problems which never have been experienced before. According to Kissell, the problems fall under six broad headings:

1. Expansion of population.
2. Burst of Technology.
3. Discovery of New Forms of Energy.
4. Extension of knowledge.
5. Rise of new nations.
6. World-wide Rivalry of Ideologies.[2]

These pressures have challenged and forced educators into developing patterns of instruction geared to a rapidly changing world. As another educator, Gladys Lees, says:

---

[1] *Marjorie Griffin, "IBM Advanced Systems Development Library in Transition," A Paper for Presentation to the Clinic on Library Applications of Data Processing at the University of Illinois, April 2 – May 1, 1963, p. 18.*
[2] *Thomas M. Kissell, "How New Trends in Education Affect Libraries," Catholic Library World, 37 (October, 1965), 109.*

"It is no longer possible for students to learn during their in-school years all of the information which they will need for adult life. New facts, materials, and techniques appearing with increasing rapidity require different attitudes, skills, and learning for students who are going to face a changing world. Instruction must no longer be geared for today, or even tomorrow, but for the unknown future, about which one cannot even hazard a guess."[3]

Dr. J. Lloyd Trump's *Images of the Future*[4] has brought about in schools the acceptance and implementation of patterns of individual study and varied group sizes and time schedules. This, in turn, has brought about a revolution in the traditional school library, resulting in the multi-media Instructional Materials Center, around which the whole instructional pattern of the school revolves.

RESPONSIBILITY OF STUDENT

The concept underlining the development of Instructional Materials Centers is based on the recognition of the need to place more responsibility on the student for the manner in which he studies and for his rate of progress. This adds emphasis on independent study and individual research, which leads to increased use of a broad variety of learning materials and devices, if the objectives involved are to be reached effectively.[5] The IMC should provide the following services to teacher, students, and, in some instances, to the public:

1. Catalog and inventory all types of teaching and learning material – books, pamphlets, films, recordings, models, exhibits, art prints, slides, filmstrips, microfilms, community resources.

2. Maintain and service all of the teaching tools used in the school.

3. Inform teachers and students about new developments in materials, equipment, and teaching technology.

4. Produce materials which are unique to a specific teaching situation.

5. Provide assistance in locating needed teaching and learning materials.

6. Assist teachers and students in the use of teaching equipment and materials.

7. Provide space and facilities for teachers and students to preview, audition, review, and try out various teaching media.

8. Serve as a comprehensive learning laboratory in which students can learn to use all types of learning materials and equipment.

9. Provide for continuous evaluation of the program and services.[6]

Carolyn Whitenack observed, "The central purpose of education (and Instructional Material Centers) is to teach students to think — to make wise, independent judgments, based upon accurate facts, clear reasoning, and understanding."

[3] Gladys L. Lees, "Mechanization Moves Into Our Libraries," AMERICAN SCHOOL BOARD JOURNAL, 151 (November, 1965), 28.
[4] J. Lloyd Trump, "Images of the Future – A New Approach to the Secondary School," Commission on the Experimental Study of the Utilization of the Staff in the Secondary School; The National Association of Secondary-School Principals (NEA), 1959.
[5] Amo De Bernardis, David M. Crossman and Thomas E. Miller, "Media Technology, and IMC Space Requirements," Audiovisual Instruction, 10 (February, 1965), 107.
[6] Ibid., p. 108.

CLASSROOMS SURROUND IMC

With this shift of emphasis in education to individual development, we find in many schools that are being built today, that the classrooms literally are being designed around Instructional Materials Centers, emphasizing their importance and relationship to the curriculum and its implementation. As David Guerin points out in an article on the influence of media on design, ". . . In one design after another, you will see the Instructional Materials Center as a hub around which classrooms radiate and from which all can be served readily and efficiently.

It might be well to point out that no one involved in the planning of an Instructional Materials Center should omit the reading of *The School Library: Facilities for Independent Study in the Secondary School,* by Ralph E. Ellsworth and Hobart D. Wagener. This publication (available free of charge from Educational Facilities Laboratories) presents a comprehensive treatment of every facet of the Instructional Materials Center. Another publication that should be read by anyone wishing to understand more fully the expanding role of the school library is the January, 1966, issue of the Bulletin of the National Association of Secondary-School Principals. This issue is completely devoted to a study of the school library − its problems and its promise.

It is time now to confine ourselves to the school libraires we have and to contrast them with the Instructional Materials Center we must begin to develop in our schools. Richard Darling aptly describes the IMC when he writes:

> "Today's school library is not only a center where students and teachers may use books and other printed materials. In the library, students use microfilmed material to do research and study in depth. They study as easily with tape and disc recordings, and with filmstrips, slides, and motion picture films, as with traditional library materials. At individual study carrels, they can assemble and use materials in a variety of media. In facilities provided by the school library, they can produce new materials of their own, such as transparencies, overlays, and slides, for use in reporting in the classroom, or simply to increase their own knowledge. The library provides them with programmed materials, with television programs, and with skillful guidance in the most effective use of all that is available."[7]

How does your school library measure up to this description?

FOUND IN SMALL ROOMS

It is feared that the majority of school libraries, particularly those in private schools, can be identified in this description by Ellsworth in *The School Library:*

> "In most of today's secondary schools the library will be found in a small room with a few hundred books around the walls. Seats for a few readers are presided over by a librarian whose main task is to keep order

[7]*Richard L. Darling, "The School Library Quarters," The Bulletin of the National Association of Secondary-School Principals, 50 (January, 1966), 38.*

over a reluctant group of students who are there, not because they want to be, but because they have been sent there to study their textbooks. The students are likely to be more interested in attracting attention than in pursuing the study of a problem. They are not there as individuals, but as captive groups."

Most of us probably have a room full of books which is called the library — with or without a librarian. (Statistics tell us that for secondary schools alone 25,000 librarians are needed right now, with at least 100,000 more needed for elementary schools).[8] If your school follows traditional, rigid period scheduling, when do the students use the library? How much training in individual research does a student in your school receive within the school? Do they have access to audiovisual materials for their own research? Does your library seat at least 30 percent of the student body — which Ellsworth says is minimal? How well-staffed is your library with *professionally* trained personnel? In a word, how far is your library from achieving the standards set forth in the *Standards for School Library Programs,* developed by the American Association of School Librarians and published by the American Library Association in 1960?[9] With the development of Instructional Materials Centers, these standards now are considered inadequate!

What is the basis underlying the necessity of change in the approach to instruction? Dr. Jerome S. Bruner, in his book, *The Process of Education,* points out:

"Mastery of the fundamental ideas of a field involves not only the grasping of general principles, but also the development of an attitude toward learning and inquiry, toward guessing and hunches, toward the possibility of solving problems on one's own . . . To instill such attitudes by teaching requires something more than the mere presentation of fundamental ideas . . . It would seem that an important ingredient is a sense of excitement about discovery — discovery of regularities of previously unrecognized relations and similarities between ideas, with a resulting sense of self-confidence in one's abilities."

It is difficult to achieve this kind of mastery in the traditional, self-contained, teacher-dominated classroom.

It might be well to indicate that it is not essential to create new facilities to to develop a comprehensive school library program. With administrative support, the librarian, if she is a dedicated professional in touch with educational change, should be able to adapt what she has — perhaps with minor renovation or remodeling — into a true instructional center. Sometimes just a rearrangement of furniture and equipment is sufficient to accommodate an instructional materials program. Darling points out: "Breaking up the reading room by the placement of

[8] *Myrl Ricking, "Recruiting New Librarians for Secondary School Level," The Bulletin of the National Association of Secondary-School Principals, 50 (January, 1966), 59.*
[9] *The American Association of School Librarians, "Standards for School Library Programs" (Chicago: American Library Association, 1960).*

shelving, with only one or two tables in each area, and using study carrels in a variety of arrangements throughout the library, creates an atmosphere appealing to secondary-school students and conducive to serious study."

PLANNING BEGINS WITH UNDERSTANDING

One may believe, as Dr. J. Lloyd Trump does, that "the study hall is the first place to eliminate in modern school construction, it having been condemned quite thoroughly on the grounds that it is a poor place for study." Here is an area in the school that could be utilized for the additional space necessary to enlarge the library into an Instructional Materials Center — but, only if the librarian and audio-visual specialist are trained as well as thoroughly alert to currents of change in education. It is axiomatic that "planning begins with an understanding of instructional communications and, through this understanding, a *conviction* that communication is a vital, necessary factor in teaching and learning."

According to Dr. Trump, five kinds of facilities are needed for comprehensive independent study:

- **A LEARNING RESOURCES CENTER** – divided into areas for study and for more active work, supervised by instruction assistants – advanced undergraduate college students, housewives, retired teachers, who have been carefully selected for their specialized knowledge of the subject area.
- **LIBRARY** – where less frequently used and specially valuable printed, audio, and visual references are kept. Strict silence is the rule.
- **CONFERENCE AREAS** – where students can get together to discuss their projects. Supervision is essential.
- **RELAXATION SPACE** (or student lounge) – with an open snack bar – – may be a section of the cafeteria.
- **FORMAL STUDY ROOM** – where pupils who cause disturbances in a Learning Resources Center, Library, Conference Room or Recreation space, and who show obvious need of constant supervision are assigned.[10]

This brings us to the burning question of centralization as opposed to decentralization. Decentralization, according to Dr. Trump's outline, is based on a definition of the library as being that section of a standard library which contains the card catalog and the reference collection, and proposes that the latter be set up in one place and that the book and materials collections be decentralized on some kind of subject divisional plan, (i.e., the social sciences, the sciences, and the humanities).

- **Knowledge cannot be compartmentalized because of the interrelations and overlapping among branches of knowledge.**
- **Decentralization costs money because it increases basic costs in two ways:**
  a. STAFF – Most schools thus far have not been able to afford ONE

[10]*Dr. J. Lloyd Trump, "Independent Study Centers: Their Relation to the Central Library," The Bulletin of the National Association of Secondary-School Principals, 50 (January, 1966), pp. 46-50.*

library staff that can adequately meet the needs of students and teachers where self-instruction or independent study is emphasized.

   b. MATERIALS — Books, records and other materials — and the space they occupy — will cost more in a decentralized system than in a centralized one because the former requires much duplication that is not necessary in a central library.

• The anatomy of a library prohibits it because the division of a library into one section containing the keys and a second containing the collection is extremely unwise.

   a. KEYS (used to help people find the information they want) are of two kinds: catalogs, leading to the contents of resources of a specific library, and bibliographies, leading to the universe of knowledge without regard to any one specific library.

   b. CARRIERS — Books, magazines, newspapers, pamphlets; official government documents, pictures on paper or canvas, posters, maps, slides, phonograph records, tapes, and various kinds of film. Each type of carrier has its specific purpose, and one of the learning skills modern students must acquire is the ability to determine which of the various types of carriers will yield the kind of information he wants.

   c. LIBRARY STAFF — The particular competence of the librarian is her mastery of the keys. She knows which ones exist and how to use them.

Satellite libraries require the services of a fully-trained librarian. Teachers are not oriented to the role of the school library in the modern school. Regarding this point Mary Gaver observes:

   "Most institutions of higher education which have teacher-education programs lack the basic resources needed to orient future teachers and school administrators to the role the school library/instructional materials can play in their future success."[11]

In support of this observation, Dr. Ralph Perkins, after finishing a study analyzing the responses of 4,170 college seniors to tests designed to measure familiarity with libraries, came to the conclusion:

   "Prospective teachers are not capable of using library materials adequately, and their knowledge of the available library resources is limited. It might be well to repeat that although prospective teachers were sampled in this study, it is highly unlikely that any other group of college students would prove to be superior in their knowledge of library fundamentals."[12]

Experience bears this out when teachers, who are subject specialists, enter a library training program. Their knowledge of library resources is meager even in their own area of specialization.

---

[11] Mary V. Gaver, "Teacher Education and School Libraries," ALA Bulletin 60 (January, 1966), p. 63.
   [12] Ibid., p. 63. Ralph Perkins, "The Prospective Teacher's Knowledge of Library Fundamentals" (1965).

To summarize: the traditional library that most of us know is ineffective and impotent in view of the explosion of knowledge and the population expansion. The Instructional Materials Center, at the heart of the diversified school program, is an important factor in the individual development of a student's potential, provided it is adequately staffed with professionally-trained experts. Without a dynamic Instructional Material Center, the total instructional program of a school is handicapped.

MORE CHANGES SEEN FOR YEAR 2000

The following facts are taken from a paper presented during the NCTE convention in San Francisco, November, 1963 (the first part has been updated to Fall, 1966), indicating that the future must depend on the Instructional Materials Center.

A child in the first grade this fall will be 40 years old in the year 2000, when he will be in the middle of his most productive years. What kind of life will he be living? We need only to take a look at the rapid changes taking place about us right now to hazard even a weak guess:

1. **Twenty percent of the jobs existing 20 years ago have disappeared or are fast disappearing.**

2. **Thirty percent of the jobs existing today were unknown before the last war.**

3. **Ninety percent of the scientists of record are living today.**

4. **Three thousand scientific journals alone are published every month.**

5. **Some types of skilled labor are moving into a four-day week.**

6. **Some types of information are building up so rapidly that electronic data processing is the only means of providing efficient retrieval.**

7. **Speed in the communication of ideas is recognized as a key to world peace, understanding and security.**[13]

[13]*Jack McClellan, "New Roles for School Libraries," Elementary English 42 (October, 1965), p. 646.*

WE DON'T WANT LIBRARIES IN OUR SCHOOLS!

Beatrice Katz

We don't want libraries in our schools. What we want and what we're working toward are "Learning Materials Resource Centers." We are no longer satisfied to have in our libraries just books and magazines with perhaps a few pictures and pamphlets. What we need is all of the appropriate educational enrichment materials and aids organized so as to encourage and expedite their use by students and teachers. We hope some day to have a center that will combine the efficiency of the modern supermarket with the service of the old-fashioned corner grocery. From the supermarket will come wide aisles with the "wares" displayed on convenient and readily accessible shelves around which the teacher can push a cart selecting films, models, books, and records to supplement the unit the class is planning. Retained from the corner grocery will be the phone order and delivery service and personal advice of an expert to suggest what is best suited, the new products, and different ways of using the familiar.

The following outline might serve as a guide for school districts working, as we are, to improve the variety of materials and to organize these into a workable indexing and circulating system.

Materials could include:
Printed matter: books, pamphlets, magazines, newspapers, charts.
Audio-visual items: films, filmstrips, music phonograph recordings, nonmusic phonograph recordings, slides, maps, globes, pictures, posters.
Other instructional aids: models, specimens, lists of resource persons, lists of community resources, organizations, services, places.

Materials are organized and housed on several levels:
Materials which are not cataloged, used by an individual classroom and kept in that classroom. These would include sets of textbooks, teacher reference books needed frequently, (e.g., teachers' manuals, guidebooks, etc.), pupil reference materials needed frequently (some maps, dictionaries, etc.), all materials purchased by the teacher.
Materials shared by two or more classrooms and stored in the school building.
    a. Housed in the building library and cataloged in the library; books, magazines, pamphlets, music records.
    b. Housed in the building and cataloged in the library: sets of supplementary textbooks, graphic materials, some models, maps, etc.
Whether materials are kept in the library or in one or more storerooms will depend on the physical space available. Ideally all materials shared within one building should be in one central location.

Reprinted by permission from the November, 1959, issue of the WILSON LIBRARY BULLETIN. Copyright © 1959 by The H. W. Wilson Company.

Materials shared by two or more buildings. These should be housed in as few as possible central locations with the organization and arrangement within these areas making for easy accessibility. These would include professional library, films, filmstrips, models, etc. There should be duplicate indexing in each building. The decision as to which materials should be duplicated for each building and which items should be owned by the system as a whole will depend upon such factors as cost, frequency of use, problems of storage, ease of transport.

Acquisition includes:
  Locating and evaluating.
  Budgeting.
  Selecting.
  Ordering.
  Receiving.
  Technical processing or preparing for use.
  Distributing to points for circulating.

The director in the special subjects has the primary responsibility for the acquisition of the materials in various fields (e.g., music by the music department). The library can assist, if desired, in locating and selecting (e.g., by supplying lists of sources) and teacher participation should be solicited and encouraged. The library could also assist in processing. Receiving and preparing materials for circulation is most efficiently done in a central workroom.

Classifying the materials would be a joint responsibility of the library and the special area directors with particular reference to the manner in which teachers and students will use them. It is important that a uniform subject classification be followed so that all materials available are readily apparent to the potential user. There should be one master alphabetical card file in each building which will include all materials. The different types of materials could be distinguished by different colored cards. The indexing system should be easily expandable to include new types of materials or added items.

Circulation procedures should be uniform, simple, speedy, and unobtrusive. There should be as few as possible persons or places to contact in order to borrow all desired materials. It should be possible either to browse and choose in person or to indicate a unit and have delivered all available suitable materials. Provision should be made for reserving materials for future use or obtaining materials at the next available date if they are temporarily out when first requested.

The intent is to organize all appropriate educational enrichment materials and aids so as to expedite their use through a readily accessible indexing and circulating system from building and district learning materials resource centers.

RELATIONSHIP OF LIBRARY SCIENCE AND AUDIOVISUAL INSTRUCTION

Clarence O. Bergeson

Questions about the relationship between library science and audiovisual instruction, between the school library and the audiovisual service center, and between the school district's head of libraries and the district's audiovisual "director" have periodically developed into deep concerns for both professional groups.

Attempts to answer such questions have led to controversy (and anxiety) in local school systems; developed tension at state levels; appeared more than once submerged in discussions of name changes for an official journal or proposals for the officially accepted name of this "area of specialization"; and at other times appeared openly as an important question in national legislation dealing with education and its materials.

Particularly during the past five years, much discussion has centered on the broadening scope of activities which both audiovisual instruction specialists and librarians recommend for their respective fields.

Librarians show a growing concern for "nonbook" materials. Many advocate the expansion of libraries to include not only books but pamphlets, films, pictures, records, models, etc., cataloged together for easy access, providing teachers and pupils a one-stop service. Some leaders advocate the library as the natural home for all types of independent study activities of pupils. This they would call an Instructional Materials Center.

Many audiovisual instruction specialists see as part of their role a concern for "verbal" as well as "nonverbal" materials. In the past they have provided non-book types of teaching materials to classrooms, ranging from small film collections to centers including everything from real objects to abstract charts. Now many specialists include programed learning materials and equipment among their service areas, thereby entering the area of linguistic-type materials. These service organizations are also named Instructional Materials Centers.

This use of the I.M.C. label by members of both organizations together with the attendant broadening spheres of activities by professional members of each group raises important questions. Are the purposes of both groups alike? Do the services provided differ? Are, perhaps, the professional contributions to the school's operation by both specialists similar and, hence, needlessly competitive and redundant?

Reprinted with permission from: Bergeson, Clarence O., "Relationship of Library Science and Audiovisual Instruction," AUDIOVISUAL INSTRUCTION, February, 1967.

ROLE OF THE LIBRARY

No discussion of library science and audiovisual instruction can go far without defining terms and inspecting the intended purpose of each area. Library science has already been described as historically book-oriented, and many persons in the field are ready to include audiovisual materials. Some definitions of the library and its role should build a basis for comparative consideration of the two specialists.

McDonald provided a definition when he wrote, "The library has been looked upon as the 'intelligence center' of the community where information is made available to the people who are making, doing, and thinking things." (12, p. 1) The *School Library Journal* in its December 1965 issue introduced its feature on "The Pattern of School Library Design" by stating that the library could fulfill its function for today's schools "by providing richer food. This, in one sentence, is the idea of the school library . . ." (10, p. 16)

Dorothy M. Broderick quoted Walter Stone as saying, "The librarian uniquely in society is charged by that society with responsibility for providing the organized reservoir of knowledge that the community needs." She then commented, "Note, the word is knowledge, not books, and the librarian who fails to use all media is narrowing the world he offers to his users." (5, p. 16)

One more comment seems in order. Eleanor A. Ahlers, the immediate past supervisor of library services for the state of Washington and current president of the American Association of School Librarians, provided a definition of the library in a recent issue of *Educational Leadership:* "A school library today, both elementary and secondary, must be a centrally organized collection, readily accessible, of many kinds of materials that, used together, enrich and support the educational program of the school of which it is an integral part." (1, pp. 452-3)

Another comment by Ahlers amplifies the role of the person in charge. "The librarian, supported by an increasing amount of a wide variety of resources and working with classroom teachers, can help children and young people solve problems, develop inquiring minds and rational powers, think and read critically, be creative, study independently, make wise decisions and accept social responsibility."

Within this scope, then, the school library operates — to be an "organized reservoir of knowledge" that, with professional help, opens horizons for children and young people and develops opportunities for their growth and maturity through guidance into the rich fruits of independent study. There can be little doubt of both the need and importance of these professional tasks.

ROLE OF AUDIOVISUAL INSTRUCTION

Discussion of library science and audiovisual instruction also requires a definition of the latter area and its specialist. Providing such a definition and succinctly presenting the specialist's role proves to be a more complicated task. Polar positions exist. In addition numerous definitions of a mixed or specialized nature appear in the literature. This discussion can only attempt to present some representative positions made by vocal members of the field.

Earlier references to the Instructional Materials Center pointed to the use of this title by both librarians and audiovisual instruction specialists. Numerous articles have appeared in *Audiovisual Instruction* describing the development and existence of such centers. To some writers such as Beggs, "An instructional materials center (IMC) is a place where ideas, in their multimedia and diverse forms, are housed, used, and distributed to classrooms and laboratories throughout the school. The IMC contains books, magazines, pamphlets, films, filmstrips, maps, pictures, electronic tapes, recordings, slides, transparencies, mockups, and learning programs." (2, p. 602) One might wonder how this definition differs from those provided by librarians or if any difference is intended.

Others, such as Ruark, feel that "the primary and well-accepted basic functions of such a Center are (1) a pool of basic and specialized materials; (2) teacher in-service training for improved utilization; (3) maintenance of equipment and materials; and (4) local production of unique materials." (15, p. 675) Note the addition of in-service training and local production as functions and the discernible emphasis on problems confronting the classroom teacher.

One working committee at the 1965 Eleventh Annual Lake Okoboji Leadership Conference proposed a somewhat different type of statement of purpose. "The functions of an educational media program include consultation, selection, preparation, dissemination-distribution and utilization of *all* instructional material, information sources, message-systems and facilities in order to promote effective learning." (7, p. 40) This definition identifies consultation and preparation as a vital role and adds a distinct emphasis on utilization.

The 1962 NEA-DAVI task force on "The Function of Media in the Public Schools" provided a different approach to this problem when they strongly suggested that patterns of organization are likely to change in the future as a result of the incorporation of all media into the schools' curriculum. (14, pp. 9-14) If one agrees, then a look at the specialist's function would be more fruitful than a concern for the IMC in its present form.

In line with this emphasis, Eboch proposed that "the prime function of the audiovisual specialist is to design and implement information transmission and display systems which are appropriate to specific instructional objectives in well-defined educational situations." (6, p. 15)

Numerous unique definitions could be presented; however, one more distinctive group deserves inclusion — that group of positions which places stress on the act-of-teaching concerns of the audiovisual instruction specialist.

The 1960 Okoboji Leadership Conference reported some paraphrased remarks by Harcleroad. Included were several areas of knowledge that he felt essential for the person charged with supervising audiovisual programs in the schools of tomorrow: "(1) principles of learning (in depth), (2) knowledge of materials and content — known in ways content specialists may not know them, (3) technological developments and their unique contributions to teaching and learning, (4) statistical skill for evaluative responsibilities, (5) principles of arranging subject matter for effective teaching, (6) process for the creation of materials and the capacity to supervise such preparation, and (7) the capacity to help teachers 'program' their own teaching." (16, p. 96)

In 1961 Bern made a case for the concept of audiovisual "engineers." He placed emphasis on information and communication theory as a basis for the field of audiovisual instruction. (4, p. 186) The January-February 1963 issue of *Audiovisual Communication Review* on definitions and roles defines audiovisual communication as "that branch of educational theory and practice concerned primarily with design and use of messages which control the learning process." (8, p. 36)

Finally, Berlo at the 1963 DAVI Denver Convention commented on the above definition and others by concluding that "in short, you are not a media specialist — you are a communication specialist. You are not just a technical advisor on the use of the media. You are a change agent, and as such, you are involved in the planning and design of messages that will attain desired objectives. The entire process, not just the message-media product, is your field of concern." (3, p. 374) A little later he added, "The dragon you must master is an understanding of the total process of effective instructional communication. . . ."

This final group of definitions places the concerns of the audiovisual instruction specialist directly on the core of the learning act. He is the one who should be qualified to improve the quality of communication in teaching and learning. Its emphasis is not on the materials themselves. It is centered rather on the process of use.

UNIQUENESS OF AUDIOVISUAL INSTRUCTION SPECIALISTS

Earlier it was pointed out that any consideration of the relationship between library science and audiovisual instruction required an understanding of the functions of each area and its respective professional personnel. Clearly, much of the present confusion stems from ambiguities surrounding the function of the audiovisual instruction specialist.

Therefore the question needs to be asked again. What ought to be the audiovisual instruction specialist's professional activity? In an interesting approach, Miles enumerated the additional preparation that he felt the director of an IMC would need if he has received basic training in library science, and, conversely, the new preparation he will need if his original competence is in audiovisual instruction. He ended this discussion by saying, "Eventually, however, we will no longer have two sides to this business." (13, p. 689)

Others contend that each area has something to offer the other without the two becoming one and that one person cannot effectively handle both areas. Many feel that the problem goes further since specialists exist within each field supported by associated organizations — television, programed learning, film production, and the like. In other words, the overlap noted in earlier definitions exists as a practical and functional necessity among professional educators whose divergent purposes delineate each as legitimate areas of specialization.

Miles' position represents those who would define the two fields as similar if not the same in educational service and purpose. The second group, however, recognizes some elements of distinction in the audiovisual instruction specialist's role. These two positions parallel the first two groups of definitions presented earlier.

A third, and in the mind of this writer, a more defensible position parallels the ideas and definitions of Bern and Berlo. Such a position holds that the audiovisual instruction specialist has his own separate tasks to perform in the educational enterprise. As a result, the field of audiovisual instruction must be considered unique, as must the professional preparation of the specialist. It is this difference from the library science specialist that needs to be pursued further.

Uniqueness of function and preparation has, indeed, been recognized historically in the field of audiovisual instruction. McClusky conducted a national survey for the NEA in 1923 about problems confronting audiovisual administration. (11, p. 8) Among the numerous concerns identified by these early audiovisual specialists were the following: training of teachers in the value and use of visual instruction, a concern for the mental development of the child, selection of materials by teachers, and the creation of new materials.

In the winter of 1953 the first issue of *Audiovisual Communication Review* appeared. It contained articles on communications, perceptual research, and research into media usefulness. This pattern of concern for the foundations and research of media use has persisted throughout that journal's history. Furthermore, the official journals of the DAVI have consistently exhibited deep concern of the instructional patterns of teachers and the role that the audiovisual instruction specialist plays in improving classroom instruction and learning.

In like manner the above-named journals and the annual conferences of the DAVI have exhibited a positive concern for the design and production of effective audiovisual materials and packages for learners. Equally evident are present concerns of the entire organization for the design, the use, and the effect of media systems, particularly those media systems developed to satisfy specific educational objectives.

Finally, it should be recognized that the audiovisual instruction field has been a regular consumer of research about instructional media and materials — primarily investigations into its structure, its needed methodology, and its influence on the user. In fact, the field of audiovisual instruction has been one of the prime generators of research about the classroom application of media and materials. As a result, the field of audiovisual instruction has been a principal promoter of those new techniques of teaching and learning that involve media.

In other words, audiovisual instruction specialists have acted in the past primarily upon concerns that dealt with the operational process level of learning — in the classroom, with the learner, with the teacher. Those other past activities which resulted in the provision of back-up services to the teacher by audiovisual specialists arose out of utilization concerns plus the obvious void of such support services in most school systems. Provision of such back-up services (library-like or not) does not remove the predominantly classroom-oriented posture of the audiovisual instruction field.

CONCLUSION

The professionally operating librarian has filled the role of providing a "reservoir of knowledge" concerned with the needs of the scholar, the learner, and the inquiring citizen of the community he serves. He has been the professional guide to the resources needed by man to study the world, the evaluator and anticipator of academic needs for knowledge and information and, in fact, the developer of required resource organizations and structures.

True to the culture around him, the librarian of the past was linguistically oriented. However, it should be noted that in that "book-oriented" society several other professional educational specialists performed complementary tasks dealing with books. Supervisors of language arts, specialists in reading, and teachers of writing worked to improve learning with language, helped and advised in the development of linguistic materials, and consulted with teachers about effective methods of teaching with the written and spoken word. Educators in the fields of language arts, reading, and writing were and are today the specialists in the "design and use" of these linguistic media.

Today the world is, in fact, faced with a multimedia milieu. In such a world a companion specialist to the language arts specialist and the writing specialist is required — someone with informed concern for the structuring of nonlinguistic media messages, with knowledge of the influence that use of these media will have on the learner, and with an understanding of the way they ought to be used. This person exists and his field of specialization is the area of audiovisual instruction.

In the past, the field of audiovisual instruction has been concerned with and has attempted to fill the role of what Berlo called the "communication specialist." In this way professionals in this field have been unique. The school of the future will need, even more, this role competently executed. Audiovisual instruction has the background, the present interest, and most important, the obligation to clearly identify itself with this role of being a specialist in the structure, application, and effect of instructional media and materials in the learning process.

It is this uniqueness that defines and differentiates the field of audiovisual instruction. It is this uniqueness that ought to characterize the future development of audiovisual instruction. It is this uniqueness that clearly identifies the role of the audiovisual instruction specialist as different from that of a competent school librarian.

BIBLIOGRAPHY

1. Ahlers, Eleanor E. "Library Service: A Changing Concept." Educational Leadership 23:451-54; March 1966.

2. Beggs, David W. "Organization Follows Use . . . The Instructional Materials Center." Audiovisual Instruction 9:602-4; November 1964.

3. Berlo, David K. "You Are in the People Business." Audiovisual Instruction 8:373-81; June 1963.

4. Bern, Henry A. "Audiovisual Engineers?" AV Communication Review 1:186-94; July-August 1961.

5. Broderick, Dorothy M. "On Misplaced Devotion." School Library Journal 11:5, 34-35; January 1965.

6. Eboch, Sidney C. "The AV Specialist: Some Reflections on an Image." Audiovisual Instruction 8:15-17; January 1963.

7. Eleventh Lake Okoboji Educational Media Leadership Conference. DAVI-NEA and The University of Iowa, 1965.

8. Ely, Donald P. "The Changing Role of the Audiovisual Process in Education: A Definition and a Glossary of Related Terms." AV Communication Review Vol. 11, Supplement 6, January-February 1963.

9. Frost, Joan Van Every. "What Are We All Here For?" School Library Journal 11:4, 29-30; December 1964.

10. Geller, Evelyn. "A Place to Nourish Learning." School Library Journal 12:4, 15-16; December 1965.

11. Harcleroad, Fred, and Allen, William. Audiovisual Administration. Dubuque, Iowa: Wm. C. Brown Co., 1951.

12. McDonald, Gerald D. Educational Motion Pictures and Libraries. Chicago: American Library Association, 1942.

13. Miles, Bruce and McJenkin, Virginia. "IMC's: A Dialogue." Audiovisual Instruction 10:688-91; November 1965.

14. Morris, Barry. "The Function of Media in the Public Schools." Audiovisual Instruction 8:9-14; January 1963.

15. Ruark, Henry C. "It's IMC for 1963." Educational Screen and Audiovisual Guide 42:673-80; December 1963.

16. Snider, Robert C. "Okoboji: The Communications Specialist in the 1960's." Audiovisual Instruction 7:96-99; February 1962.

THE EMERGING PLAN FOR MEDIA PROGRESS

Henry C. Ruark, Jr.

The school exists to provide an educational environment in which *each child* can develop to his full potential . . . on that we can pretty well agree.

If there is to be effective instruction and learning, the teacher and the learner must be able to use appropriate materials at the right time; thus, availability is the key to utilization.

But the complexities of our modern world reflect a singular and remarkable range and depth and breadth of resource materials which must be utilized to reach the levels of learning we know we must have.

The selection, evaluation, organization, distribution, application and storage of these materials, and the essential equipment for their effective utilization, presents problems of increasing significance at the school level.

Reprinted with permission from: Ruark, Henry C. Jr., "The Emerging Plan for Media Progress," EDUCATIONAL SCREEN, October, 1965.

Certain guiding principles* learned from long experience can determine the directions for planning and organization to meet and answer these problems:

First: The wide variety of instructional materials available makes it mandatory that teachers be selective; learning goals should determine both choice and functional use of instructional materials.

Second: Many materials and media, both printed and non-printed, when used in combination, greatly increase the probability of achieving desired learning goals.

Third: The instructional process can be greatly stengthened, enriched and improved by using much more extensive materials which are, or can be, made truly available.

Fourth: The increasing number of instructional materials and techniques for both group and individual learning experiences offers many new possibilities for creativity and experimentation in teaching and learning.

Fifth: Teachers need to achieve greater proficiency in their abilities to evaluate, select and use various instructional materials. Increased teacher skills and performance must depend not only on stronger pre- and in-service education, but also on proper logistics and personnel support.

If *principles* are to guide *practice,* they must be translated into *working functions;* again, experience indicates that there are four functions which must be served:

1. A pool of basic and specialized instructional materials must be readily available for teacher and learner use.

2. Teacher-in-service experiences must be supplied leading to improved selection, utilization and broad application of instructional materials.

3. Supporting services for maintenance, distribution and application must be available.

4. Local production of unique materials demanded for effective and efficient instruction must be carried on.

Over the past quarter-century, increasingly in the last decade, American schools have developed around a central building unit, often the library, and usually called an Instructional Materials (or Resources) Center. The plan and program includes:

Personnel with time free from other services and duties to plan activities and to provide services.

Materials acceptable in quantity and quality, and adequately available to support the planned instructional program.

Physical facilities and equipment to implement the levels of utilization outlined in the planned program.

An annual budget sufficient to operate the program as developed and planned by the teachers and administrators.

Organization to provide for effective use of instructional media by pupils and teachers during each period of the day.

The scope of such a plan and program, in any building, depends a great deal upon the demonstrated needs of the school, its teachers and learners; first, the relationship of the school to other schools within the school district; and second, the parallel relationship of the school district to other districts within its region.

Specific local needs and specific local structure must be the determining factors, along with the above mentioned relationships.

Experience can point the way, can outline the plan and program. It can build the foundation. Teachers, AV and library personnel, school and district administration, and others concerned with strengthening and enriching instruction must "take over" from there . . .

Winston Churchill once said, "Out of intense complexities, intense simplicities emerge."

From the intense complexities of instructional needs today, an intense simplicity is emerging: The Instructional Materials Center concept.

Don't be caught still sitting on your inertia at the end of this school year. That IMC concept can be *your* plan for media program progress in *your* school building and school district.

*Adapted from INSTRUCTIONAL MATERIALS, Illinois Curriculum Bulletin A-3, 1961, Office of the Superintendent of Public Instruction, Springfield, Ill.

MEDIA'S INFLUENCE ON DESIGN

David V. Guerin

An amazing thing has happened. We educators have at long last come to the realization that the facilitation of communication is one of the foremost responsibilities of educational institutions. We have come to realize that in order to insure that communication takes place in the teaching/learning situation we must utilize the full range of symbology (i.e., language) available to us: verbal and nonverbal, book and nonbook materials. Moreover, we have come to realize it to such an extent that our leading architects are today designing school buildings in terms of the various communications media.

It is truly wondrous for a professional educational communications specialist to contemplate these developments and to think that perhaps the time has arrived when he no longer must push his wares on teachers, plead, persuade, cajole, and try to convince them that he is there to help them, to show them that he understands the teaching problem and has something of great value to offer. Instead, a stage now has been reached where the value of the communica-

Reprinted with permission from: Guerin, David V., "Media's Influence on Design," AUDIOVISUAL INSTRUCTION, February, 1965.

tions media and the various requirements for their best utilization are guiding design factors of the very highest order of importance. Buildings today are literally being designed around instructional materials centers.

In one new design after another you will see the instructional materials center as a hub around which classrooms radiate and from which all can be served readily and efficiently. For even greater efficiency, in some instances, as in the new McPherson School in McPherson, Kansas, in addition to a large central area there are also satellite materials centers around which are clustered classrooms in which related subjects are taught. The satellite centers specialize in materials for these subject areas.

Not only is the overall design dominated by the recognized need for communications media service centers, but the shape and dimensions of the classrooms themselves also are rendered in terms of the utilization of media.

DIRECT DESIGN INFLUENCE OF MEDIA

Let us take a closer look so that you may see just how direct and powerful has become the design influence of the characteristics of media. You will notice as you look at the newer designs the repeated use of the wedge-shaped classroom set fan-wise around a central hub. It is more than a coincidence that the tapering sides of this wedge-shaped classroom match the tapering of the field of view of a projector. Here is a direct one-to-one influence having to do with projection and line-of-sight. You will notice that in some designs this influence is even carried to the point of including a sloping ceiling corresponding to the upward angle of projection.

In determining room size, designers are now taking into consideration facts long known to audiovisual specialists, such as minimum and maximum viewing distance (from a projection screen), minimum viewing angle, and maximum angle of elevation. Years of experience have shown, for example, that for optimum viewing of a projected image, the viewer should not be seated at a distance from the screen closer than two times or farther than six times the screen width. Experience also has shown that a horizontal angle of $60°$ is optimum, but may go to $120°$, depending on the screen surface. The optimum angle of elevation has been found to be $15°$, but may go to $30°$ and still be acceptable. All of these factors, well known to professional audiovisual specialists, have suddenly become meaningful to architects. Viewing area has become a direct guide to classroom area and classroom shape.

Similar considerations with respect to television viewing also are having an impact. Since the definition of a TV monitor image is less than that of a film image and the image brightness is more than that of a film image, the viewing dimensions are somewhat different. In television the minimum viewing distance is four times the image width, and the maximum is 12 times the image width. The television image is rather soft because its definition is limited by the number lines of resolution in the system – usually 525, but ranging between 380 and 600. The farther away you get from the set the sharper the image looks, but beyond the 12 times distance the details within the image begin to run together. The horizontal viewing angle on TV screens ranges only from $70°$ to $80°$ instead of ranging from 50° to 120°. These known facts about viewing areas are having definite influence on the design of new learning spaces. The hexagonal pod or wedge shape that keeps cropping up repeatedly in the new designs is indicative of this influence.

LIGHT CONTROL

The influence of communications media extends to many other elements of design. One of the most influential is the requirement for lighting control. It is an important fact, for example, that no projector can project darkness. The dark values on the screen are produced by the darkness level at the screen. You cannot see a good, sharp contrasting projected image without some measure of darkness. Yet the requirement for darkness varies from one type of projection to another; from the opaque projector which requires almost total darkness to the overhead projector which will operate in a well-lit room. Place these requirements against the fact that the eyes should not be subjected to the frequent and sudden flashing on and off of light and it becomes a design essential that lights be controlled by dimmers rather than switches, especially in multimedia presentations.

It is also highly desirable that students should be able to take notes. This further underscores the need for variable control over room lighting. Ordinary desk work calls for a light level of from 35 to 50 footcandles. In many projection situations a light level of from 10 to 15 footcandles can be tolerated. It is possible to take notes in as little as 1 or 2 footcandles of illumination. The key to what can be tolerated is the amount of ambient light at the screen plus the light intensity of the projection. To illustrate the former: if a van were parked out in full open sunlight, an image projected into its dark interior would be clearly visible to viewers on the outside. To illustrate the separate effect of light intensity: a 16mm projector employing a high intensity Xenon lamp will yield an image with references to which a 25 footcandle light level can be tolerated; whereas with the more conventional lamp, a level of 5 footcandles is advisable, though somewhat higher could be tolerated. We must seek the best combination of both factors. Dome lights recessed in the ceiling, since they do not direct light at the screen, permit the use of higher light levels in any event, and for this reason are finding their way into the newer designs.

Other electrical facilities called for by the use of the new media include extra outlets at the front and rear of the room, conduit running the length of the room for remote control cables, and 20 amp circuits and heavy-load wiring to allow for future increases in power requirements. For the running of TV cable, raceways built into hung ceilings are considered preferable to conduit. The cable is more accessible, changes can be made more easily, and more cable can be accommodated.

The need for control of light exerts another influence on school design. It makes the absence of windows a desirable feature. This, coupled with the fact that windowless buildings or buildings with a minimum of windows are best suited for air conditioning, is influencing architects away from the heavy use of glass. In the conventional classroom where one whole wall is made up of windows, room darkening and ventilation are constant problems. Room darkening is usually either total or it is incomplete, and ventilation is usually interfered with sufficiently to make rooms stuffy, inducing drowsiness in the students. Large expanses of glass are inefficient since they transfer heat and cold from the outside in as well as heat from the inside out. They are also expensive. It has been demonstrated that by keeping windows to a minimum and by following a radial or generally circular design, fully air-conditioned school buildings can be built at the same cost as conventional buildings without air conditioning. There is no question but that students will be generally more alert under conditions in which temperature and humidity are held at optimum levels.

EMPHASIS ON ACOUSTICS

Another major audiovisual influence on school building architecture is the new emphasis placed on good acoustics. Hearing well is as important to good communication as seeing well. The new designs provide acoustical treatment for all rooms. "Live" surfaces and absorbent surfaces are carefully chosen to control reverberation time. A hard surface is placed at the wall from which sound emanates to help project it. Sound absorbent material is used on the opposite wall to cut reverberation. Ceilings are kept live to bounce sound downward. Carpeting is used on the floor to cut reverberation and to eliminate the scuffing noises of shoes and chairs on hard floors. It has been proven in motels that nylon carpeting wears extremely well and is economical to use. It was found that bare floors actually require more upkeep. Carpeting is now being specified for hallways as well as classrooms, thus reducing the noise level throughout the entire school.

The shape of a room has much to do with acoustics. It is a fortunate coincidence that the wedge-shaped room which favors good projection is also conducive to good acoustics. This is because there are no equal and opposite walls to set up standing wave patterns.

DESIGNING FOR SOUND ISOLATION

One of the most difficult problems facing the architect designing the new schools is the problem of isolating sound where movable partitions are specified to permit the altering of room dimensions to accommodate groups of different sizes. In these cases, the designer often calls for folding partitions. It should be noted that complete isolation in these cases is highly unlikely, since sound isolation is dependent upon the mass and inertia of the material used. Furthermore, a large quantity of sound passes through any slight opening in the folding partition. A research report entitled "New Spaces for Learning" produced by the School of Architecture of Rensselaer Polytechnic Institute states: "Any openings in the construction of an intended sound barrier are leaks which have the same significance as leaks in waterproofing. All the sound energy that strikes a void no matter how small will go right on through. A hole of only one (1) square inch area in 100 square feet of wall having a 40-decibel loss rating will leak as much sound as the rest of the wall."

If movable partitions are to be used, particularly folding partitions, it becomes important that special attention be paid to designing them to provide maximum sound isolation. If it is found, as stated in the volume "New Spaces for Learning," that "the best barriers to sound are those which are heavy and limp," then it will be difficult to achieve a high degree of isolation with most present-day folding partitions. Therefore, other means of keeping the ambient sound level down, such as carpeting and acoustical tile, become all the more important. Likewise it becomes more important that equipment be selected which is quiet running so that it can be used on one side of a folding partition without distracting the students on the other side. I am thinking here primarily of motion-picture projectors. In this connection, it is better to use two or more speakers so that the sound may be better distributed and thereby kept at a lower level.

A fair degree of background noise can be and is tolerated in all manner of everyday situations, both in school and out. The problem is to keep it in the background. It is true that complete sound isolation is not necessary. But it is also true that in a classroom situation competition for attention of students is something we can do without. At the same time it is a great advantage to be able to change classroom dimensions to accommodate groups of different sizes. One advantage does not necessarily preclude the other. It simply behooves us to check specifications for partitions closely. The simple general rule is that the level of sound passing through the wall should be less than the level of the sound in the classroom. This means that the partition should have a transmission loss rating high enough to reduce sound intensity to a level lower than the general background noise level.

PRODUCTION FACILITIES

Still another strong influence on school design is the increasing emphasis on local production of instructional materials and programs. This has been accelerated by the demands of educational TV as well as by the visualization requirements of large-group instruction. More and more we find schools being designed with production facilities wherein all types of graphic aids can be produced, including transparencies for overhead projection, 35mm slides, motion pictures, conventional black and white still photographs, and production sets for TV, as well as various audio aids.

These production centers are most often part of the instructional materials center and are integral to it. Where the design calls for satellite instructional materials centers, it will often also call for satellite production centers. Here the teachers and/or students will create their own instructional materials employing procedures and equipment which are well within their capabilities. Here, for example, with office machines they will be able quickly to prepare transparencies from existing printed material of all kinds, or they can prepare original materials from quick sketches with the help of various lettering and other graphic arts devices. The main production center will be more elaborately equipped and staffed to provide all kinds of graphic support. In many architectual designs it is situated so that it may also provide direct projection service to surrounding classrooms, which have one wall facing toward the central production area. Under this arrangement, the projection area is located at the hub of the wheel, so to speak, and the image is projected from outside the classroom to a rear projection screen which forms part of the front wall of the classroom.

With a versatile production capability, the instructional materials center becomes a complete instrument for the facilitation of communication because it can supply not only a broad selection of ready-made instructional materials of all kinds but also can create new materials carefully designed to help a specific group of students to grasp a given concept or idea. The instructional materials production center is centrally situated so that it can render these services most directly and most efficiently.

This is the essence of the architectural influence of the instructional materials center idea. It has in the new configurations become both literally and figuratively the center of the educational design. It has achieved a classic unity wherein educational function and educational design have become one.

TODAY'S MATERIALS AND EQUIPMENT

Caroline J. Locke

ıf school buildings appear different, if new methods of teaching seem radical — they may still not be as changed as new materials and equipment.

Three powerful motivations have caused the spurt of new educational products. Most important are changes in curriculum and methods. New schemes of learning and new stress on enriched, precise content have caused a demand for new books, films, and filmstrips. Secondly, mechanical improvement and electronic equipment have simplified existing hardware and made possible new pieces. Many publishing companies and equipment producers have been acquired by larger corporations, given them new working capital. Finally, large increases in federal funds have multiplied the purchasing power of school districts.

How are materials different? Possibly the biggest change lies in their becoming multimedia in concept. More and more, the text is ceasing to be the prime source of content. Supplementary materials as such no longer exist — any source of information is basic to the learning process.

Reprinted with permission from: Locke, Caroline J., "Today's Materials and Equipment," THE INSTRUCTOR, October, 1966.

The result has been the development of systems of education and packages of learning. A company that produces a textbook either assembles its own kit of pictures, films or filmstrips, models, and other media, or contracts with other companies to produce the related materials.

The psychology that motivated programed learning has also affected the structure of textbooks. There are programed texts, and in addition, textbooks are more and more structured to develop concepts in a logical sequence.

Many schools are assembling their own multimedia packages, and the production of independent films and filmstrips is booming. Many of the new ones are excellent, with on-the-scene shooting eliminating the stereotypes once included in educational films of foreign countries.

Longer films are now being broken up into single-concept films, and new equipment has been developed to show these film loops. Filmstrips with sound tracks will be available soon.

Schools are purchasing more records, and there is an increase in available tapes. But the equipment that is causing the most excitement is the overhead projector, and almost weekly new sets of transparencies appear. Many of the new ones are animated.

Increased preschool education and revisions of many kindergarten and primary curriculums have resulted in the purchase of many manipulatives. These nonverbal materials enable the child to discover and explore. His creative urges are not stunted by a need to deal with printed symbols. Older children are using manipulatives too, especially in mathematics.

The rise in individualized reading and the interdisciplinary approach to social studies and science are giving juvenile books increased importance. The addition or expansion of elementary libraries helps to promote this trend.

Arts and crafts are receiving more attention in the school day. Inexpensive craft materials are available, and stress on process encourages teachers to forget about patterns. Schools are also buying art subjects and in some cases have their own museum.

Federal funds have increased the use of mobile units. Some are traveling television stations for educational TV; others are science laboratories, reading centers, and museums.

Computerized learning is only on the horizon for most schools, and its effectiveness is yet to be proven. Development is uneven throughout the country. Children near a computer center may be playing involved games on the computer. Others may have never seen one.

Ideally, materials implement the curriculum. All too often in the past they determined what was learned and in what order. It is somewhat irrational for schools that have let textbooks determine their course of study to suddenly become alarmed over what the computer will do. If your school develops sound curriculum goals and the guides to implement them, and if teachers adapt materials to their own program instead of letting the materials dictate their procedure, you have nothing to fear about materials in the future.

A big problem is keeping up with all that is happening. New companies, new materials, new equipment, appear all the time. A standing information committee on equipment and materials may be the answer for your school.

AV—MORE THAN MOVIES

Arnold E. Luce

In 1951 this writer asked a school administrator "What are you doing about using audio and visual materials in your school?" He replied, "Oh, we send all the children into the auditorium at 3 P.M. on Friday and show them movies for forty minutes." Fortunately for the children this is not occurring in 99 percent of the schools in 1963. Today we have a large group of teachers who do realize that good instruction includes many more materials besides "movies."

In the twelve-year interval since that incident, the state colleges and a number of private colleges have established courses of audio-visual methods and materials. Consequently, a large number of teachers are now using the newer media of instruction with varying degrees of effectiveness. Within school systems where there was a shortage of the necessary equipment to carry on this modern method of instruction, the National Defense Education Act has helped considerably to alleviate that situation. Before NDEA many teachers had never heard of the overhead projector or seen a microprojector. Now these two devices are relatively common in the schools. The electronic language laboratory is appearing frequently in an increasing number of schools.

Closed circuit television is beginning to be used to a limited extent in Minnesota although it has been successfully used in some other states for several years. It seems to have considerable promise for enriched instruction in certain areas of curriculum. Educational broadcast television has been in use in Minnesota since 1958.

The Minnesota Council of Study by Television (MCST) was organized four years ago to initiate the educational broadcasts of Spanish lessons from *KTCA-TV* Channel 2. Some 30,000 children in fourth, fifth, and sixth grades have made remarkable progress with conversational Spanish in the past three years. To accompany the live broadcasts they have magnetic recording practice tapes provided by the Minnesota Department of Education's Tapes for Teaching service.

Beginning at the middle of the second year, and continuously for the balance of the three-year program, written materials give pupils some experience with printed symbols of Spanish. Much study and some action is taking place on the possibilities of carrying on Spanish instruction in junior high school using language laboratories.

In 1959 the State Board of Education approved the regulation which requires that all persons holding the position of audio-visual director or coordinator in

Reprinted with permission from: Luce, Arnold E., "AV – More Than Movies," MINNE-SOTA JOURNAL OF EDUCATION, May, 1963.

public schools of the state must be certified for those positions by meeting certain educational requirements. As the result of this new certification requirement beginning with the school year 1962-63 many schools have qualified persons in charge of the audio-visual materials in the instructional program. These persons are not just repairmen for broken down projectors as formerly conceived, but are instructional materials resource consultants who can work with all the teachers on their curriculum problems and lesson plans. It is now possible for a teacher to receive assistance in preparing working models for science lessons, dioramas for social studies, exhibits for the public, posters for history, maps for geography, and collections of materials for the study of Minnesota resources, to name only a few of the services provided. Another area of production involves the making of transparencies for use with the overhead projector. These transparencies are being used in the teaching of penmanship, art, numbers, vocabulary, manuscript writing, cursive writing, map work, music, letter writing, language arts, mathematics, and many other subjects. It is rapidly becoming a practice in a number of schools to use the overhead projector and a permanently installed screen for most of the written instructions and diagrams which the teacher formerly laboriously placed on the chalkboard.

Another device which is experiencing an increased usage is the opaque projector. It is most useful when the teacher has only one reference book, one picture in a magazine, or one small map and wishes to have all the class see it at the same time for the purpose of discussion. The material may be placed in the opaque projector thereby producing an immediate enlarged reproduction in color on the screen. The art teachers employ this tool frequently. The language arts teachers will place a pupil's paper in the projector, and the class can study and evaluate.

In new school building planning and construction there is being included an instructional materials center to make available the proper space and facilities for all the activities previously mentioned in this article. Space for previewing projected materials and auditioning sound recordings is also being included in these plans.

The teacher of 1963 has at his disposal 25,000 classroom teaching films; hundreds of fine filmstrips; the finest recordings, both tape and disc, available in music, drama, US and world history, and language instruction. He has broadcast television which brings to the classroom world events as they happen.

No district would consider opening a school without pencils, paper, and books as they are considered basic teaching tools. Now we have additional tools for instruction which are as essential as the paper and pencils.

EDUCATIONAL MATERIALS CENTER

Patricia L. Cahn

Parnsri Wichagonrakul's main purpose in coming to Washington under the Fulbright-Hays program for foreign curriculum specialists was to work with the history departments of the D.C. schools as a specialist in area studies for Southeast Asia and, specifically, for her native Thailand. At first glance her job didn't seem difficult: to direct history and social studies teachers to the various American textbooks and trade books on Southeast Asia.

That first glance turned into a hard look and then into a frustrating search: she was unable to find an up-to-date bibliography or index to books that were designed for elementary and secondary schoolchildren. Then one day, shortly after she had arrived in Washington, she dropped by the Office of Education's Educational Materials Center. Her visit was one of many she made to different offices and agencies as part of the program set up for exchange visitors.

When she walked in the door and saw the books she asked if by any chance we had the kind of bibliography she was looking for. We told her no, but that we were having just that kind of bibliography printed. Naturally, when the bibliography came off the presses at the Government Printing Office, Miss Parnsri was one of the first to get a copy.

Hundreds of other people — some by choice, some by chance — come to the Materials Center each year from all over the United States and from all over the world. Here they find samples of the latest published teaching materials — the most up-to-date collection of its kind anywhere.

Although the Center looks for all the world like a library, it isn't. The books and other materials here are not circulated as in a library; they are read and studied only in the Center. The Center collects many of the same kinds of publications as a curriculum laboratory (in fact, it used to be called a laboratory), and it performs some of the functions that educational documentation centers handle in other countries, serving as a resource for teachers, librarians, and administrators.

In 1953, when the Center was established, it was designed to help visiting educators from abroad become acquainted with the books used in this country's schools. Today, however, domestic visitors outnumber foreign visitors almost four to one, chiefly because more and more U.S. educators are learning about our collections and services.

The Center is the result of a working partnership of the American Textbook Publishers Institute (ATPI), the Children's Book Council (CBC), the U.S. Office

Reprinted with permission from: Cahn, Patricia L., "Educational Materials Center," AMERICAN EDUCATION, July – August, 1966.

of Education, and two other Government agencies. ATPI and CBC serve as liaison with publishers who provide us with review copies of both textbooks and trade books used by schoolchildren and their teachers. The Government provides the personnel and facilities to make the partnership a going concern. Under the auspices of ATPI and CBC, various publishers send books to the Center throughout the year. We act as trustees for this collection of 15,000 books, but we never assume possession of them.

The Center's collection is constantly kept green as new editions replace outdated ones. Last year, for example, we received some 6,600 new volumes, a number of which found the way to our shelves. At the same time we culled about 6,000 older books from our collection.

The backbone of our collection is made up of 5,000 textbooks and related teaching manuals, which are selected by publishers. Each year publishing companies send us their newest textbooks planned for use in schools throughout the country. We hold on to these texts until the publishers tell us they are no longer current. Many companies send representatives to Washington several times a year to weed out their holdings here.

Since the selection of textbooks for school use is a State and local responsibility in the United States, we feel that the Center's only function is to display a current collection and to provide information about the nature and availability of the books.

The trade book collection is handled somewhat differently. By agreement with the publishers, we keep all the trade books we receive for one year. During the year the staff records reviews of the books as they appear in the standard journals covering children's literature in the United States. A book's reception by specialists in the field influences our decision whether to keep it in our permanent collection.

If the reviewers disagree about a book's merits we usually keep the book on hand. Moreover, we keep a file of all the reviews we have used in our research so that visitors may refer to them.

When we remove books from our shelves — text or trade — we send some to the Library of Congress, where they are shelved or discarded. Some of the books that are removed are still up to date and useful, and we offer these to our foreign visitors.

Not all of the Center's activities are focused on the open stacks that visitors see and walk through. Eight or ten times a year we put out reports covering our services and bibliographies of our holdings on some subject areas; for example, "Periodicals Related to International Understanding," "English as a Foreign Language," "Education — Literature of the Profession."

The Center also works closely with OE's Educational Research Information Center (ERIC); both are under the supervision of Lee G. Burchinal, director of the Division of Research Training and Dissemination. ERIC staff members were able to draw upon our resources when they compiled a packet of 1,740 documents describing programs for the disadvantaged. For example, many of the curriculum guides and bulletins prepared by local and State agencies describing their developing programs were pulled from our files and worked into this packet. These documents were put on microfiche and distributed throughout the country. The Center now has a microfiche reader and a file of ERIC materials, which gives our visitors access to a vast amount of unpublished as well as published materials.

To get the most out of what the Center has to offer, a visitor has to spend some time here. Two or three hours of browsing during an afternoon will give him only a general idea of what American publishing has made available to American schools. Some visitors spend a week at a time here; others come in groups over several days, dividing research and examination among themselves. Upon request by educators with special needs we arrange seminars and workshops lasting from a day or two to several weeks.

And now, at the request of ATPI, the Center is assembling a collection of new books related to the problems of urban education and to the work of the Research Council of the Great Cities Program for School Improvement. Included are books published since 1960 which reflect the life of city children, minority groups, the culturally different, and the disadvantaged.

All of our services and materials, no matter what their special focus, are available to American and foreign visitors alike. Government agencies other than the Office of Education support the Center. They are primarily interested in its service to foreign guests. In a small way we serve as host to participants in the various grants-in-aid programs funded by the Agency for International Development and the U.S. Department of State but administered by the Office of Education. These include exchange teachers and participants in educational-technical assistance programs and the international teacher development program.

As the Center takes on more responsibilities, provides more services, and plays host to more and more visitors, it is becoming a key source for educators and for students of children's literature. In essence, though, the work of the Center is directed to schoolchildren the world over. It is part of a worldwide effort to document, study, and compare — and by these means to improve the books that are put into the hands of children everywhere.

WHY TORONTO PUT A PROFESSIONAL CENTER IN ITS BUSINESS OFFICES

The headquarters building of a school system should do more than provide centralized offices for its administrative and business departments. It should be a place to which the public can look for intelligent and informed educational

Reprinted with permission from: "Why Toronto Put a Professional Center in its Business Office," THE NATION'S SCHOOLS, January, 1962. Copyright 1962, The Modern Hospital Publishing Co., Inc., Chicago. All rights reserved.

leadership. Above all, it should offer the teaching staff facilities for study, inquiry, research, training and professional growth.

These are some of the thoughts that found expression in the design of Toronto's new Education Centre, opened formally on November 15 by His Excellency Major-General George P. Vanier, governor-general of Canada.

Academic and business offices formerly located in various parts of this Canadian city successively were moved into the new seven-story, gray stone-faced building during preceding months. The structure meets the requirements of a modern administration building, but what makes the new headquarters unique among other buildings of its type is its curriculum center. This department, located on the fifth and sixth floors, was designed according to the latest concepts regarding facilities needed for the ongoing inservice training and self-instruction of the city's 3300 teachers.

Teachers need a place where they can receive stimulation and help after school hours. That is the conviction of Z.S. Phimister, director of education, and his fellow planners. Accordingly, the center remains open to teachers in the evening. Food is served in the cafeteria 16 hours a day, if necessary. After finishing their evening meal, teachers may remain in the building for study at the library (located on the same floor) or go across campus to the near-by University of Toronto for evening classes.

Toronto's Education Centre also houses these facilities: a professional library under the supervision of a trained librarian; an auditorium-conference room seating 250; well furnished reception, committee and waiting rooms; a teaching aids division complete with a soundproof studio equipped for radio, television and motion picture production; a special education room; a reading clinic; a research department, and (in the basement) parking for 54 cars and a large receiving and general storage area.

Within the curriculum center separate rooms have been designated for the various subjects taught. Offices of the supervisors, who planned the spaces, are in the room or near-by. Teachers here may discuss problems with counselors, get answers to questions, evaluate materials, improve their skills and teaching methods, do research, exchange ideas, and receive formal inservice instruction. Consultants, supervisors and inspectors have the resources and the space for discussion with teachers, for demonstrations, and for displays.

Forty-one supervisors and counselors are available. Teachers with specific problems usually make appointments — either for help in the classroom during the day or at the center in the late afternoon and evening. Since under the present arrangement the supervisors and counselors do more afternoon and evening work then they once did, they adjust their work schedule accordingly.

Facilities of the teaching aids division are outstanding. To make instruction more vivid and effective, teachers can get acquainted with a wide range of teaching materials — from simple printed or silk-screened items to more complex units, such as recorders and projectors. Here they can learn how to produce teaching aids not available commercially. They can evaluate projected materials in the combined screening-workroom.

The research department plans and administers carefully controlled experiments on questions of concern to teachers, administrators and trustees. Since better teaching is the ultimate goal of all experiments, cooperation between teachers and research assistants is close. Tests conducted in the schools are processed and interpreted in the research department of the center. Electronic machines and recording devices have been installed to expedite the work.

The aim of the science department is to help teachers make science instruction more meaningful to their classes. A plant and animal room, a demonstration laboratory where teachers can observe technics, a display room, and a utility room serve the area. Live and other specimens are stored here for later use by teachers in their classrooms.

Physical education quarters offer the teacher the privary not possible on the school premises. Here, with partners, the teachers can improve their skills in one or another sport away from the prying eyes of the children. Activities requiring special equipment, such as jumping pits, may be studied through film and filmstrip viewing. Curriculum planning sessions for health and safety also are held here.

Corresponding facilities are offered by the other departments — mathematics, home economics, industrial arts, music, guidance, kindergarten and special education. Each supervisor has the special books, materials and equipment needed for his particular field.

The cafeteria is located on the top floor of the building, near the library. Banks of picture windows permit a view of the surrounding landscape. The 2800 square feet of dining area can seat 164 staff members, teachers and guests. Two adjoining private dining rooms, for board members and executive personnel, accommodate 30 persons each.

A show place of the building is the two-story, walnut paneled room for the board of trustees. It has a visitors' gallery for 45 persons on the second floor level, located just off the beautiful two-story foyer near the main entrance of the building. Three automatic elevators serve the building.

The administration-business facilities of the structure have been laid out for efficiency. Executive suites are grouped on the second floor. The third floor houses the financial division, which includes the purchasing, accounting, and business machines offices. The school district's large school planning division (architectural and engineering) shares the fourth floor with the plant operations and maintenance departments. Services that call for daily contact with the public are centered on the first floor.

The cost of the building, including furniture and incidentals, approximated $5 million. Page and Steele, Toronto, were the architects.

D.S. Mewhort, coordinator of auxiliary services for the Toronto school system, including the center, made these observations about the building:

"Two generations ago, the suggestion of an education center such as this would have been accorded sparse attention, even in education circles. One generation ago the construction of such a center would have been precluded by the quality of esteem in which publicly supported education was then generally held. Rapid changes in local and in world situations have so altered the attitude of professional educators and of laymen alike, and have so enhanced the significance of public education, that the curriculum center, dedicated to education in this city, has now developed from dream to concept to reality."

At the gala formal opening, Director Phimister made this evaluation: "The unique feature of the building is that it provides rooms which serve the purpose of teachers – the important people who meet students face to face. Three floors in this seven-story building are given over to areas where teachers may find books, materials related to teaching, and devices useful in instruction. More important, perhaps, is that these rooms provide meeting places where the teacher who is seeking something will come in touch with others who are also seeking. The thoughtful, querying individual, when he comes in contact with others of his kind, is likely to develop his latent powers."

According to Dr. Phimister, the Education Centre was designed to be the heart of the Toronto educational system. It is well on its way to becoming just that. Even now more than 50 teacher groups conduct programs here for professional improvements. Moreover, the structure is destined to serve as the nerve center of the city's educational life.

THE INSTRUCTIONAL MATERIALS CENTER: DIALOGUE OR DISCORD?

Phillip J. Sleeman & Robert Goff

One of the most talked about developments in current education is the *instructional materials center*. This center, or IMC concept, is filled with hopes and promises, doubts and controversies. This paper will review the major functions of the IMC and will point up some of these hopes and promises along with the controversies. Our discussion will conclude with guidelines for future action and will be supplemented by an intensive bibliography for further reading.

The instructional materials center was to be a central source of equipment and materials, providing economy of teacher time and effort and encouraging the use of all types of instructional materials. R.A. Swanson (18) stated that the main purpose of the IMC was to benefit the pupils, teachers, and other adult residents of the community housing such a center. Further extensions of the IMC concept envisaged areas for experimentation where new types of instructional materials might be developed, produced, or evaluated for future use. In summing up the philosophy and roles of the IMC, M.G. Phillips (11) added several functions: circulation of audiovisual materials; coordination of a variety

Reprinted with permission from: Sleeman, Phillip J. and Goff, Robert, "The Instructional Materials Center: Dialogue or Discord?" AV COMMUNICATION REVIEW, Summer, 1967.

of materials; inservice education of teachers; and consultation services. Further, he advocated selection and use of every type of audiovisual material in conjunction with the use of radio and television programs.

For those who shared this philosophy, the IMC began to take on the appearance of "all things to all men" (15), and it slowly evolved into an information storage and retrieval center, with production and evaluation facilities attached. For some, the center promised to be a blending of the complete spectrum of materials services. Many saw it as the first step to a true "systems approach," eventually basing complete instructional instrumentation (mass and individual) on a completely programed curriculum with objectives formulated in behavioral terms (13). Others saw the IMC as an extension into education of the cross-discipline use of skills, knowledge, and equipment.

The evolution of the IMC concept brought about the controversy of location. Librarians naturally viewed the IMC idea as an extension of library services, and expanded library services today are often labeled "instructional materials centers" (3, 7). Audiovisual specialists also used the term "instructional materials centers" when they referred to the expanded services they provided. This is especially true today with programed instruction included in the domain of audiovisual instruction (3, 9). Both groups — the librarians and AV specialists — felt that the instructional materials center belonged in their domain (5).

This major philosophic problem leads to the many subproblems of the IMC. By its nature the IMC is not a library, and a library may not be an instructional materials center. The traditional library generally contains books, both hardbound and paperback, newspapers, periodicals, and, in many school systems, the professional library for the teaching and administrative staff. Personnel come to the library to obtain materials for immediate or home use. The atmosphere is generally quiet, restrained, and subdued.

The traditional school audiovisual center contains a variety of media production facilities and audiovisual equipment. Mainly, it is a facility to house teaching machines, projectors of several kinds, record players, and tape recorders. There may also be filmstrips, films in limited number, models, mock-ups and dioramas, study prints and flat pictures. Teachers simply sign up for needed equipment and materials. At times, a delivery or pickup service may be rendered. The atmosphere may also be quiet as the production facilities and space are unfortunately sometimes used for storage.

Today's IMC contains the materials of both library and audiovisual center and also includes curriculum guides, courses of study from other schools, specimens of standardized tests, catalogues of all types of commercial and industrial materials and equipment, and samples of textbooks from several publishers. In addition, materials in depth in all subject-matter areas are found in the collection, with production facilities to "tailor-make" instructional materials at the local level included as a necessity. Individual study stations are often found in the IMC (19).

In changing the physical elements of the IMC, there is also a change in role from *storage* to *service*. The degree of service should be measured in terms of service available for both the library and audiovisual segments of the IMC. Service involves such functions as inservice training, coordination of all instruc-

-tional media and materials, development of source lists of available materials on a system-wide basis, relationship to all kinds of instructional materials, consultation on the selection and use of instructional materials, and many other such roles.

In changing the role of the center, there is also a change in the responsibilities of individuals connected with the center. Resource person with knowledge about the wide variety of materials available, supervisor of material use in center and classroom, coordinator of several multimedia approaches toward varied classroom subjects, purchaser of materials – these are some of the functions that the supervisor of the IMC might perform. Further, this person must not only have the foresight and readiness to accept new roles for instructional materials in the teaching/learning process, but must also be acceptable to new roles for himself, roles involving planning, curriculum design, public relations, and innovation (6, 12, 17, 20, 21). He must truly function as a change agent in our educational society.

From the changed role of the persons involved, it is evident that the training of neither librarian nor audiovisualist is in itself satisfactory for supervision of an IMC. Librarians know about literature, cataloguing, indexing, budgeting, and the general and specific resources in their field (24). Audiovisualists know about the processes of communication, equipment, materials availability, budgeting, in-service needs, plant design, among other areas (23). But these are presently separate fields of specialization. Rare is the person who combines the talents of *both* fields into one general area (2, 6, 8).

Personnel problems are not the only ones which have beset the idea of the IMC. One of paramount importance is the *space* problem. The answer to the question of where to put the IMC constantly repeats itself: where the materials will be used most efficiently and effectively. Thus, planning for an IMC should begin with the individual classrooms of a building where there should be basal texts, reference volumes, periodicals, maps, charts, graphs, illustrations, filmstrip and slide sets, tapes and records (16). Within the several buildings, production facilities would be housed with circulating pools of equipment. Larger centers could be provided in separate buildings or in senior high schools (of moderate-size systems), where production areas, preview areas, film inspection areas, and repair facilities might be housed. If the system were a large one, additional equipment such as television and computers could be included (21, 26, 28).

Space could be obtained through the utilization of areas which are currently not being effectively used or through remodeling uncommitted space. As new buildings are planned, however, proper consideration must be given to the use of instructional materials as integral parts of the teaching/learning process.

Another problem which confronts the IMC concept is that of finances. The long-term objective of the IMC is to provide face-to-face instruction in small groups to the maximum degree possible within the plane of desirable teaching and learning (1). Financial support may be obtained from the Federal Government under the provisions of the Elementary and Secondary Education Act of 1965. This act provides for acquisition of library/audiovisual materials. Ironically, some school administrators seem to be trying to separate the categories and are apparently making a great problem out of a law written specifically to foster the growth of the instructional materials concept (10).

Time is another very realistic problem confronting the IMC. The school day is only so long, as is the school year. The trend seems to be in the direction of a longer school year, and if this is the case, then it might bode well for the IMC concept and its staff. Much preliminary planning can be done during the summer months. Definition of educational goals, use and evaluation of media and materials may be determined. The actual elements of organization may be established and made functional. Preliminary operation may be started with new staff and "trial runs" may be experimented with during the summer to eliminate physical drawbacks in the organization plan, should any problems become evident.

Much may be done during the school year. Consultation with department chairmen, principals, master teachers, curriculum personnel, teachers, and pupils is a continuous process. The concept of released time for designated teachers to work is a segment of the time problem. No one can expect a librarian, teacher, or audiovisual director to establish an instructional materials center while pursuing a full schedule in the office, library, or classroom. Key administrative personnel will most likely be hired for the IMC as they are usually not available within the school system.

The *personnel* problem besets education more greatly today than ever before. With the critical shortage of teachers in some areas of the country, schools are faced with an even more critical shortage of qualified staff for any venture as encompassing as the IMC (34, 35). It is anticipated that during the next ten years we will see this shortage problem grow in magnitude rather than diminish.

The foregoing pages have outlined some of the basic ideas upon which the IMC concept has developed. Developments have been touched on briefly, and some of the major problems facing the IMC today have been outlined.

What of the future? Where do we go from here with the IMC? The IMC will not advance rapidly until more attention is paid to recent trends in education. These trends are numerous and varied, but several which have taken on particular significance include: (1) focus on the individual rather than the group; (2) making the individual more responsible for his own learning; (3) true inquiry in place of memorized learning; (4) topics taught in depth in view of "fact teaching"; (5) nonclassification of children by age, but rather grouping children according to their readiness to absorb the subject matter to be learned; (6) nongraded in place of the graded school; and (7) real discovery instead of "show and tell" in education. These trends in many schools point toward the revision of curriculum in its present state of the art.

With these new trends comes a series of needs which will affect the IMC concept. The center cannot develop in a vacuum but rather must evolve in relation to other events in education which share common needs. In the overall picture, there is much need for strong administrative backing, for more effective personnel services (33), learning centers and system-wide centers each reinforcing the other (29), greater specificity of teaching objectives, and, above all, awareness that the problems in education today should be looked upon as stages in the development of an educational system involving the best cooperative use of effort (19).

In the realm of "control," there should be little problem. The major handicap exists primarily *in the minds of people* who refuse to see a delegation of authority. For those who work toward producing the best educational system possible, the IMC director's role is usually solved by thinking not in terms of "which one" but in terms of "who" is best qualified for the job.

M.G. Phillips (11) points to the person who is the coordinator of specialists, guiding them toward the optimum educational program. Paul Witt (21) stresses professional preparation and experience in education, which experience would lie in actual teaching followed by preparation in areas of supervision, curriculum development, and educational administration. This person — "Who" — should be prepared to become involved in curriculum planning, teacher and administrative concerns and use of curriculum materials as integral parts of teaching, establishing a climate suitable for the best use of media and materials, developing new procedures for evaluating the effectiveness of instructional materials, devising central classification systems to facilitate rapid location of materials for all learning situations, and developing production (locally) of materials needed for instruction.

In the areas of space and financing, school systems should look toward a unified approach. Unifying space and finances among several systems on local levels can produce cooperative efforts which can satisfy immediate local needs while long-range planning is enacted and implemented. This is especially true today when federal funds are rapidly forthcoming. The larger financial picture looks even brighter, and this means that progress on the IMC development must move forward even more rapidly. Figures and budgets must constantly be revised, and planning must be more farsighted than ever before. Planning must not be of a day-to-day nature but on the long-range basis of "What will we have ten, twenty years from now?" (14).

What is needed to bring the IMC concept to fruition is a most serious commitment to education on the part of school boards, administrators, and teachers: (1) commitment couched in terms of providing the best educational experiences possible in the best way possible; (2) commitment linked with a "hard-nosed" approach toward systems and materials, asking: "Do these do the jobs they are supposed to do? Is there something better?"; and (3) *commitment to making the students "hungry" to learn, and satisfying that hunger with high-quality instructional materials* (22, 25, 27, 30). These are the conditions necessary for making learning exciting and effective and, consequently, making the IMC function an integral and dependent part of a child's learning experience.

REFERENCES

[1] _____ . "The Instructional Materials Center." *Educational Executives' Overview* 3: 25-28; July 1962.

[2] Ahlers, Eleanor E. "Library Service." *A Changing Concept."* *Educational Leadership* 23:451-54; March 1966.

[3] Bergeson, Clarence O. *Relationship of Library Science and Audiovisual Instruction. A Position Paper.* Delivered at Delegate Assembly Meeting, 1966 DAVI Convention, San Diego, Calif. (Published in *Audiovisual Instruction* 12:100-103; February 1967.)

[4] Berlo, David K. "You Are in the People Business." *Audiovisual Instruction* 8:372-80; June 1963.

[5] Goldstein, Harold. "A/V: Has It Any Future in Libraries?" *Wilson Library Bulletin* 36:670-73ff; April 1962.

[6] Lewis, Phillip. "The Role of the Educational Communications Specialists." *American School Board Journal* 143:16-17; December 1961.

[7] McGinnis, Dorothy A. "Developing Learning Resource Centers in Secondary Schools." *NASSP Bulletin* 46:12-15; December 1962.

[8] McGuire, Alice Brooks. "The School Librarian: A New Image." *Educational Leadership* 21:227-30; January 1964.

[9] O'Connor, Olwyn. "Statement of Philosophy and Purposes of an AV Department." *Educational Screen and AV Guide* 40:488-89; September 1961.

[10] Phillips, Harry L., and Lorens, John. "Title II: Elementary and Secondary Education Act of 1965." *Audiovisual Instruction* 10:626-29; October 1965.

[11] Phillips, Murray G. "IMC – the Rationale" *The Clearing House* 37:381-83; February 1963.

[12] Preston, Ellinor O. "The Librarian Sees His Role in the Materials Center." *Educational Leadership* 21:214-16ff; January 1964.

[13] Ruark, Henry C., Jr. "A Report on the Year 1961, D.D. – Decisive Decade." *Educational Screen and AV Guide* 40:640-43ff; December 1961.

[14] _____. "The Second Year of the Decisive Decade – Sixty-two Skidoo!" *Educational Screen and AV Guide* 41:706-709; December 1962.

[15] _____. "It's IMC for 1963 – The Third Year of the Decisive Decade." *Educational Screen and AV Guide* 42:674-80; December 1963.

[16] _____. "IMC and the Concept of Levels." *Educational Screen and AV Guide* 44:11; November 1965.

[17] Sindledecker, Charles. "The Changing Role of the AV Director." *The Instructor* 74:61, 64; June 1965.

[18] Swanson, R.A. "Improving Instruction Through Materials Centers." *American School Board Journal* 139:47-48; October 1959.

[19] Taylor, Kenneth I. "The Instructional Materials Center." *Nations Schools* 66:45-50; December 1960; 67:53-60; January 1961.

[20] Whitenack, Carolyn I. "The Changing Role of the Librarian." *Wilson Library Bulletin* 38:397-400; January 1964.

[21] Witt, Paul. "High School Libraries as IMC's." *NASSP Bulletin* 43:112-18; November 1959.

For future reference and further reading on the instructional materials center concept, consult:

[22] _____. "When Media Serve People." *Educational Leadership* 23. No. 6; March 1966. (The entire issue is devoted to media.)

[23] Hammersmith, George. "Role and Function of the AV Supervisor." *Educational Screen and AV Guide* 43:89; February 1964.

[24] Alexander, Elenora. "The Librarian's Multi Media Role." *The Instructor* 74:55ff; November 1964.

[25] Ames, Robert. "A Library's Role – IMC." *Wisconsin Journal of Education* 97:9-10; December 1964.

[26] Audiovisual Instruction 10: No. 2; February 1965. (Entire issue is devoted to media influence on school design.)

[27] Dall, R.C. *Individualizing Instruction. 1964 Yearbook of the Association for Supervision and Curriculum Development.* Washington, D.C.: ASCD, National Education Association, 1964.

[28] Darling, Richard L. "Changing Concepts in Library Design." American School and University 37:98-100; May 1965.

[29] Giesy, John P. "A Working Relationship – How the Central IMC Relates to IMC's at the Building Level." Audiovisual Instruction 10:706-708; November 1965.

[30] Mesedahl, Leroy E. "The IMC: Contribution to Individualized Instruction." Audiovisual Instruction 10:704-705; November 1965.

[31] Miles, Bruce, and McJenkin, Virginia. "IMC's: A Dialogue." Audiovisual Instruction 10:688-91; November 1965.

[32] Phillips, Murray G. "Curriculum Materials Center: The Philosophy." 1965 Educational Communications Proceedings. Albany, N.Y.: State Department of Education, Division of Educational Communications, 1965.

[33] Posner, A.N. "IMC as a Means to Constructive Use of Teachers' Talents." California Journal of Secondary Education 35:250-51; April 1960.

[34] Staffing the IMC in Elementary and Secondary Schools. Bulletin No. 427. Lansing Mich.: Department of Public Instruction, 1960.

[35] The New York Times, Sunday, March 20, 1966, and every Sunday thereafter through December 25, 1966, offers evidence of the shortage of personnel in library areas. The number of vacant positions far exceeds the number of applicants.

THE IMC IN THE
CONTINUOUS PROGRESS SCHOOL

June Berry

Many solutions have been found for the traditional problems of traditional schools: team teaching, programed instruction, the Trump Plan, the Diedrich Plan, and so on. Among these, the Continuous Progress Plan is one of the few which picture the instructional materials center as the center of the plan and of the school. It is based on the educational philosophy that the student should progress at his own rate from kindergarten through college, unhampered by a lock-step curriculum or by a teacher who must give the identical lesson to 35 students.

In the Continuous Progress Plan (CPP), barriers of grade and class organization for instructional purposes are completely eliminated. Each student advances as fast as his ability and interest dictate. One may go through the curriculum of a traditional grade in four months; another will need fourteen. The plan features individual study stations, or carrels, where the student keeps his books, progress charts, and other study equipment. When he needs help he consults the teacher and librarian; or he will be called into "studios" — small groups of five or ten students who happen to need the same lecture or discussion at the same time. When the lesson is completed he returns to his carrel until he again needs help.

The instructional materials center is essential to the CP school because a wide variety of materials are needed by different students at different times and they must be kept in a convenient central location. Our IMC has virtually the same definition as that given in AASL *Standards for School Library Programs,* and it embodies almost every recommendation of the *Standards.* Indeed, it adds others, for it contains not only all the materials found in good school libraries, but the equipment and supplies offered in audio-visual centers, and the materials being used in the curriculum laboratories that are sprinkled across the nation. It also provides space and guidance for using these materials.

IMC SERVICES TO STUDENTS

Organization of materials. The IMC selects, orders, catalogs, and organizes all materials for use by student and teacher. Anything aiding instruction is an instructional material and thus a service of the IMC. We have pictures, models, maps, charts, and study kits, numbered and filed in their designated areas; our community resource file lists people in the community who can serve as resource

Reprinted with permission from: Berry, June, "The IMC in the Continuous Progress School," SCHOOL LIBRARY JOURNAL, November 15, 1964. Copyright ©1964, R. R. Bowker Company.

speakers on given subjects and indexes places that are suitable for field trips. All materials are listed in the card catalog and distinguished by color: a blue card may indicate films, yellow the study kits. Schools using this method would continue by adding colors for programed lessons, models, and exhibits.

Circulation of materials. Circulation procedures resemble those of the traditional library, except that not only books and magazines may be checked out, but filmstrips and programed lessons, and even equipment for their use. Some a/v materials are booked in advance, as they are in a/v centers, so that students and teacher may know for what day and hour the materials are reserved for them.

Use of Materials. The IMC carrels or booths can be used by the student for reading purposes and for use of film or tape recordings. The student may also use one of the conference rooms which provide electrical outlets and sound-proofing facilities. The film or filmstrip may be taken home, as books are in conventional schools, and if the student doesn't happen to have a projector of his own he may obtain one at the IMC and check it out for home use.

Guidance in Finding Materials. In the CP plan the librarian spends less time finding information for students, because they have learned their study skills early. Since students spend 60 per cent of their time in individual study, they must be proficient in finding what they need in the IMC. In his elementary years (called "entrance" and "cultural" divisions) the student may not advance in the curriculum sequences unless he has mastered certain basic study skills. More intensified and specialized IMC instruction is given in the high school (or "pre-specialization division").

IMC instruction is given in two ways: When several students are ready for advanced card catalog experiences, their teacher will direct them for small group instruction from the librarian or his assistant, though the teacher may do it himself. Or an individual student may ask to go to the IMC for help from the librarian or through some self-instructional device: a study kit, programed text, or teaching machine, on finding and using materials.

Reading Guidance. Individual reading guidance follows the pattern of the traditional school. There is as much variety in the reading levels of students as in their mastery of content. Many students, however, do read more advanced books, since they are not being paced with slower learners. They come to the library for adult books and to participate in Great Books discussions with others on the same reading level.

IMC SERVICES TO TEACHERS

In conventional school the librarian assists a teacher who must give one lesson to a class of 35; in the CP school the library personnel help a teacher who is in charge of 60 students, but who has perhaps no more than six studying the same lesson at once.

Compiling Bibiographies and Assembling Materials. The teacher will call on the IMC when she has one student or a cluster of students who need material on a given subject. A list of all the books, films, and other materials on the subject is compiled by the librarian and sent to the teacher. Often the materials themselves are gathered when the teachers request them. They may be placed on reserve for his students; or films, books, pictures, models, and exhibits are collected, checked out, and sent to the studios for the length of time they are needed, ranging from a day to a month. Because of the diversity of our collection, even bulletin board ideas and materials are available to teachers. Book jackets, charts, pictures, letters, and other objects are checked out as often as are books in a conventional school.

Preparing Teaching Materials. If the library does not contain the materials needed by the teacher, one of the IMC personnel will help him make it, or may make it for him with the help of student assistants. Pictures are enlarged on the opaque projector, transparencies are made for overhead projection; models are built; and collections of various types are assembled. The IMC includes a technical process department, often with a full-time person in charge of graphics and production of teaching aids. All materials are there: cardboard, construction paper, scissors, paper cutter, paints, all the table and counter space necessary.

Planning with Teachers. Planning takes up a large portion of time. Sometimes only a few minutes are needed to find a picture or map. More often the librarian or a/v specialist visits a studio to discuss the materials needed by a group of students and their teacher. In addition, monthly meetings are held with the various departments to discuss the needed materials. Often the librarian or a/v specialist joins the teacher in previewing a film for prospective purchase.

IMC PERSONNEL

Obviously a range of activities geared to helping all teachers and all students with their individual needs requires a larger library and a/v staff. Here the AASL *Standards* must be considered minimal, though the exact size depends on the size of the school.

Professional Staff. At least one person trained in traditional library procedures will be responsible for services involving printed materials, another, the audio-visual director or supervisor, will supervise the selection and organization of films, projectors, tapes, and teaching machines. A full- or part-time staff member, depending on the school and the teachers' needs, will be in charge of graphics and the construction of teaching materials.

Clerical and Student Assistants. To permit the librarian to engage in curriculum guidance, routine duties are shifted to one or more clerical assistants, who catalog books, films, and other materials in the IMC. Most schools will continue to use student assistants. Some students are selected because of their interest in careers in library work or "instructional technology"; others may be paid to work in the graphics department or other areas of the IMC.

IMC FACILITIES

Facilities, equipment and materials for CP schools are like those of good conventional schools although with several obvious additions. First the traditional *book storage area* must be enlarged to house films, recordings, tapes, study kits, exhibits, models, transparencies, and the various self-instructional material, and

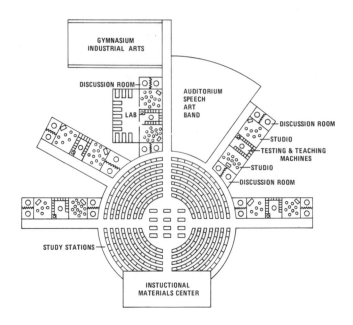

additional space provided for projectors, phonographs, teaching machines, and other a/v equipment. Special shelving must be designed to hold these various materials.

The conventional *circulation areas* must also be much larger, so that films and projectors may be checked out. Since these cumbersome objects may also create disturbance, the circulation area should be removed from the reading and study areas.

The *reading area* resembles that of any modern school library, except that fewer large tables are found, and more carrels. Various types of individual carrels and booths are scattered throughout the IMC, most equipped for use of films, filmstrips, and teaching machines.

Traditional *conference rooms* are modified only to add more complete listening and viewing facilities. In addition, a *preview and planning area* is added to the conventional library space. In small schools a large conference room may suffice.

An area considerably larger than the conventional workroom is necessary to accommodate the many supplies used in producing charts, maps, transparencies, and other instructional aids. It must have space and facilities for processing all books, films, and other materials to put into circulation, as well as space for mending books, and for repairing and maintaining a/v equipment. This area, known as the *technical processes* or *graphic area*, is also called the "curriculum lab" or teachers' workroom.

Special *production studios* and facilities are needed in schools where tapes, recording filmstrips, and/or TV programs are produced. In schools where tapes are electrically transmitted to the individual carrels, a *central control area* will be necessary, preferably in or near the IMC.

The librarian and a/v specialist each need an *office* for planning, consulting, and ordering materials. If there is a director of the entire IMC, he will also require an office.

CONCLUSION

Despite the financial problems involved in building, furnishing and staffing the Continuous Progress School, there are corresponding savings in human resources. Not only are thousands of hours saved by the bright students who now sit for hour after hour while teachers concentrate on the "middle spread," but there are fewer frustrations, behavior problems and dropouts among the slow learners who try unsuccessfully to compete with their age peers. The slow learner who needs more "experiences" can pace and duplicate his own instruction, while the gifted student uses the time to learn more about his special interests.

The library has always served individuals far more than groups. In this plan, the IMC does on a grander scale all the services which forward-looking librarians have been doing feebly without personnel and facilities. Librarians have the opportunity to use their training and skills for professional purposes — helping students with their individual needs, and helping teachers assist students in progressing at their own rate.

COMMUNICATIONS . . .

THE UNDISCOVERED COUNTRY

D. Marie Grieco

It is sheer effrontery to prepare a linear, discursive, one-word-at-a-time discourse on the concept of "multi-media," "multi-sensory" approaches to dimensions in depth. I should be an artist and create a work of art before your mind's eye. Not a line drawing, not a painting — a mosaic. I would be able to take bits and pieces of different sizes, shapes, hues, and textures and put them together with a binding agent that connects even as it separates. Or I should be a

Reprinted with permission from: Grieco, D. Marie, "Communications . . . The Undiscovered Country," SCHOOL LIBRARY JOURNAL, February 15, 1967. Copyright ©1967, R. R. Bowker Company.

musician, able to compose chords. I would strike several notes at once: sharps, flats, half notes, and rests would be orchestrated into a unified sound.

Alas, I am not a painter, and I am not a musician; but I see a mosaic and I hear a chord. For while we call ourselves school librarians, public librarians, audiovisual specialists, information retrievers, instructional materials consultants, museum curators, graphic technicians, technological engineers, communication media specialists (mediators?) — I see different labels, but one pattern; different jobs, but one role. We are the information seekers, gatherers, disseminators; we are the communication seekers, flow-ers; we are the symbol pushers. All of us, pushers; some of us, addicts; most of us need a fix.

But what fix do we need? We have all been on different drugs. Some librarians are addicted to print only and allergic to nonprint; some audiovisual people are addicted to equipment only and allergic to materials. Some public librarians are allergic to large doses of the young public; meanwhile, school librarians take time capsules which do not work after school hours. Some museum people are happy collecting all sorts of specimens except live ones; some administrators are addicted to a status quo which is fatal and are allergic to the only cure, change. Everyone would like a shot in the arm from the federal hypodermic, but not everyone can survive in the bureaucratic line.

Many of our colleagues are doped, full of preconceptions and misconceptions. Convinced of their stability in a world which no longer exists, they conform to a curriculum which cripples the unprotected victims who run its course; they adhere to schedules which stymie the students; they dote on a past which is in sore need of an antidote.

What shall we prescribe? First we must diagnose the disease. Is the concept of the materials center so new it is hard to swallow, or even see? In my most pessimistic moods I am inclined to recall that the great museum at Alexandria circa 300 B.C. was in fact a university, with library, laboratory, lecture courts, and a common dining hall. So here we sit almost 2000 years later, representing the museums, the libraries, the learning laboratories, and the lecture halls.

In my *less* pessimistic moods I marvel at the confluence of circumstances which coincided at one point in our mutual histories. Librarians will know that it was in 1876 that Melvil Dewey, age 25, launched the *Library Journal* and summoned the conference of librarians that formed the American Library Association. Museum personnel will know that it was in 1876 that George Brown Goode, age 25, superintended the exhibits of the Smithsonian Institute at the Philadelphia Centennial of 1876 and became acting secretary in charge of the U.S. National Museum, created in 1876. Audiovisual specialists will know that it was in 1876 that Edison completed the first telephone conversation. And educators will know that at the great Philadelphia Centennial Exposition in 1876 the relation of education to national progress had been a key theme. Pedagogical innovations associated rather directly with industrial prosperity had come under the closest scrutiny. It was the Russian exhibits which stole the show, for the West realized the Russian educators had scored a breakthrough. In his book *Transformation of the School,* Lawrence Cremin outlines the considerable influence and impetus directly attributable to that fair and the Russians (p. 25).

Isn't it interesting that 90 years later we are once again enjoying an impetus in educational innovation launched rather directly by the Russians along with Sputnik?

There have been moments in the past, in fact, when we seem to have been closer in conceptual compatability than we appear to be in some places today. Item: it was the Library Society of Charles Town which founded the first museum in this country three years before the Declaration of Independence. It was a librarian, John Cotton Dana, who is considered largely responsible for spurring libraries to change from mere collections of books used by a few scholars to the state where they recognized the position which they should hold in community life; and it was this librarian who started the Newark Museum and thereafter expounded his theories on the function and purpose of museums. In a book called *The Gloom of the Museum,* published in 1917, Dana lashed out against current practices and pointed the way to the future:

"To make itself alive a museum must do two things: It must teach and it must advertise. As soon as it begins to teach it will of necessity begin to form an alliance with present teaching agencies, the public schools, the colleges and universities and the art institutes of all kinds . . . Museums of the future will not only teach at home, they will travel abroad through their photographs, their textbooks, and their periodicals. Books, leaflets, and journals will assist and supplement the work of teachers and will accompany, explain, and amplify the exhibits which art museums will send out, will all help to make museum expenditures seem worthwhile." (p. 24-25)

So, when we talk about this "new" idea, the IMC, we must mean "new" not at the point of conception but at the moment of birth. And considering the length of the gestation period in education, some of our concepts should be born full-grown. Yet that long, drawn-out lag seems to affect the speed with which the new concept can travel.

Or maybe the trouble is in what we allow to be delivered into the educational mist. For example, the last few years have witnessed an extraordinary proliferation of TV sets and programming machines. I do not mean to say there is a widespread *knowledge* about the production and use of educational or instructional television or the production and use of programmed materials; a good many educators have bought the equipment and not the concepts. The potential in these areas is enormous, but there are only a few instances where this potential has any hope of being fully realized: where schools have come to terms with the uniqueness of the medium, with its influence on the learning environment, with its impact upon the learner, and where, with this basic understanding, they have created new environments and provided a variety of different learning situations and opportunities. In most systems I know at first hand, TV and programmed machines have been placed in the old school environment. The content of the TV has been the televised lecture, and the content of the program a pasted-up workbook.

My point is a bit Freudian, I guess: maybe some of these administrators really want to buy a dead baby; but, this being *too* backward, they buy the newest, the latest — and kill it with lack of proper understanding and nourishment. How easy it is to say then, and perhaps honestly to believe, "Oh well, I tried the new idea, and it didn't work. The old ideas are better. You really can't replace the human being anyway." And the status quo becomes entrenched with the empty symbols of progress, tried and failed, stored in a corner of the classroom.

Now this *is* something like throwing the baby out with the wash. It's called "killing the machine so the concept dies." Not being a very good analyst, I am not sure which is the intended victim, but the executioner is always the dominance of the past accompanied by an overdose of ignorance.

What also interests me is a kind of perverse logic. There are now more than a few schools with a TV in every classroom, a TV often no longer in use. Is there a filmstrip viewer in every classroom? Is there a library? No! Why not? *Because we can't afford that.* Aha, the fatal flaw, money. But, obviously it is not a matter merely of money. If there is a "keynote," if there is a prescription, here it is: a state of mind, an attitude toward education, an approach to learning, an understanding of media, a concept of communication, all of which has to do with perception and with people.

Simple, trite, obvious? Not at all. Terribly complex and multi-dimensional. A concept of communication. There are as many concepts of communication as there are sociologists, anthropologists, public relations men, mathematicians, artists, scientists, engineers, etc., trying to define or improve or express communication. We can narrow the field of definitions to two and still have more chaos than we can handle.

FEAST OF MEDIA, FAMINE OF CONCEPTS

We are interested in the technology of communications, living as we do in an era which has leaped into the 20th Century and into fantastic outer spaces with implications that stagger us with the range and power of their potential significance and progress. And we are interested in interpersonal, intergroup, intercultural, international communications, living as we do in an era which drags us by the hair into the Stone Age and into desolate inner spaces with implications that stagger us with the range and power of their potential impotence and destruction. This is at once the triumph and the tragedy of our age: a feast of communication *media* that really work, a famine of communication *concepts* that really work.

The answers? I don't know them, but there are directions to apprehend. For those who are looking for specific organizational approaches, I recommend the most recent book by James W. Brown and Kenneth Norberg: *Administering Educational Media.* It is neatly organized, with suggestions for physical facilities, for educational media, for administrative procedures involving both materials and equipment, and for media services in single schools, counties, districts, colleges, universities, state and regional systems. But many of you have no doubt recognized that the pattern I am using for this mosaic is Marshall McLuhan's book *Understanding Media: The Extensions of Man.* With all respect for the specialists and generalists in the field of communications and for the multitudinous studies and statistics documenting their work, I admit to a special preference for the significance of McLuhan's work, which is not a carefully controlled scientific study but a metaphorically mixed poetic exploration. The implications of his perceptions are the very essence of our interests. He has been ridiculed in educational journals to the point of absurdity. More recently, he has been interviewed or reported in the popular press in semiserious, semicynical tones. But in what is now a sort of open underground movement, he is unquestionably the unassuming leader.

I cannot begin to summarize his ideas, but I can perhaps convey the flavor of his thoughts. One of his central themes, that "the medium is the message," asserts that the medium itself, *regardless of its content,* the medium itself determines the mode of perception and the matrix of the assumptions within which our objectives are set. The "message" of any medium or technology is the change of scale or pace or pattern that it introduces into human affairs. The personal and social consequences of any medium — that is, of any extension of ourselves — result from the new scale that is introduced into our affairs by each extension of ourselves, or by any new technology. What is important is to study the effects of the medium itself on our perceptions, our attitudes.

How does the medium itself change and shape a new environment? All of our studies have been on content and the assumed effects of content, not on the effect of the medium itself.

When we try to translate this idea into our own jargon, we say: What are the characteristics of each medium? And we say: You must use each medium for its unique features. There is no substitute for a book when *only* the printed word can create a certain world; there is no substitute for the film when *only* the motion picture can create a certain world; there is no substitute for the recording when *only* the spoken word or the musical form can create a certain world, etc., to the obviously reassuring fact that there is no substitute for the human being when his presence alone can create a certain world. We know all this from the tops of our heads to the lists in our guidebooks. That is why we are objecting to the continued use of the term audiovisual *aids.* Audiovisual materials are not merely *aids,* supplementary. If they are the best, they are integral, they are unique. They do what no other media can do better.

And this is why we are objecting to the term *instructional aids.* They, too, are not merely supplementary; nor are they merely instructional in the limited sense of teacher use. They are informational and recreational and aesthetic, for individual educational and emotional and sensory experiences. But, I repeat, we know this from the tops of our heads. We have yet to reach into the subliminal realms where the meetings behind the words linger.

We all believe, of course, in the implementation of the instructional materials center philosophy. I dare say that some of us are very proud, justifiably, that we have made great strides in acquiring collections of materials. Some of us are pleased with the methods we have used for cataloging these collections or for housing them. Some of us have designed exciting new buildings with listening posts and study carrels — wet and dry. All honor, praise, and glory to us, and carry on we must, but — the needle to prick our dream world: facilities alone do not insure services, and collections alone do not insure optimal use.

More and more of us are making more and more materials available. But physical availability is not synonymous with intellectual or conceptual accessibility. Let us take stock: Do you have a card catalog of printed materials, a film catalog, a filmstrip catalog, a record catalog, a list of tapes, transparencies, a community resource file, a recorded collection of prints, photographs, etc., etc.? The lucky student or teacher! If he will just go through 22 catalogs, he will find almost everything he needs.

Oh, but some of us have interfiled catalogs. In one interfiled card catalog one can find all the materials on one subject with color-banded cards to indicate each medium, except in those schools where the librarian thinks that supplying the color codes is like "spoon feeding" the student who must, after all, learn how to use the library. And we give him plenty of practice: He looks through all our lists and/or our interfiled catalog and then he (teacher or student) goes here for a book and there for a filmstrip and somewhere else for a record and down the hall for a projector and through that door for − a rest. I am not really ridiculing; if the student has physical access to all the materials and equipment necessary, this IMC is indeed on the way. My point is that even at this stage, we have barely begun. The present state of technology gives us unprecedented opportunities for a kind of accessibility to media and materials which must restructure the entire learning environment, refashion the traditional patterns, and reform our basic assumptions.

Back to those lists. Who is compiling the lists? What cataloging system does he use, what bibliographic techniques? Are the films arranged by title alphabetically and by subject with annotations? Which subject headings will lead to the study of film *technique* itself? Which annotations will offer a variety of clues to the headings? Which will lead to the study of film *concepts?* Which will open for study of the film? Did you list that film under social studies because it traces the history of man's misuse of natural resources; or did you put it under English because the narration is in blank verse, or should you have a cross reference to music because the original score was composed by Virgil Thompson, or should there not be a card under photography because Willard van Dyke's work is a superb example of film photography; and does it not belong under film documentaries because this is a unique form in the art of film?

Of course, the *prior* question is almost too sad to ask. Do we even begin to use the artistic films in the schools, or do we confine most of our purchases and rentals only to so-called instructional films? The instructional film is to the textbook what the artistic film is to the trade book. Review your fare in the schools.

In this area the public libraries and museums lead the way, but only to a degree. The intellectual accessibility we now afford for printed materials we must begin to afford for nonprint. And the physical accessibility we now afford for print, we must begin to provide for nonprint. Technology frees us. We accept the fact that a good book or a good poem is to *re*-read. A film is to return. But a good film is also to *re*-view, to *re*-see, to study, to know. A film, too, has grammar. What are the visual metaphors? How does the film compress time, chronological time, psychological time? How does it translate from the grammar of the novel into the grammar of the film?

McLuhan has a fascinating chapter on media as translators. "All media are active metaphors in their power to translate experience into new forms. The spoken word was the first technology by which man was able to let go of his environment in order to grasp it in a new way" (p. 57).

"Our very word 'grasp' or 'apprehension' points to the process of getting at one thing through another, of handling and sensing many facets at a time through more than one sense at a time. It begins to be evident that 'touch' is not skin but the interplay of the senses and 'keeping in touch' or 'getting in touch' is a matter of a fruitful meeting of the senses, of sight translated into sound and sound into movement, and taste and smell" (p. 60).

Our educational system with its emphasis on subject matter divisions has long been based on the book, and, in one way or another, we have all been concerned with how to read a book. This is still of paramount importance, of course. But it is not enough. We must teach how to "read" a film, a photograph, a printed advertisement, a TV commercial, etc. McLuhan says – and you begin to recognize that I enjoy his metaphors: "Education is ideally civil defense against media fallout. Yet, Western man has had, so far, no education or equipment for meeting any of the new media on their own terms. Literate man is not only numb and vague in the presence of film or photo, but he intensifies his ineptness by a defensive arrogance and condescension to 'pop kulch' and 'mass entertainment' " (p. 195).

If you have lost the pattern I am trying to project – I am trying to say that if there is a keynote in the rationale for an instructional materials center, it is in your conceptual approach to learning – actually, to life. Learning is not divided into neat categories. Education is not confined to schools. We hear much talk about individualized learning. Learning has always been an individual affair. Individualized reading! Reading has always been an individual affair. And libraries and librarians have always been in the best position to invite and influence individual learning. Educators talk to us about the rates of learning and methods of learning, referring to large groups or small groups. We must hear more about methods of learning referring to media; about ways of learning referring to perceptual modes: viewing, hearing, touching, tasting, smelling. We need to heighten our perception of all the senses.

We have much to learn from the best in the museum world. Their organization of materials, their arrangements of exhibits and displays, their use of technology for individual experiences – all have bearing on our approaches. Witness the individual audio tapes providing information and appreciations at whatever pace one chooses. Witness the combination of slides with tapes with films, all operable by the user. I cannot resist mentioning the Library Museum at the Lincoln Center for the Performing Arts. This is a marriage of the worlds of print and nonprint materials and equipment, education and culture, information and appreciation; a public library which is indeed a higher institution of all levels of learning experiences.

There is much I can say about the roles and responsibilities of librarians and media specialists – all of us in the communications field – and how these roles relate and interrelate. When I first started making notes for this paper, I dwelled on all the specific examples of ways in which we mesh. For while we have developed more or less separately as spokes in the wheel, and while we are now encompassing our efforts and goals within this rim we are calling IMC, the wheel has become a web. Or, to unmix my metaphors, the web is really a mosaic. We do belong together, separately but significantly related.

And so, whatever the barriers that seem to separate us, let us be sure that the underlying meaning of "learning a life" can be the bond that interrelates us; and the name for this mosaic, this web, this IMC, this library, this museum, this college, this collage, is *Sensorium.* You are the links and the lures. You link and lure individuals to the literate world of print; the tactile world of books, or sculpture; the visual world of photos, films, fine arts, TV — micro and telescopic worlds; the aural world of records, tapes, radio. You can provide the truly "movable feasts": a taste for learning and being and becoming — and, perhaps, the thirst of a lifetime.

REFERENCES

McLuhan, H.M. *Understanding Media.* McGraw, 1964. pap.

Cremin, Lawrence. *Transformation of the Schools.* Knopf, 1961, text ed. and pap.; Vintage, pap.

Dana, John Cotton. *Gloom of the Museum.* Newark Free Public Library. New Jersey, New Museum Series, 1917, o.p.

Brown, J.W. and K.D. Norberg. *Administering Educational Media.* McGraw, 1965.

Section Two

THE ELEMENTARY
SCHOOL

SOMETHING NEW HAS
BEEN ADDED TO THE LIBRARY

Leila Ann Doyle

A new day has arrived. The elementary school library, an integral part of only the more progressive school systems during the past fifty years, has refurbished its house and is presently in the limelight. As the conscience of America has been moved to provide not only equal educational opportunities but also a better quality of education for all children, elementary libraries are being established in all schools committed to providing quality education for children. The newly planned elementary library centers are quite different and the older ones have changed too. The stereopticon has been replaced by the filmstrip viewer; the recordings are now 33 1/3 and 16 rpm; a drymount press is used for mounting pictures; "silence" signs have been replaced by "listening area," "viewing area," "recording area" and "materials preparation."

What has happened to the "reading area"? To be sure, it is there in addition to the "storytelling" corner. Reference work is not only emphasized more than ever but also introduced in the primary grades. Children are learning to study independently; to use many kinds of materials as sources of information; to evaluate and compare; to check the accuracy of information found in books and viewed on television, filmstrips or films. When more than one of the senses is involved, we know that more effective learning takes place. But we also realize that the best learning takes place when the individual is actively and emotionally involved in the learning process. The library materials center offers children unlimited opportunities for such learning experiences.

Within our schools we have a library center, the potential of which we have not yet begun to tap, which can serve all children and teachers and provide educational experiences not possible through any other organizational pattern. It has become a modern learning center by retaining the best of the traditional library while incorporating the newer materials and equipment which technology has provided; nevertheless, the change is more than this.

GROWTH OF SCHOOL LIBRARIES

Various forces have been instrumental in the growth of elementary school libraries; in the expansion of their resources, programs and services; and in

Reprinted by permission of Leila Ann Doyle and the Association for Childhood Education International, 3615 Wisconsin Avenue, N.W., Washington, D.C. from "Something New Has Been Added to the Library." CHILDHOOD EDUCATION, October, 1966. Copyright © 1966 by the Association.

focusing the attention of both educators and the public upon them. *Standards for School Libraries* (1960), a publication of the American Association of School Librarians, was the *first* major step. The School Library Development Project, which involved educators and lay groups in planning for the implementation of these standards, was a *second* major step. This was followed by the *Knapp Foundation Project,* which has made possible the establishment of pilot school library materials centers, serving as an inspiration to all of us. DAVI, the *national audiovisual organization,* has recently formulated standards for audiovisual materials and equipment, thus making a tremendous impact on education.

During the past decade elementary teachers and principals have become increasingly aware of the need for more diversified educational approaches to learning. They recognize the need to expand the content of the curriculum to include instructional materials, and to enrich children's experiences, thus insuring not only mastery of skills but also greater wealth of knowledge. To accomplish their goals and to open wide the doors of learning for each and every child, they are seeking the help of specialists in many fields. It is they who are now demanding library instructional materials specialists and a centralized library with materials, equipment, and services to enliven the learning experiences started in the classroom.

LEARNING LAB FOR CHILDREN AND TEACHERS

I search for a term that will create in the reader's mind a modern elementary school library with an array of instructional materials and areas bustling with creative activity — areas where children are in a world of dreams and fantasy as they pore over adventures of other times or places; areas where children seek answers to questions raised in the classroom, where they pursue their private quest for information on some subject that has captured their interest, or where they are guided into new fields of knowledge which expand their horizons and develop new interests. The program is varied and flexible. Classes, groups and individuals use this center as a laboratory and as a haven for quiet reading to refresh mind and spirit. Teachers as well as children frequent it for conferences on units of study and for ideas, materials and equipment.

We are closer to the realization of this ideal elementary library than we know. While our vision may be momentarily obstructed by problems close at hand, the development, which was at first gradual, is increasing with an ever-accelerated tempo throughout elementary schools. The potential of the program for children is educationally sound and exciting. Many schools have made a beginning; few, if any, have as yet developed their programs sufficiently to be able to reap the maximum in educational advantages possible.

CENTRALIZATION OF MATERIALS

The library materials center serves both children and teachers in the classroom and in the center itself. It employs an organizational pattern, making it possible to locate books, study prints, films, recordings, filmstrips, tapes and other instructional materials on any subject in a common index — the card catalog. It provides equipment for using materials on disc, tape or film at the time and place it is needed. Through this organizational pattern and centralization of materials and services, teachers and children are constantly made aware of *all* available sources of information, not only those in print or of an audiovisual nature.

Materials are then selected on the basis of the purpose they are to serve. Will a visual presentation clarify a particular concept? Will a film about children of Japan make their study of this nation more meaningful? Will a recording reenacting an historical event help children to experience vicariously this period of history? Can we locate stories that help us to understand how children lived in the Colonial period or to discover whether or not children of different national origins think as we do?

Centralization of materials, equipment and services in the library center facilitates their use by students and teachers. For example, a fifth-grade student is planning a report on certain insects. Using the card catalog, he discoveres that the library has a number of books, several filmstrips, a set of pictures and transparencies, and a film which may be obtained from a central film library. He gathers the books and filmstrips together at an individual study table or carrel where there is a filmstrip viewer. The librarian checks to see that he knows how to locate the needed information in each book and that he is recording the source of information correctly and taking meaningful notes. He is also shown how to locate articles in magazines for up-to-date information. Then he checks through the picture sets, selecting those which serve his purpose. The transparencies are viewed on the overhead projector and found to be suitable for his project. The librarian helps him to be alert for facts which are seemingly contradictory and require further checking in the most authoritative science encyclopedias. The boy may then prepare his report and record it on the tape recorder so that he may hear how it will sound when given before the class. Is it well organized? Has he emphasized important points? Is he speaking clearly so that his fellow students will understand him? Is his verbal report sufficient? Should he use the pictures he has selected on the bulletin board or use the opaque projector? Should he plan to utilize parts of the filmstrips he has previewed? What else might he do? After he has located various materials, his imagination is whetted and a truly creative project emerges.

The time, the materials and the individual guidance given to complete a simple project of this nature provides genuine learning experience in using library resources; it provides an opportunity for the pupil to seek, evaluate, compare and select; it permits him to develop creativity and the inner security and poise which result from a task well done. Study habits developed by this kind of experience are far more valuable than this same amount of time spent in "covering" a greater number of topics in the textbook which may only be memorized for a quiz and promptly forgotten.

PROVIDE FOR INDIVIDUAL DIFFERENCES

Learning is an active process, and the library center is the workshop where children can actively engage in meaningful study. The most appropriate method for each child to learn should be made available to him. As his educational experiences increase through the use of one medium, he will be better able to cope with another. It is individuals we teach, not subjects. Programmed instruction may be the answer for some children; most need the challenge of group or committee work. The library materials center can provide for these individual differences.

PERSONNEL, MATERIALS, SPACE

Three important needs for this center are: qualified personnel, well-selected materials and equipment, and adequate space. The primary need is personnel, without which we can offer only a token program. Because of both local effort and federal aid, great strides have been made in acquiring materials and equipment. Unfortunately, the space which will make possible the varied activities and flexibility is woefully lacking.

Schools and school systems committed to improving the quality of the educational program in their elementary schools are evaluating their elementary library programs. They are planning for centralization of technical services whether on a city, county or contractual basis with another school system. Provisions are being made for clerical assistance so that libraries can implement a program for children and teachers. An adequate professional staff to bring children, teachers, and the wealth of instructional materials together and thus make possible many educational experiences will make the difference between mediocre and quality education.

ORGANIZING A MATERIALS CENTER

Magdalene Glenn

How often we have heard the words. "If I'd only known this material was in the building . . ." Many a teacher has searched frantically through old cardboard boxes for a picture or newspaper clipping, only to give up the struggle as hopeless and try to explain a concept or teach a unit without benefit of some of the instructional aids that might have made the task easier.

It was just such a situation that prompted our efforts at the College Avenue School to set up a central materials center. We began the project a little more

Reprinted with permission from: Glenn, Magdalene, "Organizing a Materials Center," THE NATIONAL ELEMENTARY PRINCIPAL, January, 1961. Copyright 1961, Department of Elementary School Principals, National Education Association. All rights reserved.

than 20 years ago and have continued it ever since. The benefits have been many — pupils have been offered an enriched learning program, teachers have been stimulated, and, because we have also involved parents in the project, they have become more aware of some of the variety of experiences their children have in school.

EQUIPMENT

It is not necessary to have a vast amount of equipment before setting up a system for collecting, classifying, and storing materials. The only equipment on hand when the College Avenue School project was begun consisted of a few battered shirt boxes. This, of course, was a highly unsatisfactory method of storage and we soon realized that some other equipment was essential.

We decided to purchase three types of equipment — a four-drawer letter-sized cabinet for filing flat pictures and pamphlets, open steel shelves for larger flat pictures and portfolios, and a two-drawer steel card index cabinet to accommodate catalogue cards. Through the years, we have bought additional pieces as they were needed.

In addition, we found a number of other items necessary. Chipboard for mounting was bought in large quantities and cut into suitable sizes. For convenience in filing, we decided on two uniform sizes — 9" x 12" and 18" x 22". To make the mountings more attractive, we also purchased construction paper in a variety of colors. Stapling machines and staples, library cloth, library adhesive tape, glue, catalogue cards of several colors, Manila tab folders, and paper cutters of different sizes were among the other items acquired.

ASSEMBLING MATERIALS

The first step in our project was to assemble materials already in the school and put them into usable form. Each teacher had pictures, pamphlets, magazines, and other items which she had collected for her own use. These things, we knew, would be far more valuable if they were pooled and made available to all the staff.

The central library and small room libraries contained a substantial number of reference books, social studies readers, and fiction which had never been reviewed and catalogued by subject. If a teacher or pupil wanted information on a particular topic, hours of searching might be necessary before it could be located.

We agreed to review carefully each of the books we had on hand and catalogue them under proper headings. Pictures, pamphlets, magazines, and other materials were similarly handled. With this arrangement, when a teacher wanted material on a particular subject or unit, she needed only to consult the index cards to see what items were available.

COLLECTING MATERIALS

A valuable job had been accomplished when the work of assembling, filing, cataloguing, and storing materials already in the building had been completed.

But we didn't stop there. Teachers were now interested in looking for more and better materials — materials of wider scope, deeper interest, and more significance.

In collecting material, we have been careful to select only items that are of educational value. It is important to keep in mind the purpose for which materials will be used, and to determine their worthiness before giving them space in a collection. We find materials from a number of sources. There are several published lists of free or inexpensive materials. Professional magazines carry similar listings. Commercial ads, especially those of travel agencies, have something to offer. Many industries make materials of educational value available. The magazine sections of most Sunday newspapers frequently carry usable articles and pictures. Friends of teachers, parents, and others interested in the school make contributions when they know a worthwhile use will be made of them. Teachers themselves are more interested in collecting post cards, pamphlets, and other illustrative items if they know there is an organized way of preserving their contributions.

Clippings from old magazines have been a valuable source to us from the beginning. We have a large group of art pictures clipped from the popular pictorial magazines. Stories from the *Junior Red Cross Magazine* have proved valuable. Two extra copies of many publications are ordered so we are sure to have clipping sources.

Once one becomes a "collector," he sees things of value for the curriculum that otherwise would have gone unnoticed.

CLASSIFYING MATERIALS

If instructional materials are to contribute to the learning program, they need to be classified carefully. The classification should be done in such a way that teachers can find items appropriate for their grade levels and for particular units or subjects.

There is much discussion among our staff about how certain materials should be listed. A pamphlet, magazine article, or even a book is often held up before the group and the question asked. "If you wanted to use this material, under what subject heading would you expect to find it?"

Primary teachers select the titles under which materials for their grade levels are filed. "Pets," "The Family," and "Community Helpers" are examples of subject headings related to the primary area. Materials for the upper elementary grades are catalogued under the names of units, such as "United States (New York)," "Europe," or "Science (Fish)."

Many of the pictures are classified under broad headings and then subdivided. If they were classified simply as "art," for example, it would be necessary to go through the entire collection to locate the exact items needed. With headings such as "Art — Painting" and "Art — Appreciation," material can be located quickly.

Pamphlets, small paperback books, folders, post cards, and the like are filed under proper subject headings in the same manner as flat pictures.

One section of the central library is reserved for books that have been reviewed and found to contain material of specific curriculum value. These books are reviewed by teachers who can best classify the content. The collection contains many fictional, as well as nonfictional, books. Social studies texts and supplementary readers belonging to sets are carefully reviewed for subject content and reading difficulty and sample copies of those selected are placed on the shelves.

Sheet music is classified under subject headings and recordings are catalogued according to type — music appreciation, folk dance, march, popular.

CATALOGUING MATERIALS

If materials are to be located quickly and with a minimum of trouble, they must be properly catalogued after classification.

All books are catalogued on 3" x 5" cards — using as many cards for each book as necessary to list it under the various subject areas to which it is related. The subject cards are filed alphabetically by subject, using the Dewey decimal system. Each card gives the subject, author, title, publisher, copyright date, grade level, and any other brief description that will help the teacher. Book cards and pockets are placed in the back of books for convenience in checking them out.

In general, nonbook materials are catalogued in a similar way, but they are arranged differently. Magazines are shelved according to date of publication. There are as many catalogue cards for each magazine as there are subject areas treated in it. The card also indicates the magazine's location. Pamphlets, clippings, and flat pictures are filed alphabetically and catalogue cards simply show that there is such material and indicate the storage place. These nonbook materials are catalogued on colored cards to distinguish them from the books, which are on white cards.

Catalogue cards are also made for resource material in the community within easy reach of the school. The resource might be rabbits, a cocoon, or chickens in a neighbor's back yard, or a person who has visited coal mines or traveled abroad. It could be an industry, processing plant, or, in our part of the country, a cotton gin. For most subject headings, there is at least one card in the file which gives a brief description and the location of valuable community source material.

STORING MATERIALS

The utmost care is taken in storing our materials. The purpose is to make everything quickly accessible.

The first step in this direction was to list alphabetically the subject headings upon which we had agreed. These topics formed a basis for filing.

As 9" x 12" material is collected, it is placed in a properly labeled tab-type Manila folder and stored in the letter-size filing cabinet. Overside flat pictures, portfolios, and other materials are placed on the open steel shelves and identified by shelf label holders.

Large portfolios, 18" x 22", are very satisfactory for storing materials. A book-type portfolio may be made with two pieces of heavy chipboard bound together by strips of book cloth or adhesive cloth tape. An envelope-type portfolio can be made in a similar way, except that flaps for holding loose papers and clippings are added.

Records are stored in number racks and corresponding numbers are placed on the records. It is convenient to have separate racks for records of different classifications — folk, popular, etc. Each teacher has a list of records with their storage numbers.

We use many other types of instructional materials in our school in addition to those discussed here. Films, slides, opaque projectors, tape recorders, and similar audio-visual aids are in constant use. But they do not take the place of our books and files of pictures, clippings, pamphlets, and the like.

Our materials center has proved valuable in many ways. With a variety of resource material at hand, teachers are better able to provide for individual differences among their pupils. And since they are actively engaged in collecting, classifying, and cataloguing materials, they know what is available and how to locate it. Through the use of the materials provided, the children themselves have found their work more interesting. Parents, too, in helping to prepare materials for the center, have expressed their enthusiasm for our project.

Although we have been developing our materials center for more than 20 years, we find that the job is never done. There are always new things to be added and some that need to be discarded. But the task is more than worthwhile — we feel its value cannot be overestimated.

CHANGING OVER TO MATERIALS CENTERS

Leonella Jameson

Many school districts in the country have, over the years, developed separate audiovisual and library departments, each headed by its own supervisor. An example of this organizational pattern is found in Kalamazoo, Michigan.

Headed by a capable audiovisual supervisor, system-wide audiovisual services to all teachers have become an integral part of the teaching program. Available from this office are educational motion pictures, filmstrips, maps, globes, charts, slides, flat pictures, tapes, records, models, felt sets, and special equipment. Serving as liaison between this central service and the classroom teacher is a teacher in each building named the audiovisual coordinator for the building.

Reprinted with permission from: Jameson, Leonella, "Changing Over to Materials Centers," THE INSTRUCTOR, November 1964.

Supervision of the school library program is in the hands of the Supervisor of School Library Service, who works closely with each building's library staff. For many years the centralization of ordering, processing, and mending of books has freed building staffs so they can work on an individual basis with students and teachers. Since 1960, monthly book-order meetings conducted by the supervisor have given each school librarian an opportunity to discuss approval copies of trade books he has read and those read by classroom teachers in his building, as well as hearing many other books reviewed by fellow librarians. Book orders are placed at the close of each meeting.

The elementary library collections of the past in Kalamazoo have consisted only of books, periodicals, and pamphlets, that is, printed materials. Teachers (through individual needs for their particular grades) have acquired pictures, filmstrips, records, educational games, free and inexpensive materials, and science equipment by requisitioning them through building principals. Principals have been aware of teachers' needs and have purchased books on how to teach specific subjects and new curriculum trends. In short, they have begun basic professional libraries for each building.

The Supervisor of Audiovisual Education has advised principals of individual audiovisual purchases that would be useful in every building. (Each building is equipped at the outset with basic audiovisual equipment, based on a per room standard accepted throughout the district.)

For many years there has been a constant flow of trade books into individual elementary buildings and classrooms to support the social studies and science curricula. The Coordinator of Elementary Education has made available sample copies of these books for principals, classroom teachers, and resource teachers to examine and evaluate. He has also furnished additional pamphlets and materials which guide the teacher through the curriculum.

It can be seen then that many materials, both printed and nonprinted, have been available in abundance. However, they have been dispersed throughout the buildings with only the individual teacher knowing what is in his room. Teachers have shared materials on an informal basis but, without a master list of all materials owned, many have not been aware of materials in other classrooms that might be useful to them.

By the 1963-64 school year, the time seemed to have arrived to move ahead toward making true materials centers of our elementary school libraries. Principals and those with curriculum responsibilities at the administrative level were excited about the possibility. Classroom teachers were realizing the inadequacies of classroom collections and the values of pooling a building's holdings under the trained library staff with whom they worked. The centralized processing departments could handle an influx of materials to be catalogued and classified.

CATALOGUING CLASSROOM COLLECTIONS

A plan to meet the growing need for listing and locating all materials centrally in the buildings was presented to building principals. It was proposed that throughout the school year, a list of forty to fifty titles would be received every five weeks by each principal (with a copy for each teacher) from the Supervisor of School Library Service. These titles would be pulled from the classrooms by teachers, assembled at the building office, and sent via delivery to be catalogued and classified. The books would be out of the classroom no longer than four weeks and would be placed upon their return in the school's library area, available to all teachers. Every effort would be made to avoid calling in materials being used extensively. Books would be called in first as they form the biggest single type of material. This project should take two to three years and could be worked into the regular budget of the centralized processing departments rather than becoming a special project with all the problems and budgetary concerns inherent in special projects.

The principals agreed that this was a step in the right direction and the first group of books was processed during the Christmas vacation in 1963-64. It was also agreed that from this time on all new materials added at the building level would be routed through the centralized processing departments and then on to buildings.

This then began a move to bring all kinds of materials together to better serve students and teachers. The program toward which we are working in each elementary library is to:

1. Provide a curriculum-oriented collection of materials both printed (books, periodicals, pamphlets) and nonprinted (filmstrips, tapes, records, games, science equipment, pictures, charts, maps, slides, transparencies, models, felt sets, and realia).

2. Provide a facility equipped with individual listening and viewing equipment for students to make use of in the learning experience.

3. Provide a well trained school librarian who is knowledgeable with all types of materials and who understands the learning process and curriculum goals.

The school librarian working with students:

1. Encourages reading to develop skills and mastery of reading, and above all the enjoyment of reading.

2. Teaches research skills in the variety of materials available for student use.

3. Provides continuing encouragement and motivation for learning by guiding students to materials which will make learning exciting and more meaningful.

The school librarian working with teachers:

1. Informs them of new materials.

2. Assists teachers in preparing units of work by drawing on vast resources of materials.

3. Participates in curriculum revision and implementation by serving on curriculum committees.

At the present time most of our elementary school libraries are staffed by highly skilled paid adult clerks identified as Library Assistants. Their services have been and will continue to be invaluable in beginning elementary library service in all Kalamazoo schools. A look to the future shows movement toward adding trained librarians, full-time in schools of 500 students and half-time in schools of fewer than 500 students.

DEMONSTRATION LIBRARY

While classroom collections were beginning to be processed, simultaneously steps were being taken to demonstrate to the school district the impact of a vital elementary school library program. A demonstration elementary school library, serving as a complete instructional materials center, was established at the Vine Street Elementary School. In addition to becoming a demonstration center for Kalamazoo, the school district submitted an application to the Knapp School Libraries Project of the American Association of School Librarians, hoping to be selected as one of eight schools to serve as a demonstration center across the United States. Although the center was not selected for this project, the impetus that it gave to the growth of elementary school libraries in Kalamazoo as materials centers is noteworthy.

1. Attention was focused on the value of elementary school libraries.

2. Each person involved (supervisors, principal, librarian, library clerk, and classroom teachers) in the project gave it top priority.

3. In-service meetings with teachers to discuss uses of the library and its materials brought about a clearer understanding of the library's potential for both students and teachers.

4. A continuing opportunity is being provided for the school district to see an instructional materials program operating in an elementary school library.

5. Student teachers in the building are seeing through practical experience the values of a good elementary school library.

As was stated at the beginning of this article the responsibility for audiovisual services and library services is divided between two supervisors. This has not been a handicap toward the emergence of an instructional materials concept in the elementary school libraries. Far from it! A system-wide Instructional Materials Center has existed for some years including:

1. Audiovisual services (described earlier in this article).

2. A curriculum library containing a collection of sample textbooks in all subject areas and grades; a professional collection of more than 4000 volumes; courses of study from school systems throughout the United States; a pamphlet file of educational materials; educational magazines; supplementary books in elementary science, social studies, and secondary English; selected remedial materials.

3. An elementary book room providing a collection of supplementary books and materials in various subjects in quantity.

An opportunity to work together came when the Supervisors of Audiovisual Education and of Library Service planned and presented a multimedia demonstration for the senior high curriculum and guidance committee (a group consisting of department heads of the two high schools, the principals, and supervisors). Cooperative planning involved the two high school audiovisual coordinators and the two head librarians plus a biology teacher and the two supervisors. Each person on the planning committee contributed from his own background and a creative presentation was made. The demonstration showed how many teachers use a variety of means to reach students and how the use of instructional materials complements this approach. Student-prepared transparencies, clips from films, selected frames of filmstrips, chapters of books, drawings from texts, all brought the excitement of exploring a unit.

This successful experience in working together has helped open doors for continuing cooperation. The Supervisor of School Library Service has had frequent occasions to call upon the Supervisor of Audiovisual Education for assistance in preparing visuals for presentation to the Board of Education and the Curriculum Council. His understanding of this field brings a new dimension to library presentations.

Opportunities for cooperation at the building level continue to appear. The principal at Vine Street School suggested that the librarian serve as the audiovisual coordinator in the building beginning in the fall of 1964. The suggestion was met with enthusiasm by the librarian and both supervisors. Acting in this new capacity the librarian will serve as the liaison person between the school and the central audiovisual service, will assist in previewing nonprinted materials, and help teachers prepare visual, audio, and graphic materials. Because much of the work is clerical in nature, additional library clerical time has been scheduled in the building.

SUMMARY

School districts in which patterns of administration organization place audiovisual and library services in two separate departments *can* provide complete instructional materials programs. Suggested ways that librarians and audiovisual personnel at the building or administrative level can cooperate are:

1. To plan carefully together for future growth.

2. To work as a team moving in the same direction toward jointly determined goals.

3. To believe and talk the instructional materials concept.

4. To present coordinated demonstrations of the uses of instructional materials for teachers.

Through working together, the strengths of all concerned will come to the fore and a stronger materials program will emerge from which teachers and students will benefit every day of the school year.

AN INTEGRATED LIBRARY ... A MULTIMEDIA APPROACH TO LEARNING

Robert E. Muller

Envision, if you will, an integrated library. Picture in your mind's eye a school saturated with instructional materials, a school whose library is a rich resource of films and filmstrips as well as books, everything instantly available for use by pupils as well as teachers. This dream will become a reality in the Thomas Edison School in Daly City come next September. Name: Project Discovery.

Sponsored by Encyclopaedia Britannica Films and Bell & Howell, in cooperation with four school districts across the county, Project Discovery is designed to test the effect of maximum availability of instructional materials on curriculum, on pupil attitudes, achievement, creativity and motivation, and on teaching methods and techniques, Project Discovery's plan is to saturate a school with materials and equipment, and through a carefully developed research design, observe and test behavioral and educational changes. For a three-year period, the entire film and filmstrip library of Encyclopaedia Britannica Films will be placed in each of the participating schools: 500 16mm films and over 1,000 filmstrips, plus new materials as they are released. Bell & Howell will place a self-threading 16mm projector and an autoload filmstrip projector, a projection table and screen, in each classroom. The school district will expand and develop the school library to meet the American Association of School Librarians' standards for elementary school libraries, and provide a full-time, credentialed librarian for the school.

Four school districts have been selected to participate in Project Discovery: Shaker Heights, Ohio; Terrell, Texas; the Inner-City Target Area Program in Washington, D.C.; and the Jefferson Elementary School District in Daly City, California. Geographical, cultural, and socioeconomic conditions vary in each of the Project schools. Mercer Elementary School in Shaker Heights is a suburban, high socioeconomic school with students having relatively high ability and rich cultural backgrounds; Terrell, Texas, provides a rural area with some relatively disadvantaged students; the Inner-City Target Area is an urban area with low socioeconomic and disadvantaged students; the Thomas Edison School in Daly City is in a suburban area with students of average ability and middle-class cultural backgrounds. Because of the varied nature of each school community, each will develop Project Discovery in light of its own needs and educational perceptions. Uniformity is neither desired nor encouraged.

Reprinted with permission from: Muller, Robert E., "An Integrated Library: A Multimedia Approach to Learning," AUDIOVISUAL INSTRUCTION, April, 1965.

RESEARCH TO BE CONDUCTED

Research aspects of Project Discovery will be coordinated by the Educational Research Bureau of Ohio State University through a local research team. While a specific research design has not yet been formulated, it will be descriptive rather than experimental in nature, and will be concerned with four broad areas: (1) the effects of maximum availability and flexibility of instructional materials; (2) the effects on student achievement; (3) the effects on teaching methods; and (4) the changes in attitude toward the role of instructional media.

Project Discovery is especially interested in finding the effect of immediate availability of materials on teacher-utilization. It is anticipated that having films and filmstrips readily accessible in the school library, available instantly on need, plus the complete elimination of the necessity for scheduling projectors, will provide the impetus needed to use films as basic rather than supplementary teaching tools. The elimination of the logistical problem of booking films and projectors, combined with a thorough knowledge of the film library through intensive previewing, will open new possibilities for the use of projected materials in every area of the curriculum.

IMPLEMENTATION IN DALY CITY

In implementing Project Discovery in Daly City, we will have to start virtually from scratch. The existing library consists of one classroom (900 sq. ft.), with a book collection of some 2,500 books for grades 3-6, serviced by a librarian one and one-half days a week.

We plan to cut a 20' opening into the next classroom, expanding the library to 1,800 sq. ft. seating over 75 children. The existing shelving will be moved to other schools, and new birch-veneer standard 60" library shelving installed, some perimeter and some freestanding to create reading, reference, and storytelling areas. Study carrels will be constructed for individual study, and for film and filmstrip viewing. A listening area will be set up with earphone outlets, and storage for phonodisc and tape recordings. In the carpeted storytelling area we plan to have a rear-projector screen and a simple puppet theater to enhance this phase of the literature program.

The existing book collection will be expanded to 5,000 volumes by the opening of the project this September, with 2,000 additional volumes to be added during the first year. Films and filmstrips will be classified by broad subject areas (e.g., science, history, literature), and will be housed with the books in the same subject areas. Over 300 mounted art prints will also be available in the library.

All of these materials will be available for use by both children and teachers in classrooms and in the library. Everything except 16mm films will be circulated for home use by the children. Filmstrip viewers will be available for overnight loan.

All materials in the library will be cataloged in one card catalog. The card catalog will be divided into two parts: an author-title catalog, and a separate subject catalog. Color-banded cards will be used to indicate the various kinds of materials, but common subject headings will be used for books and audiovisual materials. In addition to the materials housed in the school library, the teachers will continue to have access to the district Instructional Materials Library (one block away, and with daily delivery) with its large book and audiovisual collections, and to the County Office (weekly delivery) and other common sources for additional 16mm films.

Professional personnel will be limited to one credentialed school librarian, but we hope to be able to recruit sufficient adult volunteers and student library assistants to handle circulation routines and housekeeping, thus enabling the librarian to devote herself entirely to professional-level teaching and library activities. All materials, book and audiovisual, will be ordered, cataloged, and processed centrally, and will be received by the school ready for use. The librarian will continue to participate in the district's book evaluation program and in the development of the district's overall library program.

The audiovisual resources provided by Project Discovery combined and totally integrated with a rich library program will provide the pupils and teachers of Edison School with one of the richest imaginable sources of the materials for learning, a source which can be tapped to extend and enrich every phase of the curriculum through printed and projected learning materials.

INTEGRATION OF EDUCATIONAL MEDIA

Integration is the operative word in this program, integration of many types of educational media to promote better teaching and better learning for every child in every classroom, to teach and extend and reinforce learning by every possible means, through every possible medium.

In addition to the development of this integrated library program, we plan an intensive in-service program for the faculty to develop and improve techniques in the effective utilization of these materials, using as consultants not only the teachers themselves, but also specialists from within the district, from the County Office and State Department of Education, from nearby teachers' colleges, and from the sponsoring firms, Encyclopaedia Britannica Films and Bell & Howell. Project Discovery is easily as exciting a prospect for teachers as for children.

Project Discovery has a rich potential for demonstration purposes, too, and we hope to share our experiences as widely as possible with visiting administrators, teachers, librarians, and student-teachers.

The potential of Project Discovery seems almost endless in its effect on pupil learning and teaching technique. We see it as a golden opportunity to demonstrate the effect of a multimedia approach to teaching and learning, to demonstrate that the full utilization of modern instructional media will create a new dimension of learning, a depth of development of children's potential, and a new concept in teaching techniques.

THE ELEMENTARY INSTRUCTIONAL MATERIALS CENTER

A. K. Trenholme

Two major trends in education emphasize the need for the elementary instructional materials center. The first of these is the recognition that a proper provision for individual differences necessitates a wide range of available materials. We must provide instructional materials of every kind on every level if we are to accomplish the goal of education for all American students.

The second major factor is the great increase in materials in the last decade. Films, filmstrips, transparencies, tapes, recordings, paperbacks, cartridge 8mm films, teaching machines, and greatly improved textbooks have added to the complexity of the elementary program. The need for many materials and their ample provision creates a situation in which an instructional materials center becomes necessary.

The elementary instructional materials center is an outgrowth of the libraries now present in some elementary schools. The modern library, such as those established by the Knapp Project, includes auditory and visual materials as well as every type of printed book and pamphlet. In addition to these, the elementary instructional materials center should include provisions for the circulation of text and supplementary books and an area for local production. Teachers find the accessibility of one facility very advantageous, and the center which is close to the classrooms probably provides the optimum of service to the extent of its materials. An elementary instructional materials center would typically include a reading room, an electronic learning room or area, and a production studio. In schools using closed-circuit television, the television studio would also be included.

The inclusion of text and supplementary materials is the most discussed feature in this definition of the elementary instructional materials center. The reasoning supporting its inclusion comes from the systems where many supplementary materials are available for temporary use in the classroom and where much of the supplementary material is of the library type. For example, in Portland, Oregon, the literature area of the elementary language arts program is dependent upon a hundred literature packets including about 1,000 titles. These books are all on the regular elementary library list and can be supplemented from the elementary depository. Since these packets are designed to circulate within the building, a central distribution point is needed. An additional reason for the inclusion of texts is that the multiplicity of titles is growing beyond casual attention and calls for a proper distribution specialist.

Reprinted with permission from: Trenholme, A.K., "The Elementary Instructional Materials Center," AUDIOVISUAL INSTRUCTION, November, 1964.

Local production has always been carried on by teachers; but the addition of teacher-produced transparencies, slides, and in some cases, filmstrips and 8mm movies has increased the need for an adequate workroom. In addition to duplicating equipment, a transparency copier, water, and in some instances photographic equipment will be needed.

In the future an extension of the viewing and listening portions of the elementary center will be into the field of electronic learning devices. Schools building facilities, particularly new buildings, should make ample provision for the addition of such equipment in the future.

The accompanying floor plan of the Sitton elementary school instructional materials center in Portland attempts to portray a facility for the introduction of these services. It will be noticed that a library reading room, an audiovisual room for viewing and listening, and a teacher workroom are provided. The center will be staffed by a library aide under the supervision of a teacher who will be in the center on a part-time basis. A number of the centers in Portland are supervised by teacher-librarians using this plan. Every system will make its own adaptations, but the concept of the instructional materials center, already so successful on the high school level, seems equally applicable to the elementary school.

The elementary instructional materials center concept is a logical extension of the elementary library, and schools with a library and librarian would have very little difficulty extending service to the whole field of instructional materials.

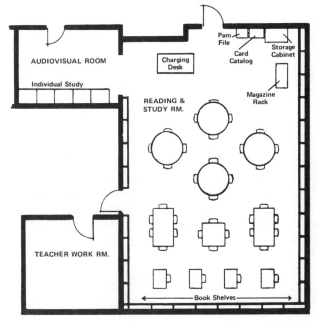

SITTON ELEMENTARY INSTRUCTIONAL MATERIALS CENTER

SET UP AN AUDIOVISUAL CENTER

Ella C. Clark

Do you want to improve learning conditions in your school? Have you audiovisual equipment and materials housed in various and sundry places in the school building? Does the resulting unavailability of some of these valuable aids to effective instruction seriously limit their usefulness? If so, why not consider the great advantages of organizing these potentially powerful tools of learning in such a way as to get maximum mileage from their use?

Last summer, Sister M. Therese, O.S.B., principal of St. Thomas More Grade School, LaCrosse, Wis., was a member of my audiovisual-aids class at Marquette University. She was one of several students who responded to the vital challenge to write a term paper on a topic or audiovisual plan that might be put into practice in her own school. After several class lectures and individual conferences, Sister M. Therese developed a carefully organized plan for what appeared to be the best possible use of the audiovisual equipment and materials already possessed by St. Thomas More School. An important part of the blueprint was a projected plan for the future wise development and expansion of the school's audiovisual program.

CONVINCE THE FACULTY

Last September, with the cooperation of colleagues, parents, and students, Sister's carefully worked out plan began to take shape with the result that currently St. Thomas More School has a well-organized, centralized collection of audiovisual equipment and materials readily available to every teacher in the school. As was pointed out in our class lectures, one of the first steps was to involve the entire faculty in this practical project. Professionally minded teachers are eager to teach as effectively as possible, and they will give complete support to a project which is designed to improve the learning of their students. Obviously, without wholehearted faculty support, any attempt to improve instruction in a school will fall far short of its potential. Research offers abundant proof that when properly organized and intelligently used, audiovisual materials increase initial and permanent learning, heighten student interest, and effect substantial timesaving.

INVENTORY MATERIALS ON HAND

Regardless of how far a school has advanced in effective use of audiovisual aids, it is wise to stop occasionally and take stock of all the equipment and

Reprinted with permission from: Clark, Ella C., "Set Up an Audiovisual Center," CATHOLIC SCHOOL JOURNAL, May, 1963.

materials the school has at its disposal, how they are being used, and what plans there are for wise future development. Making a complete inventory such as this is of particular value in schools where materials have not been centrally located and organized for ready use.

Accordingly, the staff at St. Thomas More School cooperated in inventorying all audiovisual equipment and materials it had. Their list included: two tape recorders, one 16mm. sound motion-picture projector, two filmstrip projectors, one opaque projector, two portable projection screens, two FM radios, more than 100 filmstrips, many maps, globes, and exhibits, plus an abundant supply of ordinary flat pictures useful with the opaque projector, for bulletin boards and for pupil reference.

In connection with such an inventory, it is of great value to invite the staff teachers to write out a frank assessment of the extent to which each teacher has used the various materials, along with a statement of any difficulties which, they feel, may account for limited use of any items. Usually, lack of ready availability figures as a major problem. Thus, centralizing and organizing the collection goes a far way toward the desired solution to the problem.

WHERE TO CENTRALIZE COLLECTION

A survey of every nook and cranny of even a crowded building may surprisingly reveal a small, yet adequate, space for storing the audiovisual collection. Sometimes, even a basement room may be used. At St. Thomas More School, the faculty discovered a small, little-used storage room that could be drafted into service. After readying it with paint, draperies, shelves, and storage cabinets, the school had an audiovisual center. Here they brought all the audiovisual equipment and materials not frequently needed in certain classrooms. All items were carefully listed and described, with locations noted, and a list was supplied to each teacher. Some schools develop a card index for all materials, but it is still a good idea to get a copy of the complete listing to each teacher, since she will be more apt to refer to it when planning her classes.

THE COORDINATOR OF THE CENTER

A common practice in many elementary and high schools is to appoint an interested, qualified member of the faculty to act as coordinator of the center, who with the help of colleagues and students will develop and implement plans for optimum use of all audiovisual materials owned by the school, as well as those available from various sources in the community. At St. Thomas More School, Sister M. Jolenta, O.S.B., who has a definite interest in the project, volunteered to perform this service. It should be noted that full cooperation from the entire staff is essential to the success of such an undertaking. In a similar vein of helpfulness, a mothers' group volunteered to assist in cataloging, organizing, filing, and checking materials in and out as requested by teachers. The mothers also call for and return films and other materials which are available on loan from local colleges, libraries, and film agencies — an enormously helpful service.

STUDENTS HELP, TOO

In effective school audiovisual programs, students, who are carefully selected and trained, form an integral part of the program. Wise utilization of trained students, of intermediate grades or older, who can set up, take down, and put away projectors and screens, can add much to the efficiency of the program. Moreover, if judiciously managed, with enough trained students, such an arrangement also helps pupils to render a valuable service in a democratic society without sacrifice of any pupil's classroom learning opportunities. Reliable students, trained for these tasks, enjoy the honor of serving their school by handling such routine matters, and they perform very effectively.

It usually pays high dividends to devote a few faculty meetings to looking over the available audiovisual materials and equipment and discussing the various ways each may be used more advantageously. Invite all staff members to make suggestions. Such an approach provides valuable in-service emphasis on better teaching. Many schools find it worthwhile to invite to one of their faculty meetings a consultant well versed in audiovisual materials and their most efficient uses. Simultaneously, it is well to look ahead and invite the entire staff to make suggestions for expansion of the audiovisual program. Obviously when teachers themselves have a voice in suggesting teaching materials, they are more apt to make optimum use of them.

THE PROFESSIONAL MATERIALS CENTER

Florence L. Simmons

In his article on the school library in *Elementary School Journal*,[1] Robert G. Shadick states that he often envies the school librarian his opportunities to influence what is taught in the classroom. We know, to be sure, the importance of the librarian in the school and generally recognize this insofar as students are concerned. But we tend to forget the others who can benefit from school library services – parents, principals, and especially teachers.

"The elementary school teacher," reports Dorothy Peterson in *Elementary School Journal*, "is not an avid reader of current professional literature."[2] One reason may be that the newest professional materials are simply not at hand. They are gathered in schools of education and various administrative centers, but

Reprinted by permission from the February, 1963, issue of the WILSON LIBRARY BULLETIN. Copyright © 1963 by The H. W. Wilson Company.

not where the teacher needs them most — right in the school. And it is here that the librarian, by properly organizing a materials center and keeping it up to date, can play a vital role in the professional awareness of teachers themselves.

A PROFESSIONAL LIBRARY IN EVERY SCHOOL

The most logical place for a professional library for teachers is right in the school, in a workroom conveniently located next to the school library or resource center. Though this room should have access from the corridor, it should also connect with the library, so that books will be readily available, and so that the school librarian may administer the collection with ease. Since the professional library serves many purposes, it would store not only books and periodicals, but also projectors, viewers, and records. Equipped with a conference table, vertical files, typewriter, etc., the room can provide a place for personal research or for professional meetings. And don't forget the coffee pot!

I have seen a description of such a "Curriculum Room" at the John Jacob Astor school in Portland, Oregon.[3] It is a combination work and materials center, idea exchange, meeting place and teachers' lounge. In one corner are the mathematics teaching aids with a bulletin board on which are posted recent articles listing research in this field. Another part of the room is devoted to science, and so forth. In LaCanada School, Oak Grove, California,[4] teachers place their materials for science experiments on one shelf and the professional literature they would use on a shelf nearby.

Even in a school without a separate workroom for teachers, a corner of the library can be set up for this purpose and the resources of the professional center publicized by means of various devices. A bulletin board can call attention to new items. Magazines can be routed to teachers, with notation of articles of interest. A file of publishers' catalogs, and of producers of films and filmstrips, maps and charts, science kits, craft materials, and the like would help teachers ordering new materials. A separate file, organized by type of material, can hold brochures and individual advertisements, which often appear long before the products they publicize are included in a catalog. Anything newsworthy, such as the purchase of an 8mm film projector, would be posted on the bulletin board.

PROFESSIONAL MATERIALS

Since in many schools there is no budgeted amount for professional materials, funds might be taken from the instructional materials budget. (The allocation for school library books is, of course, geared to student, not teacher, use.) Often the PTA will donate an additional sum for the professional library. The *Standards for School Library Programs*[5] gives helpful suggestions in describing the nature and importance of the professional collection.

Periodicals. One of the most important items in the professional materials center is the periodicals file. A well-stocked library would begin by subscribing to such general professional periodicals as *Elementary School Journal, National Elementary Principal, School Life, NEA Journal,* and the state educational journal. Several periodicals in specific subject fields — e.g., *Art Education, Arithmetic Teacher, Elementary English, Elementary School Science Bulletin,* and *Social Education* — are also essential; and they can prove useful not only to the teacher but to the librarian. They have frequent references to good teaching materials, book review sections, and occasional articles of immediate interest such as the useful article on picture files which appeared in a recent *NEA Journal.*[6] These magazines should not be bound. It is an expensive process and in the long run less convenient for the teacher who wants a particular item. After five years, magazines can be clipped for articles that are still of interest, and the articles then stored in the professional file with pamphlets.

Indexes. For easy reference, a copy of *Education Index* should be on hand, budget permitting. Other indexes that might be used from the central professional library are the more expensive lists of free or cheap materials, and film and filmstrip guides. The Peabody list of free or inexpensive materials[7] is a useful item to stock, and the new *Educational Media Index*[8] will bear watching when it appears this spring.

Books. If the collection of professional books is not large, more can be borrowed from the central professional library. *NEA Journal* should be checked for its annual list of "Outstanding Education Books," and other professional periodicals provide similar recommendations. A recent *Curriculum Bulletin*[9] from the University of Oregon is also helpful. Mary V. Gaver, in her article on "Building Collections"[10] in this series, mentions titles that would be useful in an elementary school professional library and we would stock most of the yearbooks suggested. Teachers will find valuable the booklets and handbooks on the preparation of audio-visual learning devices, posters, etc. The National Council for the Social Studies has a "How to do it" series[11] and there is a series on audio-visual techniques from the New Jersey State Department of Education.[12] Also useful are the texts on teaching materials, and Thomas and Swarthout's *Integrated Teaching Materials*[13] with its criteria for evaluation.

There should not be a time limit on the circulation of these materials. If, after two weeks, someone else needs a title the teachers will try to hasten their use so that it can be available to others. At midterm and the end of the school year each teacher can be reminded of items charged to him and everything not in use can be returned to the library.

Units. As teachers prepare instructional units they often place a copy in the professional collection for other teachers to examine. Courses of study from other systems are helpful. (They can be examined in the central professional library for selection purposes.) Courses of study are available for examination at the annual meetings of the Association for Supervision and Curriculum Development, and the supervisor of elementary education may check in the Association's publication *Curriculum Materials*[14] those that will be most useful for the schools. The courses of study are helpful, as they provide excellent bibliographies of books for children's use and aid the teacher in choosing materials when a unit of instruction is being prepared.

Textbooks. Teachers usually ask that a complete set of textbooks in use in the school be available for their use. To this collection can be added texts left by publishers, arranged, like the courses of study, by subject area in the curriculum rather than by the Decimal Classification. Sample workbooks, tests, etc., are useful — if they don't get into the student's hands.

Equipment. Space should be provided for materials the teachers use in their instructional program – the number games, charts, magnifiers, measuring devices, tools, etc.

THE INSTRUCTIONAL MATERIALS SPECIALIST

When we think of the professional library we think primarily of books and other printed materials, which are the guides to all tools and devices used in the educational program. When the teacher reads about the research on the use of films, he may well be doing his own experimentation with this medium. The librarian must be aware of all tools described in professional literature, the places where they may be obtained, and their relative merits. The librarian must recognize his role as an instructional materials specialist, and nowhere will this be more important than in his relations with his colleagues, the other faculty members of his school.

REFERENCES

[1] Shadick, R. G. "The School Librarian: a Key to Curriculum Development." *Elementary School Journal,* March 1962, pp. 298-303.

[2] Petersen, Dorothy G. "The Teacher's Professional Reading." *Elemenary School Journal,* Oct. 1962, pp. 1-5.

[3] *Professional Growth for Principals: The Teacher and His Teaching Tools.* Arthur C. Croft Publications, 1960.

[4] Purcell, Marge. "Science Materials Storage Shelf." *Elementary School Science Bulletin.* Feb. 1961, no. 60, p. 7.

[5] American Association for School Librarians. *Standards for School Library Programs.* A.L.A., 1960. pp. 85-86.

[6] Williams, Catherine. "A Picture File in Every School," *NEA Journal,* Feb. 1961, pp. 40-41.

[7] *Free and Inexpensive Learning Materials.* 11th ed. George Peabody College, 1962.

[8] *Educational Media Index (to be published spring 1963).* Send inquiries to the Educational Media Council, 250 W. 57th Street, New York 19.

[9] A Bibliography of the Professional Bookshelf in School Libraries. *Curriculum Bulletin no. 205,* 1960. University of Oregon. 25¢.

[10] Gaver, Mary V. "The Creative Elementary School Library: Building Collections." *Wilson Library Bulletin,* Jan. 1962, pp. 378-80.

[11] National Council for the Social Studies. *How To Do It Series: How to Use Motion Pictures; How to Use Textbooks; How to Use Local History; How to Use a Bulletin Board; How to Use Daily Newspapers; How to Conduct a Field Trip; and others.* NEA, 1954-60. 6 to 8 pages each. 25¢ ea. or 18 items for $2.50.

[12] Dunavan, C. C. and E. Fantone. "Teachers Make: Slides, Transparencies, Opaques, Tape Recordings." Available from Audio-Visual Office, State Department of Education, Trenton, N.J. 39p. 50¢.

[13] Thomas, R. M. and S. G. Swarthout. "Integrated Teaching Materials; How to Choose, Create and Use Them." *Longmans.* 1960.

[14] American Association for Supervision and Curriculum Development. "Curriculum Materials." ASCD, published annually.

MEDIA, TECHNOLOGY, AND
IMC SPACE REQUIREMENTS

Amo DeBernardis, David M. Crossman
and Thomas E. Miller

Present trends in audiovisual use and new instructional methods are definitely affecting the space requirements of audiovisual centers and instructional materials centers at various educational levels. This influence is evident in elementary and secondary schools, at the school system level, and in colleges and universities. The three specialists whose articles are presented below have been closely involved with implementing the design of facilities in response to this influence.

IMPACT ON THE IMC IN
ELEMENTARY AND SECONDARY SCHOOLS

Dramatic progress in the use of teaching media in our schools has occurred in the past decade. Coupled with rapid development of new tools and materials has come a significant broadening and improvement in utilization and a widespread strengthening of basic components for an integrated instructional media program in many school districts.

Interwoven with the development and utilization of media have been significant changes in the curriculum. A rapid overview of some of these changes will provide a context for more specific examination of facilities which will be demanded to provide the instructional materials support needed by teachers and learners in our elementary and secondary schools.

CLASS SIZE

The "magic number" given as the ideal size for an instructional group used to be 25 to 30 students. This concept is rapidly giving way to realistic groupings of pupils in various sizes depending upon instructional objectives and needs. Larger groups are brought together for functional presentation of information, and smaller groups are organized to provide an improved climate for discussion and interaction. An added factor is strongly increasing emphasis on independent study and individual research.

Reprinted with permission from: DeBernardis, Amo, et al, "Media, Technology and IMC Space Requirements," AUDIOVISUAL INSTRUCTION, February, 1965.

These developments inevitably lead to increased utilization of a broad variety of learning materials and devices if the objectives involved are to be reached effectively.

FLEXIBLE SCHEDULING

Historically, the school schedule has been among the most rigid components of the school's organization; more ideas have crashed to confusion against it than against any other barrier to change. Now the "lock-step" schedule of the secondary school is giving way to flexible systems which make it possible to plan a program designed to meet the needs of the individual rather than the convenience of the organization. Each day is divided into small time modules, thus making it possible to combine and shift modular patterns to construct varied programs. Discussion groups can meet for one hour, and labs for two or even three hours. Conferences can be set up for as little as 15 minutes of interaction time, and modules can be assigned for independent study and research.

Such close attention to individual learning needs and programing also will place strong emphasis on availability and effective utilization of many teaching-learning materials and is forcing development of resource centers providing study space and richly endowed with study materials, devices, and equipment.

TEAM TEACHING

The trend toward team teaching is a significant one. The strengths of each teacher are brought to focus on instructional problems, and through cooperative action each teacher can reinforce the others and share in the joint diagnosis and prescription of activities to implement needed learning situations.

Instructional media rapidly become an integral component of programs which teaching teams prepare, and production of specialized materials to meet specific local requirements becomes essential in this type of teaching arrangement.

INDEPENDENT STUDY

Preparing the student for independent inquiry, individual research, and broadened study is a significant trend in our schools. To accomplish this, the learner must use many types of materials and learning devices. We have already pointed out the necessity for resource centers stocked and organized for these purposes. Such centers should be strategically located throughout the building and connected with the latest communciation devices, thus enabling students to enjoy ready access to large and varied resources for the information needed. Data processing, information retrieval, and computerization of other learning--materials applications are all full of implications and impact on the planning for these spaces.

It is also now increasingly clear that all types of learning media should be available for the student to use outside of school hours. The school must be prepared to check out films, tapes, slides, equipment, and other learning components in addition to printed materials and library books.

DATA PROCESSING AND INFORMATION RETRIEVAL

Perhaps the most significant breakthrough for those who administer educational media programs are developments in data processing and information storage and retrieval. These now make it possible to store and distribute data and information in spaces and at speeds which defy the imagination, and yet they can clearly be seen to be required in the near future to meet the multiplying demands for classifying, filing, and finding the products of our well-known knowledge explosion.

It is especially significant that it will be possible to make these verbal, graphic, and pictorial data and information resources available in many areas of the school building, the district, and the geographical area or region, including most importantly, the student's own home. These same resources will be a most important link in broadening the base of "current learners" in many areas and at all levels, including parents and other adult learners.

At the present time costs are out of reach for most schools; however, it is today that we must plan for the developments which will be overwhelming us tomorrow. As in all other developments in our technological era, cost will come down as actual utilization broadens, and these systems will be part of our schools in the not-far-distant future.

TEACHING EFFICIENCY AND ECONOMY

With the increase in enrollments forcing expansion of school programs and increasing costs, educators will be called upon, more than they ever have been in the past, to provide evidence that they are doing the instructional job at the minimum effective cost per unit.

We will need to show that the uses to which we put educational media and the new technology are essential in producing a more broadly educated person who is better prepared for living in an era of change and better able to continue the self-starting learning processes demanded by that age.

The task of the educational administrator will be to provide the continuous evaluation which will furnish evidence of effectiveness in the applications of new media and technology, and the role of the instructional media specialist will be to produce these effective applications and assist in the evaluative process. These effects cannot be measured in terms of numbers of films or projectors — or even of computers — but only in demonstrably better educational programing for each student.

All in all, this overview of "the new look" in education, reflecting heavy emphasis on teaching media and new technological application, will place new responsibilities on the media specialist and in the instructional materials centers in both elementary and secondary schools.

It is obviously impractical in a single article to give detailed space allocations or to attempt to be definitive for each area; it is as obvious that local conditions, needs, and desirable functional applications will require specific local adaptation. The differentiations between elementary and secondary centers are, it will be recognized, more a matter of level and sophistication than of principles for planning.

The instructional materials center in the school should be organized to provide the following services to teachers, students, and, in some instances, to the public:

- To catalog and inventory all types of teaching and learning materials — books, pamphlets, films, recordings, models, exhibits, art prints, slides, filmstrips, microfilms, community resources.
- To maintain and service all of the teaching tools used in the school.
- To inform teachers and students about new developments in materials, equipment, and teaching technology.
- To produce materials which are unique to a specific teaching situation.
- To provide assistance in the locating of needed teaching and learning materials.
- To assist teachers and students in the use of teaching equipment and materials.
- To provide space and facilities for teachers and students to preview, audition, review, and try out various teaching media.
- To serve as a comprehensive learning laboratory in which students can learn to use all types of learning materials and equipment.
- To provide for continuous evaluation of the program and services.

Facilities to carry forward these crucial functions and services need to be carefully and thoughtfully worked out, with constant emphasis on ease and simplicity for functional use. People who will use the center are not concerned about administrative responsibilities — they just want effective media services provided with a minimum of effort on their part.

The size and complexity of any center will vary with the size of the school and the number of people to be served. The following considerations will be basic to any center.

Location. The instructional materials center will be the hub around which much of the teaching and learning activity will be built. In reality it will be the nerve center of the educational program. Its location within the building complex should provide for ease in receiving and distributing equipment and materials. Traffic flow patterns should be planned to avoid congestion and provide for an easy flow of people to and from the center. The design and plan should enforce the central theme that this is a place for learning.

Reading Area. Little imagination has gone into the planning of traditional areas which have book shelves lining the walls and rows of tables in the center. With the increased emphasis on the use of all kinds of printed materials in a research format, the reading area in the center needs a new look. The area should be designed to make it possible to change shelving arrangements easily and quickly. Spaces should be provided to have seminars and group discussions. Individual study carrels should be available. These spaces should be designed to facilitate the use of all kinds of new media; conduits or raceways to individual carrels should make it possible to hook up to a central information and retrieval system when it becomes available. The acoustical and visual environment is an important part of this area. Carpeting, individual lighting of carrels, and effective use of color will help create a more desirable learning climate. The dramatic change in media in the past decade emphasizes the need for flexibility in planning spaces for their use. Supporting walls should be kept to a minimum and utilities should be planned to be easily routed to any newly developed space.

_Learning Laboratory. Most spaces in the center should be considered as learning laboratories; however, one or more spaces should be designed for group use of films, slides, programed materials, simulated experiences, etc. These spaces should be designed for front and rear projection with good viewing and acoustical properties. In some schools this space can be used for the foreign language laboratories. It should be designed to make it easy to use all types of media. The control of lights, projection equipment, sound amplification, screens, etc. should be centrally located for use by the instructors. Because of the variety of electronic equipment which will be used in this space it is essential that conduits, raceways, or other means be provided to make it easy to provide new electronic or electrical circuits adjacent to this area. Individual and small-group viewing and listening spaces should be planned. This makes for ease of control and also for better utilization of technicians.

Television and Multipurpose Area. With the increased use of closed-circuit television, the instructional materials center must provide facilities for its use. The closed-circuit facility can be an important link in the transmission of materials to the various learning spaces throughout the school. The size of the school will determine the size and number of spaces needed. Careful consideration should be given to planning spaces for closed-circuit television and to providing a production area designed to make possible the organization of educational programs. The production space should be planned so that any type of demonstration or small-group presentation could originate from it. Large-group presentations can originate from the auditorium or gym. The teaching studio should be equipped with chalkboards, sinks, electrical outlets, demonstration benches, screens, projectors, stands, and other equipment necessary in the production of instructional programs. Storage space for such items as properties, cameras, lights, and stands should be planned. The control room which houses the monitors and central board should have good visual access to the teaching studio. The television complex should be located in close proximity to the production area of the center.

Indpendent Study Areas. Throughout the center, individual study spaces should be provided. Each space should be designed so the student can use all types of materials. These student carrels may vary from a simple study station which provides for an individual student to read, study, and do independent research to one which is in reality a self-contained study station. There the learner will be able to use not only printed materials but also to retrieve prerecorded materials, such as video tapes of lectures and demonstrations. He will have access to data stored in the computer and be able to view the filmstrips, slides, and films in the center. These same study stations should not only be provided in the instructional materials center but also be conveniently located throughout the school for greater student access to materials. It is not too idealistic to see the day when an electronic study station will be located in the student's home.

Maintenance Facilities. With an ever-increasing use of electronic teaching equipment, maintenance of this equipment and materials becomes of prime importance. Teachers and students need to be assured that their electronic devices will be in excellent condition. Too many breakdowns will discourage even the most enthusiastic person. The school materials center should have space and personnel available to carry on this maintenance program. The space should be planned and equipped to handle all types of maintenance and repair with electrical service, test equipment, lathe, and drill press. Storage for parts and stand-by equipment will be needed, plus space for repair and test benches.

Production Facilities. With the expanding curriculum and varied teaching approaches to instruction, the production of local instructional materials becomes an important function of the center. These materials will be produced to fit unique teaching and learning needs. The scope of this production will encompass everything from printed instruction sheets to video tape of a science demonstration. The production facilities will be capable of making films, slides, transparencies, tapes, models, dioramas, charts, and other teaching materials.

The production area will need photographic darkroom facilities; space for small power tools such as jigsaw, radial arm saw, and drill press; offset press; and mimeograph, photocopy, and spirit process equipment. An area should be provided for the artist-technician. Storage space for all types of construction material will be needed.

Conference Spaces. Since the materials center will serve as a focal point for a great deal of curriculum planning, meeting rooms need to be provided which will accommodate groups of varying sizes. Each room should have the capability for using all the various media housed in the center. The control of light, ventilation, and acoustics is a must in this area. Bulletin boards, chalkboards, and rear-view and front projection screens should be provided, as well as furniture which can be moved easily. Folding doors or walls will make these rooms more adaptable to varying needs.

Satellite Materials Centers. With the growing emphasis on flexible scheduling and independent study it is not feasible to store all of the materials in one central place. Materials will be used in a number of places throughout the school: the main center, the independent study station, and the satellite center. These satellite centers can be organized around specific subjects, i.e., science, social studies, math, or they can be a modification of the main center. How they are organized will depend upon the administrative structure of the school. Each satellite center must provide spaces for equipment and materials, books, filmstrips, slides, tapes, and charts. Provision for good communication between the main center and the satellite centers is a must. Student study spaces, viewing, and listening facilities are needed. Storage facilities for slides, prints, charts, filmstrips, and transparencies should be planned.

PLANNING FOR CHANGE

What has happened in educational technology and media in the past decade should give every school administrator and planner an insight into what the next decade will bring. Automated teaching devices will be a reality, computers will store all sorts of data and information, and students and teachers will have access to information not only at school but also at home. The planning and remodeling of schools must make allowances for these new developments. The school instructional materials center is an important aspect of this future development. It should be designed so that new developments in technology and media can be incorporated with a minimum of change and expense.

— Amo De Bernardis,
Portland Public Schools

IMPACT ON THE IMC AT THE
DISTRICT AND INTERDISTRICT LEVEL

Instructional materials centers vary a great deal at the district and interdistrict level in New York State. In one respect, however, virtually all are alike. They need more space.

The diversity of these space needs presents an interesting pattern indeed. I recently conducted a survey to determine the ways in which space allocated to IMC facilities is being used. Each of the school districts which responded services an average of 20 schools involving a mean student population of 13,000 students. Present square footage of usable IMC space averages 1,600 square feet. Of 12 responding institutions, all but two indicated that this space was inadequate for their needs.

CURRENT USE OF SPACE

The uses being made of existing IMC space by these institutions is tabulated below:

Use	Average Percent of Total IMC Space
Materials Storage (Including Film Library)	20
Administrative Areas	19
In-Service Training Area	13
Equipment Storage	10
Graphics Production Area	10
Equipment Repair	6
Individual Instruction Space	5
Still Photographic Production Space (Darkrooms, Studio Space)	4
Miscellaneous Use of Space	13

Reading Areas
Conference Areas
Television Areas
Listening and Preview

FUTURE SPACE NEEDS

Ten of the 12 cooperating school districts indicated that their present IMC space is insufficient for their needs. The nature of their space needs is tabulated below in the order of frequency of response:

Space Need	Of 12 Districts, Number Reporting Each Need
Graphics Production	6
In-Service Training	4
Still Photographic Studio and Darkroom Space	3
Film Library	2
Educational Television	2
Individual Instruction	2
Production Space	2
Display Area	1
AV Materials Storage	1

It seems quite clear that production and in-service training present the most pressing needs for space among those districts represented.

These needs for service space have sprung from several sources. One district puts it this way:

> New avenues to creativity in teaching brought about by the introduction of production techniques that are well within the abilities of teachers are being recognized and utilized. This has brought a new dimension to the Center, which has spurred increased interest, brought more teachers to the Center, and has increased utilization of all materials.

An interdistrict IMC indicates:

> Innovations brought about by curriculum revisions, new teaching organizations, flexible schedules, and communications media have helped to mold our IMC into a large group demonstration area, and small group and independent study carrel areas equipped with all types of programed texts, AV, and auto-instructional devices.

A third district indicates recognition of the need for increased media display areas together with expanded demonstration areas for in-service work with teachers.

ORIENTATION OF THE IMC

The theoretical orientation of the IMC determines, to a large extent, the direction which space needs take. In several of the districts reporting, for example, considerable explanation was devoted to the concept of a centralized district-wide IMC together with subcenters located in each of the member schools. In these situations, administration and major production is done in the district center, while teacher-made materials, smaller media collections, and local production characterize space use of the subcenters.

Of particular significance in the growth pattern of most instructional materials centers is its relationship to the library. Of the 12 districts questioned, seven are involved in close liaison with school and curriculum libraries, while five maintain separate services. Several of these centers began as curriculum libraries and have only recently begun to be concerned with newer media. One has complete jurisdiction over textbooks and all other media used in a large city school system. This center has become the focal point for the curriculum of that system.

Within the past year, the cooperative efforts between library and IMC facilities have taken on a new and exciting dimension. The increased interest in the individualization of instruction has led to a variety of innovations in individual learning facilities and particularly in the construction of study carrels. In some schools, the construction of carrels has taken place within an existing library facility. While the renaissance of this monastic tradition has been introduced in the simple form of separate study cubicles in some schools, considerable attention has been given to media that can be made electronically available to individual carrels on a random access basis. Obviously a system of this kind will require the extensive support of an instructional materials center. In one such installation in New York State, 15 study carrels are being constructed in a high school library with audio lines terminating in the instructional materials center. In a situation of this kind, both print and nonprint media are equally available for student use.

Another responding school began its IMC only two years ago. It started as a curriculum resources center, consisting chiefly of print materials for faculty use. A film library for classroom use is now being added, and space is being sought in which to locate a district-wide service facility.

Finally, a slightly different orientation to the IMC has developed at the interdistrict level. Designed primarily for in-service demonstration purposes, one interdistrict center has developed a unique mode of operation. This center reports that their "primary purpose is to inform teachers about significant curriculum developments within the framework of effective teaching techniques and communications technology."

In order to achieve its objective, this interdistrict center has periodically held teacher workshops within specific disciplines. "Teachers participating in these programs proceed through various learning patterns — large group, small group, independent study — using new curriculum materials, specially designed facilities, and instructional programs, and audiovisual devices pertinent to the project being studied."

— David M. Crossman,
New York State Education Department

IMPACT ON THE UNIVERSITY — AN EDUCATIONAL MEDIA SERVICE SYSTEM

All that goes together to make a university or college campus — buildings, classrooms, libraries, professors, fellow students, shaded walks — comprises a *center of educational media.* These media provide the *means* for the students' learning experiences at this center. Neither the student nor the professor can recognize "a" space or room or building which can be called the "media center" or "audiovisual center." Like love, learning experience is where you find it, and there are times when the bench beside the shaded walk yields more appropriate experience than does the textbook, motion picture, or computer-controlled classroom.

Like a projector – which should be thought of as dynamic technology tied by a light beam to a dynamic experience, not as hardware shelved in the equipment pool – educational media must be thought of as environment, and not as a static "center" somewhere. The design and provision of this environment defies any name short of "system." Services which assist with the design and provision of learning environment must be conceived as "system" rather than "center," if one is to deal effectively with *space* for these services.

One useful classification for an educational media service system is suggested here, along with comments about functions and space. Services, or elements, of this system need not be directed by one administrator or be the functions of one organization. However, they must be coordinated, and done so with design for all to see, to form a functioning system capable of identifying and serving the complex media needs of higher education.

A MATERIALS CENTER FOR EASY ACCESS

F. Edgar Lane

In the Dade County (Miami, Florida) School System the Instructional Materials Department includes audiovisual services, school library services, textbook services, the professional library and the distribution services! The philosophy is that the classroom teacher needs to be able to get all the instructional materials she needs at one location in the building. This should be as nearly central as possible. For that reason, in elementary buildings, the Administrative Area and the Instructional Materials Area are continuing parts of the same building wing. This article describes a representative elementary school materials center.

Reprinted with permission from: Lane, F. Edgar, "A Materials Center for Easy Access," EDUCATION SCREEN, September, 1959.

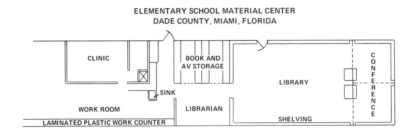

ELEMENTARY SCHOOL MATERIAL CENTER
DADE COUNTY, MIAMI, FLORIDA

A straight line flows from the principal's office through the secretarial and administrative work area to the teacher's work room, the materials work area and on through the library and conference areas. Referring to the drawing, we consider everything (except the clinic) beginning at the teachers' work space and extending through the library workroom, the library and conference rooms, as the Instructional Materials Area of the building. There is a similar area in every elementary school, old and new. A laminated plastic work surface extends through the teachers' work area and on through the library, all along one wall. Underneath this work surface are storage cabinets with at least two knee spaces having the work surface at table height. On the wall opposite this work surface (which is against the window wall), there is narrower work surface, again with cabinets underneath it, and again extending on into the library workroom.

The teachers' workroom is designed to enable teachers to construct materials of their own without the difficulty that would be entailed in locating raw materials, bringing them together, finding the tools, doing the work in their own room and dispersing tools and unused materials.

We also envisage the time when our materials personnel will have the "know-how" to give direct help in more extensive materials construction.

Note that the sink is in a projecting construction between the teachers' work area and the library work area, thus serving both. The traditional library area has been planned with carefully allocated space for functional shelving designed for the material to be stored. Thus we have shelving especially for accommodating children's picture books with their odd outsizes, for reference works, for magazines, for atlases, and of course, standard book shelves.

When new schools are planned and construction begins, a whole series of related activities begins also. For each level — elementary, junior high and senior high — there is the purchasing of a definite list of equipment that is enumerated in the Board of Public Instruction Bulletin 31A[1]. There is also the purchasing of expendable instructional materials and equipment. This last includes audiovisual equipment and library books that are centrally processed. When school opens, all equipment is in place, the processed library books are on the shelves and the catalog cards are in the catalog. The school is ready for business.

---

[1] *Bulletin 31A — Initial Equipment and Supply List for Dade County Public Elementary Schools. Keeping this bulletin current is the responsibility of the Supervisor of Instructional Materials.*

We start from the first grade[2] to indoctrinate children in seeking authoritative sources for answers to their questions, believing that the safety of our social order resides in all citizens so indoctrinated. The aim is to present balanced viewpoints through careful selection of materials. Responsiblity for the selection of materials appropriate to the course and the grade level (aside from texts which are State-adopted) resides in each principal and his faculty. Selection is generally a "team-work" situation which avails itself of expert consultants in the various fields.

Also we start from the first grade to expose children to functional training in the use of the materials centers in all elementary schools. By the time children finish the elementary school they are at ease in these centers. They know the organizational plan from long practice in finding their own materials by means of the card catalog, Readers' Guide, a wide range of reference materials (not just encyclopedias), World Almanac, books of quotations, various catalogs, etc. They know the type of information offered by each encyclopedia. They know that filmstrips can be viewed individually or by committees using table top viewers; that "earphone" record players provide a multiplicity of experiences.

To us, there is a quiet satisfaction in having public library people call us for help in regulating public school child demand for their materials. They are most cooperative, even placing book collections in our schools to augment our own. To say we appreciate this cooperation is to put it very mildly.

In the Administration Building there are other materials on which teachers can draw. There are some 4000 titles in educational motion pictures, 4500 titles in filmstrips, art reproductions in glare proof, laminated plastic, "satchel museums," models of many kinds, a professional library of over 10,000 volumes. Any of these items can be requisitioned and are then delivered or picked up on twice weekly deliveries. Teachers may also borrow 35mm still cameras, 16mm motion picture cameras, public speaker systems for outdoor events, dry mounting presses, grommeting machines, etc. Demand for all these items grows continuously.

Liason with teachers is through the materials personnel in each school. These are the librarian and an audiovisual representative. Every school has the services of a trained librarian, most of them full-time. We are moving toward having a record of all instructional materials in a school in its materials center card catalog.

We credit our Administration for having done a wonderful job of getting our public and our Board of Public Instruction to support this program. We think it is wonderful.

---

[2]*This is true of all our elementary schools — new or old.*

Section Three

THE SECONDARY SCHOOL

ORIGIN, DEVELOPMENT, AND PRESENT STATE OF THE SECONDARY SCHOOL LIBRARY AS A MATERIALS CENTER

Frederic R. Hartz and R. T. Samuelson

The active school library today in theory, and sometimes in practice, is generally described as an instructional materials center complete with motion picture films, filmstrips, phono-records, tapes, picures, maps, charts, and the traditional books, periodicals, and pamphlets. The "center" not only provides for a diversity of materials but also equipment and space to facilitate their use by both students and faculty. Schools, and hopefully school libraries, are providing more of every type of instructional media for learning – more use of technology, even though sometimes in poorly planned ways – of radio and television programs, language laboratories, and teaching machines.

During the past two decades educational literature has recorded more and more concern for quality education in the comprehensive secondary school, and the major theme indicates a shift in emphasis from group instruction to individualized independent learning and other practices which have as a goal the development of each student to his maximum potential. The curriculum that values choicemaking, independent study, and depth has brought about an increased awareness of the need for a much expanded school library program. It is estimated that in the secondary schools of the future, students will spend from 12 to 15 hours per week in school in independent study. Hopefully, this will include reading, listening, writing, viewing, and working with automated devices.

ORIGINS AND DEVELOPMENT

The philosophical development of the secondary school library as an instructional materials center can be traced by examining the library standards of the American Association of School Librarians, and through the examination of general education and library literature.

It is generally conceded that by 1940, due largely to state participation, professional efforts of library and education groups, and the large measure of generous financial assistance of such foundations as the Carnegie Corporations, Rosenwald Fund, General Education Fund, and the Rockefeller Fund, that the library . . .

Reprinted with permission from: Hartz, Frederic R. and Samuelson, R.T., "Origin, Development, and Present State of The Secondary School Library as a Materials Center," PEABODY JOURNAL OF EDUCATION, July, 1965.

". . . changed from an unwanted outside agency to the center of all
school activities. Such schoolwork as projects, problems, and units is
built around books, magazines, newspapers, clippings, maps, pictures,
slides, and exhibits. All of these are issued by the librarian."[1]

This philosophy is reflected, reinforced, and considerably expanded in the
first "Evaluative Criteria" published in 1940 by the Cooperative Study of
Secondary School Standards. The "Evaluative Criteria" contained a section on
the school library in which an attempt was made to evaluate both the quality
and quantity of library service available. It dealt with such questions as
minimum budgets, qualifications of the librarian, services to teachers and
students, and physical aspects of the library such as accessibility, adequacy, and
attractiveness. The "Statement of Guiding Principles" for the library suggests the
effective library

". . . be a center of the educational life of the school, not merely a
collection of books. It should provide the reading and reference
facilities necessary to make the educational program effective . . . the
library should provide pupils with valuable means not only of
extending their knowledge and understanding but also of developing
desirable leisure habits."[2]

Here, in this statement, one detects for the first time the possibility of moving
from a "book orientated" to a "materials orientated" library, but it is not until
the 1950 Edition that the library is designated as a resource center of
instructional materials. The "Statement of Guiding Principles" in the "Evaluative Criteria 1950 Edition" suggests that in addition to reading materials

". . . the school should have available, organized in the library or as a
separate department audio-visual materials for use in the educational
program."[3]

Two other significant recommendations are observed which were not included in
the 1940 "Statement of Guiding Principles." First, extended library services
would

". . . necessitate a qualified library staff and efficient clerical
assistance for the administration of the library services."[4]

This contrasts significantly with the older one-librarian-per-library theory.
Secondly, we notice, however vague, some indication that librarians should
participate with teachers and administrators in curriculum planning.

The "Statement of Guiding Principles" in the "Evaluative Criteria 1960
Edition," after a brief introduction on the value and necessity of the traditional
library, outlines specifically the organization and purpose of the instructional
materials center. Likewise, the educational materials suitable for housing in the
"center" are specifically stated. The following goes much further than the earlier
1950 statements of mere recommendation:

"In recent years . . . there have been developed many new and
wonderful devices which, while they cannot and should not replace

books, offer their own unique contribution to the same ends, namely the recording and communication of ideas. Many schools have developed separate administrative organizations to provide the services that are peculiarly appropriate to these newer media of communication. Others have developed an integrated administrative unit, generally called the instructional materials center, which furnishes all the services usually associated with the library, and in addition provides the services connected with audio-visual materials, radio, and television.

. . . The major purpose of the instructional materials center is to serve the established aims of the total educational program by (1) providing a rich variety of materials, including books and other printed material, recordings, still and motion pictures, filmstrips, and other audio-visual materials and resources, for use by teachers and students as individuals and in groups; (2) offering leadership in developing techniques for the use of various materials by the teachers and students; (3) making available facilities, services, and equipment necessary for the selection, organization, and use of instructional materials; and (4) furnishing facilities for and assistance in the production of instructional materials and displays."[5]

PRESENT STATE OF THE SECONDARY SCHOOL LIBRARY AS A MATERIALS CENTER

Although, the "Evaluative Criteria 1960 Edition" has had real influence in the establishment of the instructional materials center, it must be recognized that an earlier statement of the American Association of School Librarians, in 1956, pointed the way for this development and directly effected the philosophy which was stated four years later in the "Evaluative Criteria." The philosophy of school libraries as instructional materials centers is set forth in the following statement:

"The function of an instructional materials center is to locate, gather, provide, and coordinate a school's materials for learning and the equipment required for use of these materials. Primary responsibility for administering such a center, producing new instructional materials, and supervising regular programs of in-service training for use of materials may be the province of librarians, or, it may be shared. In any case, trained school librarians must be ready to cooperate with others and themselves serve as coordinators, consultants, and supervisors of instructional materials service on each level of school administration — in the individual school building, for the city or county unit and for the state."[6]

It is apparent, however, that both the statement of "Guiding Principles" in the "Evaluative Criteria 1960 Edition" and the statement by the American Association of School Librarians in 1956 were a result of the then current practices in secondary education. Since 1950, and more strongly evidenced in the 1960's, there has been an increased emphasis in our educational philosophy upon intellectual excellence, individual differences, changes in curriculum and changes in methods of instruction. (i.e., team teaching and elimination of the lock-step). Reading of these new goals in education suggest a sizeable increase in the amount and kinds of materials that the library will be responsible for.

Presently, there is an accelerated trend toward developing school libraries as instructional materials centers. The American Association of School Librarians in its "Standards for School Library Programs"[7] further supports the centralization of all materials. Supporters of the A.A.L.S. standards, and advocates of instructional materials centers are quick to point out that by combining traditional library and audiovisual materials the library can provide:

> "1. A single catalog of all the school's instructional materials, so that at a glance teachers and pupils can discover what resources are available on a topic; books, films, periodicals, filmstrips, discs, pictures, tapes, objects, and index of community resources.
>
> 2. A single charging and booking system for all of these classes of materials.
>
> 3. A unified guidance and reference service for pupils and teachers."[8]

Although the philosophy of instructional materials centers is almost universally accepted in library literature and in current library standards, there are a number of obstacles which stand in the way of full acceptance. These obstacles should be emphasized because they can, and do, limit the effectiveness of the "center":

> "1. The librarian who is solely responsible for the administration of the library, or the one who has an inadequate staff may resist any additional responsibilities. National statistics show that this type of administration applies to the majority of schools over the country.
>
> 2. The emphasis on the operation of machines has created a "hardware image" in the area of audiovisual program rather than one of selection, organization, and use of projected materials for the improvement of instruction.
>
> 3. The selection and evaluation of nonbook materials is more time consuming and inconvenient than that of printed materials. Reliable selection aids which give critical evaluations of nonbook materials are limited.
>
> 4. In a world of specialization it is hard to find leadership capable of understanding and working with all media of communication.
>
> 5. Without careful preplanning many school systems have jumped on the "band wagon" to keep abreast of the newer educational developments and are committed to an improved program of instruction without being committed to providing all of the personnel, materials, space, and equipment needed for such a program."[9]

Richard L. Darling in his 1964 "Survey of School Library Standards"[10] presents a vivid picture of inadequate standards for personnel, materials, and funds as outlined in 5, above. Darling's survey reveals that the personnel recommendations of the American Association of School Librarians, has had only a slight influence on regional and state standards pertaining to school library personnel. The regional accrediting associations and the majority of the states make no recommendation for the education of the school librarian or for additional personnel to accommodate diversification of collections.

As for the matter of materials, other than printed, a relatively small number of states recommend or require other kinds of materials. This seems to indicate that the concept of the school library as an instructional materials center has not yet had full impact on school library standards. However, enough states do include audiovisual materials of various kinds in their standards which indicates a trend towards increasing recognition of the role of the school library in providing many types of material.

Finally, none of the regional accrediting associations and only five states, at the time of this writing, — Connecticut, Florida, North Carolina, North Dakota, and Wyoming — provide recommendations for specific amounts of money for audiovisual materials. Standards for expenditures for audiovisual materials, while reflecting the trend toward administering the school library as an instructional materials center, do not provide adequate funds for the wide range of materials needed. The trend to administer school libraries as materials centers may be impeded by the failure of quantitative standards at regional and state levels to indicate specific minimum expenditures for nonbook materials.

In summary then, the newer practice of administering the school library as an instructional materials center is reflected in school library standards (though not always in a consistent way.) Some standards

> "... recommend that the school library include all types of materials in its collections, but fail to recommend the additional personnel or funds to facilitate an enlarged program. Others recommend funds, but do not recommend the additional personnel. Nevertheless, both regional and state standards show an increased emphasis on the school library as a center for many types of materials, both printed and audiovisual."[11]

For the present, however, it must be said that our school administrators have only a dim and partial perception of the gigantic task involved in revitalizing our school libraries to take account of new knowledge, technology, and the vastly enlarged dimensions of the school curriculum.

NOTES

[1] A. J. Middlebrooks, "The School Library, 1900-1935," *American School Board Journal*, 92: 20-22, June 1936.

[2] *Evaluative Criteria 1940 Edition. (Washington, D.C.: Cooperative Study of Secondary School Standards, 1939)*, p. 51.

[3] *Evaluative Criteria 1950 Edition. (Washington, D.C.: Cooperative Study of Secondary School Standards, 1950)*, p. 209.

[4] *Idem.*

[5] *Evaluative Criteria 1960 Edition.* (Washington, D.C.: National Study of Secondary School Evaluation, 1960), p. 257.

[6] This statement was passed by unanimous vote at the business meeting of the American Association of School Librarians during the American Library Association Conference, Miami Beach, June 21, 1956.

[7] American Association of School Librarians. *Standards for School Library Programs.* (Chicago: American Library Association, 1960).

[8] Louis Shores, "Library and AV Center – Combined or Separate?" *N.E.A. Journal,* 47: 342-344, May 1958.

[9] Mary Helen Mahar, Editor. *The School Library as a Materials Center: Educational Needs of Librarians and Teachers in its Administration and Use.* (Washington, D.C.: U.S. Department of Health, Education, and Welfare, U.S. Government Printing Office, 1963), p. 38-39.

[10] Richard L. Darling. *Survey of School Library Standards.* (Washington, D.C.: U.S. Department of Health, Education, and Welfare, U.S. Government Printing Office, 1964).

[11] *Ibid, p. 27.*

A LIBRARY'S ROLE—
INSTRUCTIONAL MATERIALS CENTER

Robert G. Ames

When educational innovations have proved themselves to be more than experimental techniques and are incorporated in a school's program, old ideas and facilities must often be modified or expanded to accommodate these new ways of doing things.

When the decision to organize the total Wisconsin Heights School staff into teaching teams was made, the school at Black Earth – Mazomanie was just going into the drawingboard stage and was planned with the needs of team-teaching in mind. While this was convenient, it was by no means imperative, for existing facilities could have been adapted to incorporate the new approach. Erection of a new high school had become necessary, however, as a result of school district reorganization and consolidation.

Team-teaching makes special demands on school facilities. Instruction takes place in large groups, in small groups, and in independent study. This requires

Reprinted by permission of the WISCONSIN JOURNAL OF EDUCATION from: Ames, Robert G., "A Library's Role—Instructional Materials Center." December, 1964.

rooms suitable for these varying purposes. Wisconsin Heights High School, a small, rural high school (present enrollment of 327) west of Madison, has replaced conventional-sized classrooms with large-group presentation rooms and with smaller seminar rooms. The large-group rooms can accommodate more than 100 students; the seminar rooms are designed for groups of 15 or less.

The WHHS Instructional Materials Center (IMC), the library, is looked upon as the center of learning in the school. The entire complex covers an area that is larger than the school's gymnasium.

The fact that independent study has such a prominent position in the Wisconsin Heights team approach is most important to the library. Students can, depending on their interests, motivation, ability, program, and sense of responsibility, spend as much as 30% of their school day learning independently. This demands a library with more facilities and materials than the typical high school library of the past has had to offer.

PROGRAMED MATERIALS USED

Ours is built to house 20,000 volumes, and in addition to the usual library facilities such as card files, magazine display racks, check-out and information counter, and librarian's office, it incorporates the following services.

At the present time programed learning materials in book and workbook form are being used in most of the academic areas. They provide students with the opportunity for enrichment or remedial work on an individual basis. Teachers may check out the materials for use with a student in class, or they may send a student to the IMC to complete an assigned program. Students may also request programs on their own initiative.

Students here work in the IMC at individual study carrels. When they come to the IMC, they check themselves into a carrel by taking a card for a vacant unit. In the carrel, students can work undisturbed for as long as their task takes them or for as long as their schedule permits. Wisconsin Heights High School operates on a modular schedule, and students, depending on their individual programs, may have large blocks of independent study time available on some days. When they leave the carrel they fill in the card with a brief description of what they have accomplished. The card is then returned to the vacant carrel file. The study carrels in the IMC have become the favorite place for study, and it is seldom that most of them are not in use.

REMEDIAL READING HAS ROLE

In the center of the IMC a soundproof room has been provided for the viewing of films, filmstrips or slides, and for listening to sound tapes or recordings. Students engaged in research can, for example, check out a pertinent film and view it as a resource for their study. A student who has missed a large-group presentation or who would like to review one can check out the tape of that day's lecture and listen to it. Teachers also use this room to preview films they are going to use in their classes.

Also located in the center area of the IMC is a conference room. It is available to students for committee meetings and other types of group projects.

The developmental and remedial reading laboratory is located within the IMC. Students can check into the reading laboratory during independent study time to work with the reading equipment and materials. The laboratory has individual booths equipped with shadowscopes as well as space to work with SRA reading materials and a controlled reader. The reading specialist has her desk in the reading laboratory, and is available to help students.

The language laboratory is also located in the IMC. When language classes are not in session, students may work independently on language tapes, music appreciation, dictation practice tapes and the like.

There are four team rooms located in each corner of the IMC. These rooms are located close to the materials teachers need to organize units of study and to prepare materials such as visual aids. The rooms are used for the daily team meetings held each morning before classes begin. The teams plan the work of the teacher-aides assigned to their team, and plan instruction as well as evaluate past instruction at these meetings.

All academic teachers have semi-private offices in the IMC. Wisconsin Heights considers the teacher-pupil (one-to-one) relationship an important part of the educational process, and the teachers' offices, located close to the materials of instruction, make an ideal place for students to confer with teachers as well as an ideal place for instructors to work.

A room is provided for the processing of instructional materials being added to the library or for the repair of library materials and equipment.

The traditional library with bookshelves along the walls and tables in rows to seat students during "study hall" periods is not adequate for a school organized with the team approach and interested in getting students to assume increasing responsibility for their own education. The design of these study hall libraries focuses upon supervision rather than upon learning. The Wisconsin Heights High School library provides students and teachers with access to and the opportunity for use of a wide variety of instructional materials.

LIBRARY CONVERSION POSSIBLE

While the instructional materials center library concept of WHHS is designed with the team teaching pattern in mind, it is quite possible that many schools would find this type of expanded library service not only feasible, but an important improvement in their school library service. Libraries designed on the study hall principle can be subdivided with inexpensive partitions. Library tables can be converted into individual student carrels with the addition of simple dividing panels. Materials and equipment can be added to the resources of the library.

The library of any school can become a center of learning that involves all of the media of communication and that is more adaptable to modern techniques of instruction.

THE IMC

Margaret E. Nicholsen

What is an Instructional Materials Center? It might be defined as a collection of print and nonprint materials and equipment so selected, arranged, located and staffed as to serve the needs of teachers and students and to further the purposes of the school. To be a true center it must include print and nonprint and the necessary equipment for their use. Sometimes a collection of motion pictures, filmstrips and tapes and their hardware is called an "instructional materials center." This collection may need some kind of a name, but surely it is not an Instructional Materials Center.

Test tubes are used in chemistry, baseballs in Physical Education, skeletons in anatomy, foods in Home Economics. Do these items belong in an IMC? What are "supplies" and what "materials?" What are the practical limits to the materials to be located in a center? It seems to me that it is impossible to make any hard and fast rule that would apply to every school in the country. Under certain circumstances it might be perfectly appropriate for basketballs to be distributed by the IMC or for musical instruments to be housed there for loan to students. If the IMC has the space and staff, there is no reason why it could not handle any type of material or even supplies which would help students and teachers, as well as administrators.

What materials should certainly be found in every IMC: books, filmstrips, maps, motion pictures, pamphlets, periodicals, phonograph records, slides, and tapes, as well as the necessary equipment to use them. If a collection lacks any of those nine items it is not a true IMC, in my estimation. I think most would agree that transparencies and realia should be included, as well as overhead and opaque projectors and teaching machines. There are a number of "gadgets" which are not materials and which do not use materials, but which for the sake of convenience and accessibility might be housed in the IMC. These might include book copiers (which are found in most Centers today), laminating machines, tachistoscopes, portable public address systems, cameras, radios, television sets, typewriters, duplicators, language laboratories, and adding machines. All of these would be found useful by some teachers or students at some time or other. The final decision will depend, of course, upon the space available and upon the administrative organization of the school. However, the nine items must be in the IMC before one should call it that. To repeat, those are: books, filmstrips, maps, motion pictures, pamphlets, periodicals, phonograph records, slides, and tapes, as well as the equipment necessary to use them.

Reprinted with permission from: Nicholsen, Margaret E., "The IMC," SCHOOL LIBRARIES, March, 1964.

WHY AN IMC?

Why have an Instructional Materials Center? What are the advantages of that over an old-fashioned library and an unrelated audio-visual room?

First, from the teacher's point of view: He has to go to only one place in the building, the IMC, to locate all kinds of materials and equipment. He does not have to remember that for this *I go to the library*, for that *I go to the audio-visual room*, and for these others *I ask the Principal.* When he goes to the IMC, he finds all the materials available with staff members who know them. He can ask advice, examine varied types of materials on the subject, and then select the kinds of materials which best serve the purpose for that particular class at that time. He may want to use only books and magazines for this particular lesson. He may want a filmstrip and phonograph record for the next; and he can arrange for both in the one place with no fuss or bother and without feeling that if he goes to the audio-visual room he is neglecting the "library," or if he goes to the library that he is neglecting all the new technological devices and is "old-fashioned."

Another advantage for the teacher in using the Center is that it is open every minute of the school day as well as before and after school. In some areas it is also open on Saturdays and in the evenings. Separate audio-visual rooms in many schools are often closed at certain times of the day and are not open before and after school, thus presenting the necessity for the teacher to remember the audio-visual room schedule and adapt to it. Another advantage to the teacher in having materials in one location is that bibliographies he requests will include not only books, but also pertinent filmstrips, phonograph records and other nonprint materials on the subject. Under the separate system he would have to ask the library and the audio-visual staffs to each make a list of the materials available on the subject.

Even more important than the increased service to teachers, which results from having all types of materials brought together in one place, is the increased service to students. They feel free to come to the Center for reading, for using the card catalog, for using reference books, for looking at filmstrips or for listening to phonograph records. They feel that the Center belongs to them and that the materials are there to increase their knowledge. Teaching machines for individual study, single concept films in the 8mm projectors, filmstrip viewers, tape recorders with the tapes of the lessons missed when they were ill, all these are available to them in different areas of the Center. The students are learning that when they want information and inspiration they should go to the Center and look for background knowledge and for cultural experiences in whatever media serves best the specific need.

Probably the centralization of materials is not going to result in much financial saving to the. school as the arrangement will increase the demand for materials and the efficiency with which these can be provided and will markedly increase the use made by both students and teachers. Thus, the same amount of money may be spent, but the service and the quality and effectiveness of the teaching will be improved. Likewise, a staff of approximately the same size may be needed, but it will be better utilized combined in a Center. Instead of having two staffs in charge of two separated areas, the Center would double the staff working in one area. The result — better service to both students and teachers.

PERSONNEL NEEDED

Who is needed to operate an Instructional Materials Center?

The professional staff should have training in both print and nonprint materials, their selection, organization and use. In a large staff there will be areas of specialization, but all should know literature for children or young adults as well as films, filmstrips, phonograph records, and slides suitable for use in the school. This is a large order; there is no doubt about it. However, the materials specialist is probably the only person in the school who has a picture of all types of materials suitable in all areas. Naturally, he will rely upon the subject specialists in the school for aid and assistance in selection of materials to be added to the collection. Perhaps as important as the training in both nonprint and print is the choice of professional staff members who are actively interested in all types of materials and who believe and can demonstrate that in some cases books are the perfect answer and in others filmstrips will do the job best, while in others a magazine article followed by listening to a phonograph record is the most suitable. Of the greatest importance is the philosophy that all types of materials should be so arranged and located that the professional staff member can assist the teacher or student in locating that type or types best suited to his purposes. The professional staff members must know the content of the materials; they must read books, view filmstrips,, listen to phonograph records, look at motion pictures, and read magazines. There should be specialization in large staffs, but every member should be aware of and conversant with the total resources of the Center.

In addition to professional staff there should be an adequate number of clerks. These clerks must be able to type, to be accurate, and to deal with students, and, when necessary, with a demanding or unreasonable teacher. Much of the work of checking in motion pictures, of giving out projectors, of seeing that equipment and materials are returned can be done by clerks. A professional staff member will have to work out the system of scheduling, delivering, circulating, etc., but once it is well organized, a capable clerk can handle it. A professional staff member should not need to be concerned about telling Miss Jones that she has kept a phonograph too long and must return it as soon as possible. The clerks also do all the typing needed in processing new books and in typing the catalog cards, not only for books, but also for filmstrips and phonograph records.

During the school day most IMC's will find a number of students who will volunteer to work. Their assistance is invaluable and they usually get a feeling of rendering service to the school as well as a feeling of importance. They can check out books, check in books, operate projectors, etc. However, it is sometimes a temptation to exploit these students and to give them deadly dull tasks which they must do daily. Some jobs, such as shelving books and magazines and delivering equipment, can be done before or after school. For these jobs, students should be paid and expected to come on schedule every day, working as on a regular job.

Another type of staff member who will be needed in a large IMC is a technician. He is not a professional nor on the regular faculty, nor is he on the clerical staff. He has charge of repairing the equipment and of preventive maintenance. Small Centers will find it less expensive to contract with a local commercial company to repair their equipment than to hire a technician — just as the Business Education department expects to have typewriters repaired by a local company rather than by a teacher or maintenance staff member.

The staff of an IMC, then, should consist of a director or head, professional staff, technicians, clerks, paid student help, and volunteer student aides.

LOCATION

Where should the IMC be located?

It should be located as near the center of the school as possible so that it is accessible to all students and teachers. It should be open every minute of the school day, as well as before and after school, and in some schools it should be open on Saturdays and evenings. There should be separate rooms for reading, for listening, for viewing and for the production of materials. The reading area should be able to accommodate 10% of the students, according to the standards of the American Library Association, and should have spaces for individual study. The listening area can be a small room adjacent to the reading area and equipped with booths or headphones. Some schools have placed phonographs with headphones right in the reading areas, but this makes some disturbance due to "needle talk". The viewing area should be adjacent to the reading area, and the space needed can be reduced by using a pre-view machine or a rear projection screen.

There should also be a room for the production of materials. These rooms and areas should all be in one place for the convenience of teachers and students and to increase the effectiveness of their selection of materials. The equipment should be available in the Center, so that a teacher who comes for a phonograph record does not have to go elsewhere to obtain the necessary phonograph. What good is a filmstrip projector without filmstrips? It is entirely possible to work out a system of locating large equipment, such as motion picture projectors and overhead and opaque projectors elsewhere in the school.

Those items have to be delivered to classrooms for use, but the IMC must keep previewing or auditioning equipment for each type of material to make teacher or student examination possible before deciding what to use.

All materials for reading, i.e. books, magazines, pamphlets; materials for listening, i.e. phonorecords and tapes; materials for viewing, i.e. filmstrips, motion pictures and slides, should be located in one place, the IMC, accessible to all students and teachers. Permanent classroom collections and permanent collections of books shelved in various departmental offices should be avoided.

WHEN TO START

When should an Instructional Materials Center be started? Immediately, of course. This can be done by either revolution or evolution.

The former would mean that tomorrow all materials and equipment would be brought together in one place and under one head. However, no superintendent should expect his present overworked librarians to assume responsibility tomorrow for all audio-visual and nonprint materials and equipment without additional staff and/or training. Personnel could be added who have had training in both types of materials, and present library staff could be urged (i.e. *required*) to take training in nonprint materials this summer. Likewise, no superintendent should ask his overworked audio-visual specialist to assume responsibility for the print materials unless he is given additional staff trained in both print and nonprint, and the former audio-visual staff required to take courses this summer in the organization, administration and content of print materials. The principal advantage of the quick change from two separate areas to the centralized materials is that teachers learn quickly that they are to go to just one place henceforth for all types of materials.

Changing to an IMC by evolution has the disadvantage that for some time certain materials are still in one location and others in another. Assuming that all print is in once place and all nonprint in another, it would be possible and practicable to move just the filmstrips and the filmstrip projectors and viewers to the library. Then with additional staff next Fall, the phonograph records and phonographs could be added. An additional clerk, or one transferred from the present audio-visual room, could assume responsibility for the motion picture schedule, as well as the scheduling of the overheads and opaques. Thus in a year or two all nonprint materials and equipment would have joined the print in one location and administered by one staff.

Whichever method is used, the most important job of the IMC professional staff is to gain as rapidly as possible a thorough knowledge of the content of the materials of all types.

Throughout this presentation I have obediently used the term "Instructional Materials Center", for that is supposed to be the topic of this meeting. However, the term LIBRARY is familiar to all teachers and students and means to them a place where they will find materials of communication well-selected, well--arranged, and well-cataloged, and staffed with experts who can help them find answers to their questions or find the material needed. The public library has added phonograph records and motion pictures to its collections but still is called a library. Why not enlarge our view of school library service and use the well-known term, *library* rather than the long and cumbersome "Instructional Materials Center" or "Learning Resource Center"? They mean the same thing, for a library should contain all types of materials which transmit the ideas, images, and sounds of yesterday, today, and tomorrow.

THE INSTRUCTIONAL RESOURCES CENTER, AN ENABLING FACILITY

Harry J. Ford

At its inception a new enterprise needs impatient men to mold it, restless men whose minds have broken the barrier of traditional bias. South Hills High School in Covina-Valley is just such an enterprise — designed as an educational facility to accommodate and encourage the achievement of the district's educational goals and to attain maximum efficiency in the use of time, space, and staff.

Purposefully, we endeavored to identify the needs of secondary schools as far into the future as possible; to design a building that would accommodate these needs and still enable us to conduct our current program; and to determine how to modify existing plants to meet the needs of the high school in the future.

We gave considerable thought to the promotion of instructional materials in the South Hills plant. We looked at all of our activities with a view to optimizing them in a systematic manner. Mindful of the tremendous advances in all fields of knowledge and the changes in both teaching and learning methods, we were led to a careful re-examination of the teaching tools used in secondary schools and of the way in which they relate to the newer programs of instruction. We were equally aware that any facility planned now for use in the next 20 to 40 years must be so constructed that it could accommodate instructional aids and resources currently available and at the same time provide facilities to accommodate our best predictions for the future.

We developed educational specifications by interpreting these considerations in terms of instructional needs. The result was the projection of every area of the high-school curriculum into a pattern of large-group, medium-group, small-group, independent-study, and laboratory spaces. When we translated these specifications into terms of operating activity, the instructional resource center came forth, both as an instruction and service facility.

Reflecting thus the desired educational program of the Covina-Valley district, the educational specifications for our instructional resource center call for the following areas:

• **Browsing and General Reading:** At the entrance to the library, this area serves as a focal point for all of the center's service functions. The atmosphere suggests informality, friendliness, and invitation. The area includes (a) an entrance and exit; (b) recreational reading materials; (c) small group conversational areas; (d) periodicals; (e) circulation desk; (f) card catalog; and (g) display area.

Reprinted with permission from: Ford, Harry J., "The Instructional Resources Center, An Enabling Facility," AUDIOVISUAL INSTRUCTION, October, 1962.

FLOOR PLAN: SOUTH HILLS HIGH SCHOOL, COVINA, CALIFORNIA

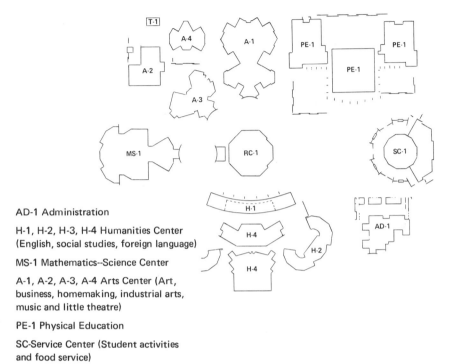

AD-1 Administration

H-1, H-2, H-3, H-4 Humanities Center
(English, social studies, foreign language)

MS-1 Mathematics--Science Center

A-1, A-2, A-3, A-4 Arts Center (Art,
business, homemaking, industrial arts,
music and little theatre)

PE-1 Physical Education

SC-Service Center (Student activities
and food service)

RC-1 Instructional Resources Center

• **Reference and Research**: Adjacent to Browsing and General Reading, this area houses the reference collection of each of the broad subject fields of the curriculum. Each section is arranged to assist the student in individual research. Flexibility is maintained through the use of low bookcases and planter room dividers. Study spaces for students doing reference work are found immediately adjacent to the material sought.

Certain reference and research collections are duplicated in the Humanities, Arts, and Science facilities.

• **Instructional Materials Laboratory**: More often called a "curriculum laboratory," this facility is intended to provide a showcase for effective learning materials. In addition, it serves as a work center for producing instructional aids, providing the teacher and selected students the kinds of tools, equipment, supplies, materials, and assistance necessary to produce all types of audio and visual materials. It includes (a) a general work area for the production of models, graphs, pictures, visuals, etc.; (b) facilities for photo production utilizing all types of photo equipment for processing, enlarging, copying, and production of all types of visuals; (c) a darkroom to be used in conjunction with the photo production equipment; (d) storage for materials, equipment, and tools needed for these activities; (e) student work area adjacent to all of the spaces above to conserve equipment and to make full use of the laboratory clerk's time; and (f) office space for the graphic technician.

• **Instructional Materials Library**: The provision of a functional program of instructional materials service is essential to the accomplishment of the district's educational goals. A realistic appraisal of this facility recognizes that good service comes only as the result of a well-planned and cooperative arrangement between this plant and the district's central instructional materials agency. South Hills High School will have its own up-to-date and appropriate collection of materials, centrally located and easily accessible to teachers and pupils.

The Instructional Materials Library is a repository for all instructional resource aids other than books and periodicals and includes space for: (a) storage of films, filmstrips, models, prints, records, tapes, etc.; (b) circulation-catalog area and work area for the instructional materials clerk; (c) limited storage area for audiovisual equipment (the majority of this equipment remaining in the classroom areas of the Humanities, Arts, Science, etc.); (d) faculty reading room; and (e) student-teacher area — individual study carrels will provide semi-private space for listening, looking, and operating teaching machines and programed learning materials. Students will be assigned to the different spaces, depending on the degree of responsibility they bring to independent study.

• **Electronic Distribution Center**: This facility represents a real potential for the future. As a district equipped with many classroom monitors and an antenna system to receive AM-FM and TV broadcast signals, it is important for us to provide facilities for originating closed-circuit telecasts. Closed circuitry will also provide a film chain, "spot" programs, programs for team teaching, etc. The electronic distribution center will operate as an electronic control center for the entire school. It will house the equipment necessary to provide closed-circuit TV or radio programing to any location on the campus. These spaces will be provided: (a) an electronic control center containing all equipment necessary for production of closed-circuit TV; film, slide, and filmstrip projection; radio, tape, and broadcast television; and facilities for live programing from any area of the circuit, plus any combination of the above; and (b) an area for preview, production, and conferences where these three functions will be accommodated through proper scheduling. This space is designed to house the production of live TV programs, the preview of films and other audiovisual materials, recording activities, and conferences.

• **Office Space** for the coordinator of instructional resources, assistant principal, librarian, materials clerk, graphic technician, secretary, and library clerks will be located in the areas where these staff members operate.

• **Storage and Workroom**: An area used primarily by librarians and library clerks for minor repairs, ordering, and storage of books and periodicals. It includes these spaces: work area with sink, counter, work tables, and equipment storage; storage space for 300 to 600 books; general library supplies, magazines, etc.

• **Textbook Storage and Issue:** These are facilities for a limited number of textbooks. Additional storage and issue facilities are located in the Humanities, Science, and Art buildings.

• **Receiving:** The receiving area is equipped with a ramp-style loading dock for loading and unloading equipment and supplies. It is designed as the receiving center for the entire school and equipped to handle receiving, shipping, checking, routing, distribution, and mailing.

• **Display:** Space will be made available throughout the center for display of all types of interesting and stimulating materials.

· · ·

The instructional resource center was conceived as an integral part of over-all curriculum planning. It was created by combining the areas just described, but the concept behind it goes beyond the mere joining of spaces. The combination provides a needed relationship among these spaces. While space is freely and efficiently gathered into a unit — the center — each area within this unit maintains its separate function. The center itself is strategically located, designed as the hub of the school plant. All academic courts — Humanities, Arts, and Science — are clustered about it. It is the core of the school's operation.

The staff of the center will identify new materials and determine how they can be used effectively in the teaching program. This will require them to keep abreast of new resources and technological advances in all fields, as well as to disseminate this information to teachers and students.

More specifically, the staff will assist in the selection of (a) materials to be used with large groups to provide the background vital to discussion and further exploration; (b) materials appropriate for medium groups to use in specialized study; and (c) individualized materials adapted both to the dullest student who must be helped to gain some knowledge and to the able student who seeks the depths of knowledge.

Students and teachers will use the center as a laboratory for reference, research, materials preparation, and program dissemination. A wide variety of resources — books, magazines, journals, pamphlets, charts, posters, graphs, models, globes, slides, filmstrips, tapes, film, phonograph records, and pro- gramed learning materials — will be checked out of the central collection to individual students and staff. Books, equipment, and materials will be ordered, received, circulated, and maintained within the center.

TRANSITIONAL BY INTENT

South Hills High School has not yet materialized as a physical entity. Construction will begin shortly, with occupancy planned for the fall of the 1964-65 school year. The very nature of the South Hills High School is transitional. The program will be evolutionary. When we have verified, through experimentation, that certain changes are desirable, we will make them on a district-wide basis. As stated by Paul B. Salmon, district superintendent, the transition will occur in reaching these objectives.

- To individualize instruction
- To make more efficient use of staff skills
- To provide for use of the growing technology of our country.

We are encouraged to believe that the instructional resource center at South Hills High School, an enabling facility, will fully exploit these objectives.

THE IMC: CONTRIBUTION TO INDIVIDUALIZED INSTRUCTION

Leroy K. Mesedahl

Many years are sure to pass before the term "IMC" becomes an active part of the layman's vocabulary, but fortunately for our young people, many educators are not only speaking, but thinking and doing in terms of the modern concept of the instructional materials center. In Duluth, Minnesota, two new elementary schools opened this fall, each with a carefully planned IMC geared to the needs of the system's promising new approach to individualized instruction.

At the new Birchwood and Rockridge schools, not only the IMC's but also the entire plant facilities are oriented to a new concept, a concept already developed and tested in one of the system's older buildings. The pilot project — called "Project Congdon" for the Congdon Park School where it took place — placed an emphasis on modern instructional materials exceeding anything previously known in this community.

At "Project Congdon" the teacher's role is far from traditional. First of all, he is a member of a team, and is able, therefore, to specialize in his area of greatest competence. He spends only a small portion of his time lecturing before the total group, and a major portion guiding students to appropriate materials for self-directed study. These include books, films and filmstrips, audio tapes, slides — the whole range of audiovisual materials — plus a battery of programed materials including some of the latest and most highly sophisticated "teaching machines" in existence.

Congdon is an older building, but the project is carried out in an addition built in 1964, with classroom space tailored to the ungraded aspects of the

Reprinted with permission from: Mesedahl, Leroy K., "The IMC: Contribution to Individualized Instruction," AUDIOVISUAL INSTRUCTION, November, 1965.

experiment. Two fifth-grade and two sixth-grade classes meet together in two large areas which become four classrooms when sliding doors are positioned. Typically, the whole four-room complex, along with the teachers' room, operates as one big and bustling unit, where unusually eager students, with unusually good discipline, self-direct themselves from one information source to another. Sometimes the information source is one of the four teachers or one of the four assistants, but more often it is an audiovisual or programed instruction device.

The project at Congdon served as the background for the new approaches at Birchwood and Rockridge. The new buildings are based on months of planning which took place both before and after the passage (by a three-to-one margin) of a bond issue which made them possible. To summarize the philosophy which guides Superintendent L. V. Rasmussen and his staff, emphasis on the individual learner is the dominant influence in building and classroom design.

The belief that each learner should be able to progress as quickly as he can or as slowly as he must has led to emphasis on such concepts as continuous progress planning, flexible scheduling, nongrading, and team teaching. It was realized that any or all of these concepts of staff and student deployment might be employed to accomplish the overall objective of individualized instruction. Thus, flexibility of instructional space became the prime consideration in planning new construction, along with careful acknowledgement of the special spatial requirements of education's new technology.

At the Birchwood and Rockridge schools, teachers in grades 3-6 teach in their areas of greatest individual strength, crossing grade levels. All teachers meet weekly for team planning sessions. This, however, is "team teaching" with a difference. It is based on the de-emphasis of large-group instruction wherever feasible, and the careful use of small-group time, with strong reliance on self-direction to the wide range of informational sources indicated.

Experience indicates that if this approach to instruction is to be successful, a materials-to-teacher ratio is needed similar to that of the EBF-Bell & Howell experiment at Shaker Heights. Similar ratios of resource materials in printed form are also essential. In order to catalog, house, and distribute the mass of instructional materials, 3,000 square feet of floor space were provided for this purpose at the 13-teacher Birchwood School. The IMC is much more than a library; it is a center where all types of media are stored, inventoried, used, and distributed to classrooms throughout the school.

In the words of William Lainen, principal of Birchwood, "the IMC is the school's nerve center or instructional resource area, where a teacher can send a student, unsupervised, at any time for any purpose." It will be the school's service center for teachers and students to facilitate the teaching-learning process. All instructional media from outside sources will be received and inventoried in this center and in many cases redistributed from it to the appropriate teaching station.

The student's substantial allotment of independent study time can take place either in the classroom or at the IMC. In these areas students may read, write up research projects, view films, listen to records or tapes, work with teaching machines, use programed materials, construct models and mock-ups, work on art projects, produce audiovisual materials, or engage in a variety of other learning activities. The area where independent study is carried on is determined by the ease with which students can make use of the available materials, equipment, and staff.

All audio equipment, including 16mm projectors, are equipped with jack boxes and headsets which provide sound isolation and eliminate the need for numerous soundproof viewing and listening booths.

The IMC at each school offers all the traditional library services and in addition provides areas for the use of all types of materials and their related hardware. Areas are also provided for a professional curriculum library, a staff preview room, materials production, equipment storage and repair, materials storage, an IMC processing area, and IMC office space.

Services of the school IMC are extended through the district audiovisual center. For reasons of cost, maintenance, and efficiency, many materials needed by teachers are circulated from the district center. To minimize red tape in ordering and using centralized materials and services, the district center provides all teachers with catalogs, telephone booking, and daily delivery. This combination puts the staff at the school IMC a telephone call away from having centralized materials delivered the following morning.

The IMC's are by no means the only forward-looking features of the new Birchwood and Rockridge schools, nor is "Project Congdon" by any means the only effort of its kind in the Duluth system. Similar projects are being planned or are in process at other elementary schools, and the junior high in which most Congdon students matriculate is preparing to greet them with a follow-up project. Duluth administrators have a strong commitment to individualized instruction, and a definite awareness of the significant role of modern educational technology in attaining this goal.

TEACHING GEOGRAPHY IN A MATERIALS CENTER

Frances A. Smith

One of the most interesting and successful methods of teaching seventh grade geography began as a result of a lack of a textbook and materials in my classroom. Two years ago when a complete revision of the curriculum in the

Reprinted with permission from: Smith, Frances A., "Teaching Geography in a Materials Center," JOURNAL OF GEOGRAPHY, February, 1962.

schools of Elkhart, Indiana, was made new social studies textbooks were adopted. In the seventh grade it was decided to teach the geography of Europe, Asia, and Africa. The textbook chosen was *Eurasia* by Glendinning, published by Ginn and Company. This book is excellent for Europe, and fair for Asia, but completely lacking materials for Africa as the title indicates. Africa is treated in another book in the series. Our problem was what to do for materials for the Africa unit.

MATERIALS CENTER

The solution was ready-made in our new school — we have a *materials center.* A materials center is a combination library and audio-visual center. In this one unit are housed all of the reference books, fiction and non-fiction books, magazines, pamphlets, pictures, films, recordings (both records and tapes), and maps. Most materials can be checked out for varying lengths of time, but the latest encyclopedia sets are not to leave the room. Older sets are on carts to leave the library. The materials center contains work space for eighty students, plus a small converence room for their use. Record players equipped with headphones are available for listening during study hours.

Early in the school year the English Department teaches a library unit on how to use the library and the students are also instructed on how to use the records and filmstrips. This is an excellent beginning for our research. It also saves the geography teacher time and gives reason to the English lesson as well.

Arrangements are made with the librarian to use the library for certain class periods until the Africa unit is finished. The children may also study extra time during study hours if they wish.

The first week of the unit is spent in the classroom viewing films and filmstrips as an introduction to Africa. After the films, a day is spent studying the map of Africa. For this, the large plastic, three dimentional, Raised Relief Map of Africa made by the Aero Service Corporation is used. We study this map to get the general layout of rivers, mountains, deserts, lakes, cities, etc. A list of countries is made and later mimeographed. A second list of items that should be known about each country is also made and mimeographed. This list contains the following information:

1. Area (also to be compared to the United States or one of its states)
2. Climate
3. The people (include numbers, religion, interesting customs, etc.)
4. Capitol
5. Government and present-day leaders
6. Natural resources
7. Agriculture
8. Industries
9. What kind of trade the United States can and does have with them
10. Miscellaneous information.

Each student makes a notebook that contains a summary of each nation plus any illustrations, newspaper and magazine articles that can be found. One boy prepared an excellent display of African stamps to go with his notebook while another one sent for free travel folders to go with his work. It is unbelievable the amount of work that a student will put into a notebook of this kind. Often the illustrations become a family affair — the whole family becomes interested and helps to get materials for the student.

Before we leave for the library we also discuss the library rules and regulations and have the understanding that it is a place to work. You cannot go in and visit with your neighbors and disturb others. When the work period ends, encyclopedias are to be shelved properly and everything is to be put in order before we leave.

Each day the class meets in the classroom to check attendance and discuss any problems of general interest before going to the materials center to work. We also briefly discuss the latest African news reports at this time.

The first year, all of the books on Africa except the encyclopedias and almanacs were pulled from the regular collections and put on a special shelf in the corner. The second year they were all listed and the students were expected to hunt them out for themselves. Each method has its advantages. It depends upon the class as to what should be done. The slower classes are helped by the special shelf method.

During the research periods the students may check out filmstrips and view them on individual viewers or check out the African records and earphones and listen to special recordings of the African folk music and folklore that are available.

Each student may begin with any part of Africa in which he is particularly interested. In fact, the students are encouraged to start at different places so that they won't all be needing the materials on Algeria at the same time, for example. The better students usually are finished before the slower students, so they are encouraged to read the travel and fiction books about Africa and make additional reports in the notebook for extra credit.

After the research is completed the children spend three to four class hours discussing the materials that they have found. Any news out of Africa is discussed here again. During this discussion period we try to see Africa as a whole and to see what the big problems are and what possible solutions might be worked out.

This unit takes eight to nine weeks to complete. The grade given on the unit is based on the following scale: three points on the notebook, one point on class attitude and participation and one point each on the two comprehensive tests given at the end of the work. One test is a comprehensive written test and the other is a map test. Since the students seem to like the research idea and will put forth much more effort than they will in a normal classroom using a textbook for their information, test grades are usually much higher.

OTHER RESULTS

Many interesting results come from a unit taught in this manner. First, there is a wider use of reference materials — one child finds some source and the news spreads. Second, there is wider reading and search in newspapers and magazines. Third, unasked-for homework occurs when students watch for things that might make their notebooks better. Fourth, you get away from textbook-type teaching and learning. Fifth, the students find different statistics and information and then begin to wonder why the differences exist and which is correct. Sixth, through the discrepancies in statistics they learn that being in a book or newspaper does not make the information correct. Seventh, parents often become very interested in the notebooks and learn along with the students. They also feel that their children are accomplishing something. Seldom do the parents complain that we are overworking their children! And eighth, the students actually accomplish more and make better grades on this type of work than they do during the other three grading periods.

The class work involved in the beginning and at the end of the unit is enormous, time consuming, but interesting. During the research period, the teacher's work is at a minimum and it allows her to give a great deal of individual attention that she would not have time for otherwise. Perhaps, this individual attention and informality are the most important parts of the method. The teacher works with her students in a much different atmosphere than she does in a more formal classroom situation.

HOW TO PLAN AND EQUIP AN INSTRUCTIONAL MATERIALS CENTER

Kenneth I. Taylor

The textbook-centered school program of the past had many advantages from the administrative point of view. Every subject was self-contained; transition from one area of study to another was simple, and the number of units and amount of material to be taught had been predetermined by outsiders. The contemporary school, however, finds these artificial divisions of subject content frequently incompatible with the kind of instruction needed for a complex world. In any school where greater coordination is essential among departments, and where modification in student schedules, teaching assignments, class groupings, and facilities for individual student research is necessary, more attention must be given to the flexibility afforded by a large variety of instructional materials.

Reprinted with permission, from: Taylor, Kenneth I., "How to Plan and Equip an Instructional Materials Center," THE NATION'S SCHOOLS, January, 1961. Copyright 1961, The Modern Hospital Publishing Co., Inc., Chicago. All rights reserved.

From an administrative position, it should seem that complete coordination of instructional materials will soon be necessary for any school. No longer can many schools afford to let departments build isolated libraries of duplicate materials to be used by themselves alone. Nor can they allow traditional library and audio-visual departments to operate independently without knowledge of what is contained in the collections of the other.

The centrally organized materials center seems to be the answer for the future school program. Based upon the premise that all types of instructional materials have more similarities than differences, the single department records, organizes and administers the materials and services related to their use for maximum efficiency.

The advantages of such a center are related more nearly to design and organization than to the size of the school. For this reason, the program can apply to small and large schools alike. The actual size of the department itself in each case must be based upon the enrollment, curriculum and services desired. It is difficult to see why any school, regardless of size, should not benefit from the economy that results from centralization, more efficient utilization of staff services, and reduced duplication of instructional materials.

* * *

Those who are planning a new school can, of course, design a materials center completely around the functions of the new department. An established school may, in many instances, be able to create a materials center with a minimum of physical change. Other schools, in which expansion of existing library and audio-visual departments is already necessary, may often take advantage of adjacent study halls or classroom areas. Underlying the concept of centralization in every case, however, is the objective of better service to students and their teachers.

What is the basis of any plan for an instructional materials center?

To design a departmental area in a school where all instructional materials (and services related to the use of these materials) are centralized. The purpose of the centralization is to help students and teachers locate all school-owned instructional materials and use them more effectively.

Who should plan the services of a materials center?

Planning should be cooperative. The advice of all consultants in instructional materials, representative classroom teachers, and the administration should result in better definition of the services needed. Once defined for a new school, the services and functions desired should be explained to the school architect. Design should be based upon function.

What services should be considered when planning?

First of all, an estimate should be made of the reading room area needed for individual and class use, including the necessary space for book shelving. Then space traditionally allotted for audio-visual services, including one or more preview and recording rooms, should be considered. Third, a combined clerical and professional staff workroom area should be added; fourth, consider the storage space needed, and, next, classroom space for group training in research methods, if desired. Finally, a teachers' workroom and a construction materials room should be considered. This total will provide the initial estimate of area needed.

How large should a materials center be?

A definite figure for a school of any particular size is difficult to give. Size is related to variables, such as enrollment, community instructional resources, and the curriculum provided. When planning a materials center, however, a school should list the services it desires, then allot an estimated area for each service.

How much seating space has been recommended for reading rooms?

Ten to 15 per cent of the student body should be seated in the reading areas. Provision also should be made for class visits and for possible expansion to meet the demands of future methods of instruction and staff utilization.

How can class visits be encouraged through planning?

By designing reading areas which can accommodate an average class and yet allow seating for students from the study hall. If more than one class is likely to visit during the same period, a large reading room might be divided with movable counter-height shelving. It has frequently been recommended that no reading room seat more than 80 students. When greater seating capacity is needed, more than one reading room should be planned.

How much room should be provided per reader?

A good rule of thumb for the reading room is 30 to 35 square feet per reader. This allows room for traffic near entrances, the card catalog, and the charging desk. It enables classes to enter and leave during a period with a minimum of difficulty.

Why is a classroom frequently included in a materials center?

For large group instruction in research methods. It often doubles for faculty meetings and lectures. It should be about the same size as other classrooms.

How large should a preview and recording room be?

A room which may double for conference purposes should be approximately 10 feet wide and 12 to 15 feet long. Some schools make the room slightly larger, then divide it with a folding curtain. Experience indicates that only a minimum of darkening is needed for preview purposes. Absolute soundproofing is seldom needed unless the room is adjacent to a reading room. Soundproofing is needed whenever a group records through a mike, of course, but in small schools classrooms are frequently adequate.

How much space should be provided for other service areas?

Audio-visual space is dependent upon the degree to which equipment is centrally stored or located in departmental areas around the school. Clerical and professional staff workroom space should be large enough so that the staff members and several student assistants can work there at the same time. Storage space should be ample. Seldom does any amount of storage space prove to be too great. Provision should be made for at least five years of periodicals. Schools may wish to use this area for storing larger equipment. A construction materials room, with running water, should be large enough to allow two or three student committees to work at one time.

Should a teachers' workroom be provided?

Such a room may be a morale factor. Many materials on methods of teaching and child development are best shelved apart from student materials. A teachers' workroom may also double for faculty committee work. Seating capacity should be based upon the number of teachers who are free during any one period.

What materials should be provided for the teachers' workroom?

Books, periodicals and pamphlets representing the best of current thinking concerning education.

Where should a center be located in a school?

Near the main entry whenever possible, but in the academic area if a choice must be made. When adjacent to the study hall, student accessibility to the center is increased.

How can adaptations be made to meet future needs?

Provision should be made in the beginning for future expansion. Modular construction in new schools may be one answer. Future educational trends may very likely create a need for more reading room area, more facilities for class visits, increased audio-visual services, and possibly specially designed areas for individual student and teacher research. Great emphasis may be placed upon the preparation of charts, transparencies and displays by students and teachers alike.

When should planning for the materials center of a new school begin?

At least two years before the opening of the school. Materials should be purchased at the same time that physical facilities are designed. In this way, good collections can be made available when a school opens, not begun on opening day.

How can the present quarters in an established school be adapted to provide a materials center?

Some schools utilize adjacent classroom or study hall areas in order to expand existing facilities. The study halls are frequently converted into reading room areas, and other areas in the school are used instead for study halls. The central records that are established in a materials center can serve as a record of the location of many materials in various departments around the school. This has the effect of increasing the storage space available, while continuing to make all materials accessible to all school personnel.

What furniture is needed in a materials center?

Furniture should conform to generally accepted library specifications, particularly for pieces such as the card catalog and charging desks. Schools frequently use wood furniture and shelving in reading rooms for beauty and noise reduction. Steel office furniture and shelving can be used in office and storage areas. Steel blueprint cabinets are useful for storage of flat maps, charts and filmstrips.

What tables are used?

In the reading rooms, a variety of tables that seat four or six students (no more) is generally best. Students should never be seated at the ends of tables because crowding results. In work areas, light tables which can be easily moved are best. For all tables, plastic tops may prove more durable under student use.

Where should entrances be placed?

One entrance for students increases control of materials. A separate entrance to the work area allows convenient receipt of packages and routing of audio-visual equipment. Another entry to the teachers' workroom may encourage greater use. If possible, an entry from the study hall to the center may reduce corridor traffic.

How can design increase the effectiveness of supervision?

Windows between separate reading rooms and work areas assist in supervision. Room arrangement should allow control from as many points in the center as possible. Doors for reading room entries within the center itself may not be needed if good acoustical treatment has been included throughout.

Is outside window space essential?

Frequent emphasis by architects and planners on decorative window effects may prove to be a luxury that many schools cannot afford. If needed shelf space is sacrificed any advantages afforded by windows are minimized. Windows may actually add distractions to readers within.

Which instructional materials should be included in a materials center?

A school should begin with an ample collection of books, magazines, maps, and language, speech and drama phonograph records. Pamphlets, music records, and filmstrips, all of which can be procured upon short notice, should be added as needed, primarily upon faculty requests.

Must all instructional materials be filed or shelved in the materials center?

No. Many materials may be kept on permanent loan in the departments. The location of these items should be indicated in the central records of the materials center, thus making them available when needed to all school personnel.

How should film rentals be handled?

All rentals, including sponsored (free) films, should be requested, scheduled and distributed to departments and returned through the materials center for most efficient use.

What is the minimum professional staff needed in the small school?

In order to have all instructional materials and services in one department, it is difficult to see how even the smallest school can have fewer than one full-time and one half-time professional materials consultant. To have only one full-time consultant means scheduling a teacher to work with school personnel every hour of the day. To schedule the teacher for less time means that some students and teachers would not have professional assistance in research methods. The addition of one half-time professional consultant provides services every hour of the day, and allows one consultant to work several hours each day on professional ordering, cataloging and organization without interruption. The half-time teacher, half-time librarian cannot operate a materials center.

How large a clerical staff is needed for the small school?

A minimum of one half-time clerical worker reduces the amount of routine clerical work to be performed by professional consultants. The clerical worker should supervise student assistants in the performance of clerical tasks as well. A flexible schedule allows the clerical worker to work with all student assistants regularly.

How many student assistants are needed?

A minimum of two or three per hour in the smallest school is needed to shelve materials, answer routine questions, perform charging operations, and assist with the utilization of instructional materials in the classroom. Their duties should be rotated frequently. The number of assistants should correspond with the size of the professional staff available in the center. Many materials centers offer a course of study for their assistants and give school credit.

What is the one major factor to be considered when designing or remodeling a materials center?

All design and organization should be based upon student needs and should encourage student use of materials. The quality of service provided to students is always a measure of successful design.

FUNCTION BEFORE FORM

Kenneth I. Taylor

Each instructional medium evolves through three distinct stages before it gains acceptance in the school program. When it first appears it is defended by its promoters. Next it is examined in isolation by educators as a separate entity for its special characteristics and contributions. Finally, as it matures and becomes more generally available, it is related to other materials for mutual reinforcement in "multimedia" teaching.

Within the past decade, the idea of the instructional materials center has reached the second stage. Articles, demonstration projects, and standards have seen it largely as a separate, though essential, department in the modern school. As the concept matures, the materials center will likely be recognized as the agency whose chief function is to stimulate and coordinate the use of materials throughout the school, rather than simply hold and organize them, and the emphasis will turn to the learning activity first, and then to materials as components in the learning structure. But this development will demand faculty commitment to a materials program, and the effective distribution of materials throughout the school. This article therefore emphasizes *programs* rather than facilities, the *use* of materials rather than the size of the collection, and the role of the materials specialist as consultant and director – functions that cannot be determined by design alone.

The *Central-University High School* in Madison, Wisconsin, provides a good example of an active library program that can be conducted despite limited quarters. In 1964-65, this school studied ways to emphasize individual, independent study for all its pupils. The plan, developed by the entire faculty as an in-service project, identified the limitations of the library quarters and pointed up the need for greater accessibility and better use of its excellent collections. To improve conditions, special collections were moved from the central library to four "branches" created in the school, and a duplicate collection of frequently consulted reference materials was placed in a learning laboratory set up in the school auditorium. Students were admitted to the library at any time *without* passes.

Beginning this fall, the school noted a most dramatic change in student use of materials. Circulation had doubled and remains at that level. Sustained use of materials in the library occurs at all hours to an unprecedented degree, and technical newspapers and periodicals, once seldom consulted, are now used frequently. As they look for information to develop their project, students are

Reprinted with permission from: Taylor, Kenneth I., "Function Before Form," SCHOOL LIBRARY JOURNAL, December 15, 1965. Copyright ©1965, R. R. Bowker Company.

using materials from ouside community sources: one boy reported with pride to his principal that he had consulted 42 books for his project, many from outside libraries.

It is true that this school's beginning toward independent work is modest. Yet faculty enthusiasm has already accelerated the plan to bring newer media into the school, and — what is of special importance to the librarian — in a library that if evaluated by national standards would not rate very high. Although the printed collections are ample in size and closely related to the curriculum, the physical facilities don't offer what is traditionally seen as adequate seating capacity. The library has compensated for this limitation in two ways: by distributing materials around the school, and by developing related study facilities in other parts of the building. The emphasis on the materials program begun here has been on accessibility and, through faculty study, teacher encouragement. There is a real probability that many — perhaps a majority of — schools throughout the United States have problems similar to those that were identified by this school faculty.

The reports of some major school libraries which made their facilities available evenings and weekends, only to find their collections unused, highlight the importance of faculty involvement. What soon became evident in these schools was that teachers were not encouraging their students to use a wide variety of materials, at least on school premises, even though their administrators apparently thought that they should be doing so.

Encouraging greater use of materials is not a matter that can be accomplished by "media specialists" alone; it needs administrative direction and faculty commitment.

A first step to enlist such involvement is a systematic method of cooperative materials selection, accompanied by in-service study on using materials.

The following six questions outline areas of investigation that can result in greater faculty understanding and participation in a school-wide instructional materials program, and may furnish a basis for local or regional qualitative evaluation of the use of materials.

1. *To what extent are materials selected in relation to school objectives and classroom activities?* The growing availability of specialized teaching media requires systematic evaluation by the total school faculty. It is becoming evident that library and a/v materials, basic and supplementary texts, professional books, and newer, untested media must be examined by those who intend to use them. A cooperative approach to selection by teachers and the media specialists results in an individualized school collection and also acquaints the librarian with the learning activities that are being designed by the faculty.

2. *To what extent are students trained in the research methods that characterize the various fields of knowledge?* As schools provide more opportunity for independent study, they will emphasize creative inquiry. Each of the major disciplines, as identified by Joseph J. Schwab — the investigative (natural sciences), the appreciative (arts), and the decisive (social sciences) — has special techniques for discovering established knowledge, for determining relationships among data, and for relating these to contemporary experiences. Instruction in these techniques, the responsibility of the entire faculty, requires

effective student use of varied materials within a process. As a result, more materials are needed today which explain these techniques. Some of these materials may have to be created by the teacher and the media specialist. In addition, facilities for the use of these materials and for the application of research techniques must not be confined to the materials center but be provided in classrooms and laboratories around the school.

3. *Are appropriate materials available for student and faculty use throughout the school?* Because most learning activities occur outside the materials center proper, collections of various media must be available throughout the school: in classrooms, laboratories, conference rooms, teachers' offices, and departmental resources centers. A coordinated materials program will eventually require that the main materials center keep central records of the locations of these materials, giving all school personnel access to school-owned materials which are decentralized throughout the building.

4. *To what extent do teachers and pupils use a variety of materials in the classroom and similar instructional areas?* To free students from dependence on limited authorities, teachers must encourage them to use many materials in every learning activity. In addition to commercially published materials, students should also be taught to use graphic procedures for explaining in a consice manner new relationships among data. A most successful method of instruction in these procedures, of course, is by teacher example. In addition to the traditional essays and term papers, graphic and audio products should also be accepted at times as evidence of successful pupil achievement.

5. *Are in-service opportunities for instructional media and utilization provided regularly for the faculty?* Successful implementation of this area of the materials program requires leadership by the school administration. Continued in-service programs can draw on the talents of all faculty members, with occasional presentations by outside resource people. From this comes the identification of mutual teaching aims that bridge grade levels and departmental boundaries.

6. *Is a plan for developing an effective program available for the next few years?* One of the most effective methods for expanding materials programs is planning how new facilities and materials services would be used if they were made available. Cooperative planning by school personnel identifies for all the goals of the materials program and relationships among the facilities, materials, services, and learning activities that support today's increasingly complex curricular goals.

DEVELOPING LEARNING RESOURCES CENTERS IN SECONDARY SCHOOLS

Dorothy A. McGinniss

Everywhere today people are talking about Learning Resources Centers or Instructional Materials Centers in schools as if they were something very new. We seem to consider ourselves innovators. I was interested in reading recently a publication of the Ministry of Education in England called *The School Library*. It brought out that, in the Ashton's Ordinances at Shrewsbury in 1578, the statement was made that buildings should include "a library and gallerie for the said schools furnished with all manner of books, mappes, spheres, instruments of astronomye and all other things apperteyninge to learning which may be either given to the schools or procured with the schoole money." The idea is not so new after all, but it seems to have taken a long time to catch hold. I heard someone mention the other day that the man who started supermarkets was inspired to do so by studying libraries where materials were organized and made easily accessible to patrons. It seems as though the supermarkets have caught up and gone one better than libraries. They are now featuring the one-stop shopping center. Isn't this what we need — a similar center where teachers can go to get all the resources they need to enrich their teaching, to give young people the best learning experiences possible, and to introduce to them all sorts of learning materials?

It has been accepted by most educators, I believe, that the one textbook approach to learning is completely out of date and that the self-contained classroom cannot possibly furnish all the materials necessary for a good learning situation. In order to meet the needs of all youth, it is necessary to expose them to the printed word in many forms at many levels of difficulty, to present to them ideas in pictures with and without sound, to use the oral approach through records and tapes, to utilize all kinds of educational media in the hope that at least one of the approaches will make an impression. The problem seems to be, then, to decide the best means of implementation.

BUYING

The first necessity is to have a wealth of materials of all kinds easily accessible to all teachers and students at the time when they can be most useful. Centralized buying of these materials will ensure economy. Centralized organization will ensure the most efficient service for all concerned. The

Reprinted by permission of the National Association of Secondary School Principals from: McGinniss, Dorothy A. "Developing Learning Resources Centers in Secondary Schools." BULLETIN OF NATIONAL ASSOCIATION OF SECONDARY SCHOOL PRINCIPALS, December, 1962. Copyright 1962 by the National Association of Secondary School Principals.

librarian has, or should have, the training in selection and in organization to play the part of centralizer. The mechanics of organization are, or should be, already set up in libraries. Each teacher is a specialist in his or her particular field. He can and should play an important role in the selection of materials. But often in the press of meeting large classes daily, preparing and correcting assignments, teachers cannot keep up with new publications in their field. The librarian has access to and knowledge of selection tools of all types and, therefore, is in a position to keep teachers informed of new materials. The mechanics of efficient, economic, and coordinated ordering can best be worked out by the librarian because of his specialized training and because he has contact with all the departments in the school. He can more easily avoid unnecessary duplication of materials. The teacher must be relieved of the mechanics connected with ordering if he is to devote more time to what he is best equipped to do – impart information, discuss ideas, and instill in students good habits of thinking and working.

AVAILABILITY

In most schools there is not room in classrooms nor in department offices for adequate and accessible storage of materials. Again the teacher does not have the time nor does he have the clerical help whereby he can adequately list material so that it will be easily accessible. The librarian, with the assistance of clerical help (which I'm assuming is available to him), is equipped by training to do an excellent job of organizing these materials so that they can be easily found when needed. He has methods already developed for charging out materials so that their whereabouts is known at all times. If there is a Learning Resources Center, every teacher knows where he can go to find all the materials he needs; he has access to all the materials in the school for his particular need; he does not have to confine himself only to those things which he has in his own room or department. Many materials are, of course, useful to various departments.

UTILIZATION

It is to be hoped that, in a Learning Resources Center, there would be books and non-book materials as well as the equipment necessary for their use. By means of the card catalog, a teacher or student can find all materials available in the school on a particular subject – books, parts of books, pamphlets, maps, pictures, recordings, films, filmstrips, tapes, *etc.* Through the magazine indexes he can find articles on his subject. He can even find community resources which will be useful for his purposes. In the Center will be the names of specialists in various areas who can lecture on a specialty, information about places the students can visit, *etc.* Available will be individual viewers so that the teacher can preview filmstrips to determine their usefulness for his purposes; and phonographs so that he can listen to recordings before deciding to use them. Here also will be a place to sign up for borrowing machines for classroom use. The librarian is ready and able to make bibliographies for any phase of a topic showing all types of materials available if this is desirable.

What I am describing is, of course, the ideal and presupposes adequate physical facilities, plenty of storage area for machines, clerical help, and technical assistance. Naturally it is obvious that more than one professional librarian is necessary to man adequately this type of Learning Resources Center. Such a Center, adequately housed and satisfactorily staffed, will enable teachers to give more attention to their subject areas and their teaching so that they can offer to the students the maximum in education. It will enable students to have access to a wealth of materials, to learn how to use them under expert guidance, and to develop to their greatest potential.

A FEW CAUTIONS

The ideal is fine for the schools which have everything needed. What about the others? Even a small school with a full-time librarian and a full-time paid clerical can have a limited Learning Resources Center. Larger schools with more adequate staff can go far in spite of inadequacies. Even though physical facilties are not suitable for housing all materials in the library; even though conditions in the area make it advisable to have films, filmstrips, or records stored elsewhere; everything can be listed in the library and everything can be ordered centrally. Unless the physical facilities are adequate, unless the clerical and technical help are available, it would be unwise for any school to rush into setting up a Learning Resources Center. Gradual changes can be made wherever possible so that more and more services can be added to provide a real Learning Resources Center which can give to students and teachers the type of service which they need and should have. As a result of these efforts will come an improved school program.

IN CONCLUSION

I like to think of the Learning Resources Center or Instructional Materials Center in terms of four E's: Economy, Efficiency, Excellence, and Enrichment. The *economy* comes from centralized and careful buying under the supervision of a person skilled in the methods and familiar with the whole school curriculum. It also applies to economy of effort because the teachers have a one-stop "shopping center" where all their needs for materials can be met. The *efficiency* results from organization by one trained for such work. The *excellence* refers to the service which can be given to teachers and students in such a center. The *enrichment* is reflected in the whole educational program, because teachers are helped to give their best efforts to the students and the students have their lives enriched by having all kinds of media of communication introduced to them and by learning to use these media.

A STUDY IN TRANSITION: WHEATON HIGH SCHOOL MAKES THE CHANGE FROM LIBRARY TO INSTRUCTIONAL MATERIALS CENTER

John L. Pilato

In 1963, it was decided by the administration of Wheaton High School in Maryland to make the transition from a traditional library to an instructional materials center. This decision necessitated changes in physical plant, changes in personnel or reassignment of existing personnel, and changes in and expansion of services offered to the school's 2,500 students and their teachers.

The first change to take place involved the physical plant. The east side of the library was redesigned to house three 16mm booths and one taping booth which would be easily accessible to students and teachers. Space for housing all portable equipment was provided adjacent to the 16mm booths. The 16mm booths were wired to allow for the use of headsets. The taping booth was constructed with acoustical wall and ceiling tile. The west side of the library was converted into a viewing and listening area capable of accommodating 25 students, and room was left for expansion. A room on the second floor was converted into a production room where a polaroid copymaker, a copying machine, and the Tecnifax system were available for use.

The instructional materials center was staffed with two librarians and two library aides. It was decided that one librarian would be in charge of all printed material, and the other would control all nonprinted material. One library aide, under the supervision of a librarian and with the help of student aides, would be in complete control of the circulation desk. The other library aide would be responsible for booking materials ouside the school, shelving, keeping up the vertical file, and taking care of routine duties, again with the assistance of student aides. This deployment of library staff was agreed upon after the instructional materials center had been in operation for a matter of months, and after it was determined that circulation had increased proportionally with the expansion of services.

The program of services rendered by the staff during the first year of operation was extensive. These services included photocopying and tape production and duplication for students and teachers; viewing of filmstrips and

Reprinted with permission from: Pilato, John L., "A Study in Transition: Wheaton High School Makes the Change From Library to Instructional Materials Center," AUDIOVISUAL INSTRUCTION, November, 1964.

listening to tapes, records, and radio programs; production of polaroid copies and overhead transparencies; booking of materials for students and teachers from the county depository and other depositories; and listing of bibliographies.

A tentative schedule of temporary exhibits to acquire on loan was drawn up. Bookmobiles travelled from the instructional materials center to the classrooms. New filmstrips, records, tapes, and books were obtained on approval to complement the various subject areas. A copy of every textbook used in the school was housed in the center. All types of free and inexpensive materials were sought to increase the vertical file. Work was begun on compiling a picture file, which eventually would become an important part of the materials to be found in the center. Every government agency was contacted for its film catalog and free materials. All materials ordered by students and teachers from outside sources were routed through the instructional materials center. Plans were formulated to compile and place in the catalog file a speakers list in hopes of encouraging interaction between school and community. All these services constituted an ambitious course of action for an instructional materials center with a total personnel complement of two librarians and two library aides.

The first month of school was used to orientate students into the old and new aspects of the program. They were shown how to use books plus filmstrips, records, tapes, and other materials; how to order outside materials; how to produce materials. As compared to the preceding year, the orientation encompassed many more materials and was much more time-consuming. The results, however, surpassed all expectations. Records proved that in the second month of operation, circulation and usage of materials doubled.

The task of completely keeping up with all the services and activities which need to be rendered by an instructional materials center staff is tremendous. Since the instructional materials center was begun, the staff has been expanded to include three librarians and four aides and additional material has been acquired. How far a full program can be achieved at Wheaton High with limited personnel is still not known. One thing is certain, however; the instructional materials center at Wheaton High School has been largely responsible for giving needed impetus toward creating a richer life for students and teachers alike.

EMMA WILLARD'S NEW LIBRARY

William M. Dietel

Planning for Emma Willard School's new library began in 1962 with a study of the total needs of the school. Founded as a female seminary in 1814, the school and its educational concepts have both come a long way in the intervening 152 years. This independent school for girls of high school age has occupied its present Troy, New York, site of 55 acres since 1910. The aging buildings and the ever young student body are no longer entirely compatible, and the administrators and trutees of the school have embarked upon a major expansion program based on a comprehensive master plan executed by architect Edward Larrabee Barnes of New York City.

Three major points of significance were immediately apparent about library needs from the 1962 study:

(1) The existing library, a handsome Gothic room with two impressive oriel windows at either end, was completely inadequate for the anticipated needs of the educational program. The room could not house the existing book collection, and there was no sensible, economical way to expand its capacity for a collection more than twice the size of the existing one.

(2) The room which housed the library was built in 1910, serving at that time as a repository for a 5,000-volume collection and as the main study room for 129 students. By 1962 the student body exceeded 350 students.

(3) The old library is just what the adjective implies. Despite its regal proportions and handsome appearance, it is old — inadequate for its main purpose of existence. We could not add to the room without destroying its architectural glory, and an infinitude of problems negated a modernization approach. We needed a new library, one that would serve well for present needs and far into the future.

A faculty-staff committee composed of myself as principal, the dean, the assistant to the principal, the librarian, and three faculty members discussed what the school would need for a library in 1967, 1977, and 1987. We posed for ourselves the questions of function, utility, service, and aesthetics.

The committee remained active for a year and a half, and its conclusions were taken up by a special new buildings committee. This second group worked directly with our master planner for the school, architect Barnes.

The original library committee examined our internal situation before it ventured to find out how other schools and small colleges had solved similar problems. We determined that, in our particular situation, a single room was

Reprinted with permission of AMERICAN SCHOOL AND UNIVERSITY, Buttenheim Publishing Corp., from: Dietel, William M., "Emma Willard's New Library." May, 1966.

totally inadequate for what we wanted our library to do. It was clear that a building was mandatory. We were largely influenced by concerns for the future of our educational goals and a desire to remain open to innovations in teaching.

Our estimates revealed that a total volume capacity of 40,000 to 50,000 would be needed over the next 30 years. We also concluded that the new library would be more than a repository for books — it would be the main resource center for all kinds of information. Centralization promised economy in operation and maintenance and, just as important, efficiency in making learning materials available to the greatest number of students in the least amount of time.

With our students living in dormitories built around 1910, we felt a strong need for a modern study space for students when not in class. The vintage dormitory rooms were clearly inadequate because of size, lighting, and furnishings for any type of study activity. Furthermore, we felt that all senior girls should be studying individually, and that all juniors, sophomores, and freshmen should move progressively to individual study. Right now four homerooms in the main building serve for organized study.

The new library, then, was to be the main study area of the school, seating 200 to 250 students (minimal figures when we consider that 310 students are residence, and all are expected to study in the evening at the same time).

As we continued to investigate future curriculum changes, we became exceedingly interested in the prospects of audio-visual education aids, and felt that some day we would be using the latest in a-v equipment as part of our instructional program.

During our explorations at other independent schools and small colleges we were impressed with the work being done at The Phillips Academy, Andover, Massachusetts, and by the use, at schools like The Groton School, Groton, Massachusetts, of information retrieval systems. Our committee determined to anticipate the future by planning our new library so that the latest in audio-visual aids could be installed when program materials warranted.

By 1965, as design work proceeded and we continued our planning sessions with the architect, we were certain that we wished to have an information retrieval system installed in all new classrooms, in the seminar rooms in the library, and in a number of individual study carrels.

The random access dial retrieval system we selected consists of equipment that stores and makes instantly available a large number of prerecorded taped programs from a remote tape library. By simply dialing a number, the student activates the remotely located tape machine and listens to any desired program.

The student position is entirely free of conventional tape equipment, except for a combination earphone-microphone and the telephone dial. Only one copy of each program is required and any number of students can listen to the same program.

The entire system consists of a student booth or study carrel, a teacher's console, and a remote library. The teacher's console contains individual switches to enable undetected monitoring of student positions, and also lights to indicate what each student is doing. Besides the taped programs, the console has nine additional program sources, and video can be added at any time.

Present plans for the Emma Willard Library call for 90 stations to have the random access dial retrieval system. The tape bank and facilities for making tape will all be located in the basement of the new library which will have a large audio-visual preparation room. Conduits will be installed in the carrels for a later introduction of visual materials – either movies, filmstrips, or TV.

Our commitment to a core program of studies in the humanities, built around a chronological study of the culture of Western man, has been a decisive influence in planning our new library, estimated at $775,000 in cost. In addition, our strong interest in the arts has made it imperative that our buildings be aesthetically pleasing. We believe that the architect has successfully fulfilled our desires.

The school's existing structures include Tudor Gothic, Georgian, and Tudor beam and mortar styles. Architect Barnes' new design will be strong enough to stand at the center of the campus without dominating these older structures. The building will be a strong statement of the importance of architecture in the lives of men.

Other building needs and the nature of our curriculum almost immediately suggested to the architect that the library be part of a complex, flanked on the left by a new music building and on the right by an art building. These three buildings will be connected by covered arcades to the chapel and the science building. Thus, the five buildings will form three sides of a quadrangle, facing the main school building on the fourth side.

We feel that the new library will have a profound impact upon the future academic life of Emma Willard School, and by design. If the building does what it is supposed to, it will lend dignity and excitement to the process of study. Through its organization of space, its aesthetic appeal, and its use of the latest available learning materials, the library will encourage learning and make it a pleasant, long-lasting experience.

TIPTOE IN TECHNOLOGY

Mary J. Egan

Federal aid is pumping money into the schools for fancy equipment and materials: industry is jumping onto the bandwagon by buying up publishing companies and putting out fancy educational gimmicks; but educators have had to remain more cautious about the new relationship of gadgets to education. While some advances are breathtaking, much in the way of equipment and materials is of dubious value. Educators must assume the responsibility for deciding what is worthwhile. As a specialist in educational materials, the librarian is at the center of the problem, for he must decide which of the new materials to buy, and how to make them accessible to students.

As Harold Howe says, "Schools have to admit the electronic age is here and that there are many ways of communication and of handling information. Education, after all, is in those two businesses — communicating and handling information. It'll have to be making more use of efficient and rapid ways of doing this ... The new media can bring the best teachers, the most carefully planned curricula, key books and manuscripts to each class and to each teacher and pupil. The teacher will be able to engage in the individual diagnosis and prescription needed to help each child learn to learn ... The media can give us a window on the world, an educational system capable of bringing the best, most real, and widest range of experience to the student." (Harold Howe II, "On Libraries and Learning." *SLJ*, February 1967, p. 28, 30; *LJ*, February 15, 1967, p. 842, 844).

Our basic conviction is that it is better to take the bull (industry) by the horns and experiment in our schools than to have industry tell educators what, when, and how to teach. This project is a start, a small but, we feel, significant experiment.

Like many projects around the country, ours is designed to transform a library into an "educational materials center" through funds from Title III of the Elementary and Secondary Education Act, with materials supplied under Title II. Individual environmental carrels, a new approach to study and research, will provide a student with *immediate access to all media* including television, films, special lessons, traditional library materials, and eventually computer-assisted instruction.

The junior high library was excellent in size, decor, and equipment. The original plan, five years ago, included a reading room, office-workroom, and classroom, a total of approximately 3000 square feet. This fall an addition containing 1170 square feet for storage and using newer media was made

Reprinted with permission from: Egan, Mary J., "Tiptoe in Technology," SCHOOL LIBRARY JOURNAL, April 15, 1967. Copyright ©1957, R. R. Bowker Company.

available. It included space for listening and viewing carrels to be installed this spring. The present facility receives excellent use.

Major objectives of the projects are: to provide materials to enhance all curricular areas; to prove the increased use of such materials when technically indexed and immediately accessible; to demonstrate the educational value of independent study and research, especially through the use of environmental carrels; to increase awareness of the need and value of the materials center by educators and local and regional communities.

Central to the project is the environmental carrel, to be provided with audio and video dial systems to provide access to a wide range of media. Portable carts will transport the materials to classrooms. A video tape recorder will allow specific lessons and research to be recorded, and a library of these tapes will be built up.

The selection of dial access equipment for the project was a very complex matter, but not of great common concern to the nation's educators. The selection of materials is a thornier problem, of immediate concern to educators in general, and to the librarian in particular. Many audio-visual materials are reviewed in professional periodicals but not with the scope found in the book reviewing world. Some commercial catalogs are excellent guides, but they represent the vendor's point of view. A paramount need to aid selection of materials for our project and others is basic lists of materials in the new media, with reliable annotations — a basic list of filmstrips, a basic list of records, a basic list of transparencies, etc.

Multimedia packages, combining more than one medium, are abundant, but evaluations of them are equally hard to find in the professional literature. More important, these "package deals" are rarely comprehensive, usually consisting of a record and filmstrip or an audio tape and filmstrip, and sometimes a script. Apparently no one publisher runs the gamut of filmstrips, pictures, records, tapes, films, and transparencies in one multimedia container. This challenge is one left for the school personnel. Assembling a multimedia kit complete with realia is fascinating and is perhaps a responsibility best left to the materials specialist and teachers in the individual school.

The state of the art of information retrieval and the status of current research on the use of nonbook media have led us to a courageous but cautious implementation in our experimental project. As can be seen, selection is a painstaking, time consuming business. The physical processing and wise use of materials also present many challenges that demand fresh approaches. There are many pitfalls for the eager innovator as there are in any field where experimentation occurs.

MATERIALS ARRIVE

Approval of ESEA Titles II and III was greeted with much excitement in our school district, especially in the junior high school where the materials center is located. Plans were firm on materials to be ordered. Overwork and overtime insured rapid placement of the orders. Materials began to arrive long before school ended last June. The boxes were piled high, and no matter how fast materials were unpacked, the mail acted like Homer Price's donut machine — there was no turning it off.

When the full processing crew tackled the task of unpacking and checking invoices, no one thought the end would come before 1970. Diligence and enthusiasm motivated the staff to dig out what they called "goodies" to put out in the open early in November. The entire faculty of the district was invited to drop in and browse during or after school to view and sample the monumental contents of that wonderful $46,000 grant before materials were in full use in the classroom. Requests for future loans were enthusiastically accepted.

In the midst of the mounds of boxes and sheaves of paper were two eager catalogers and a competent, cheerful library aide, unpacking and cataloging materials and typing shelflist cards. The project director visited such schools as Penfield to talk with capable people about processing and circulating nonbook materials. In addition to numerous meetings with the librarians of the district and ESEA staff, a workshop was conducted early in June to survey the problems and arrive at some solutions. A major debate raged during the spring about color banding. The final decision was to leave the rainbow to the sky. If the individual librarian wanted 17 shades for the wide variety of media, he could add them after materials were processed.

One day in September the typist realized that she could do complete cards for only five records in six hours (counting interruptions), a snail's pace, especially considering our lofty goals. We had requested a Xerox 914 in our Title III budget, and hastened to rent this finger-saver. In a half hour, approximately 450 cards teem out of this impressive machine. Of course, pages, of books and periodicals, transparencies, multilith masters can be quickly photocopied. But people are never satisfied! The machine goes even faster than the typist can produce *one* main entry.

The next step was to call for help. Our district's top business students at the senior high are good neighbors, good citizens, and accurate typists. They pitched in to produce main entry cards on paper slips. These were then fed to the 914 in groups of four to produce catalog cards, shelflist, plus an additional main entry card for each library in the district. This means that each school will have a listing of all materials. This list can be constantly up-dated by simply interfiling new entries as they are reproduced. Sample cards are exhibited here. No colors were used since on the photocopying machine every color is black. The marvelous machine at the disposal of the superhuman task force really made the cataloging and processing operation successful. Perhaps sometime later a book catalog can be published for every teacher in the district.

STAFFING AND CIRCULATION

How do teachers receive the materials? Our processing is too slow. Unprocessed materials are loaned for a day or a week only. This means a meticulous loan system. One of the three librarians at the junior high is becoming a media librarian, responsible for the care and circulation of all processed materials. She has set out to become knowledgeable about all of the materials, but it is her hope that her studies will help the other librarians in their special fields. The media libraian is assigned to social studies and science. Another librarian is assigned to English, and the third has art, music, shop, home economics, guidance, and you name it. Eventually bulletins containing bibliographies and evaluation of materials will be sent to all the faculty.

Evaluation sheets have been given to the faculty for their comments on the use of materials. In the interim each of the five other libraries in the district will receive a main entry card for each item cataloged. Working with Dewey classification and types of materials, the librarians in the other schools will be able to locate many materials for teacher and student use. Telephone and interschool mail aid in this loan procedure.

PROBLEMS IN CATALOGING NEWER MEDIA

Our central cataloging and processing office has been in operation for over six years, so books posed no problem under our special purpose grant. Quite naturally we turned to Dewey and Sears to organize other materials. In fact, as records and filmstrips drifted into the libraries they were cataloged and classified much as the books *Library of Congress-National Union Catalog: Music and Phonorecords,* and *National Union Catalog: Motion Pictures* and *Filmstrips* were already on our subscription lists.

The first major problem was that after hours of searching, many records and filmstrips did not have Library of Congress cards available. Original cataloging was necessary for over 50 percent of the records. Then, there were many other materials that have been orphaned by catalogers: 8mm films (single concept films, film loops, cartridges), transparencies, slides, audio tapes, video tapes and multimedia. It is extremely vital to the project to have all materials technically indexed for quick access not only for loan to teachers and students but for programming in the dial access equipment. Students in the ten experimental carrels must be able to dial listed audio or video programs. The audio and video control rooms are to be adjacent to the library for quick retrieval. In addition a quick glance at the card catalog should turn up appropriate materials. Careful indexing is indicated and annotations are included whenever possible.

Plugging gallantly through new procedures and using L.C. forms referring to Mary Gaver's *The Elementary School Library Collection,* new insights were gained. In general most problems were solved by relating the materials to the book solutions. However, some materials are not analogous. Filmstrip titles are misleading; no synopsis is printed in some publishers' catalogs. This meant the filmstrip had to be previewed for content, number of frames, color or black-and-white, and grade level. Date of publication was often not indicated. Filmstrips in a series had to be examined individually. Questions often arose about what the main entry should be — title, company, or something else.

Films were awkward to preview. What librarian dares to sit and watch movies all day? In addition, projectors were not readily available. Teachers were willing to help with evaluation and summaries, but they do not have a cataloger's approach, and don't usually check for the same identifying data. Often a date did not appear in a catalog and looked hazy on the film. Running time, price, black-and-white or color, lack of labels or reels all proved to be problems.

Loop
796.4 Trampolining, back flip. Athletic Institute and Society for Visual
Tra   Education, recd 1966.
           5 min. color 8 mm. (Gymnastics for men:
Trampolining)

35

1. Gymnastics   Series

Tape
788   Woodwind ensemble. Indiana University, recd 1966.
Woo   15 min. 7½ ips. (Each in its own voice)
         Broadcast restrictions
         Summary: Discusses what instruments are in the woodwind
       ensemble, how each is played, and what importance each has in the
       orchestra.

460

1. Wind instruments   2. Music

Transparencies
428.4 Basic reading, Part II. Visual Products, 1965.
Bas   23 transparencies b/w (English 11) with two copies of originals
           Contents: Two fixation scanning patterns.-Square-span scanning pattern.-
       Column scanning pattern.-4-letter scanning groupings.-5-letter scanning
       groupings.-6-Letter scanning groupings.-Scanning spread patterns.-Word
       scanning patterns.-Phrase scanning patterns.-Column scanning.

975-
1043   O   Remedial teaching
       1. Reading–

Sample catalog cards for audiovisuals (8mm loop, tape, and transparency), as prepared at Burnt Hills. Dewey and Sears provide basic organization

Although 8mm film loops evoked great interest and have been enthusiastically used, loops were not always as the printed title on the case stated. It was wise to preview. A few cartridges had to be returned because they were mechanically faulty. When blurbs appeared on cartridges, they were helpful for cataloging routines; but too many did not contain blurbs.

Transparencies required individual handling and meticulous care in checking upon receipt. Fingerprints show! Some could be cataloged in sets; others required individual treatment. Slides were also usually handled individually. They require special cartridges for storage and it is not easy to circulate a few at a time. The plastic strip container they come in is of no use, and we were all thumbs trying to house these little gems, until we settled on make-shift boxes.

The pictures recommended by the art department, plus various prints, charts, large maps were not always easy to subject head and were even more difficult to store. Large drawers are awkward; large shelves on rollers would be far more desirable.

Time to listen to tapes was nil. No guidance as to content, grade level, or series existed for audio tapes, which usually came on reels without labels. Some tapes even came from the manufacturer wound backwards on the reel. Fortunately, our two catalogers auditioned audio tapes on the weekends to avoid the "student look" in school. Misleading titles could only be corrected as the cataloger checked for content to classify and subject head.

For multimedia, a variety of media that must be used together to be effective, one accession number was given a unit, with individual alphabetical designations. Since the subject matter of all media was related, the classification number was no problem. The contents of the box were listed on the container for ease of circulation and inventory. (Multimedia catalogs gave no dates and often materials bordered on history when they were expected to present a current outlook. Fortunately, most dealers have been willing to exchange materials, but this is a time consuming problem.)

Records are indeed pokey. It's slow and unrewarding to search LC cards. Documentary records sometimes contain a different historical period on each side. Classification? Flip a coin or generalize. Often a film accompanies the record. If each of the media could be used independently, they were treated that way. Teachers' guides sometimes accompany records. Thick ones make for good educational use but difficult shelving.

Ephemeral materials, periodicals, globes, and microfilm, were treated in the traditional manner. The library of video tapes has been so small as to be no problem. In the future, video tapes and segments of tapes will be fully cataloged to obtain maximum use with the dial access equipment to be installed in the next few months.

What can be purchased for $40,000? The following list reveals the good news.

Books	2908
Filmstrips	1441
Tapes	527
Records	288
Films	126
Prints and pictures	109
Transparencies	2655
Slides	1368
Loops-8mm	111
Microfilm	128
Teachers' guides	220
Kits	46
SRA Career file	1
Pamphlets	360
Charts	149
Programmed Instruction	43
Multimedia kits	32
Globes, maps, map models	8

THE COMPLETE AV CENTER—
WHAT IT TAKES TO DO THE JOB

Jack Tanzman

Everyone of us has a favorite fantasy about how things *should* be. Mine has to do with the ideal instructional materials center.

Given enough funds – and a school administration willing to back me to the hilt – I would probably build a facility very like the instructional materials center at the Punahou School in Honolulu, Hawaii. For my money, this million-dollar baby is the *best* IMC around.

The way it's put together – and used – points to some important principles in instructional materials center planning and operation.

DESIGNED FOR CURRICULUM

First, the instructional materials center should be designed specifically to serve the students and the teachers.

Too many centers are simply noninstructional additions to existing library facilities built to stockpile audio-visual equipment. At the Punahou School, the center – although housing the school's books as well as its audio-visual facilities – is something entirely different. Its facilities include motion pictures, slide films, microfilms, recordings, teaching machines and taped lessons – all of them chosen and produced *expressly* to complement the school program.

Services of this center are not limited to the facility itself. An overhead projector and a ceiling-mounted tilt-screen have been installed in every one of the school's 136 instructional areas. A special random-access digital dialing system, equipped with a remote control phrase-repeating device, permits the use of 30 taped programs emanating from the center in six of the school's largest classrooms.

Second, an instructional materials center needs to be large enough. How large is this? It depends on the use the center will be put to, of course. If it's just going to be a place to keep machinery and software, the center can be limited in size – and will probably be just as limited in educational effectiveness. But the ideal center will provide independent study space for every student in the school and will include ample facilities for materials preparation and teacher training.

The Punahou School's instructional materials center fits this bill perfectly. Covering almost three-quarters of an acre, its two levels comprise 36,000 square feet – more than 10 square feet per child. In addition to ample storage space for books and other instructional materials, the building has been laid out to include

Reprinted with permission from: Tanzman, Jack, "The Complete AV Center – What It Takes To Do The Job," SCHOOL MANAGEMENT, November, 1966.

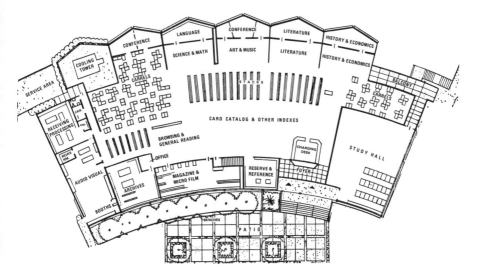

Two-level Punahou instructional materials center comprises 36,000 square feet — more than 10 square feet per child. The $1 million facility combines library facilities with audio-visual instruction areas, study halls, faculty work areas and an AV materials preparation room.

study carrel areas, study halls, conference rooms, special subject work areas, art studios and faculty work areas, as well as space for audio-visual aids and a preparation room for making new instructional materials.

Third, the ideal instructional materials center should be staffed by persons with a real feel for the multiple resource approach to education.

The heart of Punahou's instructional materials center is its staff — a tight little group of trained librarians and audio-visual specialists. Heading up the AV department is Dwain H. Hansen, a former teacher whose special knowledge is in graphic production. Hansen is in charge of materials production at the center.

The center's instructional materials preparation room includes facilities for making overhead transparencies, 35mm. slides, graphs, charts, posters, dry mounts, color lifts, laminations, duplicate and facsimile reproductions, black and white (and color) study or display prints, filmstrips, 16mm. motion pictures, enlargements or reductions from books or magazines, duplicate slides and so forth.

To ensure that these facilities are used effectively, the center's AV director spends one quarter of his time making regular visits to every classroom in the school. These are followed up with individual teacher conferences and meetings with entire departments to discuss the use of media to solve teaching problems.

An audio-visual curriculum committee works with the AV director to establish broad policies for operation and use of the center's AV facilities. Special inservice programs are available to all teachers.

Fourth, the ideal instructional materials center should be easy to get to, easy to use and pleasant to work with. All materials in the center — not just books — should circulate.

In Punahou's fan-shaped instructional materials center, all materials — including audio-visual programs — are arranged for the easiest possible access. In effect, it's a good, solid AV center — turned inside out. Look at the floor plan on page 169 and you'll see what I mean. The librarian (or, the audio-visual secretary) does not stand between the library user and the materials and equipment. Check-out procedures are simple and quickly completed. Individual study carrels provide space and adequate power to run the library's AV equipment.

More than this, students are encouraged to participate in running the center. Some 55 of them are regularly permitted to join in the production and processing of the center's audio-visual materials. Many have reached near-professional sophistication in handling the equipment.

Finally, the ideal instructional materials center should be open for use whenever it's needed. This may seem self-evident, but all too many such centers are open only on a part-time basis - i.e., eight hours a day. Punahou's instructional materials center is open from 7:30 a.m. to 5 p.m. daily as well as three nights a week, Saturday mornings and Sunday afternoons.

YOU CAN DO IT, TOO

It doesn't take $1 million to design and build an instructional materials center that really makes sense. Sure, it helps . . . but you can respect the *principles* that make the Punahou center tops, no matter how much money you have to spend. You really can't afford *not* to.

A NEW, BUT MUCH USED, MULTI-MEDIA CENTER

James L. Theodores

Scarsdale's high school students are affixing their stamp of approval to their school's new multimedia library by making it the "in" place to go in this New York suburban community. The only description that really sums up student and staff reaction to this new facility, occupied at the start of the spring semester, is "exciting." Here is a facility which, by the very nature of its design, aesthetic appeal, and function, has attracted so many students that it has created pleasant usage problems which even the most imaginative planners could not fully anticipate.

In the first blush of success, it is apparent that the new library is bursting at its seams, filled to capacity at all hours of the day. To those involved in planning

Reprinted by permission of AMERICAN SCHOOL AND UNIVERSITY, Buttenheim Publishing Corp., from: Theodores, James L., "A New, But Much Used, Multi-Media Center." April, 1966.

the library, it is rewarding to realize that the design of a facility could promote independent study to this extent. It is pleasant irony that the problem of overcrowding is caused by the success of imaginative planning, rather than by the short-sighted "too little, too late" predicament experienced by many schools today.

As with other communities, the idea for Scarsdale's library, and other phases of its construction and modernization program, emerged from the need for space and from frustration with existing facilities. Development of plans involved many people and long hours of hard-nosed work. Ideas came in all shapes and sizes. Some were good, some bad, and still others were a warmed over re-hash of "more of the same" kind of thinking. Creative ideas require imagination and daring departure from conditioned solutions — much like the multi-faceted splendor of a gem which emerges from a diamond in-the-rough, all because the imagination of the gem cutter could see beyond the surface. Creative ideas can also transform a facility into a valuable gem, while conditioned thinking often results in worthless fragmentations.

As early as 1961, a series of initial planning discussions took place to develop the framework toward most effectively meeting the program and facilities needs of Scarsdale's high school. Out of these discussions grew a firm commitment that all planning would reflect the role of independent study, which was becoming a more vital part of the total learning process.

In 1963, the architectural firm of Perkins & Will was engaged, along with the educational consulting firm of Englehardt, Englehardt & Leggett. They were to work with the school administrators and staff to develop specific proposals for additional space at the high school, and plans for modernizing and upgrading facilities in several portions of the existing building. Thus the combination of needs and basic concepts provided an opportunity to make a complete re-study of what we had, what was needed, and how to develop a package which would meet these needs most effectively.

All facilities were considered as "available space" regardless of their use at that time. With the shackles thus removed, we were free to plan for the most advantageous use of existing space, as well as to determine what the new facilities should contain. Our planning, therefore, was not concerned with merely "tacking on" needed classrooms. We were involved in a complete re-evaluation which allowed us to blend much of the old, and a little of the new, into facilities which could accommodate the educational programs of tomorrow.

This study resulted in a $2,178,000 bond issue to cover a three point construction program which included:

(1) Building a three-story addition to the high school. The addition includes on its upper floor seven new all-purpose science laboratories, four completely equipped project labs for students to work on long range experiments, central preparation rooms, science seminar room, professional library, plant growing room, and storage areas. The middle floor contains a multi-media library, library classroom, and individual offices and seminar rooms for teachers in the English and social studies departments. The ground floor contains audio-visual facilities for the entire school system, school district offices, three classrooms, and additional faculty offices.

(2) Improvements in the present high school building to serve mathematics, foreign languages, music, speech, industrial arts, and other departments. Modernization of utilities — heat, power, light, plumbing — was also included in the existing building.

(3) Conversion of a 1917 wing of the high school to house facilities for counseling services, reading and study skills instruction, student health services, student records and attendance center. This change makes more modern areas of the high school available for additional classrooms.

Significant among the new spaces developed is the multi-media library of approximately 13,000 square feet, which will accommodate 40,000 volumes and 225 students engaged in independent study. When completely equipped, this fully carpeted, air-conditioned facility will provide services for 100 electronically equipped study carrels which are arranged throughout the entire area of the library to assure privacy and easy access to materials. At present, some of the carrels are powered to accommodate television and filmstrip and slide projectors. They are also designed to include an information retrieval system by which a student will be able to dial and select taped audio programs which he can listen to in the privacy of his carrel. All carrel units can be equipped with power as the need arises and audio-visual systems are expanded. Thus, a student may work at his carrel with books, watch a taped or live closed-circuit telecast, check out a cartridge projector and view filmstrips or slides. As soon as new equipment is installed, he will be able to dial a taped audio program from a central retrieval system.

Teacher offices and seminar facilities in the library, will provide opportunity for individual and small-group conferences.

An integral and vital part of the multi-media library is the communications center. This new audio-visual communications center of approximately 3,200 square feet is located directly beneath the library to serve the information recall and technological distribution needs of the high school, as well as other schools in the system. The center includes facilities for the storage and distribution of non-printed information; a workshop for the production of teaching materials; a film preview and demonstration room; expanded facilities for television, including the use of video tape for local production and off-air broadcasts; and a professional library of audio-visual materials for teacher training.

The electronics distribution area is the nerve center of communications from which all audio-visual materials will be transmitted to the library carrels as well as to other areas of the high school, with future transmission to all schools in the district a possibility. All live programs initiated in the television studios, located in the existing portion of the high school building, will be transmitted to the nerve center and then piped to all other areas.

The new addition contains many distinctive architectural features and innovations in equipment which combine to make all spaces functional, inviting, and easy to live in. The multi-media library in particular, with its gold-colored all-wool carpeting, white walls, and warm walnut furniture of transitional design, stirkes a classic and attractive combination of colors and materials.

Furnishing the library presented many problems because of the particular student accommodations desired, the number of volumes to be housed, the wide use of audio-visual materials anticipated, the need for students to work both independently and in groups, and building code regulations which required 50 percent of the exterior wall surface be devoted to windows. Solutions had to be found for two critical problems if planning was to be successful; namely, how to house 40,000 volumes with less than half of the exterior wall space available for book stacks, and how to accommodate 100 students at carrels for independent study.

Available carrels on the market required too much space and were too inflexible for future use if we needed more stack space. It quickly became apparent that we needed a carrel unit which would serve a dual function in order to meet requirements and we set out to design one ourselves. After much deliberation, sketching, and construction of several mock-up units, we hit upon an idea to solve our problem.

The new carrel uses standard bookcase units with modified backs as the side units. A horizontal work surface and a vertical visual barrier, with a shelf for equipment, are locked into place to complete the carrel. A double carrel unit, thus formed, can accommodate two students and 500 books. It can be easily re-arranged and if additional stack space is needed, the work surface can be removed and the bookcases used separately. The horizontal work surface can be easily converted to a table by adding legs and used wherever desired.

Other unusual features of the library are:

(1) A completely packaged ceiling system which includes acoustical treatment and heating, cooling, and lighting componenets, all carefully integrated to work as a complete system. All heating coils and ductwork are located in easily accessible space above the suspended ceiling tiles, thereby eliminating the need to use valuable wall or floor space.

(2) The lighting system, best described as a recessed factory type fixture with non-glare features, is capable of producing a minimum of 70 footcandles of illumination at task level.

(3) One-foot by two-foot perforated aluminum ceiling pans, painted a flat white and backed with two inches of insulation, provide acoustical treatment, as well as radiating heat within the library. The ceiling pans are easily removed, thereby making the entire space above the ceiling accessible for installation of future utilities and ease of servicing equipment.

(4) Bronze-tinted window glass has been used throughout the new addition to reduce glare and, in certain instances, to eliminate the need for window covering. The glass also reduces solar heat gain, making possible a sizeable reduction in the requirements for air conditioning equipment. Because of air conditioning, non-operable windows were installed whenever possible to avoid air leakage, dirt, and maintenance problems.

The purpose of Scarsdale's multi-media center is to make available to all students, as well as to teachers an abundance of resource materials not available previously in a conventional library. This, then, could not be a conventional "shush" center where students could not draw a deep breath.

It was necessary to recognize the importance of modern technology in extending opportunities for independent study and group instruction. There was the problem of facilitating greater and more efficient use of new media by:

(1) Housing a wide range of equipment and materials in an attractive facility conducive to indpendent study.

(2) Organizing an abundance of appropriate material — printed and non-printed — in a way which would permit the user to find a significant body of information quickly and easily.

(3) Making a wider variety of equipment readily accessible for use by an individual without concern about complicated machinery or entangling administrative procedure.

Perhaps Scarsdale's new library can be described as an educational facility which has captured some of the vibrancy of the entertainment world. Quite like the discotheque and the au-go-go, we have tried to design a facility that is inviting, that is a fun place to go because it offers something that comes alive. It is a facility which students can share as part of a group or go solo if they wish. It is a place where they don't have to be the best in order to participate and grow.

WEST LEYDEN'S CENTER FOR

INSTRUCTIONAL MATERIALS

Kenneth I. Taylor

Since its opening in November, 1959, West Leyden's Center for Instructional Materials has received a considerable degree of local recognition and approval. There is evidence now of growing state and national interest in its plan for co-ordinated services and staff responsibilities. Floor plans, photographs, and information on design and administration are now being distributed on a national basis. Although the idea of a materials center is admittedly not new today, examples of complete coordination in actual practice are still limited in number. West Leyden's Center is actually the first in any high school in Illinois to be designed originally and entirely around the concept.

ORIGINAL OBJECTIVES

Two educational objectives influenced the design of the Center. First was the desire to bring together all instructional materials into one area of the school and

Reprinted with permission from: Taylor, Kenneth I., "West Leyden's Center for Instructional Materials," SCHOOL LIBRARY JOURNAL, April 15, 1961. Copyright ©1961, R. R. Bowker Company.

to treat them alike. The aim in particular was to facilitate student use of every media.

The second objective was to encourage class visits and allow students to use supplementary collections under the guidance of their teachers and consultants in instructional materials.

DESIGN

The triangular design allowed efficient placement of four reading rooms adjacent to the central Browsing and General Reference Room. A natural entry was created at the tip of the triangle. From this point of entry, students find the relationships of the five rooms relatively easy to understand. Windows throughout provide a maximum degree of supervision of the Center from almost any point in any reading room. Walls may be moved, whenever desired, to modify the design.

CATALOGS

Any kind of instructional material may be found through the main card catalog in the Browsing and General Reference Room. A public shelf list in this catalog indicates the classified relationship of all media in Dewey order. It also indicates the location of items which are kept on extended or permanent loan in any of the departments around the school.

In addition to this main catalog, the four other reading rooms, the Teachers' Workroom, and the Audiovisual Services Area have individual catalogs for their respective collections. Dual cataloging is thus provided for all materials.

BROWSING AND GENERAL REFERENCE ROOM

The central Browsing and General Reference Room contains the main card catalog. In this room are located light fiction, encyclopedias, magazines, general pamphlets, paperbacks, and reserve books. Two charging desks, located at each side of the entry are used, one for two-week books and the other for additional materials. Lounge furniture is located at the rear.

FOUR ADDITIONAL READING ROOMS

At the left of the Browsing and General Reference Room is the Contemporary Life Reading Room, so named because the major part of the collection pertains to the social sciences. Around its walls are shelved books from 000 to 499. At the end of the collection are the reference books for this area. National, state, and local newspapers, college catalogs, and vocational pamphlets are also here. The room seats 40 students.

At the rear left of the Browsing and General Reference Room is a collection called "Investigation and Invention." The pure and applied sciences in this area, of course, run from 500 to 699. Space is available for trade journals in a vertical file. This room, like other separate rooms, has its individual card catalog.

To the right of this room is Man's Heritage, the art, music, sports, and literature books of the 700's and 800's. Of special interest to librarians is the classification of great novels in the 823's, separated in this manner from the light fiction in the Browsing and General Reference Room. An exhibit table allows displays of small books, art prints, photographs, and similar items. A 41-by-28 inch blueprint cabinet holds a collection of 22-by-28 inch mounted art prints, which are loaned for classroom or home study.

The final reading room, Records of the Past, includes the 900's. Here is located the large biography collection characteristic of high schools. An atlas case, a vertical file, and a 48-by-36 inch blueprint cabinet are used for map storage.

CLASS USE OF THE READING ROOMS

Teachers are encouraged to schedule the reading rooms for class visits. Classes enter quietly to use the rooms for reading and reference purposes. Classroom activities such as lectures and group discussions are not carried on in reading rooms. Provisions for these activities are made in the conference rooms or the Individual Study and Directed Research Room. Moreover, a visiting class does not have a monopoly on any reading room. Individual students from study hall may enter and use the collections at any time. Members of the class, on the other hand, may leave the room for any materials which may be located in another area. They return, however, to the originally scheduled room for study.

OTHER SERVICE AREAS

The Individual Study and Directed Research Room is used for group work, lectures, debates, showing of films to several classes at one time, and experiments with television projection. The room may be divided with a folding wall. Light work tables can easily be shifted for group study.

The Audiovisual Services Area uses blueprint cabinets for storage of filmstrips and small graphic arts equipment, such as stencils, coloring pencils, and lettering devices, which are loaned to students and teachers. Projection equipment, phonographs, and tape recorders are kept on steel storage shelves. Preview and recording rooms are frequently used for conference purposes.

The Teachers' Workroom is equipped with lounge furniture and contains educational books, periodicals, and pamphlets.

SEATING CAPACITY

Each of the four reading rooms accommodates a class of 30 students plus ten to 16 students from study hall. The Center is adjacent to the one study hall of the school, located at the left but not shown on the diagram (see p. 177), and seats 160 students. Students from the study hall enter through the two doors of the Individual Study and Directed Research Room. When this room is in use, they use the corridor and the main entry.

ADDITIONAL STATISTICS

West Leyden High School was built to accommodate 2,400 students. This fall, it has 1,200 freshmen, sophomores, and juniors. Enrollment will continue to grow each year.

The Center contains 11,900 square feet of floor space. Its five reading rooms seat 210 students. The Individual Study and Directed Research Room can be arranged to seat more than 100 people for lecture purposes.

Two storage rooms, 12 by 32 feet, are available. One has two- and three-foot depth commercial steel shelving for storage of class sets and museum models. The other has shelving for the equivalent of 100 periodical titles for ten years.

The Center can shelve 18,000 books. Its present collection numbers over 8,000 volumes. It has over 600 filmstrips and more than 300 phonograph records, but can store many more. In addition, it loans maps, pamphlets, tapes, motion pictures, exhibits, museum models, and prints.

The staff consists of three consultants in instructional materials and two full-time clerical workers.

Student assistants operate equipment in classrooms and perform services in the Center. Although they specialize in certain types of services and materials, their responsibilities are rotated to provide a variety of experiences for each. A course of study is followed. One-half academic credit is given for one year's service and study. Part-time students volunteer services whenever their time permits.

One year of operation indicates the soundness of co-ordinated instructional services and materials in one area of a school. It is important, however, that departments have been encouraged to build individual collections of frequently consulted reference materials. These collections, of course, are recorded in the Center to allow maximum use of all materials by all school personnel.

Proximity of collections and uniform classification and cataloging enable staff members to find relationships among printed, graphic, projection, and transmission materials.

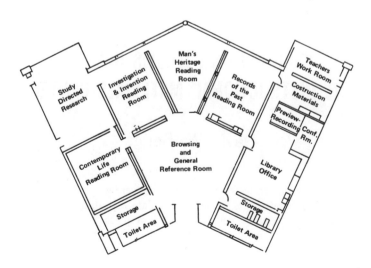

The four reading rooms, with collections numbered in sequence and clearly marked, reduce the amount of instruction in classification usually needed. Students understand the purpose of the various collections with greater ease.

Class visits increase the general activity of the Center but create few additional problems of control. In fact, an additional supervisor is gained for each group of thirty students. Needless to say, this is a lower pupil-teacher ratio than is normally granted a library staff. Thus, the more classes visiting, the greater the supervision.

Whenever collections are grouped by rooms, it is believed advisable to permit as much student freedom as possible. Students have been allowed to move from one room to another.

In the audio visual area, students have received instruction in the use of A-V materials (once thought to be for teacher use only) and in one year, there has been a definite increase in student use of audiovisual materials in individual and group projects.

The plan of the Center is not perfect. Experience will indicate where continued improvements may be made. Nevertheless, distinct advantages were originally gained by encouraging staff specialists in instructional materials to design the quarters.

It may be true that experiments in design such as this are the proper work of large schools as part of their program of educational research. If so, possibilities for continued work in design are present today as new schools are constructed. The benefits of these experiments, once proved, should, of course, be extended to all.

ORGANIZATION FOLLOWS USE . . .
THE INSTRUCTIONAL MATERIALS CENTER

David W. Beggs

The establishment of an instructional materials center in a school is a healthy sign that the school is getting its *knowing* up to date with its *doing*.

An instructional materials center (IMC) is a place where ideas, in their multimedia and diverse forms, are housed, used, and distributed to classrooms and laboratories throughout the school. The IMC contains books, magazines,

Reprinted with permission from: Beggs, David W., "Organization Follows Use . . . The Instructional Materials Center," AUDIOVISUAL INSTRUCTION, November, 1964.

pamphlets, films, filmstrips, maps, pictures electronic tapes, recordings, slides, transparencies, mock-ups, and learning programs.

An accurate description of the IMC is clouded if operational activities aren't defined. Essentially the center is a service agency for students and teachers to facilitate the teaching-learning process. It is the nerve center of the school's total instructional resources.

In accordance with the current educational psychological theory, which dictates that learning is an active process, the center is the place where students can actively pursue meaningful study. They can be observed viewing films, listening to records, working with teaching machines, constructing mock-ups, or doing research papers. The IMC is frequently built or remodeled so that "quiet" areas are provided for some activities and "noise" zones handle others. Conference rooms often surround the IMC, and teachers use it as a home base and can be seen developing teaching materials or working with students.

It is important for the effective school systematically to acquire and distribute materials to appropriate classrooms. The staff of the center keeps the flow of old and current materials going to all the classrooms in the building. The IMC is characterized by the ease with which students and teachers can use the many kinds of materials on hand. As new topics are considered in class, a rich body of information is immediately at hand for teachers and students. When a history class studies the New Deal, for example, they can make use of records of President Roosevelt's speeches, films of related events, and appropriate reference books.

LEARNING THEORY AND THE IMC

The search for ways to individualize instruction is partially fulfilled by the establishment of an IMC. Individualized instruction requires an abundance of varied materials and spaces for uninterrupted work by students operating at different rates and on different levels of investigation.

Careful analysis of the research indicates youngsters learn best when an appeal is made to several of the human senses; that is, some learn best when they hear or listen; and others learn best when they see or read. Even more effective learning may take place when a combination of seeing and hearing is employed. Therefore, the school needs to collect books and recordings, pamphlets and electronic tapes, magazines, and filmstrips, and many sources of information in as many diverse forms as possible.

Much of the learning students do is accomplished as a result of class activity, not necessarily during the class period itself. The stirring lecture or the stimulating discussion contributes to the desire for additional knowledge. The IMC is the place where students satisfy their need to know, where learners internalize their understandings.

If the sensible trend in school schedules toward more independent study time for students increases, as advocated in the guidelines of the Trump Plan, it is necessary that students have an appropriate place to carry out their individual study. The IMC is the logical place for students to work, since materials and space are available in one building.

Within the last few years, even months, a vast array of new instructional materials have been developed. In business education, for example, there are excellent tapes which students can use individually to improve shorthand skills. Recordings of the Nashville Sit-In Strike cannot help but increase students' knowledge of the racial situation. Drafting students can refine the techniques of their art by using transparencies of architectural designs, and mathematics can become clearer as the result of the use of programed learning materials. Poetry becomes more than rhyme and meter when one hears Dylan Thomas read his own poems.

In almost every subject publishers and film producers have developed materials geared to various levels of complexity. Realistic knowledge about the student population's interests and abilities are a must for the center's staff, since this understanding guides the staff in procuring the right magazines and films, appropriate books, useful mock-ups, and other learning tools.

A NEW ARRANGEMENT OF SPACE

The recognition that diverse activities will go on in the functioning IMC means adequate space needs to be provided and arranged in junctional ways for the center to meet its purposes. Areas must be set up where students can read without interruption, type or work on teaching machines freely, and view filmstrips or listen to recordings at any time. Careful planning of individual and group work spaces in quiet and noise zones will make this possible.

While it is difficult to generalize about space requirements, the IMC needs to be far bigger than the traditional school library. Certainly there is justification for an instructional materials center that is larger than a gymnasium. Indpendent study ought to have a higher priority in space allocation than basketball. The center should be of a size capable of accommodating the maximum number of pupils who will use it at any given time. If, for example, a school of 1,500 students is to be organized in such a manner that students will spend 30 percent of their time in independent study, the center should be able to handle 450 students. Division of the space within the IMC will vary in schools according to the kinds of learning activities that are to be available. For example, a school which plans on large holdings of recordings and tapes will require more listening stations than a school with less emphasis on listening activities for students.

Creative and thoughtful planning of facilities should precede any building remodeling or new construction. A few years ago special rooms were being provided for students to listen to recordings. Today, however, schools are leaning toward using special record players that are built into tables and equipped with head sets. This requires less space and expense than special acoustical rooms and, at the same time, makes it possible for several students to listen to a single recording at one time.

Tables for four to eight students are used less frequently than individual desks in instructional materials centers. Tables for four or more students are built-in communications centers; these belong in seminar rooms. Students have a right to a place to study in the center without being distracted by another student at their elbows or across a table.

The center should be located so that easy access to its many resources is possible. Often the IMC is placed in the center of the building, in the middle of the school's traffic.

It is sensible to have teachers' offices and work rooms adjoin the IMC, since this helps bring teachers, students, and materials close together. Easy access to instructors will encourage students to seek more conferences with their teachers. Constructive supervision can be given students simply by having teachers work in the same area where students are studying. Teaching is done by example instead of by direction.

MULTIMEDIA COORDINATION

Coordinated organization of materials is characteristic of a good instructional materials center. The nerve center of the IMC is the central catalog, the guide to every source of information and resource a school has. Some schools cross-reference their holdings with the city's public library. For example, the Lakeview High School in Decatur, Illinois, has included films and other teaching aids in its catalog which are housed in the central office of the city's public library. In this way students and teachers are not limited to the school's holdings in their study.

By including everything available to students in the catalog, full advantage can be taken of various learning resources. A color coding on the reference cards lets students know through what media information is presented. Books, for instance, may be on white cards, films on blue cards, transparencies on green cards, electronic tapes on pink cards, and so forth. When a teacher or student wants to locate information on World War II, for example, he will be able to study maps, electornic tapes, films, books, and magazines. Not only can he select the topic but he can also choose the media.

Instructional aids kept in classrooms should be included in the IMC catalog so they can be used for special study. Mock-ups of the human body, of steam engines, or of atomic structures, for example, may have their home base in the classrooms, but they can be made available for use by students as needed. The card catalog gives their location in the building.

Two approaches are possible in organizing materials in the IMC. Some house all materials on one topic together, regardless of media; others organize items by the media. So long as the catalog is complete and access to materials is easily available to students, the method of organization of materials isn't critical. Facilities and the judgment of IMC personnel govern the decision.

EVERY STAFF MEMBER'S BUSINESS

Orientation of teachers to the philosophy and operation of the IMC deserves prominent attention. The center is more than a library, and teachers need to understand this.

Hopefully the staff will use the center as course content is selected and learning experiences are structured. If they do this, students will follow in using the center in studying diverse routes to a single problem.

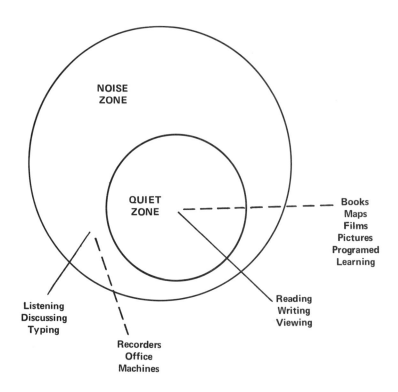

Administrative edict and a rearrangment of facilities alone will not cause the center to fulfill its purpose: an intensive on-the-job education program also is necessary. Staff meetings in the IMC aimed at failiarizing teachers with the collection will go a long way in insuring its use.

The preparation of bibliographies by the IMC staff is helpful, but there is good reason to provide some special time, perhaps in the preschool orientation week or during institute days, when teachers can work on bibliographic preparation. After each teacher has been through the stacks, studied the community resource file, listened to tapes and records, and viewed films, the IMC staff can prepare course lists secure in the knowledge that the teacher has a general knowledge of what is on hand and where it is located.

Teachers should be encouraged to contribute suggestions for additions to the center's holdings. Each staff member should have a sense of ownership of the IMC.

By placing the spirit duplicator and mimeograph machines in the center, teacher traffic will be insured. This will stimulate use of IMC materials.

The school administrator needs to exercise positive leadership in developing solid understandings of the importance of the center. The IMC shouldn't grow like Topsy, but needs frequent and sustained attention by the building principal.

Regular evaluation of the operation of the enterprise, of personnel, of procedures, and of contents will help it develop in use and effectiveness.

INDIVIDUALIZED INSTRUCTION

Every school, regardless of its size, has the beginnings of an instructional materials center. Leadership is needed to harness its resources, point out its advantages, and get it into operation. The IMC is a manifestation of the belief that *individuals* are taught, not *subjects.* The center is the place where a student can go to learn at his own rate and on his own level of understanding. As the IMC comes into its own in the school, teachers will depart from the single text to allow the goal of individualized instruction to become a reality.

The practice or requiring a pass or permit to go to the IMC is contrary to its purpose. Freedom to find, ease to use, and stimulation to seek are emblematic of the IMC.

Students should be given freedom to pursue diverse learning activities. If an adolescent can get satisfaction from his work, control problems are at a minimum. In their studying, readers should read; nonreaders should listen; notebook constructors should paste, cut, and arrange. The most appropriate method for each student to learn should be his path to understanding. In this case the means are not as critical as the end.

A BENCH MARK OF EXCELLENCE

For generations we have taught as we were taught, largely by listening to the teacher. Yet we know this results in less efficient learning than when students are highly involved and active in the learning process.

The demands of this age require better and more learning. The establishment of an instructional materials center is a means to greater effectiveness in learning. A school with an IMC has a bench mark of excellence of educational opportunity.

American education is on the move. New curricula, better patterns of organizing for instruciton, and the instructional materials center are signs of the time. While the concept of the center now is well accepted, its application still leaves much to be developed, recommended, and explored.

Section Four

THE COLLEGE
AND UNIVERSITY

CORTLAND'S TEACHING MATERIALS CENTER

Carl T. Cox

FOR SEVERAL YEARS, teachers' colleges have been faced with the problems of curriculum publications and teaching materials. Public school systems are producing an almost endless flow of courses of study and resource units; textbook publishers continue to improve their products and increase their output; new and better audio-visual materials appear daily.

From time to time articles in professional library and education journals have offered suggestions. College librarians discussed their efforts in solving the problem. Audio-visual directors have given their solution. Yet the questions still exist: How should these materials be organized? Which college agency should be responsible for the materials?

Realizing the importance of these materials to the teacher training program, the State University College of Education at Cortland has organized a Teaching Materials Center. This article is written in the hope that others who face the same questions will gain from our experiences.

In 1956 a committee from the College Library and the Education Department met to discuss the situation. Some years earlier, due to crowded physical conditions, the library had created a Seminar Library which housed all books in Dewey classifications 100's and 370's, elementary and secondary textbooks, and curriculum bulletins. This library was not staffed, doubled as a classroom, and was not meeting the needs of the student and faculty member.

After several meetings, the committee agreed that the Seminar Library should be reorganized, placed under the direction of a librarian, and open at all times to the student body.

Since the library was already understaffed, and since the new organization would be a part of the Education Department, actively engaged in its instructional program, the department filled an instructional position with a professional librarian. Funds were allocated for clerical personnel, new shelving, and additional file cabinets. The Teaching Materials Center was charged with the responsibility of acquiring, organizing, circulating, and giving instruction in the use of curriculum publications, textbooks, filmstrips, recordings, and other teaching materials. The reorganization began on September 1, 1957.

Reprinted by permission from the November, 1960, issue of the WILSON LIBRARY BUL-LETIN. Copyright © 1960 by The H. W. Wilson Company.

The first step was the collection of curriculum bulletins. Letters which explained our program were mailed to all New York State school systems and to some one hundred systems throughout the country. As they were received, these publications were placed in a vertical file. They are arranged by curriculum area and subdivided by grade level.The system used is an adaptation of Miss Eleanor Merritt's Major Filing System, which was developed at Iowa State Teachers College.

Under our system, each publication has a minimum of three cards – a shelf list card (on which are placed the tracings), a subject card and a "location-subject" card. A sample shelf list card follows:

```
┌─────────────────────────────────────────────────────────────┐
│ ┌─────────────┐                                              │
│ │ File I      │                                              │
│ │             │                                              │
│ │ Sec 15      │        Chicago, Illinois.  Public schools.   │
│ │             │           Teaching guide for mathematics; kinder-│
│ │ No A 12     │        garten through junior high school.  1957.│
│ │   TMC       │           79 p.  (Curriculum guide series).  │
│ └─────────────┘                                              │
│                                                              │
│                                                              │
│                        1. Arithmetic.  Curriculum guide.     │
│                        2. Mathematics.  Curriculum guide. 3. Chicago,│
│                        Illinois.  Mathematics.               │
│                                                              │
│                                 ◯                            │
└─────────────────────────────────────────────────────────────┘
```

Every effort is made to maintain a current collection. This requires a constant checking of the Checklist of Documents in *Education Index,* the Curriculum Bulletins sections of *Educational Leadership,* LC's *Monthly Checklist of State Publications,* and lists which appear in educational periodicals. Annually our collection is checked against ASCD's *Curriculum Materials.* There is much duplication in these lists. However, to date, they have proven to be the most useful listings available.

Working through the New York State Association of Educational Salesmen, the new program was explained to the textbook publishers. Their response was overwhelming. Within a short time, the textbook collection had grown from an outdated conglomeration of texts, manuals, and workbooks to a collection of current texts and series representing the products of forty-four publishing companies. These are arranged by subject area, subdivided by publishing company and grade level. For each series or independent text, three cards are prepared:

(1) A publisher's card contains a listing of all texts in the series and serves as an inventory to our holdings. All tracings are included on this card.

(2) A series card which is a copy of the publisher's card.

(3) A subject card which contains the note "For TMC holdings, see series card."

A sample publisher's card follows:

```
T501
G434s        Ginn and Company. Science.
G 1-8    Craig, Gerald S.
             Science today and tomorrow series, by Gerald S. Craig and
         others. Ginn, Boston, 1958.

             TMC HAS:
         Prim.  Science and you          M      T      W
         G 1    Science near you         M      T      W
         G 2    Science around you       M      T      W
         G 3    Science everywhere       M      T      W
         G 4    Discovering with science M      T      W
         G 5    Adventuring in science   M      T      W
         G 6    Experimenting in science M      T      W
                        (See card 2)
                            O
```

```
T501
G434s        Ginn and Company. Science.
G 1-8    Craig, Gerald S.
             Science today and tomorrow series . . . Card 2

             TMC HAS:
         G 7    Learning with science    M      T      W
         G 8    Facing tomorrow with     M      T      W
                Science


             1. Science. Textbooks. Elementary schools. 2. Science. Text-
         books. Junior high schools. I Science today and tomorrow series.
         II Ginn and Company. Science.
                            O
```

All texts in the series are listed. The letters M (manual), T (teacher's edition), W (workbook) and WT (teacher's edition of the workbook) are used to indicate our holdings of these titles. In the above science series, we have one copy of each teacher's edition. When other books in the series are received, the number of titles is penciled in following the title or appropriate letter. This eliminates the necessity of cataloging each item individually.

Although we automatically receive all new titles from many publishers, we annually check our holdings against *Textbooks in Print*. When new titles are discovered, a request for sample copies is made through the local publisher's representative.

In September, 1957, the College Campus School and several faculty members deposited two hundred filmstrips and seventy-five recordings in the TMC. None of these were cataloged and many were antiquated. Using these as a nucleus, the

Center has developed a fully cataloged collection of 1250 filmstrips, 223 records, and 158 record albums. Filmstrips are cataloged by title, subject and series. When possible, Library of Congress cards are used. If LC's are not available, filmstrips are cataloged locally. *Filmstrip Guide, Educator's Guide to Free Filmstrips,* producers' blurbs, and distributors' catalogs are helpful in preparing the catalog cards.

Records present a more difficult cataloging problem. Many of our recordings contain four to ten selections, while others contain only one. In all cases, the record title serves as a main entry. Each selection, author and composer and series is traced. Virginia Clarke's *Non-Book Library Materials* (Denton, North Texas State College Print Shop, 1953) proved very helpful while establishing our system. As in the case of filmstrips, record call numbers consist of a symbol followed by the accession number.

After overcoming the major hurdles in a reorganization process, the Teaching Materials Center initiated its program of instruction. During their sophomore year, all education majors are enrolled in methods and materials courses. The TMC encourages each instructor to hold a minimum of three classes in the Center.

The first class, given during the first two weeks of the course, is a general orientation period. The second class, given at the time the class is developing teaching and/or resource units, is designed to assist the student in the use of materials for his unit. The TMC staff member conducting the class develops a unit using all materials available in the Center or the College Library. A third class, held at the discretion of the instructor, may be designed to evaluate textbooks, preview filmstrips, study curriculum guides or standardized tests. The TMC staff may work directly with the students or only with the faculty member as he plans the class.

Cortland seniors, after a full semester of practice teaching, are registered in an education seminar. In cooperation with the seminar instructors, the TMC conducts workshops in teaching materials. These workshops spend five weeks studying the availability, use, and evaluation of various teaching devices. When students have accepted a position, they may use this workshop for a study of the materials which will be in their classroom the following year.

The Teaching Materials Center has not solved all problems facing the teachers colleges in the area of curriculum materials. Nor have we solved all problems facing the College of Education at Cortland. Within two years, our new library building will be completed and a new education building will be in use. Areas of responsibility must be clearly defined, staffing problems must be met, and budgetary matters must be solved. However, we feel that the Teaching Materials Center is a move in the right direction and other colleges may profit from similar organizations.

A COMPLETE MATERIALS CENTER

John Moldstad and Harvey Frye

At his televised news conference on March 23, President Kennedy alerted the nation to the dangers in the Laotian situation. To make his message more vivid, he referred to three six-by-eight-feet, staff-prepared maps of Laos to show advances made by Communist forces.

The President was showing by example the best kind of teaching – that which is strengthened with instructional aids. He was also giving example to the recommendation put forth by his predecessor's science advisory committee in its report, "Education for the Age of Science": "Finally, and perhaps most urgently, we must devote very substantial resources to developing and supplying teachers with far more adequate and up-to-date teaching and learning aids of all kinds."

Up-to-date instructional aids include a vast range of films and filmstrips, pictures and posters, magnetic and pegboard materials, models and specimens, maps and transparencies. No educator would argue that these items, and the equipment for projecting and displaying them, should be at the ready of every teacher. The only question has been the familiar one of budgeting. And tools for teaching have always run a poor third to outlay for plant expansion and teachers salaries. Now, under Title III of the National Defense Education Act, funds have been made available for audiovisual equipment and materials. Educators now face a new question: should they buy or make their own?

Certainly there is no dearth of materials available commercially. Wilson's *Educational Film Guide* lists 18,900 titles and *Filmstrip Guide* lists over 12,000. Add to this the growing stockpile of complete courses on film: the Encyclopaedia Britannica Film's 106 half-hour series on chemistry (produced by American Chemical Society), the 162 White physics films, the 120 half-hour set on biology by the American Institute of Biological Sciences, and kinescopes of the televised programs *See It Now, You Are There, Twentieth Century,* and *Continental Classroom.*

But despite this embarrassment of audiovisual riches, many instructors make little use of them. Why? Because they often aren't related specifically enough to the curriculum units they teach. Best answer, then, is to provide facilities for producing audio-visual aids on the spot to supplement those available commercially. They can be custom-made by the staff precisely to meet their own specifications – and sometimes as a cash saving over purchase or rental prices.

Locally-produced materials have several advantages over those on the market. First of all, they're up-to-the-minute. There is normally a considerable lag

Reprinted with permission of AMERICAN SCHOOL AND UNIVERSITY, Buttenheim Publishing Corp., from: Moldstad, John and Frye, Harvey, "A Complete Materials Center." May, 1961.

between the time an event happens and the time it can be worked into an instructional aid and marketed. But if they have their own production facilities, teachers can clip a map in today's newspaper or a picture on this week's *Life,* make an overhead transparency, and project it in class immediately to show the latest invention, economic crisis, or (as the President did) political development.

Another advantage of locally-produced materials is the flexibility they allow the instructor. Take the case of a closed-circuit class on physiology. The TV instructor finds the right diagram of the human digestive system in a reference book, photographs it, and makes a large photographic print to project on the TV screen. Then he has smaller duplicates made and circulates these along with the lesson outline to the teachers who will be tuning in to his lecture. Finally, he has 2 x 2 slides made up of the diagram for each teacher to use in follow-up study.

Still another advantage: with facilities for developing their own visual materials, instructors can practice "frontiersmanship" and try out new teaching methods – the "set theory" in mathematics, for example, or the use of visuals in language instruction.

The value to the student of teaching aids tailored to the specific class is obvious enough. (Imagine the vo-ag student's heightened interest in the problem of soil erosion when he sees photographic samples taken right from his own locality.) But values accrue to the instructor as well. The very act of creating a teaching aid – whether bulletin board, display model, slide, or tape recording – helps the instructor to evaluate the content of this presentation. (One university professor, highly respected in his academic specialty, revised six times a complex table he was to use in a visualized lecture before he felt it communicated precisely the point he wanted to get across.)

Too, the instructor quickly learns how to evaluate the points in his message, to decide which need to be nailed down with a visual image and which do not. As he uses the media he comes to know the advantages and limitations of each. And since he is using his own talents and energies in developing his instructional aids, he can blame no one but himself if his message is not communicated.

Some instructional aids can be produced right in the classroom, but most of them can't. To get full mileage out of locally-produced materials, the school or college should set up an audio visual studio equipped with basic production equipment. The plan sketched on the next page is a good example. It is equipped with all the equipment needed to produce instructional materials with the exception of motion pictures (and even equipment for producing these could be added, though it requires specially trained personnel).

Obviously teachers can no longer be expected to provide good instruction given only a blackboard, a few maps, and the loan of a filmstrip. They need ready access to the full range of instructional materials. Our advice to the educator who is intent on improving instruction is this: don't ignore the materials available commercially, but don't let go by default those that can be produced better right on the premises.

WHAT TO HAVE AND WHERE TO PUT IT

(O)WORKROOM
- A—air brush
- B—copy camera
- C—diazo duplicator
- D—lettering equipment
- F—dry-mounting press
- H—storage

I —light table
J —cutting board
P —sink
Q—spirit duplicator
R—stencil duplicator
T—35mm copy stand
U—work table

(G) DARKROOM
- K—enlarger
- L—trays, sink
- M—dryer
- N—washer

(S) OFFICE & STORAGE
- E—motion picture editor

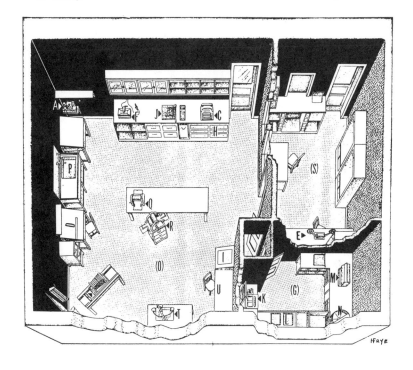

FLORIDA ATLANTIC UNIVERSITY: WHERE TOMORROW BEGINS

Len Singer

On a 1,200-acre site in Boca Raton on Florida's Gold Coast, construction is underway for a new and radically different state university which will be the embodiment of bold educational concepts.

Florida Atlantic University, the newest member of Florida's system of higher education, joins a growing family which now includes five universities, 29 community junior colleges, and an Institute for Continuing University Studies. Although it will not receive its first class until the fall of 1964, Florida Atlantic University has already been hailed by writers as "a bold new idea in education," "unique in the nation," and "a space-age dream."

A distinctive feature of FAU is that it will offer only upper-division undergraduate instruction and graduate and post-baccalaureate professional work. The responsibility for the first two years of college will be left to the community junior colleges or other institutions of higher learning. At FAU every effort will be made to minimize the lock-step, time-serving characteristics of conventional programs. Study units will be so organized that a student will progress at a rate consistent with his competence. A *minimum* of 40 percent of the student's time will be spent in independent study, and those characteristics of a specially tailored program now associated with "honors programs" will be offered to every student.

Conspicuous by their absence will be the highly competitive varsity athletic teams, the stadium, the marching bands, baton-twirlers, fraternities, sororities, and other activities normally associated with university life. In their stead will be a dynamic campus whose buildings reflect the excitement of learning and whose image will be that of a true "center of learning" rather than a "facility for teaching." In this setting, vibrant professors and mature students will benefit by FAU's new techniques of instruction, new fields of research, new areas of service, and new patterns of faculty-student contact.

These facts alone should be enough to make educators across the country regard America's newest experimental university with more than passing interest. Of particular importance to AUDIOVISUAL INSTRUCTION readers, however, is the development of a Division of Learning Resources which will unite under one administrative area all media and technology and develop a systems approach to their use.

Reprinted with permission from: Singer, Len, "Florida Atlantic University: Where Tomorrow Begins," AUDIOVISUAL INSTRUCTION, April, 1963.

The report of The Planning Commission for this institution specifically recommended that learning resources should be basic to the operation of the program and that such a program should put "at the disposal of students all of the materials and aids to learning that will enable them to achieve maximal results with minimal requirements of faculty direction and supervision."

The centrality of learning resources to the institution's program was assured with the appointment of Kenneth Rast Williams as president of the new institution. An experiment-oriented educator, President Williams is keenly aware of the significance of newer educational media and sensitive to dynamisms in each media unit that need to be explored and released. Through his work as an administrator and consultant, Kenneth Williams has become a recognized proponent of the systems approach to the use of all media and technology. One of the first staff members he appointed was a director of Learning Resources charged with the responsibility of developing a Learning Resources Division which would bring the recommendations of the Planning Commission to fruition.

LEARNING RESOURCES DEFINED

The Division of Learning Resources at Florida Atlantic University is concerned essentially with non-human tools and embraces virtually all media, technology, and services that contribute to the communication of ideas in the university life of the learner and instructor. It includes those tools and resources which will enable the professor to communicate more efficiently and thus make learning more effective for all students. These same tools and resources will also enable students to engage in more profitable independent study. We have, therefore, defined two main functions of the Learning Resources Division – which bear a remarkable similarity to the functions of media prescribed in the NEA Task Force Position Paper.

LEARNING RESOURCES – FUNCTION NO. 1

The first function of learning resources is to put at the disposal of the teaching faculty all media, technology, services, and systems which will enhance the effective communication of ideas in the pre-programed phase of learning.

LEARNING RESOURCES – FUNCTION NO. 2

The second function of learning resources is to put at the disposal of the student all media, technology, services, and systems which will enhance the effective communication of ideas in a self-programed phase of learning.

SYSTEMS DEFINED

It was immediately apparent that if learning resources were to enable students "to achieve maximal results with minimal requirements of faculty direction and supervision," a systems approach was called for – an approach that would result in less teacher-student control of classroom learning and greater dependence on

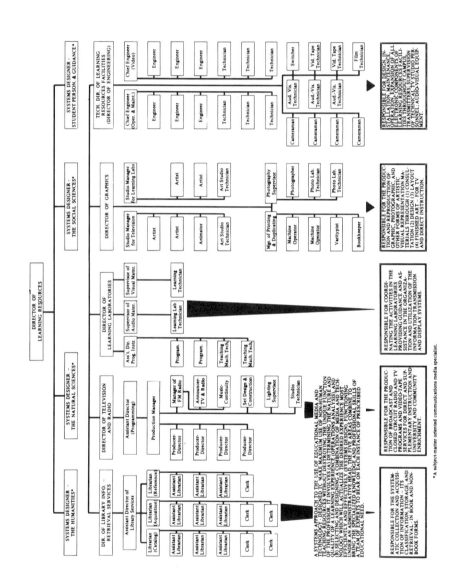

sources outside the classroom. It also became apparent that the complexity of instructional materials and sophisticated level of technology required to transmit meanings through the use of symbols called for a systematized approach rather than unguided or random selection by both the professor and student.

The systems approach to the use of learning resources at FAU will thus be a creative and imaginative use of the total complex of media and technology, achieved (1) by having the faculty prescribe the character, nature, and quality of a required educational experience and (2) by having systems designers select and create those combinations of media and technology which will actualize the prescribed experience.

The definition of instructional systems given in the NEA Task Force paper as "subject matter, procedures, and media coordinated in a program-unit design which is directed toward specific behavioral objectives" is one to which Florida Atlantic University can easily subscribe. Sidney Eboch's definition of *Systems* which also appeared in the January issue of this magazine is perhaps a more succinct description of our approach to learning resources — "a collection of parts which perform a unitary function when the parts are appropriately related and used in an organized manner."

Under this instructional system at Florida Atlantic University, the dean of Academic Affairs and Educational Research (under whom the director of Learning Resources will function) together with his faculty will construct well-defined educational situations in which the terminal behavior of learners will be identified. It will then be the responsibility of the Learning Resources staff to select, design, and create combinations of media and technology which will actualize the educational situations and bring the terminal behavior to fruition most efficiently and effectively. The specialized knowledge and professional skills of a team of experts will thus be brought to bear on each instance of educational need.

"A COLLECTION OF PARTS"

At Florida Atlantic University the "collection of parts which perform a unitary function" will consist of three distinct buildings or centers that will function in symbiosis to make up the learning-resource facilities of the University. One can appreciate the pre-eminence of learning resources in the University program when one takes into account that three of the first four buildings now under construction are its component centers.

LIBRARY AND INFORMATION STORAGE AND RETRIEVAL CENTER

The five-story Library and Information Storage and Retrieval Center, the largest building in the initial phase of construction, will provide room for 100,000 books in a gross area of 68,000 square feet. Ample land has been reserved for expanding the Library as future needs demand. At the time of the opening of the University, this expansion will most likely be imminent.

As media specialists can well imagine, to relocate the library under Learning Resources was in itself a move which aroused intense interest and excitement as well as a variety of emotions. Tradition-oriented librarians were startled to learn that the library, which had always been piously referred to as "the heart of the university," was now moved from its inviolate poistion into a learning resources complex. Some librarians expressed fear that to establish a new perspective for this facility would result in diminishing its role and scope within the university. However, at Florida Atlantic University we felt that by incorporating the library into Learning Resources we would enable it to develop its potential to the fullest and, in fact, unleash energies which had until now remained dormant. We believed that as part of Learning Resources, the library could improve its image and assume an integral role in the teaching-learning process.

There are strong indications that even the traditional university library will have to undergo drastic changes if it is to cope with the rapidly expanding body of knowledge demanded by the space age and its new curriculum. A national study revealed that in most universities, the library, instead of being the heart of the college, is more of an appendage — and not too important an appendage at that, since only ten percent of undergraduates make use of it.

Under the systems approach to learning resources, the librarian will be able to participate actively in every well-defined educational situation and will be directly involved in the problems of materials utilization. Simply to provide the student with books, journals, and other materials is no longer sufficient. The learner must be actively guided in the utilization of this material and helped with the problems of that utilization. Since the librarian will be functioning under the systems concept, he will necessarily be concerned that the information he dispenses will be used to serve the design of the system.

At Florida Atlantic University we recognized that the library would have to extend its interest far beyond traditional printed materials. As part of Learning Resources in a new experimental university, the library would have to employ new intellectual disciplines to keep pace with the rapidly developing intellectual revolution and would, therefore, have to adopt modern technology including maximum use of advanced data processing.

As part of a learning resources system, the library would no longer be thought of as "a place"; its new perspective would be that of a *function*, namely the systematic collection and acquisition of information — its classification, storage, and retrieval — in book and non-book forms.

It was encouraging that many reputable librarians were prepared to subscribe to this new role of the library. In his book *Advanced Data Processing In The University Library* (The Scarecrow Press Inc., 1962), Edward Heiliger wrote, "Librarians are eternally occupied with the need for more books, more space to put the books, and more staff to process the books. This seems to leave little time for an equally essential problem: how to make the books useful and meaningful to the users." Heiliger goes on to state that "a university library stands or falls on its contributions to the main task of the university — teaching students." He calls for a plan that would "integrate the library into a teaching program in a significant way." Heiliger recognizes that "one facet for this integration is a firsthand knowledge of each professor's work. With such a knowledge, the librarian could be forewarned of demands to be made of its services, could make the professor aware of additional library resources in course planning, and could gear its services to make the optimum contribution to the teaching situation."

Here was an outstanding leader in the library movement calling for a reconstruction of the library's image and a redefinition of its role such as the systems approach to learning resources is designed to accomplish. Librarians everywhere who share Heiliger's vision will also share in an appreciation of this significant advancement in the role and scope of the library.

THE TELEVISION AND RADIO PRODUCTION CENTER

The second center in our "collection of parts" is a highly sophisticated facility for producing broadcast and closed-circuit television programs, radio programs, and video-tape services. An open-circuit and six closed-circuit channels will serve the instructional program of the University as well as the needs of the community and other institutions and school systems. All studios and other specialized facilities necessary to this function are contained in this two-story building with an area of over 20,000 square feet. Transmitting facilities for the broadcast services will be located seven miles north of the campus where an 849-foot tower will provide 25,000-watt FM and 250,000-watt UHF coverage. The tower may eventually reach 1,049 feet and, according to James Etheridge, Jr., executive secretary of the Florida Educational TV Commission, "is really the key to educational TV in southeast Florida."

Like the library, television and radio as part of a learning resources system will have the opportunity to develop their potential to the fullest and to take on a new image. Perhaps in no other single media-unit can we find as great a source of untapped dynamisms as in television and radio. Robert Blakely, America's outstanding proponent of adult education, once said that educational television represents one of the best ways by which the individual can learn to possess himself by embracing all other men. In a commencement address in 1953, he said that "educational television challenges each finger, each neck, each stomach, each elbow to reflect on its relationship to the entire body and to learn how to express itself to other members and to the whole. Educational television can be the eyes and ears of the community looking at the various parts and learning how to be a whole." Today, ten years later, media specialists are still looking to television to fully realize this potential.

Equally challenging under the systems approach to learning resources is the opportunity to realize that television and radio are not just mass media of communication but means of selectively disseminating information to individuals and small groups of learners. This emphasis seems to have been relatively neglected in our concern for assembling more and more students in large auditoria to receive televised instruction.

At Florida Atlantic University, both perspectives of television and radio will be developed as the media are explored in an effort to release their remarkable capacities to reach, to interest, and to enlighten.

THE LEARNING LABORATORIES CENTER

The third building in our "collection of parts" is a two-story, three-sectioned building with an area of 43,000 square feet. This Center is designed to provide facilities for large-group instruction, medium-sized classes, small-group discussion, and individual learning. In these flexible learning spaces (some of which will be electronic learning laboratories), large groups, small groups, and individuals will be able to make effective use of all media and technology.

Except for science laboratories which will be housed in the fourth building now under construction, all instruction will be given in the Learning Laboratories Center where the electronic components for information transmission and display systems will be part of the structural design.

The same electronic componenets found in the independent study areas of this Center will be repeated in the dormitory rooms, student offices, and future facilities of the University, thus extending the capabilities of the Learning Laboratory Center throughout the campus.

The professional staff of the Learning Laboratories Center will coordinate the activities in the many flexible learning spaces and provide the guidance and professional assistance propaedeutic to the organization and use of programed instruction and audio and visual materials. To insure effective use of the physical plant as well as of the information and transmission and display systems, this staff will also provide instruction in the media and their utilization to the teaching faculty of all departments.

TWO SERVICE AGENCIES

In order to provide the most comprehensive professional service and back-up support for the three learning resource centers, two distinct and well-defined agencies have been brought into the system. At one time it may have been appropriate for two such agencies (graphics and technical) to operate as part of an audio-visual department, but for Florida Atlantic University this time is past. The learning resources system planned for the University will require of each agency a level of professional skill and sophistication demanding their separation.

The Graphics agency is responsible for the production and reproduction of graphic, photographic, and other forms of artistic, visual materials through (1) consultation, (2) design, (3) layout, and (4) finished art work.

For some time it has been recognized that a chief strength of television teaching is in the use of excellent visual materials, and that a graphics department is an important part of an educational television facility. More recently, the construction of auditoria with large rear-screen projection areas and automated lecterns has increased this demand for graphics. More than embarrassing, it is wasteful to place a professor behind a lectern containing rows of buttons capable of calling to the screen many forms of visual representation without providing the professional artists and craftsmen necessary for creating these materials. Then too, there's something economically and aesthetically unsound as well as pathetic about a well-paid, dynamic professor spending his time cutting out a picture from a magazine and clumsily pasting it onto a shirt cardboard in the hope of achieving a visual around which he can tailor a lecture to some 200 students.

The Graphics area of Learning Resources has been created to meet all challenges of symbology as they arise – for television, large auditorium lectures, and even for small seminar discussions. A professional staff of designers, artists, illustrators, letterers, animators, printers, and photographers trained in the science of symbology will provide services that go far beyond creating designs that are merely aesthetically satisfying.

The Technical service has been charged with the responsibility for the design, installation, maintenance, operation, and continuous expansion of all electronic components of the Learning Resources facilities. Transmitter engineers, all technical TV studio personnel, and technicians for audiovisual hardware will be assigned from this agency.

Functioning under a technical director of Learning Resources will be a staff of operations – maintenance engineers, video engineers, and technicians whose professional skills will insure the efficient operation of all electronic components used in information transmission and display systems.

SYSTEMS DESIGNERS

Exploratory discussions with Anna Hyer of DAVI and the staff of the Media Branch of the U.S. Office of Education emphasized the need for bringing a team of systems designers into the learning resources area. Accordingly, we have provided for four systems designers who will be content-oriented persons functioning as communications media specialists.

Three systems designers will represent the three instructional divisions of the University – the Humanities, the natural sciences and mathematics, and the social sciences. A fourth will relate himself to the areas of student personnel and guidance. In addition to teaching one or more courses in their respective areas, the systems designers will assume the responsibility for creating the coordinated program-unit designs directed toward specified behavioral objectives.

As new instructional programs or professional institutes are developed, they too, will be represented in the learning resources system by systems designers, thus assuring that the system will continue to function as an integral part of all university programs.

As our buildings begin to take shape, and the complexion of the old deserted airfield changes, we at Florida Atlantic University have the feeling that "we're on our way." We're not so naive as to think that the future is without problems. Many problems have already been identified and we're prepared to meet others. A particular concern at this point in our growth is the selection of a brilliant faculty that understands our objectives and subscribes to them without mental reservation. The Systems concept requires total individual and institutional-wide subscription.

Already over one thousand outstanding educators have indicated their interest in becoming associated with FAU, and a significant number of these have expressed an appreciation for the systems approach to learning resources that goes far beyond mere lip service. Their experience and backgrounds have convinced them that it makes sense to use machines to do what machines can do better than dynamic professors, and dynamic professors to do what dynamic professors can do better than machines. Many of these professors, who have read about and seen some of the new media have been like children pressing their noses against candy-store windows longing for a treat that appears beyond their reach. These educators see a learning resources system as the means for enhancing their own effectiveness as teachers and for vitalizing the independent study of their students.

These men and women are not gadgeteers — nor are we. Our mutual concern is that of discovering better ways of communicating ideas — newer and better techniques for providing quality education in an ideal center of learning. Soon, many of these educators will join the staff of this new institution and share with us in the excitement of being part of Florida Atlantic University — *where tomorrow begins.*

EMERGING INSTRUCTIONAL RESOURCES CENTERS IN STATE UNIVERSITY COLLEGES OF NEW YORK STATE

Frank Lane

In the past thirty years the ten State University of New York Colleges have undergone many changes. The most recent, and still in process, is the change to multipurpose institutions recommended in the 1960 Master Plan of the Trustees of the State University of New York. With rapidly expanding enrollments, curriculum offerings and physical facilities, the nature and function of the Colleges' audiovisual programs must also continue to alter — as indeed they have over the past thirty years. One who has known these colleges since the mid-thirties might propose a resume of the institutional changes to place in context the changes in audiovisual programs.

In the late thirties all of the institutions except the four-year degree granting Teachers College at Buffalo were "normal schools," primarily regional in nature and offering three-year curriculums. As single-purpose institutions, all prepared

Reprinted with permission from: Lane, Frank, "Emerging Instructional Resources Centers in State University Colleges of New York State," EDUCATIONAL SCREEN, April, 1964.

elementary teachers, though most also prepared teachers for one or two specialized areas such as Art, Music, Industrial Arts and Physical Education. In 1940 the nine institutions became teachers colleges and in 1942 — a mere twenty-two years ago — graduated their first four year degree candidates. In 1948 the ten colleges were among the institutions transferred from the State Education Department to the newly-established State University of New York.

The post-war expansion of higher education brought additional specialized teaching curriculums to some campuses, Master degree programs in elementary and secondary education and in administration and supervision to all ten, and more recently, programs preparing secondary school teachers. Residence halls and additional instructional facilities caused enrollments to increase from a range of 327-1004 in 1940 to 677-2022 in 1950. In 1960 the smallest college enrolled 1169 and the largest counted 3133 students. The range of 2250-8000 is anticipated by 1970. Conversion of these colleges from single-purpose institutions will be complete in 1965 when the last two will admit freshmen to the four year degree programs in arts and sciences.

During this thirty year period, the audiovisual program did not remain unchanged. Even before the term "audiovisual" was used, much of what it was to encompass was being practiced on these campuses. Courses in professional education provided the student with an understanding of the reasons for using various materials in instruction. In the campus school he observed the use of materials and equipment common in that era. Later he was expected to incorporate these in the teaching which he planned and ultimately executed as part of his training. He prepared a "materials file" — a collection predominantly of two-dimensional materials. Operation of 35mm and 3¼" x 4" slide projectors, 16mm film projectors, record players, and effective use of instructional materials outside the professional education department was unusual.

Gradually as a clearer concept of "audiovisual" emerged, as its psychological base was recognized and accepted more widely, as its first wave of enthusiasts appeared on the staffs of these colleges, course content began to be developed. Although responsible to a central administration, the State University Colleges traditionally enjoy a high degree of autonomy, particularly in curriculum design. Following workshops sponsored by the central administration some of the colleges chose to evolve discrete courses in audiovisual education, others chose to weave this content into a number of professional courses dealing with curriculum and methods — the "collecting" concept was giving way to the "communicating" concept. The student was being evaluated less on the *quantity of materials* amassed and more on the *skill in selection* and *use of materials and equipment* in the communication of knowledge, skills and attitudes.

The field was gradually "coming of age." Audiovisual Instructional Materials and Instructional Resources Centers were emerging. In some colleges these centers were established as a part of the library or the curriculum laboratory; in others they were separate. Most of these centers soon developed a "corps" of students, mainly voluntary, who served the college staff by operating and servicing the audiovisual equipment and by producing various photographic, graphic, and other instructional materials.

Though great technological changes and development have occurred in the past decade, the role of audiovisual education and of its staff continues basically the same as it was at the opening of the decade – with responsibility for the *improvement of instruction, organization* and *management,* and *service.* The excellence of its function in each of these roles provides the basis for its influence and leadership in each campus. For example, at the State University College at Brockport which is the college nearest the site of the 1964 DAVI Convention in Rochester, audiovisual education leadership is such that a discrete course is required of all students preparing for elementary and early secondary teaching. In addition, photography, television and production courses are offered as electives.

The required course in this college of 2100 students is a broad one. It is based on the principle that to be a skillfull teacher one must choose, create and use teaching materials and media appropriate to specific goals and identifiable characteristics of each learning group. General concepts are buttressed by hosts of examples brought to the attention of the student through course content (texts, and other reading materials), illustration (films, slides, tapes, graphics, etc. introduced and discussed in class), demontration (actual performance by college or campus school instructor), or experience (actual performance by the student either in the college or campus school classroom). As understanding and skill progress, the student is expected to demonstrate increasing ability to plan, select, produce, use and finally, to evaluate the contribution of the instructional resources to given teaching situations.

In organizing and managing its instructional materials and equipment, Brockport finds an "AV Center" essential. Specific equipment is assigned where it is used most frequently, but the control is centered in what is now called the *Instructional Resources Center.* Cataloguing, projecting, inspecting, servicing, scheduling, constructing, copying, laboratory instructing – all are carried on by the more than 25 students employed on a part-time basis who are responsible, under the direction of the Instructional Resources Staff, for over 300 pieces of equipment, more than 400 films and kinescopes, 4000 filmstrips and over 500 recordings owned by the college. To further aid students, it has been the policy since 1960, that a duplicate master card file of recordings showing their location on campus be available in the library. The library also has conference and teaching rooms complete with listening stations and booths.

Largely because of its strong AV program, Brockport began to experiment with closed circuit television in 1956. This first installation included two channels, a talkback system, 5 cameras and connections to 21 rooms. Although programmed and operated by a staff no longer directly responsible to the AV Director, this medium plays an important role in the students' understanding and acceptance of newer media in education. First, the medium is both audio and visual; second, it employs many of the best AV devices and practices; and third, many students have the opportunity to participate in the use of CCTV as a teaching device in either college of campus school.

CCTV provides the college student in Child Growth and Development classes the opportunity to observe the characteristics of children without the disturbance of entering their classrooms. Later, in methods and curriculum courses the student shifts his attention to observing the teacher via this medium. All students see the same thing at the same time and have the added advantage of simultaneous direction and comment by the college instructor. Kinescope recordings can be made but within the past few weeks the College has acquired a video tape recorder. It now becomes possible for the teacher himself to join observers for the analysis of an immediate re-run. Also, a college student may see his own image moments after he has taught – an experience which, with the assistance of a qualified supervisor, will aid him immeasurably in analyzing his teaching.

Geneseo, another nearby State University College, operates an FM radio station and, consequently, emphasizes this medium. Like Brockport, however, it also produces television programs in cooperation with RAETA – The Rochester Area Educational Television Association, for use by Rochester commercial TV stations.

The College of Potsdam, with a limited installation, uses its TV primarily for observation of campus school children and teaching. Open circuit television instruction has been developed on a limited exploratory basis by the colleges at Buffalo, Cortland, and Oswego.

Plattsburgh has reserved four portable tape recorders for use by student teachers in public schools to help them better analyze their work. An Oneonta professor has built his course in composition around the use of overlays with the opaque projector. Fredonia and Buffalo were recently selected by a leading business firm to receive equipment grants for proposed instructional experimentation. New Paltz has combined interest in its art certification curriculum with the AV field to improve instruction. The colleges of the State University are using and evaluating different language laboratories and programmed learning devices. AV education in these institutions has progressed from its "normal school" stage to its "college" stage and is now on the threshold of its "university" stage.

Additional education media and equipment will be available along with CCTV systems in each of the science buildings that are being constructed on each of these campuses. A telemicroscope will enable students in lecture halls to view simultaneously the same minute subject via projected television. Provisions are also being made for CCTV in new campus schools to enable education majors of other colleges to profit from the experience gained at Brockport.

For the campuses not already equipped, plans envision television installations in individual buildings to create an all-campus system, college lecture rooms with rear projection systems for slides, films and filmstrips and television, a planetarium and a communication-lecture hall building whch will become the nerve center for all campus AV operations. As the purpose of the State University of New York Colleges expands beyond that of solely preparing teachers, *change*, that constant modifier of concept, is creating *learning centers* where audiovisual programs existed only a few years ago. College curricula must be examined to see what they can offer students preparing for careers in radio, television, theatre arts, advertising and other fields which, even though they are not "teaching," are closely allied to audiovisual education.

Expanding enrollments, increased curriculum offerings and changing purposes, combined with the "University" concept, still a new mantle on the shoulders of these colleges, will lead university administrators to seek answers concerning the efficiency and effectiveness of the newer educational media.

Is greater functionalism achieved by consolidating or dispersing instructional resources on the campus? What degree of coordination is possible and desirable among colleges to avoid unreasonable duplication? What means are most effective in making available on a campus, and among campuses, information and findings relative to promising developments in educational communication? Should certain colleges be designated to build collections of particular types of materials? What means are most effective in stimulating the general faculty to use instructional resources and techniques selectively? Is a state-wide system of television and information transmittal feasible in terms of function and cost? What systems should be used in storing and retrieving basic information? The answers to these and many other questions will shape the future in our State University of New York Colleges.

SOME MATERIALS CENTERS IN THE MIDWEST

Louise Stull and E. G. Holley

For the last ten years librarians, teachers, and professors in colleges of education have been talking about materials centers. When the term is used by the educational *avant garde* it is taken to mean a comprehensive collection of all media of communication which might be useful for instructional purposes. The term used to describe such centers is not always the same, however. Nor can one assume that an institution describing its own "materials center" implies much more than a couple of hundred textbooks in a back room. Just what is a materials center? What can one obtain from such a center as it actually exists?

In 1957, in an attempt to answer these questions, such centers in 14 teacher education institutions of the Midwest were surveyed. Among the schools were seven state teachers colleges, three private colleges, two private universities, and three state universities. Nine replies came from Illinois, four from Indiana, and only two from Iowa. Results derived from questionnaires sent to these institutions may be helpful in assessing the current status of the materials-center

Reprinted with permission from: Stull, Louise, and Holley, E. G., "Some Materials Centers in the Midwest," THE JOURNAL OF TEACHER EDUCATION 11:570-72.

Materials in Fourteen Midwest Centers

Materials	Ball State	Bradley	Butler	Chicago T.C.	Eastern Ill.	Goshen	Indiana State T.C.	Northern Ill.	Northwestern	Southern Ill.	State Univ. of Ia.	Univ. of Ill.	Wartburg	Western Ill.
Books:														
Children's	x		o	x	o	x	x		x	x		o		
Adolescent	x			x		x						o		
Textbooks	x	x	x	x	x	x	x	x	x	x	x	x	x	x
Manuals	x			x		x		x		x				
Workbooks	x			x		x		x		x				
Courses of Study	x			x	x		x	x	x	x	x	x	x	
Units of Study	x						x	x	x	x		x		
Periodicals						x	x	x				o		
Children's											x			
Professional					x						x			
Pamphlets	x			x	x	x	x	x	x	x	o	o		x
Maps		o	o			x	x	x	x		o	o		
Posters						x	x	x						
Pictures	x	o	o			o	x	x	x	x	o			
Tests and Measurements	x			x	o	x	x	x			x	x	x	
Charts								x						
Diagrams														
Catalogues	x				x		x	x				x		
Letter Sets											x			
Toys and Games				x	x			x						
Films	o	o	o	o	o	o	x		o			o	o	
Filmstrips	o	o	o	o	o	o	x		o			o	o	
Records, Transcriptions	o	o	o	o	o	o	x		x			o		
Educational Tapes	o						x							
Realia	x						x							
Free and Inexpensive Learning Materials	x				x					x		x	x	
Equipment														
Projectors	o	o	o	o	o	o	x		o			o	o	
Screens	o	o	o	o	o	o	x		o			o	o	
Readers for Micro Cards and Films							x						o	
Listening Posts							x				o			
Turntables							x				o			

x = Materials found in the material center.
o = Materials not in lab but elsewhere on campus.

concept in the Midwest and in determining how far theory has been put into practice.

The survey revealed that the materials center is normally administered by the education librarian. It may be housed in the education library, in an adjacent room, or as a completely separate unit; but it is still under the administrative control of the education librarian. Examples of the first type are the University of Illinois and Southern Illinois University; of the second type, the State University of Iowa; and of the third type, the Indiana State Teachers College. Staff in the 14 centers range from none in those physically located in or near the education library to two professional librarians and five half-time graduate assistants in the Teaching Materials Center at Indiana State Teachers College. However, the well-staffed center with adequate funds of its own was not predominant in the 14 institutions in this study.

Most of the centers were organized to serve students in the materials and methods courses in departments of education. They have therefore developed largely from collections of textbooks donated by publishers. An examination of the materials housed in the various schools revealed that textbooks still form the backbones of such centers. All of the centers have textbooks.[1]

The next most frequently mentioned type of material was the course of study which the institutions reported. Other frequently mentioned materials were units of study, manuals, workbooks, tests, and pamphlets. However, when one breaks away from the printed word, most centers are very bare. Only three have toys and games, only four have maps, and only one has charts. In view of the increased emphasis upon films, filmstrips, records, and tapes, it is somewhat surprising that only Indiana State Teachers College reported a full range of audio visual materials plus the equipment with which these can be used. Nine other centers did indicate that audio visual materials were available elsewhere on the campus, but there is no indication of how easily accessible they are to students in the teacher education program.

From this survey it would seem that few teacher education institutions even approach in practice what has long been advocated in theory. After almost 15 years of talking about the multi-materials approach to teacher education, the typical "materials center," "curriculum laboratory," or whatever else one cares to call it, still does little to provide anything except textbooks and courses of study. From this survey it is apparent that not only *can* prospective teachers leave their colleges without coming into contact with all media of communication, but frequently they do. One hopes that another study of the same subject three years later would reveal significant changes in the types of materials provided by these 14 centers.

[1]MacVean's study of curriculum laboratories in 1955 reveals a similar pattern for materials in these centers. One should note that Ball State purposefully limits its center to the printed word and has an audio visual center elsewhere in the library building. See Donald S. MacVean, "Type of Materials Found in Curriculum Laboratories" (Table 18) in *A Study of Curriculum Laboratories in Midwestern Teacher Training Institutions* (Ed. D. thesis, University of Michigan, Ann Arbor, 1958) p. 64.

THE INSTRUCTIONAL MATERIALS CENTER

Donald W. Johnson

The Instructional Materials Center at Colorado State College, Greeley, is directed by Dr. Harold Bowman. It has three major functions: to train teachers in audio-visual education; to maintain a rental film library; and to give service to the local campus. The campus services performed by the Center are many and varied.

All of the film orders from the faculty are processed by the Center. Approximately one-half of the orders are supplied from the local film library, the remainder are obtained from other sources. A small collection of filmstrips, slides, records, and tapes is maintained for campus use. All materials are delivered directly to faculty members, at their request.

All of the equipment for the College is centrally controlled, supplied, and maintained. Most of the equipment is permanently located in campus departments but a small inventory of special purpose equipment is housed in the Center for special use. Nearly any type of equipment can be delivered to any location on the campus to fill special needs.

The Center provides students to operate all types of equipment. According to Dr. Bowman, motion picture projector operators are requested most often but students are available to operate other types of equipment, such as tape recorders, public address systems, slide projectors or any equipment a faculty member may desire.

A campus recording service is operated within the Instructional Materials Center. The installation of telephone lines enables the Center to record, from a central location, conferences, speeches, and other special events. Equipment is available to cut disks, as well as duplicate tape recordings. These services are provided on a limited basis.

Graphic production is an important part of the campus service. Poster and sign making occupy the major portion of the student graphic artist's time. Other production facilities are available, however, and are becoming more in demand by the faculty. They include: facilities for transparency production; production of photographic slides in color or black and white; slide duplication; and photography for instructional use, although publicity photographs are produced by another department. All of the student identification cards are laminated by the graphics service. Faculty members are encouraged to use the graphic production facilities themselves, but they can obtain assistance from the staff if it is needed.

Motion pictures of all athletic events and other special events are produced by

Reprinted with permission from: Johnson, Donald W., "The Instructional Materials Center," EDUCATIONAL SCREEN, April, 1963.

the students and staff of the Center. Last fall, the football game films were actually shot by one of the coaches with a film technician standing by to take care of the mechanics of camera operation. According to Dr. Bowman, the head coach is very pleased with the results because the coach, while not a photographer, was able to anticipate just the right action to photograph.

Public announcements are amplified over a campus public address system operated by the Center. All campus events, student activities, and other announcements are pre-recorded on tape and automatically played back during class breaks.

Recently closed-circuit television was installed in the campus laboratory school. At present, the facilities are being used to train student crews. When trained crews are available, the system will be used for observation of students in the laboratory school by education and psychology classes and by student teachers at the college.

The CCTV system consists of two vidicon cameras, audio and video control, a film chain, tape deck, and a turntable. This equipment is housed in one studio and a control room in the laboratory school and will be received in special viewing rooms in the same building.

Dr. Bowman says, "We supply anything in the way of service." It seems all a faculty member need do is ask for it.

THE TEACHING MATERIALS CENTER

Thelma C. Bird

The collection of a college teaching materials center is composed of many facets each with its individual characteristics, but emerging as a whole in the form of multi-purpose materials which play an essential role in an effective program of professional education. These materials provide a cross-media approach to the selection, coordination, and evaluation of elementary and secondary instructional aids for both laboratory and demonstration purposes.

The I.S.U. Teaching Materials Center, based on the preceding philosophy, was organized and developed to complement the program of professional education. Services and materials are offered to individuals, informal groups, and classes which meet in the Center for orientation and instructions. Library instruction is

Reprinted with permission from: Bird, Thelma C., "The Teaching Materials Center," TEACHERS COLLEGE JOURNAL, January, 1965.

directed toward materials of interest to each individual group. Student teachers use the resources extensively in planning, selecting, and coordinating materials for teaching; and special loans permit borrowing for extended periods of time. Other students plan and organize assignments around specific materials which are then used for demonstration purposes in the classroom.

Although primarily planned around the program of professional education, the Center provides materials, services, and special facilities for all instructional departments, particularly those of Music and Art. A sound system, through which record, tape, and radio programs can be channeled to selected locations in the library, makes group listening possible for several hundred students in "Introduction to Music Literature" classes. Similar planning with the Art Department enables the Center to make slides available to the faculty for classroom instruction for a like number of students in the course, "Arts in Civilization."

In addition to on-campus services, the librarian frequently serves as consultant in developing similar collections and services, and in the selection of materials for curriculum planning and revision. The Center also cooperates with other area colleges and with various civic and professional groups in lending materials not available elsewhere in the community.

The collection includes a sampling of almost all types of instructional aids with the exception of films: elementary and secondary textbooks and supplementary reading materials; curriculum bulletins; recordings; filmstrips; slides; art prints and flat pictures; maps and globes; and exhibits and models. While textbooks and supplementary reading materials constitute the major bulk of the collection, some of the special areas are worthy of additional comment. Among them are:

1. A specialized reference collection includes the major selection tools, such as the *Children's Catalog;* the *Standard Catalog for High School Libraries;* the basic book collections published by the American Library Association; indexes to poetry, short stories, and fairy tales; subject bibliographies; general and subject catalogs listing free and inexpensive materials; encyclopedias, dictionaries, and atlases for the children and young people; and indexes to audio visual materials.

2. A special collection provides student and supervising teachers with the Association for Student Teaching *Bulletins, Yearbooks,* and *Resource Bulletins;* books intended for student and supervising teachers; and the *Yearbooks* and other publications of the Association for Supervision and Curriculum Development.

3. In addition to pamphlets, units of work, and other curriculum materials, the pamphlet files contain two highly specialized collections. A survey was made of colleges and universities offering teacher training programs in an effort to locate manuals and handbooks for the student and supervising teacher. Those which were available were acquired. The second specialized collection is concerned with school administration and includes samples of handbooks for administrators, teachers, parents, and students; student evaluation forms; reports of school surveys; annual reports; and cumulative records. This file provides

information on school costs, pupil accounting, school-community relationships, lunch room programs, and school bus safety.

4. While the collection of more than 8,000 slides encompasses many subjects, the majority pertain to forms of art. Among the outstanding groups of art slides are: *The Arts of the United States,* a set of 2,500 subsidized by a grant from the Carnegie Corporation of New York, which illustrate the history of American art from the 17th Century to modern times; and complete sets to accompany Janson's *History of Art* and Gardiner's *Art Through the Ages.*

5. The Center's collection of curriculum bulletins is one of the most comprehensive of its type. The bulletins are obtained from state departments and city boards of education, and represent the majority of the states. In an effort to maintain a file of current materials, the collection is checked each year against the list of those bulletins which have been exhibited at the annual meeting of the Association for Supervision and Curriculum Development. In addition, periodic surveys are made of issuing agencies for lists of their most recent bulletins and other curriculum materials.

6. The extensive record collection represents all forms and styles of music, from the early Middle Ages to contemporary composers. Non-musical recordings include children's literature, drama, poetry, essays, literature in several modern foreign languages, foreign languages for study and teaching, education, science, social studies, speech, and special programs.

As the program of education of the University expands, that of the Teaching Materials Center will grow proportionately. There will be continued recognition of, and emphasis on, instructional materials to promote the student's professional curiosity. There will be continued need for encouragement to explore, to experiment, and to evaluate if the prospective teacher is to develop fully his potential resourcefulness for more effective teaching.

NEW LEARNING CENTERS STIMULATE
MEDIA INNOVATION AT MIAMI-DADE

Peter Masiko, Jr. and Frank Bouwsma

To plan a building for learning is an especially difficult task; so is the design of a structure for high use of today's media. It is next to impossible, then, to create a learning resources center which will facilitate an increased use of media and yet meet requirements for a very proper learning facility. We at Miami-Dade Junior College have been involved in this next-to-the-impossible with our two new Learning Resources Centers, and we believe our experiences will have implications for other colleges planning similar facilities.

The design and planning path toward our new buildings began with the formulation of educational philosophy and behavioral objectives. After a decision was reached concerning innovative projects to be included in the building, the staff and faculty worked out the student and academic needs which had to be met.

Next, the college building committee, a seven-member group composed of the president, appointed administrative officials, and the school architect, met with representatives of the architectural firm to discuss the project and define broad objectives and specifications.

M-DJC's campus planning director Donald C. Bulat and his staff worked with Pancoast, Ferendino, Grafton and Skeels, the architectural firm commissioned to design both Miami-Dade campuses, to make on-site studies of other learning resources centers, analyze design solutions, call in special consultants for advice, and finally to prepare their findings and recommendations for presentation to the building committee.

When a proposed design solution by the architects was approved by the college planners and administrators, final schemes were completed with the joint cooperation of the building committee and the architects.

The design of the Learning Resources Centers came to grips with the gargantuan growth patterns of Miami-Dade Junior College. We have 18,000 (full-time equivalent) students in six years of existence and our computers predict a continuance of this pattern. We believe the LRC is the focal point for the media aspects of education and the central structure of the academic forum.

We have tried to design the campus for the very best possible education for each student who comes to us, and the LRC is the center of that campus pattern. The building design offers students attending college in a high

Reprinted by permission of AMERICAN SCHOOL AND UNIVERSITY, Buttenheim Publishing Corp., from: Masiko, Peter Jr., and Bouwsma, Frank, "New Learning Centers Stimulate Media Innovation at Miami-Dade." May, 1967.

enrollment situation a feeling of small campus intimacy and small group learning cohesion.

To plan for high utilization of our centers, we made certain imperative stipulations clear to the architects:

The student should be near the learning media while at study to insure ease of use of the equipment; the acceptance of media and their programs depends largely on faculty awareness of their potential, and faculty involvement in production or selection as a content specialist; a well planned lecture, when properly enhanced, is a prime stimulus for learning; the acquisition program for equipment should be based on the latest in technological development and on assured student use; the present state of media is color, and all black and white programs are regarded as having an unnatural educational value; there will be interchanges of top quality productions and we will in time produce such programs; the uses of the building will change drastically and often, and we must strive for the ultimate in flexibility in the original structure and with ensuing changes.

The LRC building must be able to change to improve itself according to changes in teaching on the campus. Teaching and learning methodology result from faculty action and adminsitrative encouragement. The administration at M-DJC has committed itself to innovation which improves student learning and which is practically feasible. With this encouragement, the faculty has developed new and different instructional programs, and the new buildings and their flexibility are already being challenged.

BUILDING FEATURES

The buildings were designed for low maintenance and climate control. The exterior of the Learning Resources Center-North, for instance, is exposed concrete and precast wall units faced with quartz. The aluminum window walls have a glazing in neoprene structural gaskets. The air conditioning distribution system is combined with polarized lighting panels in the library. The overall effect is a luminous ceiling broken into areas expressing the structural bays of the building. Carpeting in the library is wool, other floors are cork, vinyl asbestos, and terrazzo.

To achieve high quality productions for learning and thus help insure high utilization of the centers, we selected a staff of professional caliber and equipped them with exceptionally professional gear. Obviously such a group and their equipment could not be duplicated, so only one production center was designed and it is located at the North Campus. This production center has special design features, notably a high 28-foot ceiling to help dissipate the intensive heat of quartz lighting needed for color.

Each program presented in a teaching auditorium or through the color television system requires six to eight weeks of production time. Most of this time is spent in art work, photography, editing, sound track mixing, animation stand work, and narration dubbing. Actual studio facilities time is only 10 per cent maximum of total production time.

The architects set aside a production room space where it was possible to set up the exact configurations to meet academic needs.

Within the learning areas of the centers new methods of acoustical control make it possible to satisfy the commuter students' need for an academic "bull session" area. Discussion tables are located in the middle of the reading rooms and group study is both encouraged and modulated.

The library stack is used as a divider, thereby creating many small libraries in the large reading room. The stack also is an effective acoustical barrier and, by its location, places the instructional material next to student study positions at tables or carrels. The shelving is placed on legs to give an impression of lightness and also for easy maintenance of the carpeting.

Specially designed individual carrels are placed near the outer walls, creating alcoves of private study. Many carrels are also located between stacks, permitting private study throughout the library.

To promote the efficient flow of materials, the library has automated circulation procedures with a computer system. All circulation records are computer-produced. The periodicals department maintains its extensive records by use of paper tape-punch machine which generates data reports, including a weekly inventory print-out.

The most notable difference between the North and South Campus buildings is the location of 32 peripheral classrooms around the South library. These classrooms are separated from the library reading room by sliding glass doors and draperies and are located to encourage classroom-library projects. Eventually these classrooms will convert to library space as future growth dictates.

The teaching auditoriums in the Learning Resources Centers are planned to emphasize the viewing of well planned faculty lectures. Rear projection is used, although we intend to experiment with front TV projection to transmit a color picture of high quality.

Auditorium lecterns have remote controls for the faculty which are only a start-stop- button system. Faculty members cannot be expected to operate up to four different projection projects for one auditorium with split second timing. This task rests with the projection technician.

COLOR TELEVISION

The color television system is more a means of program distribution than a production system. The distribution of programs by 16mm. color film through the television system, through a classroom projector, or in a carrel as an 8mm. film, gives us the flexibility that such diversified media approaches for higher education require.

The special study carrel employed in the centers for individual audio visual instruction is deeper than usual and has a one-foot shelf which holds notebooks and/or tape recorders, creating a shadow box effect on the inside front wall. The inside front wall, itself, is made of white formica and is used as a viewing screen or front projection.

A generous amount of electrical, central audio, and RF cable is coiled around brackets beneath the carrel. Each carrel can be plugged into the systems individually or in series groups. After seeing how the faculty changed carrel locations during the first weeks of use in the South Campus, we conclude that this sort of flexibility is highly essential.

When a college accepts innovation in its instructional pattern, it faces certain involvements. The faculty, for instance, must keep aware of projects and studies being conducted elsewhere, and they should know they are involved in decisions to try new projects. We have created an Innovations Library for faculty and staff on each campus. and we have been stocking them generously with reports, studies, journals, and materials. We believe that faculty awareness creates faculty innovation and use.

We hope the new spaces for learning and the new materials and equipment we have provided will increase the learning potential of our students and give our faculty more time to foster in each student the feeling of belonging.

We also hope that our students will be able to work toward knowledge and understanding rather than toward the mere accumulation of information. We want to be able to provide not only the best education, but the most effective stimulus for education to each student who comes to us.

SPACE AND SCHOLARSHIP –
NEW CHICAGO TEACHERS COLLEGE – NORTH

Robert Walker

Chicago Teachers College-North opened its doors to a select group of freshmen and transfer students in September 1961. Both faculty and students are delighted with the design of the buildings and are busy equipping the 275,771 square feet with modern teaching devices. When fully equipped the instructional plant on this 10-acre site will combine space and technology to fill every type of instructional need required to prepare tomorrow's teacher. Here are flexible and multi-purpose classrooms built in "open spaces" design to accommodate both large groups and the many seminars and discussion groups necessary to maintain student-teacher contact; independent study spaces equipped with self-instructional devices and tied into a central communication

Reprinted with permission from: Walker, Robert, "Space and Scholarship – New Chicago Teachers College-North," AUDIOVISUAL INSTRUCTION, April, 1963.

system; and an amphitheater type of auditorium where multi-screen projection is employed to bring mass instruction to a peak of effectiveness.

Classrooms are located on only one side of each corridor, and the hexagonal design of most rooms provides an interesting shape that may enhance group interaction. The two main wings are divided by spacious student lounges; exterior walkways and benches provide a pleasant break between classes. Individual study carrels line the outside wall, providing 200 quest spaces, each equipped with a lighting fixture, a locker, and storage space. These spaces will be wired with coaxial cable, communication cable, and tied into the communcations center and the language lab. At present portable AV equipment is used.

Portability of equipment was desirable when the college first opened, because this was an experimental college. Now the College is undertaking to equip each division with their unique teaching tools as the newly formed faculty groups plan their curricula. Meanwhile, since the College is built in ranch style, the portable AV equipment on carts has no trouble getting from room to room.

Flexibility in shaping the classroom area is provided by accordion-type partitions in 11 of the large classrooms. Nine of the smaller classrooms also have sound-deadening partitions of hollow wood or vertically-controlled electric curtains of layered plastic. Eighty percent of the instructional area is thus subject to control.

A three-channel perimeter language laboratory is now installed in one of the medium-size classrooms which houses 32 students. The audio-lingual method of teaching in reinforced by the use of movies and slides. Spanish, Russian, and Chinese are currently taught, with French and German scheduled for next fall. The permanent language lab being installed in one of the large classrooms will seat 36 persons, expandable to sixty.

An adjoining room will be used as a "switch-room" where students will go for half of the 50-minute lab period before exchanging places with students in the laboratory. A small seminar room will be converted into studio, storage, remote tape recorder station, etc. A teacher's console will permit the remote control of slide projectors, film projectors, and television for the programed use of visuals.

Telemation in the Auditorium represents an epitome of new instructional media. Through an array of five AV devices, the instructor can program his lessons to an audience of over 600 students. The Auditorium is a beautiful, almost Graeco-Roman type of amphitheater, with curtains to create stage areas. Installed in the cyclorama are two large plastic screens that are covered by draperies when not in use. Any effect desired from the five projection devices behind the screens can be controlled at the lectern by the speaker, at the equipment by a technician-monitor, or can be entirely automated.

The units controlled by this installation (the second employed in an educational institution) are two 2x2-inch projectors, a 3½x4-inch projector, 16mm sound projector, TV projector, and audio input of tape or disc. Automated control of complex cues is handled by solenoids and relays activated by a unit that reads punched cue cards. These cards are capable of giving 12 different orders to the equipment. Cards are advanced and read when metallic cue strips placed on the lecturer's video-script pass a solenoid in the video-script reader. This cued script is a carbon of the two copies of the script that the lecturer is reading from and is paced by an attentive technician. Script readers with reflective glass plates at the top, permitting easy reading as well as visibility and contact with the audience, are placed in front of the lectern.

Programing is done by the instructor or one of the two full-time programers. With the addition of the latest model EDEX classroom console, faculty members can work out lectures for mass instruction. Although the EDEX system has only four AV devices controlled by cues added to the second track of a dual track tape, it adds the feature of 40 student responder units which tell the instructor how each student is responding and give him a percentage read-out of every answer on a multiple choice question.

Our responder units in the Auditorium are still in the experimental stage, but when completed they will tie in with the IBM computer adjacent to the Teleprompter control room. With this mechanism, an instructor will be able to do an item analysis, before the end of the class period, on any tests given during the lecture.

Entire courses have been programed in American English (Structure and Function), and many sequences have been done in Comparative World Cultures, Social Science, Speech, Writing, and Art. Supporting these lectures are a full-time artist working out of a production workshop and a photographer equipped to do color photography. The completely telemated lecture can be televised and sent to monitor screens in any part of the college. When necessary, as during the dedication ceremonies last year, the Little Theatre can accommodate an overflow crowd for TV viewing.

After one of these telemated lectures each week, the large group of students breaks up for two discussion periods and often for a workshop. This is where room scheduling and flexible classrooms synthesize.

The Auditorium has its own sound system for taping all lectures as well as for feeding monaural or stereo to the ceiling speakers or to the new stereo speakers. Beneath the Auditorium are the efficiently laid-out rooms for costumes, scene construction, make-up, chorus, and band. These rooms currently house the art and photography shops.

Each wing of the building is designated for one of the five major teaching divisions of the college, and has been especially created to induce the interaction necessary for good teaching situations.

The Fine Arts wing houses two art studios on either side of the Little Theatre. Space dividers are utilized for exhibits on one side, and for teaching lessons and assignments on the inner side. Many college projects originate in these well-supplied, creatively staffed studios. The Little Theatre again emphasizes the flexibility aspect of all rooms. It has no permanent furniture, but seats 225 persons in comfortable folding chairs. The area is used for lectures, laboratories, film showings, club activities, variety shows, TV viewing, and faculty meetings. It is equipped with a P.A. system, but the low ceiling and acoustical plaster make the use of this system unnecessary. Programs from Midwest Airborne Television are used for instruction in language workshops. The three monitors are also used to receive programs from within the school on our closed-circuit television system.

With our orthicon camera and the micro-projector, we have one of the finest teaching tools available. We have run experiments using inschool television for teaching Spanish, Art, and Psychology. When the coaxial cable is finally installed, we will originate programs from any of ten locations or from any classroom. Any program on television can now be projected to about 8'x10' via rear-screen projection in the auditorium. The College also expects to make good use of open-circuit TV. It has been cooperating with the Junior College of the Air in co-sponsoring telecasts in Art, Shakespeare, Audiovisual Communications, American Public Education, Human Relations, and Tests and Measurements. Programs planned for telecast during school hours next fall will permit students to study on or off campus over Channel 11.

The audiovisual services are operated out of a temporary home by a full-time Civil Service technician and several student aides. There has been no attempt to standardize on certain items, so the storage room looks like that of any other rapidly expanding school service. Besides the usual equipment for standard classroom usage, our AV center makes field recordings, transparencies, 8mm sound film, 16mm film, 35mm slides, 3½x4-inch slides, and photographs. The reproductions room handles duplicator, mimeograph, and offset stencils. Two professional journals, *Hexagon* and the *Data ProcessingNewsletter* are edited and published at the college. The faculty, too, makes a heavy demand on printed media in developing syllabi for new courses.

The Library also offers many audiovisual services as a part of its normal function. Listening posts and storage facilities occupy the mezzanine; study carrels and study corners permit the use of teaching machines; and the periodical room has four microfilm viewers. The Curriculum Center maintains an up-to-the-minute display of the latest software and some of the new hardware. There are open stacks in the basement, photocopy services, and disply booths. The color and the furniture provide a congenial atmosphere.

The Data Processing Center includes key punches, a verifier, a document writer, a card sorter, an interpreter, and an IBM 1620 computer. Three full-time employees and as many student aides have developed systems for registration, grade recording, grade reporting, admissions, class lists, mailing lists, punching plastic ID cards, and numerous activities in testing and research.

Rising above the classrooms is the six-story Administration Building dubbed, "beehive," "honeycomb," or simply "the tower." The first floor houses the registrar and bursar, the second floor the dean and his two assistant deans, the secretarial section, and admissions. The faculty is housed on the top four floors in single and double offices that line the perimeter. In the core of the building are the rest rooms, broom closets, two elevators and on each floor, a large conference room. Shared by students and faculty alike, these conference rooms house instructional devices, and projection and playback equipment. They are windowless rooms with bulletin-board walls that are much in use.

Heating throughout the College is provided by a high-temperature hot-water nitrogen pressure system that flows heat in baseboard convector units.

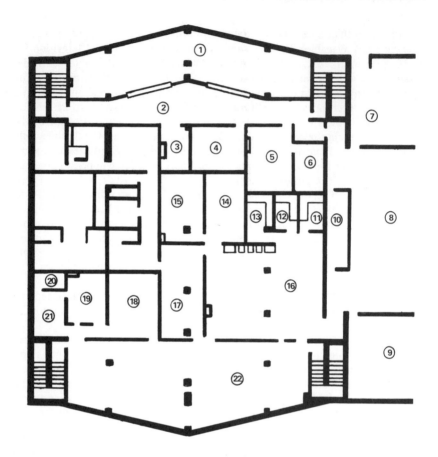

Floor Plan: Instructional Materials Center

KEY TO FLOOR PLAN

1. Coat room	12. Dark room
2. Corridor	13. Dark room
3. Telephone switchboard room	14. Storage
4. Telephone switchgear room	15. Film preview room
5. Sound console room	16. Photocopy preparation
6. Storage	17. Multilith room
7. Model shop	18. Staff office
8. Art shop	19. Reception area
9. Visual aids storage	20. Storage
10. Control Center office	21. Administrative office
11. Dark room	22. Future expansion area

Thus at Chicago Teachers College-North we see classrooms built to receive any type of portable equipment with the faculty working steadily to utilize a wide variety of equipment. Small seminars, discussion groups, or large lecture sessions are possible. A variety of teacher-classroom arrangements emphasize informal grouping, scattered buzz sessions, or the more formal chevron of rows for teacher-dominated classes. Students enjoy the variety during their school day and often arrange the room and the chairs to suit themselves and the dynamics of their assignments. The individual quest spaces will have six TV channels; remote controlled audio-active-record positions tied into the central communications setup which will offer programs in foreign languages, linguistics, speech, literature, and all lectures; and a tie-in with the language lab console and the intercom system.

The Instructional Materials Center in the basement of the Student Union Building will supply the school with all types of graphics for use in class and in practice teaching. Photography, model-making, recording and programing of language lessons, and a TV studio will be housed in the other basement space available.

The use of media is moving the instruction along the lines of programed learning, and short courses are offered from time to time in the use of the EDEX system, the Telemation system, and the Computer Center. With an experienced faculty cognizant of the best methodology from the past and sensitive to the demands of the future, our space and use of new media are making a definite contribution to the classroom of the future.

A NEW A-V TECHNOLOGY

FOR WIDE-ANGLED LEARNING

The use of audio visual devices at all educational levels is fast approaching dimensions of a billion dollar market.

Since statistical records were begun for the nontheatrical film and audio-visual field in 1956, the market has grown twice as fast as the nation's economy, showing an 83 percent growth.

While the market continues to grow, it also becomes more sophisticated, and flexible, with new approaches and dimensions in the area reaching the education

Reprinted by permission of AMERICAN SCHOOL AND UNIVERSITY, Buttenheim Publishing Corp., from "New A-V Technology for Wide-Angled Learning." April, 1967.

field each day. Federal funds, especially those from the ESEA, have pushed the a-v market to its present high.

BLACKBOARD-BY-WIRE

Last fall, Purdue University introduced a new audio-visual concept, the "blackboard-by-wire," a teaching system that transmits voice communications and handwriting over telephone lines at a relatively low cost.

The "blackboard-by-wire" has since been installed at various institutions throughout the country, backing up the prediction of James S. Miles, the articulate director of television at Purdue, who said: "the system has many applications in education, particularly for continuing education to sparsely populated areas distant from colleges or universities. Costs of the system appear to make such an effort economically viable."

The new system offers transmission costs susbtantially lower than those for closed-circuit TV. For example, a one hour closed-circuit TV transmission with one-way audio between Los Angeles and New York City would cost about $3,700 in comparison with about $900 for a similar transimission via the blackboard-by-wire system. The blackboard-by-wire circuit, utilizing leased telephone lines, also would allow two-way audio transmission.

During a demonstration program, Purdue faculty members used the system to transmit segments of typical classroom lectures in entomology and mathematics — complete with line drawings, equations and symbols — over telephone circuits provided by the General Telephone Companies of Indiana and Illinois. The voice and graphic signals were sent to the headquarters of the Illinois company in Bloomington, and returned instantly to a receiver on the Purdue campus in Lafayette, Indiana, completing a round trip of 220 miles.

The new electronic system enables distinguished scholars and leaders in many fields to present, from a centralized point, illustrated lectures to one or more remote locations anywhere in the country, with any number of TV monitors being utilized for display purposes at each reception site. At Purdue, for example, a lecture by a prominent scholar could be originated on the Lafayette campus, and be transmitted with two-way transmission to any of its branch campuses scattered around the state.

While speaking from his classroom, office, or home, the instructor illustrates his remarks with an electronic writing unit on the system's transmitting console. The handwriting is transmitted over telephone circuits in the form of voice-frequency electrical tones to the TV monitors at each remote location.

In addition to the TV monitor and loudspeaker at each classroom reception point, the system includes an audio unit and a question-indicator panel and microphone which allow the students to ask questions and discuss ideas with the instructor. A light-indicator panel on the desk-type transmitting console signals the instructor when a sutdent wishes to comment or ask a question.

As the instructor talks, he uses an electronic pen on the eight-by-six inch writing surface of the console. The electrical tones generated by the unit are decoded at the reception points and electronically etched on a storage tube in a graphic receiver unit.

A small TV camera, also in the receiver unit, then transmits the image from the storage tube to the screen on the TV sets where it is displayed in a fashion similar to the conventional school blackboard — a white image on a black background. The image remains on the TV screen until the instructor pushes an erase button on his console, which clears the blackboard instantly for further use.

In a more recent application of the system, college classrooms in Kentucky, Tennessee, and New York were linked together before an audience of more than 400 mid-Appalachia educators at Union College in Barbourville, Kentucky, and Carson-Newman College in Jefferson City, Tenn., as an illustrated class in physics was transmitted from Union College to Carson-Newman.

Thereafter, Carson-Newman sent blackboard lectures on art and the humanities to Union, and both schools received a voice-and-graphics demonstration in metallurgy from Cornell University in Ithaca, New York, 700 miles away, the greatest distance covered in a demonstration of the new system. The mid-Appalachia council is investigating the system as a means of connecting its 13 member colleges through an economical communications system, said Dr. Mahlon A. Miller, Union College president, who also heads the council.

At the University of Wisconsin in Madison, a demonstration program reaching Wausau, Wisconsin, cost $150 for two full days of use, in comparison to an expenditure of $750, that would have been required for just one hour's use of closed-circuit TV transmission.

THE ELECTROWRITER

Similar to the "blackboard-by-wire" is a device called the Electrowriter, which is also utilized with two-way telephone lines at a remarkably low cost. On the Electrowriter, however, all handwritten notations, mathematical formulas, chemical annotations, drawings and graphs are enlarged to blackboard size or larger as they are written and are received on a large screen.

The instructors illustrate their method with a stylus on the Electrowriter, a shoebox-sized device to transmit handwriting. Telephone amplifiers and microphones are used.

The Electrowriter has been employed in many installations throughout the country, including elementary and secondary schools, as well as colleges and universities.

One of the most interesting adaptations is in the remote village of New Shoreham, Rhode Island, located on Block Island, some 13 miles off the coast of Rhode Island in the Atlantic Ocean. Children from kindergarten through 12th grade, all of whom attend the one consolidated school on Block Island, are now receiving expert teaching in the "New Math", via the Electrowriter, which connects them with their instructor, a Rhode Island College professor on the mainland.

"Block Islanders feel they are pioneers in showing how an outpost community can draw live, visual instruction from any point," said Dr. Albert Lindia, Block Island School Superintendent. Island adults have also expressed an interest in an evening series.

The system was funded under some of the first applications for grants under

Title III of ESEA. Because the community is so inaccessible, retraining teachers in the newer concepts of instruction in mathematics, or sending consultants to the island has been practically impossible because there is a great turnover of teachers. Now two teachers at Rhode Island College in Providence teach mathematics to the students 65 miles away.

With the amplified telephone and Electrowriter, the students are able to talk with the teacher, and whatever the teacher writes or illustrates is projected on a large screen.

The students are divided into two groups. One teacher will instruct children from kindergarten through fifth grade, and the other those in the sixth through 12th.

DIAL-ACCESS SYSTEMS

Oklahoma Christian College in Oklahoma City was the first school in the nation to provide every student with a "total communications center" specifically designed for independent study.

Each carrel is a permanently assigned, fulltime study center, where students can use the learning system, read, type, write papers and have immediate access to the library and visual aids. All can be viewed and heard in an ideal study environment.

The system is a dial-access, programmed learning unit that consists mostly of tape recordings in individual terminals, although records, AM-FM tuners, live microphones, slow-scan television, and other components can be used.

At Oklahoma Christian, the initial installation consisted of 720 student positions having access to 136 programs which were recorded on magnetic tapes. The system allows all 720 student lines to be connected to the same program at the same time, if desired, but the 136 programs are usually more evenly distributed over the student lines.

The student's request for service, initiated by a switch on the student position, is noted by a solid-state processor in the system's equipment room. The processor – a special purpose digital computer designed expressly for controlling a switching network - notes the demand for service and returns a dial tone to the student. The processor continuously scans each student line for a demand for service and is capable of scanning thousands of lines for these status changes in a fraction of a second.

Each program source is assigned a three-digit directory number, and, upon receiving a dial tone, the student, who sits in his carrel and wears a headset, dials the directory number of the desired program. The processor receives the dial pulses, equates the dialed number to a particular program terminal, and sends control signals to the crossbar switching matrix. Selected crossbar switches then close a path between the student line and the desired program.

PORTABLE SCIENCE A-V UNIT

The Armstrong School District in the Ford City, Pa. area (seven high schools with 12,000 students covering 516 square miles) employs a portable audiovisual operation, moving a special science classroom to each high school periodically rather than attempting to duplicate the facilities in each building.

Because a planetarium is the dominant facet of the unit, the entire classroom is portable. The first of its kind ever delivered to Pennsylvania, it is completely self-contained and air conditioned with results in a constant temperature winter or summer and a complete air change every ten minutes.

The interior includes a planetarium capable of seating 20 students. Projections of the star system appear on the dome above a circular couch; all projections are motorized and synchronized to display valid astral movements. Headphones are worn by students enabling them to listen to a direct lecture by the teacher or to a tape-recorded lecture from the console. The planetarium consumes about one-third of the interior space of the trailer, which is 40 feet long, 11 feet, 8 inches wide, with a cieling height of 12 feet.

The balance of the unit includes a weather station with instruments identical to those used by the U.S. Weather Bureau. Other equipment available for student use includes a microprojector, radioactivity demonstrator, vacuum pump, electroscope, soil-testing kit, radiometer, electroplating outfit, dissection kit, rear screen projector, and a variety of optical, electrical, and mechanical demonstration boards, science films and filmstrips.

Purchased under federal funds from Title I of ESEA, the unit is assigned to each high school for periods of from six to 10 weeks.

PROJECT DISCOVERY

Project Discovery – a cooperative experiment started two years ago in Shaker Heights, Ohio, and now becoming increasingly popular across the country – could actually be defined as an encyclopedia on filmstrip.

Each school participating in the project was equipped with projection equipment for each classroom and a complete library of 600 classroom films, plus more than 1,200 filmstrips on most grade school subjects.

"The real researchers on this project," says Dr. Wayne Howell, director of Project Discovery, "are the teachers and students themselves, working and developing film utilization on their own."

Mary Koontz, a second grade teacher at Shaker Heights, said: "With motion and vision we are able to teach more science and social studies in greater depth than ever before – and to develop concepts more rapidly. Yet you fit the tool to whatever the particular need is at the time. If the films and projectors were not as accessible as they are, I would not use them so much."

"Films take us many places we can't take students. For example, they show water freezing. To approach such a degree of realism – well, we could hardly put the youngsters inside a refrigerator!"

Research teams of educational media specialists representing several universities are studying the effects of a number of audio-visual materials and equipment on pupil achievement and on changes in student, teacher and parental attitudes toward educational experiences.

Aside from the Shaker Heights program, which encompasses the highest income area in the U.S., other schools participating in Project Discovery include Edison Elementary School in suburban San Francisco, a typical middle-income community, Scott Montgomery School, in the heart of Washington D.C.'s inner city redevelopment program, and Terrell, Texas, a rural community 30 miles east of Dallas.

A COMPLETE A-V CENTER

A centralized audio-visual department results in a high degree of efficiency at Foothill College in Los Altos Hills, California.

Audio-visual and library services are organized as an instructional materials center to assist the faculty in effective teaching and to supply students with facilities for optimum learning. The audio-visual center occupies one wing of the library building.

The center provides a film service, photographic and graphic services including the preparation of slides, films, transparencies, charts, and audio tape recording service for the faculty. Materials such as maps and recordings, both disc and tape, are housed in the center and issued for classroom use on either short time or term loan.

Audio-visual personnel set up the classrooms and auditorium for the use of equipment, maintaining it, and keeping audio-visual installations in top operating condition.

The center's staff is headed by the audio-visual coordinator and includes a graphic artist, photographer, a listening room supervisor, audiovisual and television technicians, student assistants, and a booking clerk and secretary.

Among the facilities are a listening room with 12 stereophonic channels and 200 stations, fed by the listening room control desk, which includes four record players, two tape recorders, a stereo cartridge system, and 12 amplifiers.

Small listening rooms contain from six to 12 speakers, include loudspeakers, blackboards and ceiling mounted screen. Other facilities include a preview room complete with projection equipment; a graphics room with drafting table, drafting machine, light table, dry mount press and two duplicators; a photographic darkroom and dry room, a studio and control room, and two tape recording booths.

COMPUTERIZED INFORMATION RETRIEVAL

A sophisticated combination of audio and video learning devices is put to good use at Oral Roberts University in Tulsa, Oklahoma.

An Oral Roberts staff headed by Dr. Paul I. McClendon, director of learning resources, helped design the $500,000 system, which is officially described as a "computerized dial access information retrieval system."

The system is composed of many equipment items common to the current electronic age of education, but the inventive blending of these elements has produced an electronic study system surpassing in versatility the sum total of its individual parts.

The ORU system is housed in the six-story Learning Resources Center whose soaring columns dominate the campus scene. Behind its facade are enough "live" and film TV cameras, videotape machines, and switching and control equipment to outfit a moderate-size commercial television station.

The vidicon cameras are the same as those used by commercial TV stations around the country. The TV film systems comprise "islands" — motion picture projectors, slide projector, optical multiplexer and the film camera grouped together in an array common to broadcasting.

A tape recorder, used for video playbacks, is a compact "tea cart" machine mounted on large casters which can easily be rolled from classroom to laboratory, or elsewhere, when a tape recording job is called for. A companion machine used at ORU, is the industry's first "tape player." Its function in video tape corresponds to that of the projector in motion pictures as it is used to play back tapes.

Section Five

OPERATION OF
AN IMC

THE INSTRUCTIONAL MATERIALS CENTER: WHOSE EMPIRE?

Raymond Wyman

There is no doubt in any modern educator's mind that the wide and good use of all kinds of print and nonprint media is needed if teachers are to teach and students are to learn effectively and efficiently in our schools. There was a time when printed and audiovisual materials were optional and on the fringes of the teachers' central concern. Library and audiovisual specialists established little empires that made little difference to anyone, least of all the students. But times have changed. Books, periodicals, films, transparencies, recordings and programs —the "software" of education—are now recognized as essential to education. So, too, are the equipment and spaces—"hardware"—necessary to handle and use them. The new status of educational software and hardware is due to research, experimentation, evaluation, and most of all, to federal support for their acquisition and use.

The media program, or more commonly programs, have now grown to the point where they are worth fighting for, and the outcome of the battle does make a difference. The two protagonists are the audiovisual person and the librarian. Who shall be the person in charge of the wealth of media resources now being purchased and about to be purchased for education?

It is easy for the established and traditional audiovisual person and librarian to look at the new horn of plenty and make plans to include all of the new media in his own area. There may be a battle, and it may hurt everyone.

An attractive solution is to combine all books and nonbook media into a single instructional materials center (IMC) presided over by a general media person who is equally capable of dealing with and partial to all of the media and their utilization. We have been talking about this utopia for some years with very few operating examples to point to.

Maybe the time has come to try an entirely different approach. Franklin Roosevelt made history by proclaiming to divided labor, "A plague on both your houses." Maybe the traditional librarian and traditional audiovisual specialist should neither be combined nor preserved.

Reprinted with permission from: Wyman, Raymond, "The Instructional Materials Center: Whose Empire?" AUDIOVISUAL INSTRUCTION, February, 1967.

Let's go back to the essential process of education and assume that neither library nor audiovisual empire existed. What media support is needed if modern education is to be most effective?

We start with the curriculum which includes the total body of what the students need to know. The curriculum is fed into the teaching-learning experience by professional educators and, if they are successful, desirably changed or educated students result. We have learned much about improving the teaching-learning experience in recent years, and the schools are in ferment as new techniques with software and hardware are incorporated.

Much progress is made by dividing educational experience into group activities and individual learning.

The group of from twenty-five to hundreds is most efficient for the one-way communication of common instructional messages needed by all of the students at the same time. As modern communication devices and techniques are employed, the term "lecture" is inadequate and "presentation" is more descriptive. Special presentation areas are being constructed to make it easy to communicate, even with large members of students and a variety of media.

A group of about a dozen is most efficient for the essential interaction part of education where students are discussing, questioning, debating, proposing, etc. This is best done in special areas where students are seated around a table with some degree of privacy. Few, if any, media are used in this part of education.

Individual learning is growing rapidly as we discover that most students are ready, willing, and able to assume much responsibility for their own education. The materials available for individual study have never been so good, so abundant, and so needed. We can at last really do something about the unique needs of each individual student. Individual learning can take place in ordinary classrooms, study halls, libraries, and homes. It can be much more effective in individual study spaces called carrels which may be equipped with sophisticated hardware to permit the use of all kinds of newer media, as well as printed materials.

CARRELS
For Individual Study

Group presentations and individual study both need hardware and software in order to be effective, and their acquisition, or production, storage, maintenance, cataloging, scheduling, operation, and evaluation become substantial operations. Let us consider three separate service areas.

We need a software or media library that includes all of the books (other than texts), films, slides, strips, recordings, etc., that will be needed in presentations and individual study. These materials need to be acquired, cataloged, stored, and maintained. Most of all, they need to be readily available to both teachers and students.

We need a hardware or equipment shop where projectors, previewers, recorders, amplifiers, etc., are acquired, stored, serviced, and ready for loan to a teacher or student to use in presentations or individual study.

We also need a local production center where recordings, brief movies, slides, transparencies, graphics, booklets, and hand-out sheets can be prepared to answer special needs for media that cannot be satisfied with commercial materials.

The software library can be operated by nonprofessional people who have been trained in the handling of media. A two-year library training program is the closest thing that presently exists.

The hardware within and outside of the shop can be best serviced and operated by trained technical personnel who have completed a two-year postsecondary technical program. Presently these men tend to have either electronic or photographic training. For our purposes, they need to have a combination of both.

The local production center needs a photographic, graphics, and audio person to operate cameras, duplicators, tape recorders, lettering and drawing devices, etc. A new two-year training program is needed for this person.

It appears so far that we have taken care of the whole library and audiovisual empires without having any need for professional personnel, other than the teachers. This is not the case.

We do need two new professional people who have not yet appeared on the scene in any appreciable numbers. We need a specialist in presentation design and techniques, and a specialist in individual study design and techniques.

The presentation specialist would know the contents and capabilities of the software, hardware, and production centers and be a cosupervisor of their personnel and activities. He would also know much about projection, lighting, acoustics, group dynamics, and sophisticated presentation techniques. He would be to the presentation what the producer is to a television show. He would work with many teachers to make the most effective presentations possible. He would work with administrators on the design of new presentation areas and with curriculum groups on the design of new courses. He would know how to evaluate the outcomes of group instruction.

The specialist in individual study would also know the contents and capabilities of the software, hardware, and production centers and be a cosupervisor of their personnel and activities. He would, in addition, be an expert in working with individual students as they search for, select, and use reference books, supplementary texts, films, recordings, slides, newspapers, periodicals, and especially programed materials. He would have particular competencies in choosing carrels and systems to go with them. He would be a sympathetic and patient helper to the student with a problem. He would do much of the evaluation of learning outcomes.

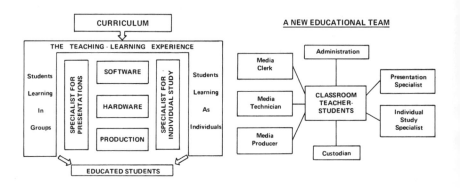

These two specialists and the three technical people might work in one large school or a number of smaller ones. They might need secretarial assistance. They would work on a team directly with the teachers and with each other so that every student could learn from all modern media, as well as the traditional ones.

Where would the specialists come from? Audiovisual people would most likely move into the presentation area as they learned about producing presentations, group dynamics, research design, room construction, etc. Librarians would most likely move into the individual study area as they learned about newer media used in individual study, carrels, evaluation, guidance, and particularly programed instruction. Graduate programs could be established for the future training of these new educational specialists.

HOW THE CENTRAL IMC RELATES
TO IMC'S AT THE BUILDING LEVEL

John P. Giesy

In 1961, the Flint School District in Michigan established a central instructional materials center and appointed a director with the title of instructional materials consultant. Administratively this center is under a director of instructional services, who in turn is directly under the associate superintendent for K-12.

Establishment of an IMC in Flint was based on experience gained over many years which has shown that a few teachers will collect and use many types of teaching-learning materials. The large majority of teachers, however, plead inadequate time, nonavailability of materials, and other reasons for not using the resources available. Records kept by the central instructional materials center show conclusively that if these materials can be gathered together, cataloged, publicized, and made readily available to a reasonable degree, teachers *will* use them. In some cases it is almost necessary to place the material in the teacher's hands and instruct him in its use. The circulation charts for Flint's central IMC, after four years of operation, still show increases in the neighborhood of 300 percent for some types of materials from one year to the next and from one quarter to the next.

THE CENTRAL IMC

The central instructional materials center houses vertical file materials cataloged according to broad teaching units, such as health, transportation, life sciences, physical sciences, and earth sciences. The vertical file also has subunits cataloged; for example under health one can find materials on anatomy and physiology, and dental health and teeth. Models, scientific apparatus, charts, pictures and posters, maps, projectuals, filmstrips, motion pictures, slides, single concept films, tapes, recordings, multimedia kits, dry mounted art reproductions, framed art reproductions, and projection and listening equipment are also located in the IMC. In addition, the center does laminating and dry mounting, and makes projectuals on a cost basis.

The normal loan period for most items is three weeks; motion pictures, filmstrips, tapes, recordings, and multimedia kits must be booked in advance for one week and are transported to and from the schools on a twice-a-week basis. Spot booking of these materials may also be made, in which case the return date is predicated upon the next booked date, but in no case can the period of loan

Reprinted with permission from: Giesy, John P., "How the Central IMC Relates to IMC's at the Building Level," AUDIOVISUAL INSTRUCTION, November, 1965.

exceed one week. Normal procedure is for all patrons to pick up from the central IMC and return to it all articles except booked items. For the convenience of the patrons the center maintains the following hours: Mondays through Thursdays, 8:00 A.M. to 10:00 P.M.; Fridays, 8:00 A.M. to 5:00 P.M.; and Saturdays, 8:00 A.M. to 12:00 noon.

BUILDING IMC'S

The instructional materials centers in individual buildings in the Flint School District are combination library-instructional materials centers. The objectives of these centers are to provide a wealth of materials that are readily available to teachers and to develop needed materials for specific local learning sessions. All new buildings have space built in for these centers. Older buildings are being provided with this space as additions are completed or improvements and modifications are carried out. Each of these building centers is staffed by a teacher on a half-time basis at the elementary school level; a full-time school librarian and a released-time coordinator at the junior high school level; and two full-time school librarians and sometimes a released-time coordinator at the senior high school level. The junior and senior high school librarians have library degrees; the professionals in charge of the elementary school centers need not be trained librarians.

During the school year 1964-65 three building level centers in elementary schools were established. The relationship between each of these three centers and the central instructional materials center is the basis for this article.

Two of these centers, A and B in the table accompanying this article, were staffed half time. The same teacher served both schools. The third center, C in the accompanying table, had a materials person full time because of its size.

RELATIONSHIPS DIFFER

With two of the three building materials centers which began operation in the 1964-65 school year, the central IMC had direct, positive relationships from the very beginning. Personnel from the central IMC, in conjunction with the library and textbook consultant, helped with the initial planning. After this, in cooperation with the principals of the two schools and the professional in charge of the two building centers, the central IMC staff developed general plans of operation and laid ground rules. One of the fundamental agreements reached was that the professional in charge of the building centers (who was to devote half-time to each center) was not to become involved in routine clerical work, but was to carry out those professional duties necessary to establish and operate a successful library-materials center. Experiences of the past year were so successful that the Flint schools will have eight building-level materials centers in elementary schools in operation before the end of the 1965-66 school year.

It was agreed from the start that the professional in charge of the building IMC also would be the instructional materials coordinator for that building. All materials requested for usage on specific dates, such as motion pictures, filmstrips, and other booked items, would be consolidated by the coordinator, delivered to the coordinator, and collected and prepared for return to the central

IMC by the coordinator. This arrangement worked extremely well. Provisions for the transportation of the items to and from the building centers were handled by the library consultant. Board of education mail trucks were used for this purpose, since the central IMC has no trucks of its own.

The opening of the three centers necessitated several changes in the operating procedures of the central center. Before these opened, signatures were required to obtain all materials except booked ones, and only booked items were normally transported to and from the schools because of the lack of adequate transportation facilities. After the three centers were established, shipments to the building centers were made without signatures and by advance arrangements with the business office, and the mail trucks transported all materials to and from the centers.

The relationships between the third building center and the central IMC were quite different from those with the first two centers. Located near the business district of the city, the third center was housed in one of 13 schools participating in a special program called B.T.U. (Better Tomorrows for Urban Youth). Since special resources were available to this center, it concentrated on the preparation and acquisition of materials to be permanently housed there. Midway through the school year the central IMC urged the third building center to request quantities of materials for shipment to that building. After that, no appreciable demand was made upon the central IMC for anything except booked items.

The table included with this article compares circulation of materials from the central IMC to the three schools for the year previous to the establishment of the building centers, and circulation for the first year of operation of the building centers.

Circulation from Central Instructional Materials Center
To Three Building Materials Centers, 1964 1965

School		1963-64	1964-65	Increase	Percent Change from 1963-64
A	Booked Items[1]	329	831	502	+ 153
	Other Items	51	4856	4805	+ 9411
B	Booked Items	222	655	433	+ 195
	Other Items	439	6596	6157	+ 1403
C[2]	Booked Items	316	666	350	+ 111
	Other Items	452	276	− 176	− 39
	Totals	1809	13,880	12,071	+ 667

[1] Motion pictures, filmstrips, slides, tapes, recordings, multimedia kits, 8mm single concept films, and projection and listening equipment.
[2] Full-time professional and late central center involvement.

CONCLUSIONS

The following conclusions are based primarily on the author's four years of experience in operating a central instructional materials center and on one year of experience in serving building level centers.

1. When there are instructional materials centers in individual school buildings, the use of instructional materials other than books increases significantly.

2. Some provision must be made to handle the clerical work involved in establishing and operating building materials centers. At the present time, all of the books for school libraries are processed by the Flint Public Library, a division of the Flint City Board of Education. During the past summer the central materials center processed 40 projectuals for each of the eight building centers to be in operation this fall. When these projectuals are delivered to the building centers, the catalog cards will be delivered with them. As the year progresses, it is hoped that more items can be processed for these centers.

3. Of all the materials shipped to the centers served, only one small pamphlet was lost. This is a far better average than that experienced when items were circulated to individuals.

4. Certain types of instructional materials should be readily available at the building level. Plans in Flint call for each building center to have its own projectors, record players, tape recorders, records, filmstrips, vertical file materials, and inexpensive high-use models and apparatus.

5. The central center should have on hand for short loan to building centers the following: projectors, record players, tape recorders, specialized projection and listening equipment, and expensive and low-use items.

6. The central center staff must be in a position to recommend items of equipment and teaching-learning materials for inclusion in building centers. This necessitates an evaluation program. In Flint the central materials center staff handles most of the recommendations for equipment, but relies heavily on teachers and consultants for recommendations concerning teaching-learning materials.

7. The central center can handle the previewing of materials more efficiently than can the numerous building centers. In Flint most previewing is scheduled through the central materials center which requests the materials; notifies the interested parties upon arrival; supplies personnel, equipment, and space for previewing; returns the materials; and maintains records of the previews and evaluations.

8. Each building center should maintain a card file of all materials and equipment available with a notation as to where they may be found. Not all instructional items in a building need to be in the materials center when not in use. The temporary location, however, should be entered on the catalog or charge card if the material is to remain out of the center for any length of time. As an example, if a 16mm motion picture projector is to be kept on the second floor of a building, and the materials center is on the first floor, the appropriate notation should be made.

9. Professionals in charge of building centers must resist pressures to perform clerical tasks to the extent that the organization and operation of the center

suffer. Adequate clerical staff must be made available to the building materials center professional.

10. In developing building centers, the school principal must participate in the establishment of procedures for the center in his building and must be kept informed of activities and developments at all times.

11. Motion pictures should remain at the central materials center and be circulated from there because of the cost, need for constant care and upkeep, and occasional and specific use.

FILM LIBRARIES AREN'T EXPENSIVE

It isn't hard to find reasons why schools don't usually have their own film libraries. Having to purchase thousands of films, and having to find space and hire the personnel to manage them, simply provides most school administrations with another set of problems to solve.

In Milwaukee, Wis., however, school officials *have* found an efficient way to operate a local audio-visual library. In cooperation with a Milwaukee museum, they share space, personnel and financing. Both the school district and the museum have access to each other's resources—a total of nearly 15,000 films, 5,000 filmstrips and thousands of other items such as slides and recordings.

Because the museum is supported by city taxes, it also makes these audio-visual materials available on a loan basis to private and to parochial schools; it also operates a rental service for some 6,400 local registered adult groups and other organizations.

The museum cooperates with the schools by sponsoring museum field trips for elementary school children. These field trips include film showings and other exhibits relating to classwork. A teacher, in turn, may borrow a film from the cooperative library to elaborate on a class field trip.

"Other school districts could do the same thing, but they aren't restricted to working with museums," points out Mrs. Ellen McComb, director of the audio-visual center in Milwaukee. "In the same manner that our museum works with the local schools, other agencies could work with schools—agencies such as public libraries or even civic clubs. There is much mutual benefit in such a relationship."

Reprinted with permission from: "Film Libraries Aren't Expensive," SCHOOL MANAGEMENT, April, 1963.

HOW THE LIBRARY WORKS

The center's films are selected and evaluated by Mrs. McComb and three persons representing the school district — the director of audio-visual education, his assistant, and the director of curriculum. Last year, more than 1,000 films were added to the center's collection, but Mrs. McComb also reports, that because the center's activities reach many influences in the community, many films are donated. More than 100 donations were received last year.

Even though the museum pays for the materials it desires, and the school district pays for those materials it wants, each evaluates the other's acquisitions for its own uses. Films purchased by the public schools, however, are considered "deposits" and are not distributed to private or parochial schools.

Both the museum center and the public schools are on the automatic "preview list" for new releases by educational film producers, such as Coronet Instructional Films. Coronet, for example, issues an average of six new titles a month. The library usually retains these preview copies, even if additional copies aren't bought immediately.

The audio-visual center distributes a catalog to all teachers in Milwaukee advising them of available titles and, in particular, new additions. When requesting a film, a teacher simply submits a written request to the center. Twice-weekly deliveries are made by truck to each school.

On her request form, which is made out in triplicate, the teacher lists the film title and catalog number, and the date on which it is to be used. The top copy is retained by the museum. The second copy is returned to the teacher to confirm the reservation date. The third copy serves as a "delivery-and-return" record, and is attached to the film's container. When the container and film are returned to the center after use, the teacher indicates on this third copy whether the film needs repairs, how many times she has shown it, and the approximate number of viewers. Clerks in the film library check these forms to ascertain when films should be replaced, if additional copies are needed, etc.

Check-out time for films, recordings or other audio-visual materials is usually one week. The center discourages passing a film from teacher to teacher in the same school; this, in turn, encourages teachers to reserve their films well in advance.

The audio-visual center is located in the museum, and is operated entirely by the museum. As for finances, the school district pays about 25% of the center's operational and maintenance budget.

COSTS SCHOOLS LESS

"All told," says Mrs. McComb, "it probably costs the school district less to have its own library than to rent films through the mail. The schools don't have to pay a rental fee for each showing, and the films are always here ready for showing whenever they are desired—no waiting. Most important, many teachers seem to be using more films, more often, more effectively."

EASY AND INEXPENSIVE AV CATALOGING

Gardner L. Hart

One of the major problems that faces every audiovisual department is the necessity of keeping teachers and principals informed of the available audiovisual materials for classroom use. When audiovisual departments were small and materials were limited, the problem was simple; but with the expansion of the curriculum and the extensive amount of materials available for school use, the problem of producing catalogs has become very complicated.

In the Oakland Public Schools in California, for example, it was taking almost five years to completely revise each of the 18 catalogs from the kindergarten through the senior high school. Each one of these catalogs parallels a course of study. There are 91 schools and 3,000 teachers in the Oakland system, and a sufficient number of copies are reproduced to enable each teacher to have a copy of each catalog that lists the materials he may wish to use. If he teaches a subject that covers more than an area or grade level, he may easily need more than a single catalog. A complete file of catalogs is also placed in each school library, as well as in the hands of curriculum and supervisory personnel.

Due to the tremendous amount of new audiovisual materials being added each year and the many changes being made in the curriculum, the Oakland Audiovisual Department found it necessary to develop a faster and more efficient method of producing catalogs. The system in use was not only too slow, but it also was becoming too costly.

BASIC REQUIREMENTS ARE MET

Upon contacting various companies and checking into types of equipment available for this job, it was found that while some offered certain advantages over the system in use, none appeared to be able to do the necessary job and at the same time maintain the flexibility which was needed. Therefore the Oakland schools, in cooperation with the AM Corporation, determined that the addressograph principle basically met the requirements of the audiovisual procedures. However, it was recognized that additional research and development were needed to perfect the system to perform all of the operations necessary.

Even in this machine age, man must still master the machine, and therefore the first step was to find out just what the equipment should do. It was essential to bear in mind the need to convert a wide variety of audiovisual operations while keeping the operations themselves very simple. Following is a partial list of the tasks which had to be done with one operator and one machine:

Reprinted with permission from: Hart, Gardner L., "Easy and Inexpensive AV Cataloging," AUDIOVISUAL INSTRUCTION, November, 1964.

· AV Catalogs: Make 8½ x 11 offset masters for high-speed duplication.
· AV Catalogs and Special Listings: Select materials for imprinting in predetermined categories ranging from 30 to 60 in number.
· Bulletins and Classified Directories of Sources, etc.: Change the position of lines so that any one line may be printed in any position. This is possible due to the ability of the machine to pick out any given information from the plate and imprint on any desired position on the form.
· Cards: Print catalog and inventory cards, by imprinting full plate on 3 x 5 cards. Also, print titles and other necessary information on 5 x 8 motion picture booking cards.
· Label AV Materials for Circulation to Schools: Print titles and related information directly on art prints, pictures, phonograph record envelopes, and other audiovisual materials. Also, print titles and related information on gummed labels to be affixed to boxes containing recorded tapes and other audiovisual materials.

THE PROCESS IS PERFECTED

To devise a system capable of performing all these tasks was a big order, but with the cooperation of the technical staff of the local firm it was accomplished. The following step-by-step description of the process shows the satisfactory way in which the equipment works.

First, a single metal plate capable of holding a maximum of 38 characters to a line, 9 lines to a plate, is embossed for each of the 30,000 articles in the Audiovisual Department. Each plate holds information similar to that on the following sample:

DISCOVERING PERSPECTIVE   MP
    col 15 min FilmA 61   Art gr5-10
Describes the methods used to create the appearance of distance or depth on a flat surface. A variety of techniques is shown. Especially useful for seventh grade art classes when beginning study of perspective.

These plates are then tabbed so that each plate can be selected in any one of 60 other classifications if so desired, and then filed in drawers in the order in which they are to appear in the catalog. Each time a new audiovisual aid is purchased, a plate is cut and an imprint is made on a 3 x 5 card for cataloging and inventory purposes. The plate is immediately inserted into the proper place in the file drawer. Thus a complete master record, or inventory, which is never behind for more than one day, is maintained.

Once the metal plates are completed, the reproducing of catalogs becomes a very simple matter. For continuous operation where hundreds of plates are to be imprinted on offset masters, a special control is used which enables the machine to operate continuously until the last impression is listed on the form. Plates are transferred from the file drawers to the machine in one fast motion, and as the plates complete their passage through the machine they are automatically refiled in their original order in the filing drawer. In one minute's time, the machine will reproduce four 8½ x 11 offset masters which may be used immediately on any number of high-speed duplicators.

A change of a single setting on the machine makes it possible to print special list of materials, either by subject or grade level. The automatic selector attachment automatically selects certain plates to imprint and passes others through the machine without imprinting. Lists of materials by producers with titles of films, date of production, and other information also can be automatically reproduced.

Manual controls covering "consecutive," "repeat," and "skip" operations are used when manual feeding is necessary, as in the case in printing titles and related information directly on art prints and similar materials. Motion picture booking cards are hand-fed into the machine at the rate of 1,000 an hour, and the first two lines—title, subject, grade level, running time, and producer—are printed on both sides of the card. The labeling of recorded tapes is also handled by this machine. A full imprint is made on gummed labels which are affixed to the box containing the tape.

Additional attachments such as the two-column and three-column lister make it possible to list part of the information from a plate in one column on a sheet, and another part of the information from the same plate in adjacent columns. This is used when it is desired to have the information appear in tabulated form in several columns across the sheet.

OTHER BENEFITS ACCRUE

Although this equipment was developed especially to meet the needs of the Audiovisual Department, other departments also have found that the same machine can be of benefit to them. The library, for example, has found that library catalog cards, shelf cards, circulation cards, and book pockets can be printed much more efficiently by this equipment than by other methods. Therefore, nearly 400,000 items have been run for the library department of the Oakland schools.

The production of audiovisual catalogs, which formerly took months of careful, painstaking, and time-consuming typing, proof-reading, and reproducing, has now been reduced to a fast and simple mechanical operation. And this in turn has made available to teachers catalogs of up-to-date audiovisual materials to help them toward more efficient teaching.

MORE NOTES ON AV CATALOGING

Robert G. Harding

In the November 1964 issue of AVI (see pp. 241-243), Gardner L. Hart described a fine inexpensive method of cataloging AV materials for district-wide library services. Mr. Hart's method assumes, however, that expensive duplicating equipment, storage devices, and operating personnel are available. Preparing a catalog in a smaller or less centralized school district still entails a great deal of handwork. If your audiovisual service exists within a smaller district, or in one in which the service is just emerging, consider the following procedures for creating an AV catalog.

Every member of your faculty should have immediate access to information about your collection of school-owned audiovisual materials. If such data is not readily available, plan now to prepare a printed catalog for distribution to every teacher. Detailed card catalogs are best for analysis of specific needs, but every user must come to it; it can't be taken home, or put into the teacher's desk. Circulation of media will increase if each teacher can refer to a personal copy of the catalog, and although detailed descriptions of each entry may not be practicable, abbreviated information will cause the teacher to visit the campus AV center to examine the materials personally.

If your school already owns several hundred items and has not cataloged them previously, plan to produce your first publication during the summer when the school clerical staff will have more time for new projects. Preparing a sizable catalog with a limited staff while school is in session is difficult, since the myriad details required to do the job well can't be dealt with while other work is in progress.

To begin the work, determine the kinds of materials to be included in your publication. If some of the types considered are already recorded in other curriculum library resources, it may not be necessary to duplicate that data in your efforts. Will you include school-made teaching tools in the catalog? If the material is as good as a commercially made item, it should be represented.

Next, take an inventory of the classrooms, noting the types of items you have decided to include in the catalog. A duplicated form may assist you in completing your description of each classroom item. This phase of the work is by far the most exhausting if you have a great many rooms to visit, but if your work is to be complete, every item you own should be included. In addition, a review of your district's business records will reveal acquisitions you would not have known about otherwise. If you cannot locate titles previously purchased, ask the teachers and department chairmen most likely to have received and used the lost materials.

Reprinted with permission from: Harding, Robert G., "More Notes on AV Cataloging," AUDIOVISUAL INSTRUCTION, January, 1966.

Before continuing, make sure that the school administration understands the importance of your cataloging effort, and devise procedures which bring newly purchased titles to your desk for cataloging before they reach anyone else on campus. Then with all existing media accounted for, you can begin designing the format of the catalog — type of reproduction, e.g., mimeograph, photo-offset, or letterpress; paper size and weight; cover design; color; binding style; and quantity. Will school equipment and personnel do all of the work or should quotations be obtained from commercial firms? It may be most economical to have your staff do the inside pages and have the collation and binding done commercially. The catalog should include a description of how teachers can obtain the items listed if they are to be circulated from a central location. A statement on how to acquire additional titles would also be useful.

Finally, the last stage of the project is the promotion, distribution, and supplementation of the campus catalog. Faculty orientation sessions are ideal for the initial distribution. Departmental meetings hold potential for directing attention to specific subject categories of media in the publication.

Producing supplements for the general catalog should be considered carefully. If media purchases are infrequent, perahps an annual revision of the catalog will suffice. But if the school services expand rapidly and new acquisitions abound, one or two supplements for the year will be necessary. Remember, several supplements for each edition are cumbersome to work with and can be lost easily.

So, after what could be several weeks of preparation, you have made available to your faculty a new dimension of audiovisual service. Watch your increase in business!

GUIDELINES FOR THE SELECTION OF INSTRUCTIONAL MATERIALS

Horace C. Hartsell and R. A. Margoles

We are observing change in teaching. A shift in content interest, teaching methods, and instructional development strategy are but a few examples of such change. The current trend for applying the newer educational technology to teaching and to learning is being reflected in varying degrees of acceptance, or rejection. In selecting instructional materials, educators find themselves at a crossroad of either confrontation or stimulation, smugness or involvement. The difficulty most frequently occurs due to lack of a plan and because of ineffective communications among the researcher, the administrator, the teacher, and the educational specialists, i.e., media, learning, and evaluation.

David K. Berlo, chairman, Department of Communications, Michigan State University, in an address to the DAVI Denver Convention[1] challenged media professionals to develop theory with which to establish guidelines for selection and/or production of instructional materials. He charged us with failure to realize that we were in the "people business" and that our "bucket theory" of communications places the meaning upon the symbols used rather than in the people who produce and receive the symbols. The materials used in a given mode of instruction must do more than transport and dump a load of facts and things on the learner.

In addressing ourselves to the question of guidelines II for the selection of instructional materials, we must fill the gap between what we know should be done and what is being done. Decisions are based on either wants, needs, or oughts. Too frequently instructional materials selection has been based on the *wants* of the teacher and not on what *ought* to be available to the learner. The key curriculum issues appear to be: (a) need for establishing priority, (b) importance of learning how to learn, (c) need to see the school program as a totality, and (d) caution in promotion of "easy to adopt" packaged programs. A quantity of instructional materials is no assurance that the learner will reach his behavioral goals.

Before listing guidelines for selection of instructional materials, permit us to propose a rationale and the criteria for stating objectives for the selection of media.

---

[1] *Berlo, David K. "You Are In The People Business." Audiovisual Instruction 8:273-81; June 1963.*

Reprinted with permission from: Hartsell, Horace C. and Margoles, R. A., "Guidelines for the Selection of Instructional Materials," AUDIOVISUAL INSTRUCTION, January, 1967.

CRITERIA FOR SETTING FORTH OBJECTIVES FOR THE SELECTION OF MEDIA

"The sum of the parts is equal to the whole" may be an erroneous concept on the part of many educators. It is founded on the stabilization of the school's social environmental system. When factors such as those identified by the Sub-committee on Economic Progress of the Joint Economic Committee of Congress[2] are fitted into a regimental pattern for consideration, the results are prescriptive communications that allow many teachers the opportunity to acclaim a new idea but remain apathetic toward it.

Taking the view that people talk with each other, it is suggested that the sum of the parts is greater than the whole. In this case, the "parts" deal with standards for setting up objectives for the selection of media. These parts are human involvement links, namely, clerical, communication, and judgment. Although these links are interdependent, it is thought that some consideration should be focused on each. Perhaps in this way some insight into the questions of "How sophisticated should criteria become?" and "Where are the best points to intervene?" can be accomplished.

Clerical Link: The clerical link refers to the audiovisual adage of the "Four R's" – right materials, at the right place, at the right time, used in the right way. Educators can create conditions where media adjustment is possible instead of simply accepting things as they are. These conditions center about the avail-ability and the capability of media. The logistics of media is a continuous prob-lem which ranges from what is available to when it is available. This problem is not resolved as easily as allocating newly found funds toward purchases. Most frequently, the addition of learning resources compounds the problem when the learning needs are not thoroughly analyzed. The clerical links should be opera-tionalized in order to answer the classroom teachers' questions: What is there to use? How do we learn to understand proper use? How do we maximize the effec-tiveness of the instructional materials available?

Certainly many schools have made known to their staffs what is available and how to get the materials. However, it is an assumption of these authors that teachers go through stages of media utilization, i.e., awareness, pragmatic manip-ulation, and strategy for utilization. It may be that many teachers are only in the "awareness stage." They are willing to use media, but without knowing why. At the awareness stage many teachers, whose media requests are not filled, are still able to conduct their class without remorse.

Schools must not only consider the teachers' knowledge of what is there, but they must also let teachers know what new materials are being used elsewhere. Curricular dissemination is needed for media acknowledgment by the teachers. At the same time, the school administration must make the distribution of

---

[2] *Education U.S.A., Washington Monitor, September 8, 1966, p. 11. (These factors as reported are as follows: (1) Effectiveness of research in learning theory and its application to the development of education; (2) improvement of curriculum programing, particularly in respect to meeting educational objectives; (3) organization of school systems and intelligent planning of curriculum; (4) more effective use of teachers; and (5) recognition on the part of educators of the great potential in the new communications technology.)*

instructional materials easy and efficient. As one in-service teacher taking a media course aptly stated, "Many of us do not use media simply because we do not know how or why."

These clerical services are important as a building block for teachers' awareness. Teachers must be aware that audiovisual materials exist, and that the school is interested in helping the teacher to mature in the use of media. Without this first step, awareness, the criteria for the selection of media is not going to become an internalized aspect of the teacher's instructional interaction with the student.

By putting into action the clerical links, teachers can become aware of what is available and begin to suggest what ought to be available. At the same time, teachers should become aware that the school is interested in them by the fact that information relating to media instruction has been obtained for them. Awareness is a necessity for laying the groundwork for criteria. The clerical link creates the conditions where media adjustment is possible. What follows is the communication link.

Communication Link: The communication link sets the mode for what form of freedom is possible in the school's social environment. No sooner has the teacher become resourceful in the use of media than he finds himself in the stage of "pragmatic manipulation." In other words, the teacher is quick to select but then neglects the rationale on which instructional strategy and behavioral consequences must be based. In consequence, the teacher places himself in social coercion which cooperation entails. Does this cooperation invade his autonomy? Indeed it does, for now the teacher must follow prescribed rules and roles for the use of media. Whether these rules and roles are in connection with the ordering of media or by suggested use of media, the teacher feels his self-expression curtailed. If autonomy interests are challenged at this stage, can one expect there to be a common outlook on the objectives for media?

If an educational system is designed to bring about prescribed and/or predicted changes in the capabilities and attitudes of the students, then it follows that the same system brings about changes in the capabilities and attitudes of the teachers. This may be true, but it does not follow that one teacher understands and comprehends why another teacher used certain instructional materials. The sharing of experiences among teachers tells little about the process of change. The communicability of success persuades one to duplicate another's efforts. What may follow is a feeling of non-accomplishment, or the thought by the teacher who states, "This is not fulfilling what I had hoped to do."

Those pragmatic manipulators who think they have accommodated themselves to the times of media find themselves rejecting or becoming displeased with media. They are quick to communicate their dissatisfaction. One favorite reason for their frustration is the gripe that they cannot always obtain the materials when they need them. Perhaps what they are really trying to say is that they have learned to identify themselves with the media as an extension of their body. Thus, the teacher feels frustrated when denied its use, not frustrated for organizing and structuring learning with content, but rather frustrated for having an extension of himself taken away.

Educators are quick to resolve problems through communications. However, communications in a social environment take on the character of a hierarchy of channels. In other words, communications between line and staff facilitate, whereas communications between staff and staff explicate. To carry this flow of communications further, those using media in the pragmatic manipulator category talk to those in the awareness category. Hence, an uncertain or biased feeling is conveyed about the significance of media.

What school personnel can do is to set up through in-service content meetings, social policies which represent an inductive process from the unique insights and experiences of every person concerned with the use of media as an interrelated part of the instructional process. Remember that the statement of the sum equaling the parts was negated in favor of the parts being greater than the whole. This was to illustrate that the involvement of members could not be written off as a problem resolved. But rather, it means that much time, effort, and understanding must be undertaken in order to bring a staff up from the awareness stage and through the pragmatic manipulation stage. Only when there is recognition that many of the groups are at this stage, can efforts be made for escalation to the "strategy-for-utilization" stage. The energy involvement at the communication link entails a socio-psychological process of change. The best that one can expect from this process is a mutual goal setting. But this is expecting too much. Rather a mutual consensus, as to where one is in regard to his views of media, is sought. For when a group is at a minimal level of agreement and understanding, the third link can be entered. That is to say that the judgment link must be undertaken only when the communication and clerical links have been operationalized. Parallel to these links are the assumptions of teacher advancement through the awareness and pragmatic manipulator stages. Perhaps diagnostic instruments can be constructed to confirm the establishment of these links and stages. However, it may be unnecessary if the teachers feel themselves to be at these levels.

The Judgment Link: Teachers approaching the strategy-for-utilization stage frequently demand time and assistance in instructional planning in order to develop the potential of media. However, difficulty occurs when the teachers are asked to identify the commonalities on which the planning was based. In many instances, the teachers only identify abstract-level objectives. This is not surprising since it is via this abstraction of objectives that teachers can reach some general agreement. But when teachers attempt to break down these abstractions into concrete descriptions of action, divergence appears. Hence, communications become misunderstood and insights and experiences cannot be shared and evaluated. The judgment link consists of teachers not looking at pieces of content information but rather of teachers asking themselves: What are our tasks? What are the learners' tasks? What are the behaviors sought? and, What are the alternative modes of instruction?

Given that a heterogenous group of teachers is involved with setting up objectives for the selection of media, and if the school has developed through the clerical link and the communication link as well as the parallel stages of awareness and pragmatic manipulation, then the group would be able to agree upon certain action, content, and an instructional mode. This is the characteristic of the judgment link.

The judgment link can be focused on the following components: (a) socioeconomic factors such as budget allocations, logistics, and environmental adaptability; (b) knowledge, understanding, and synthesis of content in terms of affective, cognitive, and psychomotor behaviors; and (c) perpetuation of selection through evaluation which includes efficiency and performance.

The groundwork for the judgment link which is paralleled by the strategy-for-utilization stage is explicated in the writings of Bloom, Gagne, and more recently, Briggs. The contention of their works is beginning to be realized. In a two-page publication, Briggs[3] succinctly outlines a hierarchy of decisions to be employed in the selection of the specified stimuli with the most advantageous form of media. Others have realized such a stage of strategy for media utilization. An example is the Instructional Systems Development Project (coordinated by Michigan State University) which is now being carried on at four institutions of higher learning.

The judgment link can and should be shared by two distinct groups, namely the instructor(s) and the educational specialist(s). Both have a common interest in improving instruction and maximizing the learner's environment. At the same time, they both have a common background of knowledge and understanding which complements the analyzing of the learning task and states the entry and exit behaviors. No threat of autonomy invasion is present. The teacher realizes his need for acquiring knowledge which concerns the conditions of instruction required for each type of learning.

Thus, the real problem is to develop the teacher through links which are paralleled by the hierarchial stages of awareness, pragmatic manipulator, and strategy for utilization. It is quite probable that these stages may be necessary but are not sufficient for describing a teacher involved in the judgment link. Certainly they need to be operationalized and verified.

In any case, these criteria of setting up human links in a school social system are advocated. It is suspected that these operating links would promote the maturation levels of the media field. Although these stages may be accelerated by attending courses in media instruction, it is thought that the returning teacher would find it hard to communicate and demonstrate his proficiencies in an environment not yet ready for adoption.

What has been suggested may lead to unanticipated consequences if school personnel follow the strategy of business. The rationale in business is that a systems specialist can do an amazing amount of planning and thinking which leads to sound decisions because he is not involved in the day-to-day operations. This is probably true for business, but not in education. It is the teacher who must acquire a new insight, a new self-reliance. Otherwise, the best strategies laid out for a teacher can still fall short of established goals. The teacher's enthusiasm, contribution, and understanding enable him to work with the media for the students.

---

[3] *Briggs, Leslie J. "A Procedure For The Design Of Multimedia Instruction," Palo Alto, Calif.: American Institutes for Research, 1966.*

GUIDELINES FOR SELECTION OF INSTRUCTIONAL MATERIALS

Guidelines for selection of instructional materials have been suggested in a collection of position papers reported in Media Competencies for Teachers Project directed by W. C. Meierhenry,[4] University of Nebraska. The Vern Gerlach paper entitled, "Selecting an Instructional Medium,"[5] presents rationale and criteria for stating guidelines. Gerlach stated, "Media selection ought to be dependent upon a list of specific determiners."[6] He differentiated between stimulus-oriented materials and response-oriented materials and emphasized the importance of clearly stated behaviors prior to selecting and/or producing instructional materials. The instructional strategy developed from the statement of objectives should determine whether the materials possess a high degree of internal control or whether the materials provide a support base for the teacher, i.e., external control with the material aiding the teacher. In reference to the Gerlach paper, Meierhenry stated, "What Gerlach attempts to show is the way in which each specific behavioral objective can be approached initially by the way of learning strategies . . . it is evident that he comes to grips with the basic problem."[7]

If strategy is needed to select instructional materials, then it would seem that all efforts should be directed toward the acceptance of an identified instructional development system.

When instructional strategy has been developed and a mode of instruction has been established, guidelines for selection of materials will be determined. If this concept could be accepted as a major guideline for selecting instructional materials, it would serve as a control for the treatment of media. A control can be exercised in terms of the following: by the teacher, by the materials, or on the student. Treatment of media as a control by the teacher would lead to decisions as to the proper sequence of materials for the student at the desired time. Treatment of media as a control by the materials would lead to decisions as to which additional materials should be considered. Treatment of media as a control on the student would lead to responses made by the student at the desired time.

Many of the audiovisual textbooks consider general criteria for selecting instructional materials. They cover such aspects as cost, technical quality, flexibility, authenticity, organization in terms of stated goals, appropriateness, length of time, lending itself well for additional learning, and availability. Along with these instructional and technological criteria, we suggest criteria in terms of what the teacher must know: that is, what the teacher must know in terms of the learning environment and the school environment.

Before the teacher makes a decision as to what to do with media, he is advised to think through these ideas with others:

[4]*Meierhenry, W.C. "Media Competencies For Teachers." U.S.O.E. Contract No. 5-0730-2-12-6. Lincoln: Teachers College, University of Nebraska, 1966. 229 pp.*

[5]*Ibid., pp. 70-101.*

[6]*Ibid., p. 71.*

[7]*Op. cit., p. 68.*

1. What order of hierarchial events constitutes the day's objective(s) and/or the weekly lesson plan?

2. What sequence of knowledge (in behavioral terms) has been already attained by the student(s)?

3. What behavior is expected to be exhibited by the student after the utilization of the media?

4. What are the characteristics of the media?

5. What forms of evaluation can determine where the students are in terms of the expected behaviors?

6. How should one set up a variety of experiences in order to coordinate the acquired learning experience(s)?

Before the teacher can make decisions about the use of media, he needs to know the types of assistance that the school can provide. Some types of such assistance are suggested below.

1. Information about media should be made available by school personnel. Such information should include what is available, where it is available, and when it is available. Information should be made available as to production services and educational services which will help the teacher to understand how media can be utilized efficiently.

2. Information about the capabilities of media for transmitting the desired experience might include the following: (a) flexibility range that a vehicle has in arranging, prearranging, and alternating the desired bits of audiovisual information; (b) utilizing a vehicle at one or more teaching stations, simultaneously; and (c) alternative advantages for manual or automatic teaching situations.

3. Personal consultation with those involved with the curriculum in order that agreement can be obtained as to what experience best matches an anticipated learning behavior.

4. Knowledge of timing in the use of media is needed. This would lead the teacher to question whether or not the student is fatigued by the constant involvement with one medium.

5. Opportunities made available to the teacher in order to explain to colleagues what strategy was considered in order to follow a specific instructional mode.

ELECTRONIC DATA PROCESSING APPLIED TO AV CENTERS

Robert C. Gerletti

Until a few years ago typewriters, adding machines, and rotating files were about the only means of speeding up data processing in audiovisual centers. New methods are now possible. By using the electronic principles of magnetism and electricity, one can process data without moving great volumes of paper and performing arithmetical computations.

Consider a booking operation. Orders come in, are stored for a short time, are processed and shipped out. Figures 1 through 4 show the four general steps — input, storage, processing, and output. Until recently most of the developments in speeding up operations had been in the processing step; very little had been done about input, storage, or output. It was inevitable that these three remaining areas should be brought up to date. Thus, a system of punch cards was created.

The holes in the cards represent coded information punched from source documents. Electrical components sense the presence or absence of the holes. Electrical impulses are generated and control panels, previously wired, direct the operation of the machine. The machines produce other cards, arrange cards, or produce printed documents.

The basic principles involved in moving data electronically are (1) that positive and negative electrical charges can be stored, (2) that an electric current can be started and stopped, and (3) that information can be translated into a code which can be changed into electrical charges.

Let's take a brief look at how each part — input, storage, processing, and output — operates in an electronic data processing system.

INPUT

Information from source documents, such as orders, is coded to be used later. Coding can be done in four ways: holes in punched cards, paper tape, minute magnetic spots on magnetic disks or drums, actual characters which are decipherable by man as well as by machine. The print is a magnetic ink. The coded information is fed into the input machines. No matter which system of coding is used, electronic signals are generated as the information is fed in.

Reprinted with permission from: Gerletti, Robert C., "Electronic Data Processing Applied to AV Centers," AUDIOVISUAL INSTRUCTION, December, 1961.

STORAGE

The electronic signals are stored as positive or negative electrical charges on magnetic cores, drums, disks, or tapes. It is interesting to note that information stored as an electrical charge can be read at about the speed of light when retrieved. You can see some advantages. The information is stored in small bits, transferred by an electric current, and turned out the same way.

Which method to use for storage is a critical question. Getting the information out depends on how it was put in. Random access, the process by which information can be stored in any order and retrieved almost immediately in any order, is a promising development for the audiovisual center. The information stored may be a number, letter, digit, word, or complete record. The information is assigned to a specific area and is located by using an identifying number. An example of the compactness of storage is shown in the fact that an inch of magnetic tape may hold as much as 550 bits of information.

Three types of basic data can be stored: facts and figures, reference tables, and operating instructions which direct the equipment.

PROCESSING

The processing unit performs these operations: (1) controls traffic to and from the various components; (2) tells the computer where to store information; (3) calls for data when needed; (4) performs necessary calculations; (5) compares pieces of information; and (6) tells components what to do. The system must be told how to perform; in other words, it must be programed. Each operation is designed to perform in response to a specific command. Programing is hard work, but useful because it forces you to think through established routines.

The controls for the electronic processing unit are stored internally. The information which tells the machine what to do is stored like the input information − as electrical charges on tape, drum, disk, or core. Once this is set up, the system will perform.

OUTPUT

Output can be in the form of punched cards, punched paper tape, magnetic tape, or printed information. What you wish to do determines which form you use. To assure accuracy in output, controls and checks are built into the system. Again this takes time, but so does washing out the bugs in a manual operation.

*   *   *

Some advantages of the electronic system are: faster reporting, fewer peak-and-valley work loads, compact storage of information, random access to information at high speeds, easier auditing, and almost simultaneous input and output. (Solid state circuitry is helping to reduce the size of components.)

Among disadvantages are the necessity to retrain personnel, high initial costs, difficulty of handling exceptional material, and problems when the machinery breaks down.

Electronic processing is a way of storing data in very small areas and providing for retrieval at high speeds. Its purpose in an audiovisual center is to facilitate tasks and reduce time-consuming procedures.

CHANGING CONCEPTS IN LIBRARY DESIGN

Richard L. Darling

Today's educators and architects must plan new schools and school libraries to accommodate a virtual revolution in instruction. The scope, content and number of courses offered in both elementary and secondary schools, influenced by federal programs and privately sponsored curriculum studies, have expanded so rapidly in the last decade that new patterns of administrative organization for instruction have emerged. Flexible scheduling, large group instruction, and ungraded schools, among others, have encouraged teachers to use different methods of instruction.

With team teaching, which has won widespread approval, teachers may work part of the time with small groups and thereby individualize instruction. Individualized reading programs in elementary schools, often in conjunction with ungraded plans of organization, have led to increased emphasis on individualized instruction in other subjects as well. Important characteristics of current teaching methods are this individual work with children and extensive use of a wide variety of materials.

New learning materials, also, have effected changes in teaching. Motion picture films, filmstrips, slides, recordings, and other nonprint materials have assumed an important place in instruction. Schools now use programmed materials for teaching machines, and television as aids in teaching. Teachers find that transparencies and overlays for use on overhead projectors are effective instructional devices.

LIBRARY PROGRAM CHANGES

School library programs are changing rapidly to support these new methods in teaching and learning, and to accommodate newer educational media. An increasing number of school libraries are administered as comprehensive instruc-

Reprinted by permission of AMERICAN SCHOOL AND UNIVERSITY, Buttenheim Publishing Corp. from: Darling, Richard L., "Changing Concepts in Library Design." May, 1965.

tional materials centers, including a wide range of different types of materials in their collections and providing new services related to these materials.

Both students and teachers now use the school library according to the dictates of the instructional program. In both elementary and secondary schools, scheduled use of the school library by entire classes has given way to individual and small group use with free movement from the classroom to the library, and back again, of both students and materials. Teachers recognize that many children can learn independently, using materials in the library, just as effectively as they can during formal instruction in the classroom, and permit their students to visit the library whenever a need arises. In this manner they permit children to take advantage, individually, of what has been described as the "teachable moment." When an entire class uses the library, it does so for a specific purpose, related to classroom study, and not according to the old ways of unchanging schedules — to check out books or learn a "library lesson."

What has happened is that the school library program has been integrated with the instructional program and, at best, has become indistinguishable from it. Instead of existing as another teaching station in the school with its own special program, the school library has become the undergirding for the entire curriculum — a service agency supplying materials, and guidance in their use, for all instruction.

In connection with increased use of audio and visual aids in the classroom has come recognition that students may also profitably use them for individual study. Students are encouraged to use tape and disc recordings, filmstrips, slides, and motion picture films in independent study, just as they use books and other printed materials. The school library, which traditionally has provided the printed material, now also supplies the materials and facilities for study with non-print instructional materials.

NEW CONCEPTS IN FACILITIES

Concepts in the planning and design of school libraries have changed to facilitate the use of new materials, and to enable teachers and students to use library materials in new ways. Because of the great emphasis on independent study, school planners have questioned the value of traditional large reading rooms and have either decreased their size, or subdivided them with shelving to create the feeling of several smaller rooms.

Many libraries designed in the last few years have several small reading rooms instead of one large one, often with collections divided by subject. Schools planned for team teaching may have satellite reading rooms located near the subject department classrooms, but administered by the central library.

Within the reading rooms the common multi-student round or rectangular library tables have been partially replaced by individual study carrels. Many schools report that students, given a choice, prefer to work in small rooms and in the semi-isolation provided by a carrel. Both elementary and secondary schools are using them more and more.

ELEMENTARY LIBRARIES

In elementary school libraries, the traditional rows of tables are also likely to give ground to low tables, stools, and other furniture designed to the size of young children. The floor covering often is carpet and, in these schools, the floor is probably where many of the children will be sitting.

Among new facilities included in school libraries are areas for listening and viewing. In some schools these activities are housed in separate rooms included in the library suite. In others, particularly in elementary schools, they may be provided as part of the reading room. Booths, equipped with electrical outlets or with electronic devices, are frequently planned by the architect and built into listening and viewing areas. Here, students use filmstrips, slides, tape and disc recordings, and even motion picture films for individual study, just as they use printed materials. Connected with the listening and viewing area, there is often a sound proof recording booth where students or teachers can make their own tape recordings.

Shelving or cabinets to house nonprint materials, and equipment storage areas, need to be located adjacent to listening and viewing areas for easy accessibility and use. Not only should storage rooms for equipment adjoin the listening and viewing areas, but they should also have direct access to a corridor so that equipment may be moved to classrooms without interfering with any of the library activities.

Each classroom should have a screen for projecting materials so that viewing areas for large groups of students will not be necessary. Instead, many libraries will have a small viewing room where several students may see a motion picture film, or where teachers may preview them. A television receiver could also be included here.

An individual student may also use this room for viewing, although with earphones he can just as readily study a sound film in an individual viewing booth. In general, the library must be planned so that it provides facilities for both individual and small group use of nonprint materials and can supply teachers with materials and equipment for class use of a-v aids.

Another library facility, in a separate room because of noise, is the typing room. Students engaged in research can take materials to the library typing room in order to type notes and prepare reports. The typing room is equipped with counters or tables of proper height for comfortable use of standard typewriters supplied by the school.

Perhaps the most radical change in school library facilities is in the workroom. Schools which depend upon school system processing centers or commercial firms to do their cataloging and processing of books and other materials no longer need large workrooms for these activities. But instead of decreasing the workroom's size, planners have designed it for new purposes. The library workroom has become a center where teachers, librarians, and students produce instructional materials.

They may work together to produce transparencies, overlays, slides, and other materials which cannot be procured from commercial sources. Equipment located in the work-instructional materials production room may include copying machines, photoprinters, camera copying stands, dry-mount presses, spirit duplicators, and other machines used in production of materials. The room must be designed with appropriate counters and electrical outlets to handle the equipment, and with storage cabinets designed to accommodate film and other needed materials. At the same time the area must provide for the more traditional workroom activities — mending, poster-making, preparing exhibits, unpacking books, and so forth. With such a range of activities, the workroom actually turns out to be larger than those in traditional school libraries.

Storage areas have become increasingly important in school libraries, but are usually different from their predecessors. In the past, storage areas have housed back issues of periodicals, primarily, and copies of infrequently used books. Often these areas have only been large enough to house from three to five years of back issues of periodicals most frequently used for student research.

The current emphasis on independent study and research has revealed a need for longer runs of periodicals in school libraries. To overcome a shortage of space, libraries have turned to microfilm. If this trend continues, school libraries probably will not need larger storage areas for periodicals.

However, the same emphasis on individual study has created a need for much larger book collections, larger than school libraries can expect to house in ordinary reading rooms. The need is for stack rooms or areas with sufficient shelving for the larger book collections, perhaps using space formerly reserved for periodicals.

The audio-visual program requires storage areas especially designed for large and small projectors, viewers, record players, projection tables, and equipment. Special shelving must house machines, extension cords, lamps, and other auxiliary items. Projection tables require open floor space out of the way of traffic into and out of the equipment storage area. Though some equipment, particularly in multi-story buildings, may conveniently be stored in other parts of the school, at the same time, a sizable equipment storage area needs to be planned as part of the library suite.

The school library has changed to accommodate and provide new materials and new services. Its physical facilities have also been changing and must continue to change if the school library is to support instruction in the best possible way. Schoolmen and architects must look closely at changing concepts of school library service so that the facilities they plan will be appropriate to changing programs.

CATALOGING AND ADMINISTERING A TAPE COLLECTION FOR THE LANGUAGE LABORATORY

J. C. Sager

The first hundred tapes, especially when in the hands of one teacher and used exclusively by him, offer no difficulties. But as soon as the number of tapes increases, more staff become involved in their use and it is recognized that there is an advantage in a tape collection being made available for the free access of students, the problem of how to administer an ever increasing collection of tapes becomes more serious.

In our third year of laboratory administration with a staff of about twenty, five languages on the curriculum and hundreds of tapes of all kinds of origin and a variety of purposes, we have developed a system of cataloguing for our tape collections which in a modified form might serve as a guiding line for colleagues facing similar problems.

USE OF TAPES

In deciding upon a system for the classification of our tape holdings we had to consider first of all the various uses to which we wanted to put our tapes.

1. There were our intensive courses to consider in which staff monitored laboratory classes. This offered no difficulty provided the course instructor held all the tapes and prepared and monitored the exercise. But as soon as a technician prepared the laboratory and a native speaker monitored the exercise it was necessary to classify every tape and every exercise on it.

2. Then students wanted to go back and repeat a certain tape they had already covered. So we issued every student with two blank tapes which they could exchange at the end of every laboratory period against the recorded tape. But very soon students wanted to work on tapes of which they had not been able to retain copies. They approached the technician for copies giving what indications they could about the tape. The technician complied with their request but not being conversant with the spoken form of the five languages involved, he wasted considerable time in finding appropriate sections of tapes.

3. Lecturers found it convenient to set tape work to be dealt with in the students' own time but limited within a specified period. To copy the appropriate number of tapes required work beyond the time and availability of our technician and copying machines. The need for a fully catalogued student collection of tapes arose which students could use like an open shelf library.

Reprinted with permission from: Sager, J. C., "Cataloging and Administering a Tape Collection for the Language Laboratory," AUDIO VISUAL LANGUAGE JOURNAL, Summer, 1966.

4. Finally, for purposes of revision or private learning by any member of our institution, a tape classification independent of any courses and a subject catalogue of all the material on tape seemed to be the only answer to deal with the numerous demands made upon the laboratories.

The nature of the material involved very soon extended beyond the strict requirements of organized semi-programmed courses. We began to collect readings, lectures, dialogues, songs; in a word, all manifestations of the spoken language in self-made or commercially produced tapes.

TECHNICAL CONSIDERATIONS

Two of the basic questions we had to decide upon were the recording speed and suitable length of tapes, but they were partly decided by the nature of our equipment. So we chose a speed of 3¾" per sec., as this would allow us a transfer speed of 7½" per sec. and a copying speed of 15" per sec. We needed strong tape that would resist quick stopping after a high winding speed and our tape decks limited the size of spools to be used. We chose tapes of 45 minutes duration as the average, as a full period of 50 minutes would seldom yield more than a maximum of 45 minutes actual work. These tapes had the advantage of being quickly rewound, and even if used only for half hour periods the time spent in winding to the appropriate section would be inconsiderable. We were also conditioned by the need to look for convenient storage boxes which we found in units of three and in strong plastic material for 4½" to 5" reels. Single units would be space wasting and not so easily kept in order. Larger units might not suit items in our collection consisting of only two or three tapes. The boxes used as standard also have the advantage that they can stand upright on a shelf. Students are given cardboard boxes with their tapes. These boxes have their name imprinted and allow the students to write on the back what material they want copied. These tapes, of one standard length, go into an "In" tray from where they are collected by a technician, recorded, and returned to an "Out" tray.

There is an order book in the technician's room where staff enter full details of material required with entries for dates, hours, sections of tape and number of student positions to be prepared. It is preferable to have the laboratory positions set up with pre-recorded tapes before the beginning of a drill lesson. In this way students can themselves control their tapes. Besides it always allows the transfer of a recording to another group of students in an emergency.

RECORDING

With an increasing number of staff writing and recording material it was necessary to recommend certain common procedures for scripting and recording:

1. Always record at a speed of 3¾" on the master track and on one side of the tape only. (This may be more expensive but it saves time in using tapes. While two track recordings are possible on master tapes they are inadvisable on student collection tapes. In order to avoid a dual system of classification of tapes for master and student this more costly procedure seemed preferable.)

2. Indications to numbers of tape and number and/or letters and types of drills should always be given in English, e.g. "German grammar drills, second series, one a. substitution drill" (text), "one b. transformation drill", etc. (This will allow the technician to find the relevant section of tape more easily.)

3. If you follow a text book (this applies particularly to tapes for a semi-programmed course) it is convenient to maintain the units of the lesson designating them as 1, 2, 3, etc. and designate the drills to each lesson by letters, e.g. 1a, 1b to 1z, 2a, 2b, etc. A similar division might be useful for other tapes as well, as it helps to locate the drills more easily. If you hear drill 239, you are confused and have to consult a chart telling you that 215-240 belong to lesson, or unit, 14.

4. Do not use the Greek alphabet as technicians, students, or staff for that matter, might get mixed up and pronunciation could create misunderstandings.

5. Always state "end of tape . . . " as often you will have to leave the end of a tape unrecorded as it is not long enough for one drill.

6. In the interest of easy understanding it is advisable to use the conventional names for drills, e.g. Transformation Drill, Substitution Drill, Expansion Drill, Reduction Drill, Repetition Drill, etc. (These two words in English are often more helpful to the technician in finding the beginning of a drill than to the student.)

7. If your larger units are shorter than 45 minutes you may prefer to use shorter tapes.

CATALOGUING

As soon as a tape is recorded it must be catalogued before it is incorporated into the collection. This involves several procedures:

1. The script must be deposited in an appropriate folder stating clearly beginning and end of tape especially when the text is continuous. This script need not contain the corrected answers to the students' responses, but must otherwise be a faithful copy of the material on tape.

2. The tape and its appropriate box must be fully labeled.

3. A catalogue card with full details must be made out for each tape and placed in the appropriate filing box. If necessary a subject reference card has to be made up as well.

NOMENCLATURE FOR TAPES

There is a colour code for languages for easier identification of tapes, script folders, and catalogue card boxes.

We have chosen white for French, blue for German, green for Italian, red for Russian, and yellow for Spanish.

On scripts, cards, and tape boxes where no colour label is used the first capital letter indicates the language, and we have chosen the English names, i.e. G for German, D for Dutch, etc. The second capital indicates the nature of the material on tape.

So far we have used the following subject symbol:

L − language, i.e. semi-programmed material in connection with a course taught;

G − grammar;

S − syntax and **W** − word formation and derivation, for exercises that do not follow a course where these subjects would come together, but are ordered by types of words, inflective systems, types of groups or sentences, etc.;

P − phonetics and intonation;

C − comprehension, only for passages, dialogue or prose, which are followed by questions on the passage or other exercises in connection with it;

R − prose-reading;

V − verse reading;

D − drama and dialogue;

M − music.

Finally for our specific purposes, **T** − Technical glossaries, **I** − interpreting dialogues and **C** − conference speeches.

Should there be more than one series of any material this can be classified by roman numerals. Series can indicate simply material ordered by another criterion, or in the case of material connected with a course, degrees of difficulty such as beginners, intermediate, advanced. But such a division is also possible by drill numbers. Every tape in any series has a number. This is necessary as the material on tapes seldom can be divided up into exact units of 600 feet of tape or 45 minutes.

The label on a tape box could then read GL II. 4. 25r - 26m; the same information would appear on the catalogue card. But the very small label on the tape itself, relying on the colour code and serving merely as an additional identification, can be as short as L II 4.

While recording from the typewritten script, which already contains the language, subject and drill classification, the number and beginning and end of tapes must be entered on the script.

The beginning of a tape would then sound as follows:

"French Grammar, third series, tape six, twenty five c, transformation drill . . ."

and the next drill would be introduced by

"twenty five d, transformation drill."

The tapes themselves would be ordered on the shelves first by languages, secondly by alphabetical order according to the subject index, thirdly by the series and finally by the tape number.

The same system applies to scripts, where several ring-file folders are required for every language; and to the card catalogue, where every language is kept in a separate filing box.

CARD CATALOGUE

Every tape is represented by a card in the catalogue, and contains as a heading the same data as the tape box. It contains information on the source of the tape, i.e., the author of the script and whether it was done in conjunction with a specific textbook. It also indicates the date of the recording, the speaker of the tape, the length of the tape, and the type of drills or exercises on the tape, e.g. continuous text, open ended drill, two, three or four phase drill, etc. While this information has only technical relevance, the list of contents which follows is of great importance to students. Here every drill or every small unit of drills dealing with the same point is listed, and the purpose of the drill given, e.g. "26g. number: agreement subject-predicate" or "29r. contrast of initial and final s". When the tape does not contain drills, the titles of songs, short stories, etc. are given here with indication of author, composer, etc.

The subject index will have to look partly like the index of a good grammar which lists grammatical topics in detail and at the same time words and expressions specially treated. But it will also have the titles of short stories, poems, songs, as well as their authors. Reference must be made to sections of a tape, and in material other than drills where length is relatively uniform, length in minutes should be given, but this is a point of refinement we have not as yet introduced.

The subject index can be divided into as many parts as there are subjects in the card catalogue and could, for that matter, stand together with the tape catalogue, either preceding or following the cards for tapes. This system may be useful in a small collection, but in a larger one it may not yield the information required, and therefore I think it is better to have an alphabetical subject catalogue completely apart from the tape catalogue. It will also be found that the tape catalogue will be required mostly by staff in connection with the collection of master tapes, whereas the subject index is a guide to the student collection, which should in any case be housed in the open laboratory itself where students have permanent access to it.

SPEEDY REPAIR EQUALS GOOD UTILIZATION

Robert L. Pryor

AUDIOVISUAL EQUIPMENT is of little value unless a definite plan of maintenance and repair can assure teachers that equipment will be available when needed. Equipment taken from the school for long periods of time tends to lose its effectiveness as a teaching tool.

For many years, the Instructional Aids Department of the Spokane Public Schools has operated a maintenance and repair section as part of its service. At present this means 3,000 pieces of equipment to be kept in working condition, including 300 television sets used every day. A sizable task by any standard, this phase of the Department's operation is manned by three men — the assistant to the Department supervisor and two technicians.

In the fall of 1960 the Department experimentally installed a system of two-way radio communication, operating on Citizens Band between the maintenance truck and the Instructional Aids Department. We believed that many miles could be saved by this installation because trouble calls frequently originate in areas where the truck is already operating. We found the system highly satisfactory, and after the first year, made it a permanent part of our activity. We also installed a unit in the truck that delivers audiovisual materials and mail to all of the district schools.

Work orders are taken over the telephone by a Department clerk, written up on order forms, and sent directly to the maintenance section of the Department. There the work orders are clipped to the dispatch board under labels indicating the four sections of the city. A colored pin is placed on a large city map above the sectional clips to indicate the location of the school requesting service. When a piece of equipment has been repaired, another color-coded pin is located on the map to indicate a return delivery. This system enables the technician to tell at a glance where deliveries and pick-ups are needed, and thus facilitates the routing of the maintenance truck.

The end result of the maintenance service has been speedier repair, giving teachers their audiovisual tools when they need them. Out-of-service time has decreased on individual items, and much of the maintenance work can now be completed at the school.

Does it pay the school district to operate its own equipment and maintenance service? Comparisons with other districts indicate that our operation has been more economical than commercial service — both in dollars and cents, and from the standpoint of cutting down on out-of-service time for equipment. It may be of interest to note that the maintenance staff also adds to the versatility of the

Reprinted with permission from: Pryor, Robert L.; "Speedy Repair Equals Good Utilization," AUDIOVISUAL INSTRUCTION, March, 1963.

department, permitting it to operate graphic and photographic laboratories, train projectionists, give demonstrations and workshops, and perform innumerable unusual services.

We are convinced that we have a sound program.

AV FOR INDEPENDENT STUDY

L. D. Miller

During the 1960-61 school year, 27,400 students at Purdue University made use of the Audiovisual Center's facilities for independent study. This was an increase of more than 20,000 students over 1958-59 when a little less than 7,000 persons used these same facilities. Student demands have made it advisable to keep the Center open 90 hours per week and pressure is strong to have this increased still more.

Current plans are to install a network of audio lines by which eventually the majority of the classrooms on campus can, at the wish of the professor, be connected to tape centers in the individual buildings or to the consoles in the AV Center. This will permit the Center to record lectures at the instructor's request and make them available for student use. The number of these requests are encouraging even now, but the possibilities for the future are almost unlimited.

Students began viewing films independently at Purdue as early as 1950, and in 1955 all students on campus were invited to use the Center's library of films and filmstrips. The following year tapes were made available. In spite of poor equipment and drab surroundings, sufficient numbers came to demonstrate the value of the program. When the center moved into larger quarters in 1958, the volume of independent study began to climb sharply upward.

An analysis covering the 12 months ending in June 1961 showed that 19 percent of student activity at the Center was devoted to viewing films and 76 percent to listening to tapes. This preponderance of tape listening reflects the fact that students in the modern language department are familiar with tapes and tape recorders and that the language instructors encourage their students to spend extra time in the AV Center. Another factor has been the development of special taped materials for some courses in English and General Studies.

The rapid increase in the number of tapes, with consequently greater potential for listeners, has been made possible through the activities of students and

Reprinted with permission from: Miller, L.D., "AV for Independent Study," AUDIO-VISUAL INSTRUCTION, November, 1961.

staff. For instance, a Freshman physics section recorded their class sessions and deposited the tape lectures in the Center. They considered this profitable since the professor was of foreign extraction and somewhat difficult to understand. The opportunity to re-run portions of the tapes solved the problem.

Another series of tapes receiving heavy usage were the ones developed by an instructor in the English department for his course in folk lore. After playing selections in class to illustrate points or to give an overview, he directed the students to the AV Center's tapes for specifics. This worked so well that the same pattern was followed in a course of music appreciation.

Procedures in the AV library are kept as simple as possible. They are the same for staff as for students, except that the student is required to present his identification card (referred to as "passport"). Presentation of this card bearing the student's name and picture entitles him to use any film, filmstrip, or recording in the Center but does not permit him to carry it from the premises. Taking materials home would undoubtedly be advantageous to the student but would necessitate an investment in materials prohibitive at the present time.

The student can, however, bring his own recorder to the Center and copy all of the non-copyrighted material he desires. The Center also will make copies for him for a small charge. Many of these taped copies are stockpiled in residence halls where they reportedly get considerable use, especially before examination. Others are used by students who find it inconvenient to spend time at the Center.

The method by which a student secures and uses materials (in this case a film) are as follows: (1) He makes his selection from the card file and, (2) on a special keysort card places the name of the film and its call number. (3) This and his ID card are given to the staff member on duty who, (4) secures the film and stamps the card in a special machine. (5) The ID card is returned to the student along with the film, take-up reel and a key to a viewing room. (6) The student operates his own equipment and (7) when he is finished he returns the film, reel, and key to the counter.

Since the Center inspects films after each showing, maintains careful supervision, and keeps projectors in good condition, film damage has been surprisingly small. Records indicate that there has been much less damage from threading errors during individual viewing than from comparable use by off-campus borrowers. To reduce operating mistakes still further the Center is planning to install mechanical instructional devices in each viewing room. These are expected to carry the load of introducing and training persons in the operation of the equipment. One room equipped for a time with a conventional slide projector and auxiliary equipment demonstrated that no other help is necessary in learning to operate a 16mm sound projector. As soon as a compact, less expensive device can be purchased or made locally, it will be put to use, thus reducing the sometimes exasperating demands upon the Center staff.

As previously noted, individual requests are made on a special card. Information such as the type of material, its shelf number, room to which the person is assigned, date, and hour are punched into this card. The cards are sorted regularly providing data for persons or departments concerned. This information also helps in planning for growth of the program.

The increase in demands for individual use of AV materials has raised many questions about the students who participate. Are they the slow, average, or brilliant ones. How many are saved from failing courses through the extra work at the Center. Is there any correlation between long hours with tape and film and success in school? A study has been planned by which a start may be made toward answering some of these questions. Presently it appears that results justify the expenditure of time and money.

MANAGING MODERN MEDIA

Vincent Lanier

The disadvantages of using newer media in teaching art are difficult to face. Yet, there are educational liabilities in the uses of media which can be ameliorated only by thoughtful consideration.

One of these problems is quality control, which we have previously discussed. Another is the possibility, however remote, of teacher dependence on the supportive qualities of media materials. For example, it is not the best teaching procedure to delay a lesson on perspective to a ready class simply because the film ordered on that subject has not arrived. This type of incident may seem unlikely at the moment because most of us are not used to teaching consistently with media, but it is not uncommon in the home to hear the helpless cry of "What shall I do?" when the television set breaks down.

Perhaps the most serious disadvantage of newer media is one which is mentioned the least, the problem of mechanical failure. We all recognize a slide jammed in a projector, a burnt out lamp, and broken film as ever-present hazards and all too frequent occurrences. However, in many cases, it is human error rather than mechanical failure which causes a breakdown. Carelessness, unfamiliarity with a particular device, and lack of adequate preparation or testing all may contribute to an unfortunate interruption of the media process.

One answer to the breakdown problem may lie in the development of simpler systems. If we look at media as a means for data processing—the storage and retrieval of data—visual and verbal, our problems of mechanical failure lie primarily in the area of retrieval. For example, information or data in the form of pictures is stored on slides. That information is retrieved or presented by projec-

Reprinted with permission from: Lanier, Vincent, "Managing Modern Media", ARTS AND ACTIVITIES, September, 1966.

ting the slides on a screen. When a slide jams in a projector, we can say the retrieval system has failed.

We also can look at the need for a simplified retrieval system from another direction. As we move into an era of multi-media presentations, the chances of a breakdown in the presentation process becomes much greater. In making my report, "Uses of Newer Media Project", to the NAEA regional conferences, I used one screen, one slide projector with two trays of slides, one super 8mm motion picture projector and one 16mm projector. To a nonspecialist such as myself, this was an impressive array of equipment and its coordination and proper functioning was a serious concern.

Most of this problem can be solved with the development of a simple, single projection system. What we need, and will ultimately have, is an all purpose sight-sound projector, drawing its works and pictures from the vast storage source of a computer memory bank. The specific characteristics of this system are technological issues on which I can shed no light, but the particulars of our requirements may be profitably discussed here.

Most instructors who teach art, whatever the level and circumstances, use pictorial material to illustrate what they say to students. To talk about art without some visual point of reference is usually a weak, if not fruitless, effort. Of course, this is less true, or even untrue, in some aspects of the field, such as philosophy of art education or aesthetics. Or, it may be that pictorial reference for students at a higher learning level becomes less necessary since we are able, when familiar with a field, to hold pictures in our minds for reference purposes. Interestingly enough, it is usually necessary to use words in the teaching of art. Can you visualize a completely silent art class?

In the majority of instructional situations, the availability of visual material is of paramount importance to effective learning. Therefore, what the art teacher needs is a large reservoir of visual images—paintings, photographs, diagrams, etc. —which can be called up individually or in prearranged series, with, if desired, spoken or printed verbal support. The technologist will have to decide just what devices and procedures will be appropriate to the task of presenting these programs as required by the art teacher. Perhaps a system similar to closed-circuit television may be the best we can get, or a further sophistication of a process similar to the Westinghouse Phonovoid in which visual images are stored on a disc similar to a phonograph record, or a completely new system which is unknown or unpublicized today.

Whatever the alternative or final choice, this aspect of the issue belongs primarily to the engineer rather than the art educator. We can be confident that our modern technology will fulfill our demands, however stringent, given sufficient time and funds for research and development. The portion of the issue that is the responsibility of the art educator is the selection of the visual and verbal data to be stored.

It is easy enough to decide that Renoir's *Moulin de la Galette* should be represented in our storage computer, and it would not be too difficult to find experts knowledgeable enough to select the most authentic slides, reproductions or whatever form the storage and retrieval system dictates. However, it is another matter to decide which views of Taliesin West are essential, or whether that building or another particular drawing or craft item is essential for storage. Many of the thousands of art objects created by the human race will probably have to be left out, and it is this type of decision that only the art educator can make. Fortunately, the growing maturity of our field and the increasing effectiveness of our organization suggests that this task may be efficiently accomplished.

A move in this direction in the near future raises one more critical problem— the activity curtailment of commercial organizations now producing and distributing media. As a comparable example, recent developments in photocopying techniques make it possible for one copy of a book, in one library, to serve as a master and be distributed, by photocopy, to the entire nation—thereby virtually destroying the publisher as a social and commercial institution. The existence of one or several media storage banks from which teachers may draw visual materials without duplication may almost eliminate the media producer or distributor.

We must be aware of all these implications and not ignore them in our thinking, as it is convenient to do.

Section Six

PERSONNEL OF
AN IMC

THE ROLE OF THE EDUCATIONAL COMMUNICATIONS SPECIALIST

Philip Lewis

In many instances last year's answers are no longer valid in terms of improving the educational program for our schools. Our major objectives, in the larger sense, may still be quite similar, but educational technology has advanced at such a rapid clip that we are now at the point where progress can be made toward the realization of goals that seemed quite distant only months ago.

The key to progress will be our willingness to go the distance to reexamine current practices, to determine necessary changes, and to apply the accumulated evidence of research to the solution of emerging problems. For example, it is no longer a question of merely requesting more money to do on a larger scale the usual things to meet the student population explosion. Similarly, the knowledge explosion is changing the role of the teacher. No longer is he the source of all knowledge, but rather assumes the function of a resource person who can guide, direct and work on an individual basis with students to meet their special needs— to enable them to realize their full potential in the pursuit of learning.

We must face the fact that some of the things we are now doing are inefficient in light of available know-how. Perhaps our dilemma is due to the situation that we have never really evaluated current practices in terms of current possibilities. It may seem comfortable to continue with familiar practices, but can it be said with validity that the approaches are sound in terms of the established goals? When educational television appeared on the scene, a real effort was made to test, to appraise, and to evaluate this new medium. How many other technological contributions to education have been similarly and promptly treated.

EDUCATION OF THE COMMUNICATIONS SPECIALIST

In considering the role of the Educational Communications Specialist, do we really know what to expect of him or what he should be able to do? It is certain that practitioners in the field of educational communications are necessary to reinforce or complement the more narrowly specialized materials and equipment

Reprinted with permission from: Lewis, Philip, "The Role of the Educational Communications Specialist," SCHOOL BOARD JOURNAL, December, 1961.

handler. It is an easy out to decide that this new person should take a prescribed list of courses for preparation for such an assignment. However, the indications are that since instructional procedures, learning theory, and classroom methodology are undergoing significant changes, the communications specialist must be conversant with the broad field of education as well as with his specialization in instructional materials and new media.

During the Seventh Lake Okoboji Audio-Visual Leadership Conference, sponsored by the State University of Iowa and the Department of Audio-Visual Instruction, NEA (April 1961), a proposed organization was submitted for discussion purposes to indicate the possible place of this specialist in the hierarchy of school districts, county schools and individual schools. This position would, of course, take many different forms in organizational patterns. The small school might utilize a single person for curriculum direction as well as for communications and instructional materials administration. In large institutions, the Educational Communications Specialist might head up a series of sections or divisions including library, audio-visual, ETV, teaching machines, reading laboratories, language laboratories, et cetera.

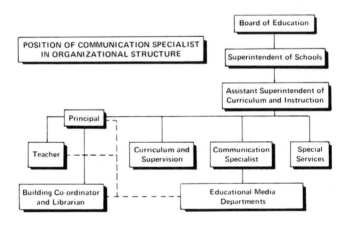

To the degree dictated by the local circumstances, the Educational Communications Specialist should be prepared to:

1. Be directly involved in curriculum planning.

2. Promote among teachers, administrators, school governing bodies, and school patrons the concept that the use of resource materials is integral to instruction and not an adjunct to be used when time permits.

3. Establish an educational climate suitable for the optimum use of instructional media and materials.

4. Develop new measures for determining the effectiveness of instructional materials in specific applications.

5. Be responsible for evaluating emerging innovations for possible introduction into the learning process and for interpreting and promoting those innovations which can make a significant contribution.

6. Become involved in the development of central classification systems that will permit rapid location of related instructional materials for specific learning situations.

7. Arrange for the acquisition or production of instructional materials which are not readily available but are necessary for the instructional program and provide the incentive, training, and materials for production by teachers and others.

8. Provide consultation opportunities for all teachers, including teachers-in-training, to secure assistance in the use of new media and materials in their lesson planning.

9. Contribute to the improvement of methods of communication within the profession on matters relative to the emerging practices and innovations, the exchanging of ideas, and the establishing of liaison with outside agencies—the "clearinghouse" idea.

10. Be involved in decision-making activities on such matters as building-planning, classroom design, etc., as they affect the instructional materials program.

11. Assume the leadership responsibility for initiating programs or activities that will bring about needed improvements and innovations.

12. Develop and implement instructional systems involving automation approaches to expedite free flow of information and ideas (communications centers, learning laboratories, random access devices, etc.).

13. Make use of research results.

14. Provide a variety of well-selected instructional materials and equipment, easily accessible for use by teachers and pupils and give encouragement and/or administrative support for the effective use of these materials.

COMPETENCIES OF THE COMMUNICATIONS SPECIALIST

In order to be prepared to function effectively in the ways listed above, the Educational Communication Specialist must possess certain competencies. He must:

1. Have a knowledge of curriculum theory and of the dynamics of curriculum change and development.

2. Have a background of successful teaching experience and specialized education to assure a high degree of proficiency as a demonstrator of effective utilization techniques, as a proponent of the best educational methodology, and as one possessing thorough knowledge of the strengths and weaknesses of all types of materials.

3. Be able to communicate ideas clearly and succinctly to professional and lay people through the use of appropriate media.

4. Be able to delegate responsibilities, other than supervision, when a project reaches the level of development where it is a functional operation.

5. Have ability to initiate interaction with his colleagues to explore the possibilities inherent in new ideas or proposals prior to actual experimentation.

6. Be a communicator, interpreter, and promoter of the research results in the field.

7. Have a knowledge of classification and cataloging procedures and the ability to implement them.

8. Be professionally prepared and aggressive enough to acquire that status which will involve him in decision-making activities at high administrative levels.

9. Maintain intellectual curiosity and display a willingness to keep abreast of new developments by participating in conferences, conventions, and workshops, by keeping up to date with the literature of the field, and by engaging in the additional training which the new demands of his position make necessary.

10. Have a knowledge of building design and facilities which will permit optimum use of materials and equipment.

11. Be able to work effectively with individuals and with groups.

Although only a few educational systems and institutions have moved in the direction of establishing an organization and position for handling instructional materials and media along the lines proposed, there is great urgency that this movement is accelerated. Here is an opportunity to help streamline teaching and learning—to actually begin to meet the challenge to bring about more learning in less time at a higher level of effectiveness.

THE NEW LIBRARIAN

"When I went away to library school," recalls Maryan Reynolds of Olympia, Wash., "my father warned me: 'Don't come back with your hair in a bun, white cuffs slightly soiled, looking as if you should be hung on the line for a good airing'." Hair buns and white cuffs could be found among the 9,000 librarians in New York last week for the 85th annual convention of the American Library Association, but so could a new spirit: thanks to the information explosion, libraries are where the action is.

The demand for information—and for librarians to give order to the mountains of paper, recordings, film and microfilm that pour into libraries every day—has grown enormously in recent years. Though there are 70,000 librarians in the U.S., one expert estimates that at least 100,000 more are needed just to fill current needs.

Jobs are being created in new types of libraries, many of them operated by industry for specialized information. IBM, for instance, runs 25 libraries in the U.S. and fifteen overseas, and 67 of the industrial firms on Fortune magazine's list of the top 500 have libraries in the U.S. and abroad. As companies demand more information, predicts Paul Wasserman, dean of the University of Maryland's new library school, company librarians will be included in decision-making groups. Even the title has changed: firms advertise for "information retrieval specialists."

Modern Hero: Libraries in secondary and elementary schools are also growing rapidly, with the help of Federal dollars. Title II of the Elementary and Secondary School Act alone has authorized some $100 million for libraries.

Because of the new demand for librarians and the high education-level required, salaries are rising—a graduate from library school with a science background can expect $9,000 to $12,000 as starting pay in some research libraries. The financial lure and new technologies are drawing hundreds of innovation-minded new librarians into the stacks. The dean of the University of Chicago's graduate library school, 41-year-old Don R. Swanson, is a physicist. "Physicists like to tackle new problems," he explains, "and there are more unsolved problems today in information science than in any other field."

The solution, clearly, lies primarily in automation, and the computer is steadily changing both libraries and librarians. While libraries tend to be conservative institutions, says Wasserman, "the data-processing expert has assumed the role of the modern hero of librarianship."

Transformation: When Western Reserve University's library school offered its first computer course in 1955, recalls dean Jesse H. Shera, "we were told we were ruining librarianship." Soon it will be impossible to run a large library without a computer-librarian. This fall sixteen research libraries will begin receiving experimental computer tapes containing catalogue information on all new

Reprinted with permission from: "The New Librarian," NEWSWEEK, July 25, 1966.

English-language monographs received and catalogued by the Library of Congress. LC director L. Quincy Mumford predicts that the entire LC catalogue will be computerized by 1972.

Machine catalogues, however, seem modest compared to the automation facilities at some science libraries. The National Library of Medicine in Bethesda, Md., is one leader with its Index Medicus, a computerized reference to medical literature. Each year the library prepares abstracts of more than 175,000 articles published in about 2,500 of the world's leading biomedical journals. The abstracts are indexed and transferred to magnetic tapes. From the tapes computers print a monthly Index and answer requests for specialized articles.

The NLM also uses a mobile camera which goes into the stacks and copies specific book pages for doctors upon request. Developments such as this seem to herald the end of the book and to confirm Marshall McLuhan's vision of the future. Martin M. Cummings, director of the NLM, predicts that complete texts and articles eventually will be stored in computers and be made available through a national network of retrieval devices. "I think such a system will be operational by 1975," he says. "The literature explosion is so vast that everything will break down first."

NASA is already into the McLuhanesque 1970s. Its red-brick, two-story library in College Park, Md., is almost as advanced as the space research it supports. One section of the building contains 50,000 square feet of stacks with all the NASA reports. Upstairs, the same information is condensed onto microfiche cards stored in a space smaller than a single bowling alley. And in the computer area, 18 reels of tape hold all available NASA information.

No Waiting: In addition to providing quick access to material, computer tapes serve another purpose. Through the Selective Dissemination of Information (SDI) system NASA is able to send to some 900 scientists lists of reports published in their fields. Both the articles and the interests of the scientists are coded and fed into the computer. If a scientist wants to read an article called to his attention by SDI, he sends back a punched card which tells the machine to send him a copy.

Herbert S. White, who directs the system, is as good an example as any of the new librarians. "Our responsibility," he told NEWSWEEK'S Steve Saler, "is to get information out rapidly. Too many libraries are waiting for people to ask them for something." But, adds White, "a machine won't tell you whether the material is any good. Human evaluation is still necessary."

IMPLICATIONS OF DATA PROCESSING TECHNOLOGY FOR MEDIA SPECIALISTS

Glenn D. McMurry

Designed to inform the media specialist of the present state of the art of the application of computer technology to instruction, this preconvention symposium featured three presentations and the reactions of a six-man panel.

PRESENTATIONS

R. Louis Bright, U.S. Office of Education, in his discussion of "The Educator's Need for Computer Understanding" pointed out that the educator's fear reaction to computers can well be understood, especially when one looks at the changes that have taken place in other fields as a direct result of the new technology introduced by computers. The educator's role will change and has already changed in some areas such as administration. He discussed some of the uses of the computer in schools — grading, testing, and attendance. "Why educators need to know about computers is obvious," said Mr. Bright. "What they need to know is less obvious."

The educator does not need to know programing, but it helps. It gives him a background of knowledge and helps him to know what other people are talking about. Mr. Bright explained why the computer is so important these days — it can manipulate symbols extremely fast, can make logical decisions depending upon the program routines, and has the ability to branch out to an almost endless number of subroutines. The computer does more than multiply and divide; in fact, most computer applications do not involve mathematics at all. Most of the present load is in language translation — in other words, translating the language of the programer into the language of the computer. The computer can measure response times with ease. One thing that the computer cannot do, however, is to develop self-confidence in people or handle the relations between them.

Mr. Bright emphasized the importance of allowing for program expense. In setting up a budget, one should allocate as much for programing costs as for equipment rental. Computer-assisted instruction seems to be a very practical use for the equipment. Although expensive to begin.with, present developments are bringing these costs down. Mr. Bright concluded with the statement that "the applications of the computer are mainly limited by the imagination of the people using them."

Donald D. Bushnell of the Brooks Foundation reported on "The Columbia City, Maryland, Computerized Media Project." A planned community of some

Reprinted with permission from: McMurry, Glenn D., "Implications of Data Processing Technology for Media Specialists," AUDIOVISUAL INSTRUCTION, June-July, 1966.

400,000 people, Columbia City will have each home connected by a coaxial cable which not only transmits video, but is linked to a computer to allow for feedback. This feedback from the user can be utilized to individualize instruction. Many unique applications are being explored. One extremely interesting facet of the project is that the information will be available at any time to anyone, and anyone can have access to all information.

Mr. Bushnell explained the rationale for the project in detail. He also explained some of the systems for improving instruction that were developed at System Development Corporation. The insights gained at SDC provided a superior instructional program which could take care of slow as well as fast learners. He discussed further the development of remedial materials and how the instructional system was modified as a result of the knowledge gained through feedback. These experiences and many others were combined to build the Columbia City instructional program which is expected to take two years to develop.

The presentation made by Ronald L. Hunt, Brooks Foundation, was entitled "Data Processing in the Administration of Media Programs." Mr. Hunt indicated that the number of school systems using computers will increase sharply in the near future. He emphasized that computers will not only improve the existing administrative programs, but will completely change some of them. These improvements and changes will affect all aspects of the administrative program, for computers will perform jobs ranging from simple reporting to complex electronic transmission of materials. Technical assistance is necessary if we are going to handle the deluge of data being acquired as a result of individual instruction, observed Mr. Hunt, and data processing can handle these programs. The equipment and systems are presently available, he explained, but studies need to be made to assess their effectiveness and economic feasibility.

REACTOR PANEL

"To whom should we address this new technology?" asked Albert L. Goldberg of Honeywell, Inc. The equipment and technology are here. Finding enough money to put these two together into an integrated system seems to be the problem. He pointed out that costs are reasonable these days; installing a computer, for example, is comparable in cost to installing a vocational automobile shop in the public school. Also, there is legislation that includes the rental for installing data processing equipment. Manufacturers are offering training for educators in the operation and management of their equipment, and they can help educators solve these problems. However, the problem must be defined by the educators themselves, and then their real needs for equipment can be determined. There is no doubt but that this type of equipment is different from conventional audiovisual equipment, stressed Mr. Goldberg, for it is very complex.

Mr. Goldberg further emphasized that media people are not involved in decision making when it comes to data processing. Someone else "up there" decides and may offer some "leftover" time to the audiovisual director. Media people need to be in early on the decisions that are made on data processing equipment, concluded Mr. Goldberg.

Glenn D. McMurry, University of Southern California, stressed several points based upon his experiences with automated cataloging. He pointed out the need to obtain accurate information about computer equipment available and to learn all one can about data processing. Such knowledge will help one get what he wants from the equipment, he explained. He also emphasized the importance of improving the appearance of the computer print-out; resistance to the upper case print-out can be minimized. Since no two computer configurations are alike, one must know his computer's capabilities. If possible, he stated, demand accessibility to the computer. Some prime time of the day should be reserved for sign-up time.

Before one can manipulate any data, it must be gathered and accurately stored in the computer, noted Mr. McMurry. He also observed that keypunch cards should not be discounted; because of their utility value, they will probably be used for some time. Be ready to accept standards in the media field, he cautioned. Hire a competent programer and learn how to communicate with computer people.

Charles J. Vento, also of the University of Southern California, then indicated that unless media specialists accept the standards set up by the Automated Cataloging Project, each job is a hand job, not a computerized one. He emphasized further that media people must get into management before they can expect any real success in data processing. Management in this instance, according to Mr. Vento, will mean administration or curriculum development.

With all of the technology at our disposal, observed Amo De Bernardis, Portland, Oregon, Community College, we still must hold meetings in non-air-conditioned rooms, we still have equipment that will not work, and we never get our material when we want it. Perhaps, he said, the head may be the best computer. With a very light touch, Mr. De Bernardis pointed out that whereas he used to get his reports in two days, now he is lucky to have them in three months. No one gets his grades until all grades are in. He concluded by expressing the thought that technology is fine; however, whatever the gadget, it must assit the teacher. Furthermore, the children want someone to talk to; they must be able to talk to someone. We want more time for teachers with their own pupils, not more time in the coffee shop.

"The educator must learn what the computer does," stated Theodore Carp, General Electric Company. He pointed out that it is cheaper to build a general-purpose computer than a specialized one. Therefore, in order to ask for specific pieces of equipment, the educator must know his equipment. Special requirements in education require particular equipment, and only when the educator can communicate the special needs to industry will this equipment be forthcoming.

Eugene K. Oxhandler of Syracuse, New York, University stated that computers will never replace the teacher unless he is merely a dispenser of information and facts. In its right context, the computer will assist the teacher.

Mr. Oxhandler described the feasibility project at Syracuse University, where 20 cooperating film libraries in New York State are being used to simulate a library service. They are experimenting and simulating library situations while the real program continues. Mr. Oxhandler feels that much work needs to be done before we start on school children themselves. The role of the teacher as a communicator was emphasized, as well as the fact that the computer must increase the time the teacher is able to spend with each child. According to Mr. Oxhandler, teachers will have three basic roles in future educational systems: the gatherers of information, the programers of the information to be taught, and the teachers of the information.

THE HIGH-SCHOOL LIBRARY
AS A CURRICULUM MATERIAL CENTER

John J. Farley

At the first faculty meeting of the year, the new audio-visual co-ordinator at a New Jersey high school was introduced to his colleagues. Asked to say a few words about his proposed A-V program, he began, "My area will be the learning that takes place through seeing and hearing . . ."

At this point, a crusty old veteran of twenty-six years in the classroom muttered cynically in my ear, "Good. The rest of us will worry about the learning that takes place through smelling."

Actually, this A-V man was a pretty competent fellow, and he didn't mean to lay claim to as broad a field as his opening remarks seemed to indicate, but they do bring up the question of just what an audio-visual specialist is supposed to specialize in. Since the administration of audio-visual education is a relatively new field, there is still a great deal of vagueness about what it entails.

One concept of the A-V man's job, and a fairly common one, would have him in charge of films, filmstrips, slides, records, and tapes, together with the equipment necessary for use of them. Surely this notion is such a narrow one that it would hardly justify the presence of a full-time audio-visual expert on the staff of any but the very largest high schools.

The trend in the audio-visual field seems instead to be in the direction of general instructional materials service.

The materials used in teaching and learning are today so many and so varied that no teacher can know all about them, even in his own field, much less

Reprinted with permission from: Farley, John J., "The High School Library as a Curriculum Materials Center." THE CLEARING HOUSE, November, 1959, and February, 1963.

attempt to acquire, handle, and store them efficiently for classroom use. They comprise not only the usual audio-visual materials but maps, globes, charts, pictures, prints, models, posters, and textbooks. Even the people and places in the community can be used as instructional aids. So can commercial motion pictures and radio and television programs. There is also the vast store of free and inexpensive sponsored materials available to every teacher, a surprising number of them of very high quality. And there are, best of all, books. Not only textbooks but library books, supplementary classroom books, magazines, pamphlets, paperbacks.

Someone is needed in the school who will be an instructional materials expert, not just a film-and-record man. The instructional materials specialist should be an audio-visual expert on the side but should range much more widely and be concerned with all of the materials that can aid and improve teaching and learning. He would, incidentally, be an ex officio member of every curriculum committee.

It is my belief that the person who is best qualified for such service in the high school is the top-notch librarian.

Many librarians turn an attractive shade of purple when anyone suggests broadening the scope of their duties, and perhaps they have good cause. They're usually bogged down with so much clerical work and so little assistance that they despair of ever getting their real professional duties accomplished. But actually only the librarian (the real librarian, not the one who is, in every sense of the word, a bookkeeper) has the training, the experience, and the broad grasp of the high-school curriculum that are necessary for good materials service. The "audio-visual' expert" usually doesn't. He is overspecialized. He is concerned with only a few kinds of instructional materials, and not necessarily the most important ones, and if he has had any training in his field it has usually been too narrow.

What is needed is a person who is familiar with all instructional materials, not an electronics engineer. The school librarian has been trained to know the sources and the values of all kinds of learning materials, including visual aids. He may not know the intricacies of projection and recording equipment, but he doesn't need to. This is a custodial and not a professional function. What he needs to know about the equipment he can learn easily.

Accepting the librarian as the school's instructional materials expert would involve some changes in the usual concept of the school library, but some changes in this concept are long overdue anyway. The high-school library should be a curriculum materials center. All of the school's resources for learning should be there, including audio-visual materials. It should be a learning and information center for students and faculty. A teacher or student gathering material on a given unit of knowledge shouldn't need to visit library, textbook office, audio-visual center, and then try the local phone book for sources of aid. All of these sources should be at the fingertips of one person in the school, and the logical fingertips are the librarian's. If we were to accept this concept of library service we might eventually make the library what librarians have wistfully been hoping for years it might become, "the heart of the school."

It would give the librarian a chance to put his real competencies at the service of faculty and students, and lift him out of the status of study-hall monitor and clerk. It would enhance his case for more professional and clerical aid. It would possibly even free him from the burden of giving "library instruction," a time-consuming job that is better done by the classroom teacher, but which the classroom teacher prefers to have done by the librarian so that the teacher can brighten his day with a cigarette and coffee.

A school which is fortunate enough to have a really professional librarian and a halfway decent budget can go far in the improvement of instruction by centralizing all curriculum materials in the library. Such a school is not only increasing its administrative efficiency but is making the job of good teaching easier.

AV AND LIBRARY: COMPLEMENT OR MERGE?

James W. Brown

While separate audiovisual and library services in our schools are likely to be inefficient and certainly out of step with modern educational trends; in the long run merely merging the facilities may not really be a more satisfactory answer.

For unless merging enables us to catalyze, to release, and to magnify the beneficial effects of professional educational media services, the process seems hardly worth the effort. And while such magnification is entirely feasible and possible, it may be difficult to achieve without considerable change in our professional viewpoints.

If our merger is only a formality, and afterward we continue doing things in the old inefficient compartmentalized ways, we might just as well maintain separateness.

The time has never been more propitious for us to remake the educational media field; to strike boldly out toward integration; to offer a combined, comprehensive educational media service that heretofore has been only a dream which we really never believed could be achieved.

Recent circumstances and conditions pointing to the desirability of *merging* library and audiovisual services in our single schools are:

1. Vastly expanding general attention to the improvement of teaching and learning.

Reprinted with permission from: Brown, James W., "AV and Library: Complement or Merge?" EDUCATIONAL SCREEN, January, 1967.

2. Recognizing the great importance of all kinds of media in teaching and learning and a disposition on the part of national and state legislatures and local boards of education to support purchases of significantly larger quantities of media than ever before.

Virginia's $1¼ million appropriation in 1946 was something of a "shaker" in its time, but it would hardly be noticed today. Provisions of the Elementary and Secondary Education Act, the Higher Education Act, and all others give a kind of largesse we of the 1946 era would never have dared to dream about. But it is here with us now and we *must* deal with it efficiently.

3. More and more individuals, many of them highly qualified or capable of becoming so, are professionally involved with "educational media." Included are the school librarians.

The ALA Standards for School Library Programs, to name one publication, contains recommendations resembling those of "pure" audiovisual groups. The list of job functions of school librarians as prepared by the American Association of School Librarians and those of audiovisual coordinators prepared by the NEA's Department of Audio-Visual Instruction have a tendency (probably a good one) to overlap. It's hard, in such cases, to see any real differences in professed professional purposes.

4. As more and more school superintendents become involved with educational media enrichment programs supported by various federal government appropriations, they turn anxiously toward professional audiovisual and school librarian associations in an effort to locate suitably trained professional personnel capable of grasping and handling the myriad responsibilities of educational media.

Too often we hear that they are dissapointed in their quest. They can hire librarians; they can even hire educational media *specialists* of various kinds; but they find it most difficult to locate qualified *generalists* who are at home in several aspects of the field.

Somehow these individuals seem to be missing. "You people are talking a good game," say these same superintendents, "but where are the graduates who can handle a comprehensive media program in our schools?"

What will the new merged or combined instructional materials or learning resources center of the single school of the future be like? What services will it provide? How will it differ from the separately organized library and AV center? I see it as a vital link in the teaching-learning endeavors of the single school.

The following will occur there:

• A teacher and a materials generalist will work together to *clarify objectives* of unit study; they will give special attention to the background, ability, needs, and interests of the student group.

• IMC personnel working closely with teacher (perhaps, too, with a student committee) will choose a variety of suitable materials from the IMC collection; printed, audiovisual, real.

• The materials generalist and teacher together will give students a *prefatory overview* of what is available, its characteristics, and special values in the study to be undertaken.

• Decentralized room libraries or subject laboratories will be set up for convenience of those using materials. Students may serve as room librarians to control materials sources.

• The materials generalist and teacher (still working together) will continue to guide students in selecting and using materials throughout the study period. As they find need for using the other IMC resources, suitable schedules are arranged for independent study materials, auditioning, and the like. Special displays also are arranged in the IMC or in the classroom with the aid of IMC staff.

• Center service facilities will be provided as needed for production of slides, transparencies, duplicated materials, charts, and the like.

• The materials generalist will indicate the availability of other suitable materials not in the center collection; films in the district IMC, a field trip to a valuable site, or others.

• The materials generalist will schedule and monitor student use of teaching machines, small group conference rooms, listening booths, carrels, recording studio, projection or viewing room, and other facilities.

-• At the conclusion of the unit study, the teacher, class, and materials generalist will *evaluate* the suitability and adequacy of the materials, facilities, equipment and services used and recommend needed improvements or additions.

What *is* this "generalist" about whom I speak? What kind of person must he be? What does *he* do?

1. A professional resource person for teachers first and foremost, for media center professional and paraprofessional staff, for administrators, and for students. As such, he must have full knowledge of teaching; be trained as a teacher and yet be imbued with a deep commitment to the improvement of teaching and learning (of others) through effective use of excellent educational media.

He must be *credible* in his resource relationships with other teachers. They must know that he speaks from experience, and that he knows what teaching is about; what good teaching *is*.

2. A knowledgeable curriculum worker; one who is familiar with theoretical aspects of curriculum development, who knows good objectives when he reads them, who recognizes the differences between effective and ineffective means of translating objectives into learning experiences, and who realizes the contribution of well-selected and well-used materials of instruction.

3. An administrator; one who, although he happens to specialize in educational media, must study and solve problems like those being met and solved by administrators in nearly every other aspect of education.

He must develop bases for approved policies and guidelines. He must deal with specifications and purchases, with authorizations for payment, and develop enough business sense to know when he is getting his or the school's money's worth in the bargain. He must be capable of supervising and motivating the professional and para-professional staff directly responsible to him.

Perhaps even more important, he must also know a good deal about the special capabilities of his own school's teaching staff and be able to stimulate a kind of "mutual assistance" program that draws on their particular strengths;

upon the kinds of things done well by different individuals in the group. We now know enough about how people change and improve in their teaching to appreciate the value of these kinds of relationships.

In addition, he must manage the very essential liaison relationships of his media program with those of his district, the county, or the state. As a generalist, he must know enough about all aspects of his program to permit its effective integration in the total school effort.

4. A professional practitioner; one who knows sources of media; equipment; services; one who is capable of guiding various professional groups in developing and applying defensible criteria in the selection of materials; one who knows enough about local production activities to assist others (students as well as teachers, although in the larger school his relationship to such production might be only supervisory); one who is similarly familiar with the many technical aspects of his program such as arranging and equipping classrooms, auditoria, and special rooms to make full use of audiovisual materials.

And he is one who is capable of classifying and cataloging his materials collections to facilitate their easy use by students and teachers whether or not he actually *performs* these activities or supervises the work of others who do.

5. A catalyst for innovation and for the extension of practices of proven worth, a student of the process of educational change and especially of human relations and motivations; one who recognizes the worth or applicability of proposed innovations in relation to the situation in which he works; one who is aware of innovational trends, of new programs of promise coming to notice across the country; one who understands enough about human nature, particularly the nature of teachers, students, administrators, and school patrons, to guide his efforts and to avoid all the well-known pitfalls in effecting curricular and instructional changes in the school program.

Of course, he should be a catalyst with his feet on the ground, sufficiently experienced to be able to recognize most of the worthwhile alternatives and eschew those that are not.

6. An evaluator; one capable of serving an especially valuable feedback function for district, county, state, and national programs. He knows a great deal about the students of his school, particularly about aspects of their interest, economic and social status, goals, and needs that bear upon his school's selection and use of educational media.

The district-developed course of study, the "systems" approach, the district-wide textbook selection program, the centralized media production service in the downtown office, the individualized film catalog arrangement all should be subjected to the proof of utility and validity of purpose. The media generalist stands in a uniquely good position to provide and report such assessments.

To have an instructional materials center provide all these services in merged and integrated fashion would result in the kind of magnification of results that is needed. For too long our schools have gone without good libraries, just as they have gone without good audiovisual services. The attention both these services are getting today is justly deserved. We should not be content with merely makeshift, half-adequate materials; resource services and facilities. The schools need better.

The time is ripe, as it has been for some time, for us to make a breakthrough in preparing competent materials generalists for our schools. Professional school library and audiovisual associations can and should work together on this problem; and our colleges and universities should march along with them in developing and improving graduate programs to accomplish this end. If these things are done, we can effect a small but much-needed revolution in classroom teaching and learning.

IMC'S: A DIALOGUE

Bruce Miles and Virginia McJenkin

Bruce: Hello, Virginia. How are things down in Fulton County, Georgia . . . or haven't you been home lately?

Virginia: Well, I haven't been home too often. My official duties have kept me pretty occupied. How about Fairfax County, Virginia?

Bruce: Great. Last I heard we passed a whopping big budget, a nice portion of which will come our way for the instructional materials center. You know, Virginia, people often ask what an IMC is . . . the kind we have in schools nowadays. I like to answer that an IMC is a place where . . . where there are all kinds of resources and lots of interesting things taking place.

Virginia: Bruce, how do you think a modern IMC differs from the traditional school library?

Bruce: Of course, "traditional" means many things to many people. After all, what is new and exciting today will become traditional within a relatively short time. Some people in charge of what we presently refer to as instructional materials centers have facilities which are probably as traditional as any library ever has been. Other IMC personnel have accepted − indeed have gone out seeking − new ways and new materials to serve the needs of their school.

Virginia: Actually, the traditional library served only pupils and teachers with printed materials of several kinds. Today we are attempting to serve a much

Reprinted with permission from: Miles, Bruce and McJenkins, Virginia, "IMC's: A Dialogue," AUDIOVISUAL INSTRUCTION, November, 1965.

broader cross section of people – pupils, teachers, adults enrolled in adult education programs and in vocational programs, and so forth. At the same time we are serving the needs of these groups with many new types of media in addition to the traditional printed material.

Bruce: True, Virginia. I have even been able to secure a repair manual for my MG sports car in one of our high school instructional materials centers. We have branched out from traditional printed materials with the result that more and more students are being helped with or through the use of other important types of communication media, such as slides and filmstrips, flat pictures for research or plain display, museum-type collections, phonograph records, tape recordings, and 8mm films in many IMC's. It is not at all uncommon now to see production of media taking place in an easy, attractive environment that once was pretty stiff, formal, and above all, quiet.

Virginia:: As much as I hate to admit it, the atmosphere certainly was like that in many instances.

Bruce: And the new facilities and materials are only a part of the picture. Another change involves the staffing of IMC's. This includes the training, philosophy, and most important, attitude of the head of the operation. The traditional librarian was often characterized as a rather mean old woman, bent on silence and keeping her books neatly arranged on well-dusted shelves. Obviously this is an erroneous characterization; yet all of us have probably had experiences with such people.

Virginia: How do you characterize the IMC librarian now? Has the image changed for the better?

Bruce: Oh, indeed. The librarian now associated with the modern IMC is equally bent on getting the books off the shelves and seeing that they are well utilized in the overall instructional program. The modern librarian must have a broad educational background. He or she must understand the problems and theories of communication. Above all, the IMC director must know and understand children. This cannot be emphasized too much. Hopefully the IMC also is staffed with well-trained librarians, media specialists, assistants, and clerks.

Virginia: Also, the IMC person is quite aware of the total school program and must particiapte in all types of activities related to curriculum, scheduling, selection of materials, in-service education, and so on. She works closely with teachers, department heads, and the administration as well as with students in producing a more effective program. In short, the IMC has become a vital part of the overall teaching-learning picture.

Bruce: IMC's will differ widely from one school system to the next and, as a matter of fact, will differ within a given school system. Such differences may stem from philosophy, the unique needs of a school or school system, and always from the budget. Budget is often necessary to accomplish the goals set for a program. Thus, possibly the best thing to say about the difference between traditional libraries and the modern concept of the IMC is that the new service is one dedicated to the necessity and opportunity of providing a wide variety of critical learning resources to many people within the community served. It may be that the word "service" is the all-important word in such an attempt to define this difference.

Virginia: This description is supported by the official statement of the American Association of School Librarians on school libraries as instructional materials centers. You will recall the opening statement: "The AASL believes that the school library, in addition to doing its vital work of individual reading guidance and development of the school curriculum, should serve the school as a center for instructional materials. Instructional materials include books – the literature of children, young people, and adults – other printed materials, films, recordings, and media developed to aid learning."

Bruce: Obviously all of this necessarily leads us to suspect that the modern IMC person must have much broader competencies than the so-called traditional librarian. His world has certainly expanded.

Virginia: It certainly has. Actually, we probably should consider this aspect in two ways: the competencies of the director or administrative head of the operation, and those of the supporting staff.

Bruce: Well, I would think that the director first of all should have a good background in teaching. Secondly, the director should have the best possible training at the graduate level in all appropriate areas of the service he or she is to administer. I am not talking about courses in running projectors or cataloging books. I really am thinking about the types of things that will help the person to better understand how children learn, what can be done to increase the effectiveness of both teaching and learning, and how to really operate a service-type operation. However, the director cannot overlook more down-to-earth matters in his training. I would think that he or she should have a working familiarity with the various aspects of both the library and audiovisual facets of the total operation. If the person is essentially library-oriented, then I would think it logical to expect that person to become very familiar with production techniques. Our director will certainly find it necessary to know how to get a student's art work copied to be shown at the final PTA meeting in the spring, how to use and select maps and globes, how to use the overhead projector to accomplish near miracles, how to get a borrowed record on tape for use the following week in the English Department, and a host of other things. And if our director has spent his life oiling projectors, he will certainly have to get into a training program which will allow him to understand and function as a true IMC specialist. Eventually, however, we will no longer have two sides to this business.

Virginia: I would like to add two ideas at this point, Bruce. You already have suggested them, but I think they are important enough to reiterate. A competent director of an IMC must have a wide knowledge of materials, the whole gamut of media, and must give expert guidance in the selection of these materials. This director must be skilled in the organization of a diversity of materials. I do not mean that he must be a slave to classification and cataloging, but rather that he be competent in planning simple and flexible procedures to organize materials for easy and effective use that he be sensitive to automated techniques. Now our supporting staff presents another problem. They could be professionally trained persons. It would seem that much depends upon the size of the school served, and also on the size of the system. After all, the staffing of an IMC must be accomplished within the framework of the available budget. It is possible that most or all of the staff members could be locally trained lay people. Many tasks and services can and should be performed by semiskilled individuals. There is no need to waste a professional person's time on making minor repairs to equipment or placing materials back on shelves. It is quite possible for leadership and staffing to develop in many equally productive ways. Our real concern lies not so much in who handles this as in the fact that *it is done and done properly.*

Bruce: I couldn't agree more. Now then, let's take a look at the nuts and bolts aspects of the IMC.

Virginia: A good idea! You know, Bruce, the so-called "nuts and bolts" aspects of the audiovisual business bother a lot of people. How does this get handled in the IMC concept, or doesn't it?

Bruce: First of all, Virginia, we should remember that there are nuts and bolts aspects to the library program, also − too many of them, if I am hearing correctly during our yearly budget discussions. But let me expound on this a bit. I'm not only concerned about the job's being done, but I'm also concerned about the attitude of many people on this question − and not just librarians. As mentioned before, it's frightening to think of the waste that is imposed on professional time in pursuit of such activities. The nuts and bolts responsibilities in a center are important, however, and must be taken care of. Contrary to what many people may think, the remainder of the instructional materials program simply will not function without constant attention to the nuts and bolts aspects. This often holds everything else together. In a small IMC situation it is possible that the administrative head of the organization must assume some of these chores. By this I certainly do not refer to utilizing a screwdriver in the repair of a record player; rather, I mean training teachers or pupils in the proper utilization of materials. Certainly librarians cannot resist this opportunity in teaching teachers and pupils how to utilize books. We must remember always that equipment is important insofar as it is the carrier of the materials which actually provide learning. We might logically assume, therfore, that one is dependent upon the other, and that both aspects must be served. In my own situation we are seriously considering the training of lay people to do some of these jobs. In fact, we already are using such personnel in our county center.

Virginia: I've sensed another real concern on the part of some librarians, Bruce, about this business of centralization as opposed to decentralization within schools. Recommendations made by J. Lloyd Trump in his report *Images of the Future* are having a definite effect on school design. This is particularly true at the secondary school level. You will recall that Mr. Trump and his associates suggest grouping departments with a resource laboratory for each subject area. This calls for decentralizing materials collections and placing most of them in the resource centers. The library, as such, becomes a central reference area with a complex of study spaces or carrels surrounding it. The theory of placing appropriate materials close to the departments which will use them is sound. In large schools this is an excellent way to provide the space and arrangement to take care of many users and many materials. In actual practice, however, there are some obvious problems: First, it is expensive to provide the staff needed to supervise and service these resource centers. (I grant that these staff members do not all need to be professionally trained librarians or media specialists. Some can be clerical help, but some must have a knowledge of the subject area materials.) Second, there necessarily must be duplication of materials from department to department and to some extent in the central collection. *This is expensive!* It is true, however, that the new federal funds will make this easier. Third, in many instances the materials in resource laboratories are not processed or cataloged. This means they are not easily accessible for use and are easily lost. Several schools which are experimenting with resource laboratories have arranged for all materials services to be under the supervision of the central library or instructional materials center. The IMC staff (including professionals, subject specialists, and clerical aides) has been increased to supervise the services in the resource laboratories. Permanent or temporary collections of materials are placed in the resource laboratories. There is regular truck service to the laboratory from the central IMC. Ridgewood High School in Norridge, Illinois, and Oak Park and River Forest High School in Oak Park, Illinois, have this arrangement. Other schools, such as Decatur-Lakeview School and West Leyden High School, have found that a centralized IMC is better. In these situations arrangements have been made to house all types of materials, arranged in broad subject groups, in one area. Provision has been made for large deposits of these materials or book truck service to various teaching areas throughout the building.

Bruce: A lot of work, and probably research, needs to be put in on this important question.

Virginia: Yes, and as we get more and more material and equipment, the need becomes very clear. Speaking of this reminds me of the impact of federal aid in our programs. How do you think the new federal legislation can stimulate the development or expansion of IMC's?

Bruce: Of course, the NDEA program has been expanded to cover many areas and already has had great impact on stimualting the development of some of these areas. In many cases, however, I am afraid that materials purchased under various sections of the title — science, math, and modern foreign language — have ended up being placed in departmental libraries ... and I use the term loosely. There has been, because of the nature of the program, a feeling that this new science material is "all mine" on the part of the departmental chairman. Actually, we find many cases where material secured for one of these three areas is almost equally useful in other curriculum areas, and there certainly is nothing by way of intent which restricts the use of this material in other departments.

But try and get it . . . that is something else. I think that this is a good case for the centralization of materials — good because otherwise there is an obvious waste of money and poor material utilization. Of the new federal legislation, we think specifically of Titles I, II, and III of the Elementary and Secondary Education Act of 1965. Title I will certainly make lots of materials available to schools. In our own county, nearly $350,000 will be allocated under Title I, and much of this will be spent on the purchase of materials. While some of these will be placed in division-wide centers, the very nature of the act and its attempt to serve children will require that many of the items be placed in schools and issued from a point which can serve all students equally well. Other programs such as Project Head Start will also inspire the need for proper utilization of materials. The purpose of an act such as this, if we strip all political and other considerations aside, is actually to improve instruction for specific groups of students. I don't know of anyone now who denies the fact that films and filmstrips, records, tapes, and other materials are important and indeed integral parts of an instructional program. From this point it seems to me that it becomes the responsibility of the librarian or the media person in a system or in a building to inspire the teachers, students, and the administration to want a place which will help everyone make better use of materials.

Virginia: We can expect a great deal of help under Title II, which specifically makes provision for "library resources." Francis Keppel has stressed the need for expanding the book collections in all school libraries in a number of statements: "At all levels of education, effective teaching has become increasingly contingent on well-stocked libraries, the services of professional librarians, and up-to-date testbooks." "The school library will provide a variety of resources, including recordings, microfilms, slide films, video tapes, charts, maps, and pictures. The most important of the resources offered, however, will be books in abundance in the humanities, the social studies, the sciences, and the practical arts — books of such range and variety that there will be something to arouse the interest and further the learning of the dull and the bright, the practical and the theoretical, the poor reader, and the advanced student." "Title II proposes to correct these inadequacies with a five-year program which would make books and other printed materials available to the school children of our nation." "Library books, textbooks, periodicals, magnetic tapes, phonograph records, and other materials essential to the education of our junior citizens could be purchased with these funds." Incidentally, at the suggestion of officials in the U.S. Office of Education, ASSL, is publishing a brochure giving guidelines and sources of selection of materials (both print and nonprint) to assist in implementing Title II and the expanded Title III of NDEA. You have mentioned opportunities under Title I. Under Title III supplementary educational centers could well be instructional materials centers. Title V makes it possible to employ state school library supervisors or media specialists to serve as consultants. It is all quite exciting, Bruce, isn't it? The opportunities are so great they seem overwhelming at times.

Bruce: Yes, Virginia, the opportunities are great — and now is the time to begin taking advantage of them.

THE MISSING LINK IN INSTRUCTIONAL SUPPORT

Robert M. Diamond

Audiovisual services are in a period of transition. The cafeteria-type center with a simple film and equipment check-out system is rapidly being replaced by a complex organization offering to the teacher a wider range of services and a far greater variety of tools and techniques than ever before.

Teachers fortunate enough to be in a college or school district where a communciations or instructional resources center exists can have a wide variety of materials designed for their specific use. These range from simple mountings, 2x2 slides, and overhead transparencies to 8mm films in cartridges for use in seminars or for independent student study. Along with the standard projection and sound equipment and materials library, the teacher also may have the use of a duplicating center, audio laboratory, a single-room for overhead television unit, and a library of programmed materials. In some instances he may actually have the opportunity to request that a particular television presentation be prepared for his students. Some centers now provide the instructor with assistance in the preparation of programed materials. In short, the instructional resources center today has become a complex operation consisting of a wide variety of services and a skilled staff of specialists.

With this growth have come problems. Along with the expected administrative changes that come with size there are other areas of basic concern. When all of these services and techniques are available, how can the individual teacher be most efficiently, and effectively contacted and served? Where is a decision made as to what approach will be most effective and, in effect, will make the most sense? Who can identify common problems that deserve wider attention? Who can bring to the teachers new developments, products, and techniques that may be of interest?

In the past these functions were served by the audiovisual director, members of the graphic-photographic staff, and in fact, anyone within the operation who happened to be working directly with the teacher. However, with the larger operation this laissez faire approach is not only inefficient and impractical but also raises the question, should highly skilled individuals, to the neglect of their primary functions, spend their time with work that can be done by others?

COMMUNICATION COORDINATORS

It is for these basic reasons that we in communications need to develop a new member of our team — an individual to serve as the "middle man" between the instructors and the service organization. Basically it is proposed that the functions of the coordinator should be to —

Reprinted with permission from: Diamond, Robert M., "The Missing Link in Instructional Support," AUDIOVISUAL INSTRUCTION, November, 1964.

- Work with the instructor in the definition of specific objectives so that when he meets with the graphic artist or other members of the center staff, the preliminary planning is already accomplished and work can begin with minimum delay.
- Work directly with instructors in the improvement and evaluation of their teaching effectiveness. This would include instructional television where the coordinator would work with the TV teacher in a support function throughout the lesson planning process, suggesting techniques and generally evaluating the lesson.
- Present to the faculty new developments and materials related to their specific subject area.
- Direct instructors toward those techniques that are most logical for their particular application.
- Bring together faculty members with common kinds of problems.
- Coordinate research proposals in the use of the technology.

In the November 1963 issue of AUDIOVISUAL INSTRUCTION, Marie McMahan[1] gives much of this responsibility to the building coordinator. This approach, while sensible for the majority of public school districts, is obviously impractical within most colleges. As Miss McMahan notes, the building coordinator needs released time to perform these functions. Unfortunately, at the present, such a schedule is the exception rather than the rule.

THE REQUIREMENTS

Obviously the person who can serve this function is a rarity. He must understand both instruction and the new technology; he must be creative and work well with people. The problem: Where do you find such an individual.

At the University of Miami, we have been attempting to develop such people within our program as part of a grant from the Fund for the Advancement of Education.

Last summer a workshop was held for three weeks for two members of each department in University College (social science, natural science, humanities), who were to serve as communication coordinators. During this period each participant had direct experience with the writing of specific and measurable objectives (as set forth by Robert Mager[2]), were introduced to the wide range of instructional techniques now available, and had the experience of planning and presenting a short televised lesson.

At the same time a coordination of service was developed and a Lesson Preparation Flow Chart was designed. (See illustration.) In this process, the objectives for both the large-group and seminar instruction are designated; and then the coordinators work directly with the instructional staff in planning and preparing the lesson and the related material.

[1] McMahan, Marie. "Building Coordinator: Professional Partner?" AUDIOVISUAL INSTRUCTION 8: 662-65; November 1963.
[2] Mager, Robert. Preparing Objectives for Programmed Instruction. San Francisco: Fearon Publishers, 1961, 62 pp.

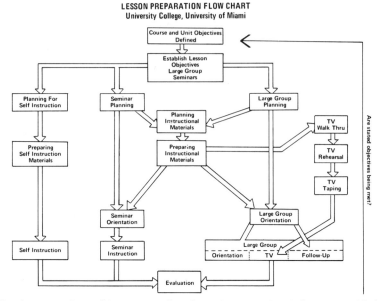

LESSON PREPARATION FLOW CHART
University College, University of Miami

In the year since this program has been in operation it has met with both success and failure. From these experiences several conclusions can be reached:

• A support program of this type will only succeed when the course and lesson have prestated, well-defined goals. Objectives must be stated if the coordinators are to be able to work effectively with the faculty in the preparation of materials and in evaluating the results. In several cases the main effort of the communication coordinator was in the definition of objectives, not in the support function for which the position was originally designed.

• The communication coordinator must realize that his function is one of service and support and that the content of the lesson must remain the responsibility of the instructor or instructors involved. Too often the meeting on implementing specific objectives degenerated into a debate on what should and should not be taught. For this reason it may make sense to have most communication specialists work in subject fields other than their own.

• There must be a service organization backing up the communication coordinator because once an instructor becomes interested, his requests and needs must be filled well and at once.

• To be most effective in his role the coordinator should have been a successful classroom teacher and ideally might be teaching a minimum load while serving as coordinator.

In short, if the instructional resources center is to succeed, its program must be sold to the teacher. A new type of person is needed for this — an individual in a new position whose responsibility is contacting the instructional staff, bringing to the teacher information concerning the materials and devices that are available, and then preparing the instructor to use the services of the center. Only in this way can the center provide its ultimate in service and perform the role for which it is capable.

PROPOSED: A MEDIA CLERK-TECHNICIAN

Elwood E. Miller

I created or designed a piece of instructional material, other than a routine chalkboard illustration, for use in your classroom. How long since you searched for and used a really good visual or audio instructional aid?

All right, so you have plenty of good and legitimate reasons why you would probably have to say, "It's been a long, long time." The fact that this is an unfortunate situation is not altered by the reasons you might advance for not creating instructional materials that could cause you to do much better work with your classes.

Vast quantities of excellent materials await your use. Simple devices of a graphic nature are not complicated to dream up. Why don't you use some of these proven materials?

Research and study in the audiovisual field demonstrate over and over that it is simply the lack of time on your part that prevents your involvement. Time from your teaching is not available to search for appropriate material, to construct the teaching materials that you might like for your own class. Suitable back-up help of a clerical and technical nature is not available to you, nor is it available to the vast majority of teachers in every institution, regardless of the level of instruction.

School building audiovisual coordinators should not be expected to provide a solution to this problem, for most of them are certified teachers who should not carry this clerical or technical burden. It is another matter if they are used as consultants concerning the proper use and place of instructional material within the curriculum. Building coordinators' with training and ability are important to a strong program of instruction. If their function is to work as clerk-technicians, however, then their time and talents are badly wasted.

I should like to propose that a new position be created to fill this important gap between teacher and media. Why not incorporate into the school staff a trained person who can help the instructor find and create suitable instructional materials and effectively use the machines of audiovisual instruction. This person would be called a *media clerk-technician.* This teacher assistant, who could equally well be a man or a woman, should have a high school diploma and perhaps two years of training at the community college level. This training should center around the technical aspects of media use and production of instructional materials. This person could become a vital cog in the program of instruction in any school large enough to financially justify back-up assistance for the instructional personnel.

Reprinted with permission from: Miller, Elwood E. "Proposed: A Media Clerk-Technician," AUDIOVISUAL INSTRUCTION, November, 1964.

Why not let teachers teach and furnish real instructional leadership, and leave the "nuts and bolts" responsibility to a trained person who is interested in this type of work and who is efficient at it?

The media clerk-technician could be budgeted at the general level of clerk or typist in the school system. Mature people who have an interest in education are available in most communities for work of this type.

This would demand some new thinking on the part of the audiovisual professionals. As the educators most interested in innovation and change, this new look should not present much of a problem. Community college curriculum people would need to be involved in the design of such a program. Their interest in developing new technical fields is evident, and should present no serious problem.

The major attitude change would have to come from school and college administrators. Positions of the type suggested would have to be created, and financial provision would be essential in order to place people trained in such a field.

It is my biased opinion that nearly every school and college in the country today could improve to a marked degree the instructional program of their institution by the careful use of a trained media clerk-technician. Back-up assistance for teachers is long overdue.

TRAINING

The training of a media clerk-technician might include work in the following areas:

• General education at the community college level. The media clerk-technician must communicate and work with trained. and highly educated teachers and/or professors, and should have a good command of the basic language and communciations tools needed by anyone working in the educational atmosphere.

• Technical training to include: (a) Operation and use of the typical tools of the audiovisual department; (b) simple maintenance and trouble shooting of a "first aid" nature on such equipment; (c) knowledge of sources of material of all types; (d) basic graphics production for use in television; (e) some basic understanding and ability to use photography; (f) television technician work, including such things as lighting, camera work, floor direction, prop and scene construction; and (g) audio work in the production of sound tapes for instruction.

This proposal would in no way change the present audiovisual philosophy in teacher education programs. A basic understanding of the potentials of the audiovisual field and the proven strength of audiovisual methods is still essential for all who would call themselves teachers. With resource help of this type, teachers would need to be even more versed in the effective use of educational media.

Under this proposal, teachers would be free to work at the design and utilization level of instruction and would leave to the media clerk-technician such typical mechanical details as machine and material schedules, keeping equipment in a healthy condition for daily use, making routine graphic aids, and supervising student projectionists.

The experienced teacher knows full well that lack of technical assistance in their desire to use the media of instruction causes more failure in the effective use of educational media and instructional materials than any other single factor.

THE PRESENT AV BUILDING COORDINATOR

What might a position of this type do to the present building audiovisual coordinator in most schools?

Let's face the fact that most buildings do not really have a building coordinator other than a teacher assigned to account for the machines in the building and that such duties are nearly always asked of the teacher in addition to his normal teaching load. A point bears repeating here: that qualified teachers should be involved in teaching and instruction, and use of such personnel as machine accountants is a waste of valuable and expensive instructional resources.

Buildings that do have a functioning building coordinator should elevate this person to the role of material and methods consultant, and relieve him of the routine jobs described in this paper. This implies that this person is a professional, has training in instructional media and some sophistication in its effective use. This is what the audiovisual profession has been trying to do for years, and so the position of media clerk-technician should help to raise the standards and effectiveness of the school building media specialist or audiovisual coordinator.

QUESTIONS TO CONSIDER

In closing this set of suggestions, three major questions remain to be asked:

• *Teachers* – Would you use the services of a media clerk-technician in your instructional planning?

• *Presidents of Community Colleges* – Are you willing to design a training program in your institution to prepare these media clerk-technologists?

• *Superintendents and School Board Members* – Are you really serious about the effective use of media and materials in your school system? Serious enough to spend some funds for support of personnel of this kind for your teachers?

The educational media clerk-technician can answer a real need in an instructional program. As programs grow and strengthen, more personnel of this kind will be needed. Will we in education make the necessary effort to fill this need?

THE NEW CHALLENGE FOR COMMUNITY COLLEGES

Amo De Bernardis

Most innovations in education to be effective and have an impact on the learning process must eventually be implemented by the classroom teacher, and the use of new media is no exception. The multiplicity of newer teaching and learning materials will no doubt increase the teacher's power to enhance and make more effective the instructional process. However, to insure that this takes place, the teacher must be kept aware of these new developments in media and perhaps more important is that the logistic support be provided to make these materials and teaching equipment easily accessible. Without this support teachers cannot be expected to make effective use of these resources.

Just as the engineer and the doctor have looked to technicians for assistance in their work, so must the teacher rely on technical help in the complex task of organizing for teaching. The use of a single textbook as the source for planning learning experiences is no longer adequate.

The teaching task has become most complex. Teachers have to be concerned with the explosion of knowledge. They now have at their command a multitude of teaching materials and equipment and the public demands that the teacher be a professional who will deal with their children with the same degree of knowledge and skill of the doctor and the dentist. The non-professional aspects of the teaching act can and should be delegated to assistants or aides.

AIDES FOR MEDIA

More and more schools are turning to aides and assistants for this support. Where else could these aides be used more successfully than in the area of media? Teachers should know how to use and operate equipment and be knowledgeable in the local production of audiovisual materials.

However, there are more important tasks to which a teacher should devote his professional talents. An employee who is skillful in the production of audiovisual aids can operate the equipment, duplicate materials, and do numerous other jobs which are required in the use of these materials. In short, this person can be an important part of the instructional team. Too often secretaries or other clerical personnel are assigned these duties with the belief that the needed skills and insights will be developed on the job.

This approach to the problem of providing teacher aides to assist in the use of audiovisual materials is not the most productive. These aides must be skillful and know their job well if they are to be effective in assisting the teacher in the use of the many and varied teaching and learning resources.

Reprinted with permission from: De Bernardis, Amo, "The New Challenge For Community Colleges," EDUCATIONAL SCREEN, December, 1965.

AIDE TRAINING

Where should these aides be trained? The training for instructional materials assistants fits logically into the educational philosophy and function of a community college, which is to provide educational opportunities for people beyond high school. The Portland Community College, after preliminary exploration, found that there was need for instructional materials aides. The principals and superintendents of the metropolitan areas indicated that if a person were properly trained, there would be employment for them in their schools.

As a result of this preliminary survey, officials of the college met with the representatives of the employment services to determine if this type of instruction would meet the requirements set forth in the Manpower Development Training Act. All agreed that this was the type of training which the Act was intended to fulfill — that is, to provide training for people who are underemployed or unemployable.

VARIED CURRICULUM

As a result of these meetings, a training program for instructional materials was developed. The course was designed to cover a period of six months with students attending class six hours a day; however, the training period was later extended six weeks in order to provide more experience in depth in the use of offset press and other duplicating equipment.

The curriculum was designed to provide as varied experience with the materials and equipment as possible, in order to furnish the teacher with the backup needed to use media more efficiently. The major areas covered in the course were: orientation in use of media in instruction, place of instructional materials aides in the teaching and learning process, operation and use of the various types of audiovisual equipment.

From the course description it may appear that there was too much to cover in a short period of time. However, it should be emphasized that the program was not intended to train instructional materials specialists or technicians, but rather to train an aide who could perform for the teacher some of the tasks which did not require a professional.

Experience may indicate that the program should be lengthened. A follow-up is planned to determine how well these aides are performing their task and how they relate to the teaching team.

LEARNING BY DOING

The training program was centered on "learning by doing" and over-the-shoulder instruction. Students were given as much practical experience as possible. As they progressed and gained skill in each unit of the course, they were assigned work projects in the college's instructional materials center. They made transparencies, recorded lectures, produced slides, operated duplicators, cleaned equipment, and planned displays and bulletin boards. Guest speakers were brought in to explain the various instructional materials organization in the schools. Field trips were taken to schools and area instructional materials centers, thus providing trainees with a greater insight of the job requirements. Perhaps as important as developing the skills in the operation of equipment and in the production of instructional materials was the emphasis on the role of the instructional materials aide in the teaching and learning process.

The program is too new to draw any definite conclusion about the training program. The college plans to make a thorough follow-up on each student to determine strengths and weaknesses. There is no doubt that as more and varied teaching resources become available, the need for these materials aides will grow. The Portland Community College expects to be in a position to fill these needs with well qualified instructional materials aides.

THE AV SPECIALIST: SOME REFLECTIONS ON AN IMAGE

Sidney C. Eboch

A colleague once described the audiovisual specialist in this way: "His only real virtue is that he truly cares about teaching and learning, even when he doesn't understand either one. He started as a screwdriver mechanic, became a swivel-chair administrator, and is finally developing an egg head. Now that he is thinking about it, he might find out who and what he really is. If he ever does, American education will be better."

Cynical as it may sound, the above quote gives the sense of this paper which attempts to sketch what the audiovisual specialist might become: if we are to determine what the audiovisual specialist is, and should be, the audiovisual specialist must specify the most important things he believes about himself and his role in education.

SOME BASIC BELIEFS

Audiovisual specialization is but one part of education. It is not all, perhaps not even a major part, of education. The growth of the audiovisual specialization will depend upon the value and effectiveness of specific functions being well performed.

Reprinted with permission from: Eboch, Sidney C., "The Audiovisual Specialist: Some Reflections on an Image," AUDIOVISUAL INSTRUCTION, January, 1963.

The prime function of the audiovisual specialist is to design and implement information transmission and display systems which are appropriate to specific instructional objectives in well-defined educational situations.

This basic function rests upon two major premises:

a. *Each student is entitled to the most useful information presented in the most effective manner at the most appropriate time.*

b. *Each teacher is entitled to the most precise information display which is operationally effective for specific instructional goals.*

The key phrase in the above statements is "information transmission and display systems." The meaning is simple and old, yet complex and new. The four basic words can be interpreted in the common meanings of the terms.

Information is news, facts, knowledge, data, lore.

Transmission is communication, conveyance, transfer passage between one person or place and another.

Display is to exhibit, to present, to show.

Systems refer to a collection of parts which perform a unitary function when the parts are appropriately related and used in an organized manner.

Thus, an "information transmission and display system" is two or more items organized in such a manner that knowledge is conveyed and presented from one person or place to another. To state it another way: An information transmission and display system is an organized method for communicating knowledge between two points.

It is the function of the audiovisual specialist to develop information transmission and display systems appropriate to the educational situation in which he works. It should be recognized that a teacher is an information transmission and display system in some functions performed in the classroom. A book is an information transmission and display system. A motion picture, a television program, a teaching machine program, a demonstration, a study hall experience, a discussion — nearly every educational experience involves information transmission and display in *some* aspects. Under these circumstances, the audiovisual specialist should develop only those aspects which are not within the immediate scope and capability of the average teacher being served. This means, for example, the audiovisual specialist would not determine the content of a college lecture; he might produce the television broadcast which transmits and displays the lecture. The audiovisual specialist would not select the concepts to be taught by a classroom motion picture experience, but he would relieve the teacher of all concerns with the transmission and display of the film's content. The audiovisual specialist would not select the instructional objectives for a teaching machine program for a single student; he would relieve the instructional staff and the student of all concerns relative to the transmission and display of the information to be studied.

THE RELATIONSHIP TO EDUCATION

The rationale which establishes the relationship between the audiovisual specialization and education could be defined as follows.

A prime function of education is instruction. While education may perform many social services, a prime function is that of instruction.

A major part of any instruction is the transmission and display of information. Teachers must "teach" something; students must "learn" something. Although many interpretations are possible and many factors are involved, instruction centers around information. Even skills and attitudes depend in part upon basic information. Transmission and display may be more or less complex and more or less effective. Information may be more or less correct and more or less useful. However, some kind of information is somehow transmitted as part of instruction.

Students and teachers are entitled to the best possible information trans *mission and display system.* (See premises a. and b. above.) If information is important, students and teachers are entitled to the most favorable conditions of effective use. This can begin only when efficient transmission and display are achieved

Information transmission and display systems are becoming increasingly complex; they require design and control management. It is a long way from McGuffey's readers to Telstar. Television production and textbook production are both extremely complex operations which require many and varied specialists of high competence. The design and management of information and display systems also require several skills of high order if information and the rights of teachers and students are to be treated adequately.

Thus, the audiovisual specialist rests his case on: (a) the centrality of instruction, (b) the role of information in instruction, (c) the rights of teachers and students to the most efficient support conditions, and (d) the complexity of information transmission and display systems.

DELINEATION OF FUNCTIONS AND RESOURCES

If the audiovisual specialist is to perform efficiently as a designer of information transmission and display systems, he must recognize the broad outlines of his functions and resources.

Information. Ideas are to be communicated; therefore, information (or curriculum content) is the first requirement. The specialist will ask that information be specified along with instructional objectives. Curriculum and subject-matter specialists are the major resources in this instance. The audiovisual specialist will bring to information his special skills in the analysis of forms and structure in content and his abilities to translate one form or structure to another. Once content (information) is determined, the audiovisual specialist should be able to translate words into pictures, and graphics into words and other possible combinations required by other elements in the transmission system. He should be able to analyze the structure and form of content into instructional problems to be solved. This means the ability to determine emphasis, sequence, repetition, time patterns, and space requirements.

Instrumentation. Obviously, ideas will have to appear in some form (media) and these forms will require some type of transmission and display. Ideas become media and all media require instruments of transmission or display.

Textbooks have to be delivered and, more important, the type (print) size and clarity should be adequate before the text is ever committed to a press. Motion pictures require a projector — with a functioning lamp. Television viewing requires a set of adequate size and a picture of adequate quality.

The problem for the audiovisual specialist is to give up the concepts of machines *and* materials. A motion picture projector is virtually nothing without a film; the projector is an instrument just as the film is an instrument to transmit and display the ideas *in* the film. A programed auto-instructional course uses an *instrument* to transmit and display information; the form of the instrument may be a textbook or a machine plus text materials.

The instrumentation element requires varied levels of technical skills in instrument maintenance and repair. The audiovisual specialist needs the talents and support of industrial personnel from electro-mechanical fields. The instrumentation element requires an efficient storage and retrieval system for the multiple and varied uses made of instruments. Here the professional librarian is probably the best resource. However, the needs indicate the librarian must be one who is aware of and capable of handling the various modern and developing systems of information storage and retrieval.

The function of the audiovisual specialist is to know the capacities of various instruments and their combinations, particularly in relationship to specific types of instructional problems. The specialist must be able to select the most efficient instrumentation and arrange all the processes which would result in effective use.

Personnel. The translation of information formats and structure require what we call production personnel — the artists and photographers of today's "graphics" or "materials preparation" activities in audiovisual education. Instrumentation requires technical personnel for repair, maintenance, storage, and retrieval. Transmission and display require additional personnel in varying degrees. The personnel requirement might be as simple as a nine-year-old projector operator or it might be 50 highly trained professionals and technicians producing a motion picture or a television broadcast.

It is the function of the audiovisual specialist to plan and provide the personnel requirements for any specific information transmission and display system.

Environment Analysis. All transmission and display will occur in a physical and socio-psychological environment. It is the job of the audiovisual specialist to analyze the audience characteristics and the physical setting in which any specific presentation of information will take place.

Design: the Prime Function. The ultimate expression of the audiovisual specialist's contribution to education will occur in the design function. The specialist should perform all the functions indicated above under Information, Instrumentation, Personnel, and Environment Analysis in a coordinated plan that will result in a systematic organization of the final information transmission and display. The audiovisual specialist will recognize that all these elements and resources are interacting to determine the nature of the total result. This is why design is needed.

There is an optimum combination of elements and circumstances for the effective solution of every instructional problem. It is the audiovisual designer's job to analyze, predict, and deliver that optimum solution.

Evaluation. Finally, the audiovisual specialist should measure the effectiveness of his work after practical use. The major resource here will be the specialists in educational testing and measurement. After measuring the results of his efforts, the audiovisual specialist should use the information to improve the basic design function. This evaluation problem should include the experimental exploration of the relative effectiveness of single elements and combinations of elements.

THE DEVELOPMENT OF STANDARDS

It is customary, as specializations develop, for the professional group to develop a set of standards which become a basis for judging the practice of the specialization. These standards assume many and sometimes multiple forms. One set of standards usually relates to training and experience requirements of the practitioners. Another set relates to something like minimum working conditions; this is most frequently expressed in terms of minimum facilities in which the specialist can practice. Another set of standards describes appropriate and inappropriate functions within the specialization; these are most frequently called the "code of ethics."

In my view, standards cannot be developed for an ill-defined specialization; if attempted, they become either non-functional or delimiting. I believe that, if the definition of the audiovisual specialization given here could be developed and accepted throughout the field, standards could be developed. This is not the only definition of the field which is possible; no suggestion is made that it is the best, or complete as it stands. It is offered as an example of the type of specification needed. Audiovisual specialists usually have been described in such vague and general terms that it is difficult to decide how this person is different from any conventional supervisor in public school systems. The one exceptional element is that the audiovisual specialist-supervisor always "supervises" machines and materials, and sometimes people (but not so they notice it).

If audiovisual personnel could agree on the definition of their function, could appropriate standards be developed for publication to outside groups and educational agencies? The answer is yes. But only after a lot of homework by the audiovisual field.

Standards to match the beliefs and resources given above would not be the conventional standards of buildings, space, number of pupils or teachers, machine or materials. They would be related to (a) types of instructional problems, (b) types of information form and structure, (c) capacities and characteristics of instrumentation combinations, (d) types of teacher and student activities, and (e) levels of demonstrated achievement by students.

To develop standards that express these characteristics of the profession will require a depth exploration of much accumulated research and the re-structuring of this knowledge into "formulas" useful for measuring overall accomplishment or well-defined relationships. It is suggested there are *continuums* of (a) multiple content forms, (b) instrumentation capabilities, (c) multiple talents of personnel, (d) multiple environments, and (e) multiple and varied audiences. Each of these continuums have several characteristics which are intra-dependent, and each has inter-dependent relationships with the others.

Some of the "homework" required to develop standards of this type is already completed. Much has already been done on the analysis of content-difficulty and interest levels in reading materials. Less but equally competent research into the nature of graphic and pictorial factors is available. Benjamin Bloom's *Taxonomy of Education* and Hoban and VanOrmer's *Instructional Film Research* have much to contribute to the development of our analytical tools. A great amount of communications research relates to audience measurement.

Some of the "homework" is about to be produced. James D. Finn, through the Technological Development Project, is making an assessment of the technological world available to education and the extent of education's reception of and reaction to this world. Francis Noel's study of the audiovisual activities of state departments of education will provide another sidelight. Eleanor Godfrey's study will give a measure of audiovisual equipment and materials and factors related to the use of these tools. Fred Harcleroad and Bob Hall are studying the audiovisual personnel training situation. These and many other studies financed through the U.S. Office of Education are bringing to fruition some first-time answers to elementary questions in audiovisual education.

THE FUNCTION OF STANDARDS DEVELOPMENT

There is a climate of change within education. Already proceeding in a number of specialites within education are works that are successfully changing concepts and modes of action. The climate of the times does not call for more of the old standards or evolutionary goals; the climate is revolution based on much tough thinking over a period of years.

Bigger organization and much teamwork is in the nature of today's social world. The audiovisual specialist will be part of a team of curriculum experts, technical personnel, and testing specialists. But if he expects to function on this team, his relationships and related functions should be clearly specified. Team members do not appreciate the "dead wood" members or the self-appointed leader who asks, "What do we do now?"

The audiovisual field is still somewhat confused about its proper definition. The cry for theory and the cry for standards are but two facets of the same question: Who and what is the audiovisual specialist? Only through homework can we come to the proper definition of the specialist's role and functional relationships.

The entire conceptual structure presented here grows out of attention to the writings of three men: C. Ray Carpenter, Charles F. Hoban Jr., and James D. Finn. Of the three, Finn represents the strongest influence and is the leading voice of the audiovisual field. The problem of the field was never so clearly reflected as in his definition of the audiovisual specialist's role. Many an audiovisual specialist as well as the educational field in general has been quick to interpret Finn's work as too "gadget-oriented" because he frequently speaks of machines as instruments. Yet his own words state the problem in two senses.

Technology includes processes, systems, management and control mechanisms both human and non-human, and above all . . . *a way of looking at problems* as to their interest, and difficulty, the feasibility of technical solutions, and the economic values – broadly considered – of those solutions.

If the audiovisual specialist is to develop a new public image, he must develop a clear view of himself, and he must find a new way of looking at problems.

THE MARGINAL MEDIA MAN — THE GREAT PARADOX *

James D. Finn

In spite of the cliches currently in vogue about the progress and challenges of professionalism in the educational media field today, a hard, honest look at the problem reveals that our business, field, profession – whatever you choose to call it – is actually in serious trouble.

It is the thesis of this article that traditional concepts about the professionalization of the educational media field[1] will probably have to be changed and that the organization of DAVI ought to be changed in order to accommodate the demands of the times on the media man. For the media man *must* be, and must always remain, marginal to many fields, organizations, events, and institutions, and any move toward greater professionalism must take this stubborn fact into account.

The statement that we are in trouble can be countered by overwhelming evidence that the educational communications field as a professional specialization is not only *not* in trouble, but is enjoying its best days. And here is the beginning of what might be called the great professional paradox. On one hand,

This is the first in a series of articles by the author published in Audiovisual Instruction – The Editors.

[1] *In the course of this discussion I shall use all of the names now under consideration by DAVI (see the March 1965 issue of AVI) more or less interchangeably for purposes of style. Incidentally, the name itself is of almost crucial importance in this problem of professionalism.*

Reprinted with permission from: Finn, James D., "The Marginal Media Man, Part I: The Great Paradox," AUDIOVISUAL INSTRUCTION, December, 1965.

it is true that the audiovisual communication field has been growing; its practitioners are becoming more professional; and its many professional contributions to American education over the last 30 years finally are being recognized. On the other hand, it increasingly seems that our destiny is being taken out of our hands; we are gradually being demeaned; and the educational media field, once our domain, is now either too important to be left to educational media specialists or too insignificant to admit the importance – or even the existence – of the need for an educational media specialist, except as he temporarily may be useful as a technician in repairing a projector, hooking up a TV set, or, in extreme cases, locating a film that the librarian could not find.

Let us first make the case for progress toward professionalization within DAVI. In January 1952 there was no *Audiovisual Communication Review.* As of this year, AVCR appears in Volume 13, embracing almost 60 issues, including six special supplements. In January 1952 *Educational Screen* was the official publication of DAVI and, as such, carried little professional content directly related to the concerns of the organization. Nineteen hundred and sixty-five marks the tenth year of publication of DAVI's own professional magazine, AUDIOVISUAL INSTRUCTION.

In the span of about 13 years, the publication program of DAVI has had some remarkable successes, topped by the monumental Lumsdaine and Glaser work, *Teaching Machines and Programmed Learning: A Source Book,* and by the subsequent publication of *Teaching Machines and Programed Learning, II: Data and Directions.* There have been yearbooks, monographs, and other substantial contributions, such as the Williams' book, *Learning from Pictures.* By any standard, the publications program argues that tremendous professional growth and success have been achieved.

A list of other outstanding successes can readily be put together: the growth and increasing influence of the national conventions; the contributions of the Okoboji conferences; the effect of the influential joint media conferences held with ASCD in 28 states a few years ago under a Title VII contract; the invitations to representatives of DAVI to participate in meetings overseas; and the great influence of DAVI thinking in the Educational Media Council (at one time there were five DAVI past presidents sitting on the Council).

The list could go on to embrace legislative activities and many other important contributions. A word should be said concerning DAVI's relationship with the NEA hierarchy and with the complex of NEA affiliated organizations. Over the last 13 years or so, because the Division of Audiovisual Instructional Service of the NEA and the Department of Audiovisual Instruction were, in effect, one and the same, the counsel of the educational media specialist has been heard increasingly in the general educational community; in some cases, as with the current copyright situation, leadership for the whole educational community has fallen to us.

So far the discussion has centered principally upon the professional growth of the field through activities and developments within DAVI and its symbiotic partner, the NEA Division. There are, of course, many elements within the overall field of instructional technology itself that project change, growth in importance, and the move toward professionalism. In that same January of 1952 used as a benchmark before, educational television did not exist except on paper; teaching machines and programed instruction had not been exhumed from their premature burial at Ohio State University 20 years earlier; the language laboratory was a gleam in its developers' eyes; computers were discussed in popular science articles as "giant electronic brains" with no conceivable relation to education; and even such simple devices as the overhead transparency projector (over a decade old at the time) were almost unknown to the majority of American educators.

Money, which is equivalent to energy, was inserted into American education during the years following 1952 by the great foundations and the federal government for the development and use of audiovisual communications devices and materials. Title III of the National Defense Education Act, for example, which provided the school systems of America with a great deal of equipment and materials, forced a certain amount of professional direction upon both state departments of education and school districts. Title VII, the research and dissemination title, had been expanding the intellectual horizons of the media field since its first implementation in 1958 or 1959. Other legislative programs associated with the Great Society concept of the Johnson administration are all having these same effects.

In response, professional programs for training and development have shown some increase. At this writing, approximately 20 NDEA fellows are working on doctorates in the educational communications field in four institutions of higher education. There were over 35 institutes for educational media specialists in the summer of 1965, funded under Title XI of the NDEA. Other graduate programs within a small cluster of institutions have shown increases. Placement requests for instructional technologists with the doctorate are impossible to fill at the present time.

Finally, the professional organizations have grown as well. DAVI had approximately 1,200 members in 1952. It now enrolls 6,000. The National Association of Educational Broadcasters was reorganized and refinanced during this period and has now become very powerful. The National Society for Programmed Instruction was founded. Both NAEB and NSPI have engaged in joint projects with DAVI. The Educational Media Council was created about 1961 and now includes representatives of 14 national organizations and maintains headquarters in Washington, D.C. Professional organizations outside of the field, such as the American Association of Colleges for Teacher Education and the Association for Higher Education, have become interested in media.

Space prevents a further catalog of events, organizations, and achievements which point to great professional development on the part of the educational communications field. Enough has been said, however, to make the case. And the case sounds great. The only trouble with the case is that it is true only if you look at it from the optimistic side. *For the paradox in which we live our professional lives is that while things professional in the audiovisual field seem very good, they are also very, very bad.*

Let us now make the case for retrogression of professional development in audiovisual communication. When I use the term "retrogression," in a way I mean it to be thought of in a "what-might-have-been" sense. The positive development of the field described above *did* happen. However, while it was happening, somebody else picked up and carried off most of the balls in the park. We had a few short years — from about 1952 to about 1958 — to achieve true professional status and, at least, give some effective professional direction to the field. The truth of the matter is that we didn't make it. At this writing it remains in the balance whether we ever will.

The case for retrogression may be seen most clearly by examining two factors: the downgrading of the educational media field by the U.S. Office of Education and the complete lack of attention given to educational media at the White House Conference.

THE DOWNGRADING OF THE EDUCATIONAL MEDIA FIELD BY THE U.S. OFFICE OF EDUCATION

The Commissioner of Education, Francis Keppel, recently reorganized the U.S. Office of Education. In the process, he wiped out the Educational Media Branch, separating the functions of Title VII-A (Research) and Title VII-B (Development-Dissemination) within the larger bureaucracy. At least for Title VII-B projects, the monitoring of the projects will be scattered throughout the Office; for example, the monitor of the new contract of the Educational Media Council is to be a nonmedia person.

The Commissioner never replaced Walter Stone, head of the Media Branch, after he left the USOE a few years ago. Seth Spaulding, Thomas Clemens, and John Gough all occupied the position on an acting basis. Several other excellent professionals have paraded swiftly through the Media Branch, either back to where they came from or on to better things, notably Gerald Torkelson and Hugh McKeegan. Obviously, if Commissioner Keppel had had a real concern for the media field, he would have obtained and appointed a permanent head long ago and made conditions such that the parade of experts might have stopped short of a general exodus. Now the Commissioner doesn't need to concern himself — the Branch is gone.

The Commissioner's recent decision not to allow the proposed revision of the *Educational Media Index* to continue as the unique partnership it was between the government, private industry (McGraw-Hill), and the Educational Media Council, but rather to force it into the public domain, was a direct blow at the field of instructional technology and a direct measure of the significance the field has within USOE thinking.

Finally, the support and conduct of the New Media Demonstration Center within the U.S. Office is almost a scandal. The Center was grandly conceived as a place where school people from the United States and abroad could see all types of new equipment and materials in a demonstration situation. To that end, many manufacturers and producers, with high hopes, I am sure, placed their equipment and materials in the Center. The Center has gradually declined into a sort of unofficial audiovisual service for USOE agencies, and the room is considered an adjunct meeting room for USOE staff functions. In my last two visits there, much of the demonstration equipment was piled into the corners gathering dust. I hasten to add that it was not the fault of the staff assigned to manage the operation. The staff was too small, overworked, and lacked the proper logistical support to do a good job. It can be concluded that the Commissioner does not even care about the public image the media field has within the U.S. Office of Education.

THE WHITE HOUSE CONFERENCE AND THE MEDIA THAT WEREN'T THERE

The much publicized White House Conference on Education held in July of this year erased any doubts as to the group not running American education for any person at all knowledgeable concerning the national educational scene. The New Educational Establishment which has been put together in the last 15 years was revealed in all its glory from Grandfather James Bryant Conant on down the line.

Although there were political, geographical, and other dimensions associated with the invitations in addition to educational eligibility, the fact remains that only two members of the old-line audiovisual field were invited as participants — and they were there by virtue of the fact that they had worked on the Educators for Johnson and Humphrey National Committee during the last campaign, not for their connections with the educational media field. As far as I know, the only other people associated one way or another with educational communications were a couple of programed learning specialists from industry, several big-time publishers, and, of course, Senator Benton and his associates from Encyclopaedia Britannica.[2]

The Program was also revealing. Many of the panel topics might or might not have had representatives from the media field, as, for example, "Pre-School Education." However, it would be expected that the two panels on educational innovation — one for elementary and secondary schools and one for higher institutions — ought to have had such representation since much of what is referred to as educational innovation either is or is related to educational technology. The closest one might come to this requirement was the fact that Alvin C. Eurich, formerly of the Fund for the Advancement of Education of the Ford Foundation, was on the panel for innovations in higher education. While Mr. Eurich has had more influence on the audiovisual field than most of us put together, it is stretching a point to consider him as a professional representative.

Further, the vice-chairman of the Conference in charge of these two panels, Ralph Tyler, director of the Center for Advanced Study in the Behavioral Sciences, could hardly plead ignorance. After all, his brother Keith has had his entire professional career in the educational broadcasting field, and one of Ralph Tyler's oldest friends is Edgar Dale. The conclusion is inescapable: from the point of view of the planners and directors of the White House Conference, the educational media field deserved no attention whatever.

One of the major addresses of the Conference was given by Mr. Tyler under the title, "Innovations in Our Schools and Colleges." In this address he did

---

[2] *William Harley, president of the National Association of Educational Broadcasters, was allowed in as an "observer" — one grade lower than a "participant."*

mention educational technology as one of five promising areas of innovation. It could be argued, therefore, that there was some consideration. However, from the professional point of view of people who have pledged their careers to educational media, his words are hardly comforting. Read this quotation carefully:

> At the present time, however, the yield from the innovative efforts (in educational technology) has been small. Too many of the projects undertaken have been guided by those whose training and competence are in the technology and they have not been wholly familiar with the educational tasks, the aims sought, the conditions of learning to be maintained, and the like. However, today some experiments have been started by persons who have the educational competence as well as having knowledge of the technology being used. We need many more efforts of this sort . . . [3]

Mr. Tyler is plainly saying that, in his opinion, the audiovisual or educational media professional isn't good enough and that other educators must take over his function.

There were also two consultants' papers (published prior to the Conference) which had bearing on the media field. These papers paralleled the two sections on innovation. One, by Lewis B. Mayhew of the Stanford School of Education, was concerned with innovation in higher education and devoted a great deal of space to the newer educational media. Professor Mayhew quoted extensively from the Stevens College report of 1959, a well-known document in our field. He also referred to some newer developments, such as Florida Atlantic University. Significantly, there is no evidence that Professor Mayhew was acquainted with the DAVI-AHE book on newer media in higher education. That, and his reliance on a 1959 statement in 1965 during a period of accelerating change, suggests that his acquaintance with our field and with the central literature is woefully inadequate. Of course, a scholar would not go looking for literature generated within a profession that he didn't know existed . . . and that is hardly his fault.

Dwight W. Allen, also of Stanford, prepared the paper on innovations in elementary and secondary education. He devoted about two paragraphs to media, but since he was considering innovation broadly, this seems fair enough. In general, he took the Trump position with respect to audiovisual communication devices and materials. *Nothing in either of these papers suggests the need for professional direction of media programs, the existence of a professional media literature, or even of media professionals.* The conclusion one is forced to come to is that, in the eyes of the Establishment, such media programs, after all, are pretty simple and can be managed by any amateur (with the possible help of a "technician").

Finally, the discussion in the two meetings on innovation merely reinforced the general trend of downgrading instructional technology. In effect, all of the discussion could be summarized as stating somewhere fairly early in the proceedings that there were such things as films, television, and teaching

---

[3] *Tyler, Ralph W. "Innovations in Our Schools and Colleges." White House Conference on Education: A Milestone for Educational Progress (printed for the use of the Committee on Labor and Public Welfare of the U.S. Senate). Washington, D.C.: Government Printing Office, 1965. p. 188.*

machines; that such things had their small place; and that it was now time to get on with the business of talking about innovation. If I may editorialize even more directly for the moment, I thought both innovation meetings were very poor, particularly when compared to the excellent coverage given the subject at the last DAVI national convention. The cavalier shunting of the audiovisual field to one side early in the meetings and the general low quality of the meetings themselves were especially horrifying under the circumstances, as when Mr. Tyler announced that 35 of the 50 state superintendents of public instruction were in that particular audience!

Quite a lot of wordage has been devoted to the White House Conference because it is significant as a bellwether for American education and will be for some time to come; and the media field, as a field or as a profession, came off badly. There were, it should be added, two positive factors — one minor and one major. The National Audio-Visual Association (NAVA) supplied the briefcases for the participants, and Vice-President Humphrey (still perhaps influenced by the Minnesota DAVI Convention) gave educational media a plug in his speech.

Basically, the White House Conference must be seen as an expression of the new power structure in American education — the New Educational Establishment. If the National Education Association, the loose coalition of state education associations, the chief state school officers, professors of education generally, and the American Association of School Administrators continue to think of themselves as *the* Educational Establishment (so often criticized in the decade beginning in 1950), they had better forget it. There is a New Educational Establishment, and what this power group thinks about educational media or audiovisual communication is absolutely crucial to the professional development of instructional technology.

Therefore, the New Educational Establishment and its general attitude toward and performance with educational media needs further exploration as a major part of the negative side of the professional paradox. And there are other elements, such as the absolutely decisive role of Jerrold Zacharias in media development, the disappearance of some of our old friends, the low condition of state-level audiovisual administration, the fundamental lack of understanding and support of our field among teacher and administrator organizations, etc.

Once these somewhat dismal factors have been explored in the next article, attention can be directed to the mixed and troublesome situation within the media profession itself. While we may not yet be in the position of appreciating our enemies more than our friends, we will probably get to that stage fairly soon. Such incidents as the recent anti-intellectual memorandum submitted by the Audio-Visual Education Association of California to the DAVI Delegate Assembly need to be scrutinized, as well as the state and nature of our training and certification programs, the national organization power struggle, the inability of the profession to develop standards, and the general commitment to footdragging.

After the exasperating state of affairs within the profession of instructional technology is located within the paradox of success and failure, the problem will have been defined. It then may be possible, in the concluding article, to suggest new dimensions for the marginal media man and how these dimensions may be drawn. All in all, it is an uncomfortable pattern of thinking that we face, but, if there is to be salvation in media, it will be because we persisted with, as the sportwriters say, a hard nose.

ROLE AND FUNCTION
OF THE AUDIOVISUAL SUPERVISOR

George Hammersmith

All professionals in education are, in reality, engaged in the same task of providing democratic teaching-learning situations through which and by which the student learns what the democratic-process is and how to use it.

In this report an effort will be made to show that the main role and function of a special supervisor is to use his specialty as a channel for promoting democratic living by helping to improve instruction through the more effective use of audiovisual aids or instructional materials.

The main function of the audiovisual supervisor is to see that the curriculum needs, as expressed through teachers' committees and the Curriculum Department, are provided; to have a visual aids building coordinator in each school as a vital connecting link; to encourage high school department chairmen to assist the visual aids building coordinator through the assistant principal in charge of curriculum; to work with the Curriculum Department as a consultant; to procure the best equipment; to conduct an in-service training program for teachers; and to make the teaching tools available.

The director of the Visual Aids Department is on the Curriculum Staff and directly responsible to the Assistant Superintendent in charge of the Curriculum Department. The director attends the many curriculum meetings as a curriculum member and specialist in teaching-tools matters.

The charge of the audiovisual supervisor is to perform the services of helping to make the curriculum alive by furnishing tested and approved instructional materials that are needed to serve the youngsters in a dynamic society.

The curriculum-coordinators, with the help of classroom teachers' preview committees, select the aids which best supplement the teaching units. In this

Reprinted with permission from: Hammersmith, George, "Role and Function of the Audiovisual Supervisor," EDUCATIONAL SCREEN, February, 1964.

manner text-films, slides, filmstrips, and other instructional materials are obtained for the various subject-areas and grade-levels as is done in textbook selection. Here is the statement governing this procedure in Toledo!

VISUAL EDUCATION ADVISORY COMMITTEES

1. Visual education advisory committees shall be set up as outlined below, the following areas: Kindergarten, Primary, Intermediate, Language Arts and English — Grades 7-12, Mathematics — Grades 7-12, Science — Grades 7-12, Foreign Language — Grades 7-12. (In other fields, the director of Visual Education will work with the supervisory staff.)

2. The functions of these committees will be:
   a) to evaluate, annually, the visual aids currently available through the Department, giving advice with regard to films which are essential and basic; identifying those which are of questionable value, either because they do not fit the curriculum or because they are out-dated; and suggesting curricular areas for which new materials should be found.
   b) to preview and evaluate new films and to make recommendations for purchase.
   c) to aid in determining the specific grade-level or subject in which a film has primary use.

3. It is expected that each committee will meet at least once each year in connection with 2(a) above, and such other times as are required for 2(b). (Some of the previewing could be localized.)

4. The Director of Visual Education shall be responsible for staff service to these committees: setting dates for meetings, sending out notices, keeping records of meetings.

5. The Director of Visual Education shall prepare a summary report covering the items in 2, based on the recommendations of the committees, by the end of each school year.

6. The Director of Visual Education will base his purchase orders on the recommendations of the advisory committees. These purchase orders and copies of the report referred to in 5 shall be submitted to the appropriate coordinator of instruction for approval prior to purchase.

7. The Advisory committees shall be appointed annually by the Assistant Superintendent-Instruction, in consultation with the coordinators of instruction and the Director of Visual Education. All members of the committees should be teachers of several years of experience in the Toledo Schools (so they will be familiar with our inventory) and be recognized for their skill in the utilization of visual aids. Each year there should be some members who carry over from the previous committees.

The kindergarten, primary and intermediate committees shall be composed of approximately ten members of the general supervisory staff.

THE CHANGING ROLE OF THE LIBRARIAN

Carolyn I. Whitenack

There is no more challenging and exciting field in which to work than the broad field of communications, nor is there any more important task than the management of knowledge — which is the business of librarians. Today we are witnessing extraordinary changes: the expansion of population, the development of entirely new fields of knowledge, the introduction of new techniques, and the spread of a literate "student" group comprising a wide age range. These changes shape our role as librarians; they are the challenges which we must now meet.

The first challenge is that of expanding populations. In his latest book, *People,* William Vogt has compared the growth of human population with the human pulse rate. "Count it for a few seconds," he suggests. "Assuming that you have a normal pulse beat, it will not quite keep up with the increase in world population. ... Every time your pulse throbs, the population of the world will have added more than one human being." Marston Bates has stated that somewhere between 80 and 100 individuals are born every minute — about 270,000 a day; and about 142,000 people die — a net gain of 128,000. A great challenge to librarians in every type of library is the marshalling of the forces of education and librarianship to raise the level of educational and technical competence of these large population groups. According to the Office of Education, the United States may well have over 260 million population by 1980 and close to 400 million by the end of the century. All or almost all of the increase in population between 1960 and 1980 will be in urban territory, most of it in metropolitan areas. This increase will leave between 75 and 80 per cent of our population in urban territory and almost 70 per cent in metropolitan areas. Within metropolitan areas, close to 60 per cent of the population will be in suburbs. These suburban industrial complexes will require high-level library and research support. Also the affluent middle classes living in these areas will continue to expect good library facilities and services. College and university enrollment in 1980 is projected to be between 3 and 3½ times the 1960 figure. The population will be younger in 1980 than in 1960, but the underlying long-term increase in the proportion 65 years of age and over will continue. The most striking development during the sixties and seventies will be the increase of 80 per cent in persons 18 to 29 years of age. Educational attainment levels will continue to rise so that, by 1980, the "average" adult 25 years of age and over will have received more than a high school education. By 1980 close to 60 per cent of the persons 18 years of age and over will be high school graduates; 10 per cent of those 22 years of age and over, college graduates. Our nonwhite population, mostly Negro, growing more

Reprinted by permission from the January, 1964, issue of the WILSON LIBRARY BULLE-TIN. Copyright ©1964 by The H. W. Wilson Company.

rapidly than the white population, will increase in importance and may well approach 13 per cent of the total by 1980. Many of these people are now located in metropolitan centers and are looking to libraries to improve their educational competence.

A large majority of these expanding populations are students – elementary, secondary and college students – monopolizing library services wherever they find them. As we have learned from the recent Conference Within a Conference at the 1963 ALA meeting in Chicago, lifelong education is making a "student" of every age level. Librarians must understand the goals and structures of the educational system of which the library is a part. Librarians must know what is involved in the complicated process of learning. At present we must acknowledge that we are poorly prepared to meet the psychological and sociological problems of the learner, as well as poorly equipped to meet the needs of these expanding populations: 18,000,000 Americans with no public library service; 10,000,000 students in schools without central libraries; 66 per cent of all elementary schools without libraries; over 75 per cent of our junior college libraries substandard by one or more norms and 55 per cent of our college libraries likewise substandard. And perhaps the greatest challenge is that these needs must be met with an estimated shortage of 100,000 professional librarians.

THE EXPANSION OF KNOWLEDGE

The expansion of knowledge is our second challenge. Recent reports concerning production and distribution of new information indicate a very rapid increase in volume as well as complexity of ideas and multiplicity of languages. Fields of knowledge unheard of a generation ago have become complete disciplines with journals, societies and specialization. This growth is just beginning. Half of all we know in science we have learned in the last ten years, according to Dr. J.A. Stratton, president of Massachusetts Institute of Technology. And he predicts that our scientific knowledge will double in the next five years and continue to multiply at an ever-increasing rate. Erection of an automated national science information center would "double the effectiveness of American scientists," Congress was recently told. Dr. F. Ellis Kelsey of the U.S. Public Health Service reported to a House education and labor subcommittee that the average scientist and researcher now spends "half of every working day in the library trying to find information already in existence, to advance his work." Cutting down that library time, by making information readily available through a computerized science data center, "would make our scientists twice as effective," he asserted. Though a real question has been raised by some librarians, especially Ralph Shaw, professor of Rutgers Graduate School of Library Service, as to the extent automation will help us, there will be ever-increasing need for effective management of many services in libraries. Certainly the problems of indexing and cataloging lend themselves to computer technolgoy. One example is the *Educational Media Index,* which is using the advantages of computer technology in assembling, controlling, storing and retrieving the information. The *Index* is being compiled by Educational Media Council and McGraw-Hill and will be published soon.

THE THIRD CHALLENGE

The third challenge involves new technology and new media in education. Mechanization and automation have been increasingly displacing human employees. Obsolescence is a continuing problem. All of us wish to "return to normality," but there can be no return to a less troubled past. Our crisis is here, now, present and demanding. With the mass media, TV, radio, books, newspapers, magazines and teaching machines, public opinion is very easily shaped. American society has created a flow of information unparalleled in its magnitude. For example, we have more television sets — 91 per cent of our homes — and we consume more newsprint — 90-95 per cent of our families take a daily newspaper — than all the rest of the world together.

The number and diversity of our magazines and the size of their circulation are nowhere else approached. Our research libraries are the largest and our public libraries with all their inadequacy are the most numerous, with the possible exception of the Soviet Union. Contrary to the general impression, the United States leads all nations in the per capita production of books. The intensified use of books in student reading may be the first mass use of books in our culture — a mass made up of individuals.

The daily flow of communication to Americans is certainly the largest in history. And it is a free flow, not under government control and probably less restricted by censorship than anywhere else in the world. In this complex society it is obvious that each person must receive a constant flow of information enabling him to adapt his behavior to changing requirements. Libraries, as always, will be among those places where man may explore the alternatives in making choices.

LIFELONG LEARNING

Related to this third challenge is the fourth: the challenge of organizing lifelong learning resources in school libraries, public libraries, college and university libraries and special libraries so that the "student" of whatever age will be served. The great numbers of students may call for drastic changes in technique. The greater degree of responsibility on the individual for self-direction and self-learning suggests that librarians must look for new approaches in organizing services so that students may pursue their inquiries.

In public education there are many new ways of structuring the curriculum. It has been said that changing the curriculum is like moving a cemetery: No matter how long what's there has been dead, it still has lots of friends. Of much importance are new ways of organizing instruction which have brought together educationists, psychologists, mathematicians and scientists to devleop a framework for the improvement of the teaching of mathematics and science. These specialists have developed a core of materials — films, filmstrips, tests, tapes and other laboratory materials for national distribution. Team teaching, individual carrels, clusters of learning centers and new devices such as two-way audio, two-way video, instructional television, electronic tapes, teaching machines and other modern technical tools, which Dr. Campion will develop more fully, demand special attention and planning for library use.

In the public schools with which I am most familiar, the following units are grouped in various administrative patterns: a textbook center, library and/or instructional materials center, film library, a radio and/or television unit, photographic laboratory, teaching machines center, language laboratory, multiple teaching center and the like. Often these are competitive in operations. In the interest of improving the quality of education, coordinating services and resources, and reducing the high cost of duplicate services, central organization of all types of materials is being explored and tried in schools, colleges, and in some public libraries. Professional standards and opinions of at least two national groups — The American Association of School Librarians and the Department of Audio-Visual Instruction — now call for improved service arrangements. Agreement has not yet been reached concerning numbers and kinds of "professional" jobs and types of special training and areas needed, but conferences, workshops and much discussion are in process. It is my opinion that communication is being improved and that appreciation of the special competencies of each specialist — librarians, audio-visual personnel, radio and television personnel, documentalists — in the broad field of communications is being enhanced. However, it will certainly require a broadening and deepening of library education to include the research and experimentation which librarians have too long neglected. Suffice it to say that there must be available all recognized forms of library materials, audio-visual resources, television, teaching machines, computers and newly developing tools such as sound slides and concept films so arranged and in such amounts as are needed in libraries for ready access by "students."

Never before in history, and in no other nation, have librarians been offered so great a feedom to throw their energy, their intelligence and their knowledge into constructive use. And never before have the stakes been so high. It is very easy to be afraid of chance and dissent. History furnishes no evidence that men who face challenges in fear and reaction survive to win great rewards. In fact nineteen of twenty-three civilizations of the world were not destroyed by forces from without, but by forces from within — a death of the spirit.

Our task is simply to organize a system of recording and managing knowledge in relation to current flow. This may mean information retrieval and automation. The real purpose of library automation is to accomplish with ease and efficiency those tasks which our present techniques either cannot do or have difficulty in performing. One suggested solution is the use of an electronic network that will tie in regional, national and even international sources and depositories based on a television-microfilm principle for interstation transfer. Automation will include centralized processing of books and non-book materials, book catalogs for certain bibliographic situations, and special projects similar to those shown at Library 21 with its Univac to carry on conversations with great minds of the past.

QUALITY IN THE PROFESSION

Another task facing librarians is the recruiting of quality as well as numbers in our profession. We must go beyond identifying promising young people — we must revise our curricula to make more learning opportunities available. Frankly,

I believe we should develop programs of training for various levels of service, perhaps similar to the Trump plan for improving secondary teaching staff. We need library technicians. We also need junior professionals, college graduates, primarily women, returning to the labor force after their children are in school, who take a basic core of courses or workshops in librarianship. We also need pre-professional education similar to the program at Purdue of pre-general and pre-technical librarianship, for the recruiting of good subject-matter specialists who complete the basic core and go immediately to graduate library school. Of course we will continue the fifth-year program; we need more sixth-year programs for specialization and the Ph.D. We also must improve our in-service training and retraining programs. Especially we must improve our professional education in new media and technology.

Librarians must tell "the library story" to win support for expanded library legislation. There is a fight for dollars — a fight for public support. Everyone is clamoring for attention. Who are the opinion makers in a community? Certainly a major group is its business men. This public is organized. They are a captive audience at lunch. You can tell your story. Be bold, be positive, be imaginative, be enthusiastic and be brief.

We need to encourage reflective thought and free inquiry. I believe with Congressman Judd that we are fighting a new kind of warfare in which you hold with arms and win with ideas and concepts. We must work to spread the doctrine of freedom. It would be tragic indeed if, after chasing the Russians to the moon, we should obstinately refuse to plan for a future here on earth. Our preoccupation with things, money and technical processes causes us to forget that fundamentally our main task is to work with people. If we want people to grow, to get new vision and to create a better society, we must bring people, community resources, money and new techniques together in a unified community, state, regional, national and world educational effort. Librarians can be key people in this effort. All we need is imagination in relating our task to our opportunity.

There is a limit to how much a man can eat, how many cars he can drive and how many suits he can wear, but there is no limit to what a man may know. If we as librarians will take a larger look at where mankind is today and if we would take an overview of librarianship, we might enlarge our vision to see the opportunity of transcending some of the limitations of space, time, money and personalities to reinforce the unity and interdependence of man. It would be fortunate indeed if we could say with Aeneas:

> Many of these things I saw
> And some of them I was.

I believe that we can improve the world, if not save it, through an enlightened generation. Life holds nothing more precious than the process by which, to the fullest stretches of which we are capable, we stretch our minds and hearts to see the opportunities before us. And on seeing these opportunities, may we have courage to act.

THE CHANGING ROLE OF THE AV DIRECTOR

Charles Singledecker

From equipment manager to the new role of educator specialist — the duties of the Audio-Visual Director in a school are changing completely. In the past, he has functioned primarily as a coordinator with teachers. Today, he is becoming a member of the instructional team and an integral part of pupil learning activities.

Increasingly, the Audio-Visual Director is being given the opportunity to help plan the methods by which the objectives of the school curriculum may be reached. Working closely with supervisors, principals, and administrators provides the director with the task of planning many avenues of learning for the student through the multimedia approach to learning.

In addition to coordinating teaching media, the new director-specialist is called upon to help select and provide materials and equipment for children to use for independent study, learning, and research. The reorganization of some libraries into total multimedia Learning Centers is a vital concern to the AV Director and demands a thorough understanding of the learning problems of pupils within his school or schools.

More than ever before, the AV Director functions as a teacher in large-group instruction of work-study skills, so pupils can learn to use efficiently all resources, facilities, and equipment. Often, the director instructs individuals or small groups so they can independently use each piece of equipment for research and in their classroom reports.

Working with teacher committees, the Audio-Visual Director helps to select new materials to be used in classrooms and in the Learning Center. His knowledge and judgment are the backbone of a successful teaching media program. Cooperation and planning with the teachers enable progress in pupil enrichment at all levels and with the use of all media. New teachers who need orientation into such programs find help from the audio-visual leader.

Along with the librarian, the new director works with helping students find information from the printed word and from many forms of projected visuals and listening lessons. His suggestions and recommendations help in the ordering and purchasing of new supplies, and he must see that materials and equipment are kept in good repair. The indexing and color coding of library index cards according to media also require his attention.

The Audio-Visual Director of today is aware that learning situations must be created; they are not miracles that just happen. Under the guidance and direction of his teacher, and with the help of the AV Director, the student learns to use the correct media to present his ideas.

Reprinted with permission from: Singledecker, Charles, "The Changing Role of the AV Director," THE INSTRUCTOR, June, 1965.

The multimedia approach, allowing pupils to use transparencies, tapes, filmstrips, records, and other aids, has created a more worthwhile learning situation, because of pupil involvement, than the past practice of entrusting only the teacher with materials and equipment. The information shared in a learning environment at school is furthered at home, because of children's eagerness to carry home both materials and equipment for the family to enjoy. The child who becomes an active participant, *both* at school and at home, will be helped to make desired changes in behavior and attitude.

The new role of the Audio-Visual Director demands a mind open to change and research. Because of the expanding duties, a knowledge of the curriculum from kindergarten through grade 12 is necessary, as well as a capability for working closely with many different personalities and methods of teaching. An understanding of teacher and pupil problems must be coupled with the philosophy that instruction depends upon the concept being taught, rather than upon the equipment being used.

Because instructional methods vary according to the needs of the pupils and the best talents of the teachers, there is no one criterion to serve all AV Directors or to guide the establishment of new Learning Centers. We must of necessity be flexible in any operational procedures and receptive to the implementation of innovations that will help us meet our needs.

However, Executive Secretary of The American Association of School Librarians, Dorothy A. McGinnis, has succinctly stated four "E's" which may act as a guide for us all.

1. *Economy* – Economy in a multimedia setting is achieved by careful selection and purchasing of materials and equipment under the supervision of teachers, librarians, and a skilled AV Director.

2. *Efficiency* – The Learning Center and the use of all equipment by pupils and teachers are planned and developed through careful organization in order to provide maximum efficiency.

3. *Excellence* – Knowledge of operation and findings of resources by pupils and teachers in an efficient organization results in excellence in services.

4. *Enrichment* – Enrichment is revealed in the total educational program when teachers put forth their best efforts and strive for improvement, and when students in turn are enriched by the many media of learning resources.

Many schools are becoming more and more interested in coordinating multimedia learning activities by their pupils into the regular curriculum. Such experiences are becoming an integral part of independent learning programs, and they are proving to be vital in single concept learning.

For many years we have used all sorts of materials and equipment in the classroom for instruction, but increased multimedia learning experiences by children develop a need and an interest for a greater and more flexible use of visual aids in more subject-matter areas. We have discovered the value of the use of varied learning tools in many areas where they were not used in the past. Some schools are now in the process of equipping every classroom with basic equipment for maximum availability and use. Teachers, therefore, more than ever, need careful instruction in the use of equipment as well as successful methods to use it as a teaching tool. The AV Director is being called upon to help coordinate and supply materials for almost all areas of the elementary school curriculum.

The new emphasis on elementary school libraries has brought about a noteworthy revitalization. Along with updating and renewing a well equipped school library, many are expanding to include all forms of research material.

Our research project in Shaker Heights has created interest in all parts of the country in creating Learning Centers within the present framework of school libraries. The development of such a center can be the "hallmark" of all learning activities within a school. We have found a Learning Center necessary to any concentrated program in developing independent work-study skills in grades four, five, and six.

The success of such a center depends upon the guidance, preparation, and organization done by teachers, principals, and the Audio-Visual Director in his new role of coordinator-teacher-specialist.

Section Seven

EVALUATION OF
AN IMC

DEVELOPING A SELF-EVALUATION INSTRUMENT FOR APPRAISING EDUCATIONAL MEDIA PROGRAMS*

William R. Fulton

In the past few years there have been unusual developments in the field of educational media and an increased interest among schools and colleges concerning the use of such media.[1] These developments have frequently occurred in response to immediate needs and pressures within the school or institution rather than in response to a long-range plan. Too often the school administrator is inclined to make assessments of the adequacy of his educational media program or to formulate plans intended to improve the organization, administration, and financing of a media program on only a short-term basis.

In order to evaluate adequately his educational media program, an administrator should possess accurate information about the current status of his program as well as other information that makes it possible for him to make valid judgments relative to his program. Too often this information is not readily available to the school administrator.

Consequently, when confronted with the problem of reactivating the consultant services of the Department of Audiovisual Instruction, the DAVI Consultant Service Committee decided that some effort should be made to develop an instrument which would enable a school administrator to appraise his own program and to determine whether he needed consultative help of a more scientific nature.

A proposal was submitted to the U.S. Office of Education for a grant for the purpose of developing criteria and an instrument which could be used by local school administrators to assess the value of their educational media programs.

* The study reported herein was performed pursuant to a contract with the United States Office of Education, Department of Health, Education, and Welfare, under the provisions of Title VII, Public Law 85-864.

[1] The term "educational media" as used in this article includes all of the equipment, materials, and services traditionally called "audiovisual materials" and all of the newer media such as television and programed materials.

Reprinted with permission from: Fulton, William R., "Developing a Self-Evaluation Instrument for Appraising an Educational Media Program," AUDIOVISUAL INSTRUCTION, January, 1966.

The proposal was subsequently contracted and funded through the University of Oklahoma. The objective of the contract was to develop and validate one or more instruments which could be self-administered and which would yield necessary information for determining the functional status of educational media programs in elementary and secondary schools of all sizes and in colleges and multi-purpose institutions of higher education.

Developing an instrument for evaluating educational media programs proved a difficult problem. The task was complicated by the fact that educational media programs vary markedly from one institution to another. Some faculty members use fewer media because of the nature of their fields, while others use more media because of their methods of teaching. Some use media at a high level of sophistication, while the level of utilization of others is much less sophisticated. These and other factors enter into a determination of the adequacy of an educational media program, and they also make it difficult to establish precise guidelines for judging a particular program. Nevertheless, there are fundamental elements which appear to be common to all educational media programs, and around these some guidelines were developed. Obviously, the first step in developing the evaluative instrument was to identify these common elements and to use them as a basis for the construction of the instrument.

The entire process of developing the instrument was undergirded with the concept that (1) evaluation is the process of ascertaining the value of something, which involves the passing of judgment on the degree of its worthiness, and that (2) the degree of validity of such a judgment is largely determined by the validity and comprehensiveness of the information available to the person making the judgment. This seemed to indicate that any evaluative instrument should be accompanied by criteria which would assist the evaluator in making judgments compatible with the purposes or goals of the program being judged. Consequently, in addition to developing an instrument through which a person might self-evaluate his own program, it seemed necessary to develop supportive information and documents which would bear upon the evaluative process.

To make a valid judgment concerning a local program, for instance, one should know which educational media are available to the particular school being evaluated. Thus, a comprehensive inventory checksheet was developed for use in gathering such information. The checksheet was designed to elicit detailed data relating to the components of the evaluative checklist.

In order to make valid judgments about a particular program, it was necessary also to develop some guidelines or criteria pertaining to those elements thought to be common to all educational media programs. The development of such criteria involved two major steps. One, a thorough review of the literature was made in an attempt to identify advocated criteria. This resulted in the compilation of an annotated bibliography for further use in developing criteria. The second step involved the use of a panel of consultants, all of whom were expert practitioners. The panel consisted of 12 prominent educational media people representing all areas of the country. Three consultants were from relatively small school systems, three from relatively large school systems, three from single-purpose institutions of higher education, and three from multi-purpose institutions.

Each consultant was requested to write a paper describing what he considered to be the characteristics of a model educational media program for the institution of the category he represented. After these papers were collated, the 12 consultants were called together for a one-week workshop designed to develop a list of criteria. Using the annotated bibliography and the collated list compiled from their papers, the consultants formulated some preliminary criteria, and a tentative decision was made relative to the format of the evaluative instrument.

The project staff then developed a tentative list of criteria and a tentative draft of a self-evaluative checklist and circulated these to the consultants for their criticism and suggestions, after which both the self-evaluative checklist and the criteria were revised.

The revised draft of the self-evaluative checklist was pilot tested in six school systems in widely separated geographical regions of the United States and in nine colleges and universities similarly located. Each pilot test was made in the presence of a member of the project staff, thus making it possible for him to identify unclear items and to clarify procedural problems in administering the instrument. On the basis of this experience, the instrument was again revised into what is thought to be a fairly valid instrument for evaluating an educational media program. Due to the differences in terminology peculiar to school systems and to institutions of higher education, it was found that two forms of the instrument would be necessary. For example, a school system is seldom referred to as an institution, and neither is a college referred to as a school system. Other than the variations in terminology, there is essentially no difference between the forms. Each form is designed to yield the kind of information which makes it possible for an administrator to infer the adequacy of his educational media program and to support the basis for developing a minimally acceptable program.

The self-evaluative checklist, the comprehensive list of criteria, and the comprehensive inventory checksheet were mailed to approximately 200 schools and institutions of higher education for field testing. The field test was self-administered, and one copy was returned to the project director for analysis. The results of this survey, along with comments from the evaluators, led to some minor revisions of the instrument. The results of the field test indicated the following: (1) the instrument is fairly reliable in yielding the kind of information on which judgments may be made; and (2) it is possible for a local school administrator to evaluate his own program and determine the strong and weak points. It is anticipated that the self-administrative nature of the instrument will motivate the administrator to improve his educational media program. This may be accomplished by local in-service self-effort or by calling in outside consultants.

Six elements identified as being essential to an adequate educational media program constitute the components or sections of the evaluative instrument: (1) administrative commitment to a system-wide or institution-wide educational media program; (2) educational media as an integral part of curriculum and instruction; (3) an educational media center; (4) adequate physical facilities for the use of educational media; (5) an adequate budget for the educational media program; and (6) an adequate educational media staff. Each section is preceded by a brief statement of pertinent criteria selected from the more comprehensive list of criteria which accompanies the instrument.

Section I, dealing with the Commitment of the Administration to an Educational Media Program, involves five subtopics which include: (a) general commitment to educational media, (b) commitment to educational media as an integral part of instruction, (c) commitment to the provision of adequate facilities for educational media use, (d) commitment to adequate financing of the educational media program, and (e) commitment to adequate staffing for the educational media program.

Section II, entitled Educational Media Services and the Curriculum and Instruction, has four subsections: (a) consultative services in the use of educational media, (b) media services to educational preparation programs in school systems, (c) faculty-student use of educational media, and (d) involvement of media staff in planning.

Section III, concerning the Educational Media Center, includes six subtopics: (a) location and accessibility of educational media, (b) dissemination of information about educational media, (c) availability of educational media for instructional purposes, (d) storage and retrieval of educational media, (e) maintenance of educational media, and (f) production of educational media.

Section IV, Physical Facilities for Educational Media, deals with two subtopics: (a) facilities existing in classrooms already in use, and (b) educational media facilities for newly constructed classrooms.

Section V, Budget and Finance of the Educational Media Program, includes three subtopics: (a) reporting of financial needs to the administration, (b) basis on which budget allocations are made for educational media, and (c) developing the educational media budget.

Section VI, entitled Educational Media Staff, has one part for institutions of higher education which deals with the number and qualifications of staff necessary for an adequate educational media program and another part dealing with the educational media staff for the school system, which has two subtopics: (a) adequacy of the staff and quality of training of the staff for carrying on the educational media program at the central media center, and (b) quantity and kind of staff necessary for carrying on the educational media program in school buildings.

The seventh part of the instrument, the profile sheet, is designed to project an image of the particular program being evaluated. The evaluator may do this by simply transferring his responses from the evaluative checklist to the profile sheet and connecting them with straight lines. This depicts pictorially the peaks and valleys of attainment for the particular program being evaluated.

In order to complete the evaluative checklist, the respondent is required to continually formulate judgments as to the adequacy of his educational media program. The format of the evaluative checklist is not like that of the usual checklist which simply requires a response as to the presence or absence of something. Three different descriptions of situations that may prevail in educational media programs are presented for each program element included in the instrument. These three descriptive statements vary in the degree to which each meets the criteria on which the evaluative checklist is based.

The respondent selects the statement that best describes each element of his program and then judges whether that element of his program is on, above, or below the level of the situation described in the checklist. Example:

1	2	3	There is no full-time director of the media program.
4	5	6	There is a full-time director in charge of the media program.
7	8	9	There is a full-time director and a sufficient number of clerical and technical personnel.

The instrument and supportive information are now being used by the audio-visual coordinators of the state of Minnesota in a state-wide evaluation of their audiovisual programs. These materials are also being used for a similar purpose by the Oregon State Department of Education.

Copies of the instrument together with supportive information and forms may be obtained from the Department of Audiovisual Instruction, National Education Association, Washington, D.C. Single copies or quantity orders are available at prices subject to quotation.

SELECTING INSTRUCTIONAL MATERIALS FOR THE CLASSROOM

Mary Ellen Oliverio

The contemporary teacher would hardly believe that a few decades ago the teacher was fortunate if he had sufficient copies of a basic book for all the students in his class, for today the teacher faces a range of teaching materials that would leave the uninitiated overwhelmed and perplexed. The laboratory with individual stations, the tape recorder, the overhead projector, the opaque delineascope, the transistor radio, the 16 mm film, the 8 mm film — these are merely some of the devices available to transmit, display, present, and communicate a fast-growing body of knowledge on every subject in the modern school curriculum. This knowledge is in original documents of various types, in textbooks written expressly for certain students, in reports with varying points of view, in

Reprinted with permission from: Oliverio, Mary Ellen, "Selecting Instructional Materials for the Classroom," BALANCE SHEET, December, 1965.

data available from institutions of all types, in periodicals, and in scientific investigations. The task of selection of these instructional materials is indeed a formidable one, for the wisdom of the teacher in choosing will determine, to a large extent, the success of his students in fulfilling the objectives of the course.

The teacher who attempts to use dozens of materials and introduce students to a hundred devices for learning is likely to end the year with youngsters breathless from the confusion of competing aids to learning. Unfortunately, abundance of materials does not automatically assure a teacher of an enriched learning environment. To select haphazardly is foolhardy because the quality of present-day materials ranges from the useless to the highly valuable.

Two present dangers in use of instructional materials. One danger that the teacher faces as he makes decisions about instructional materials is that he will become so enamoured of each new publication or each new device that comes to his attention that he will purchase it and shortly thereafter incorporate it into his teaching scheme. The novelty of new devices is generally sufficient to prove them superior in initial attempts at determining the effectiveness of their use. However, the teacher must be wary of such claims and make his assessments on the basis of the best professional judgment he possesses.

The second danger that needs to be mentioned is that of concluding that one book or one teaching device is the best material on the market and that there is absolutely no need to introduce students to any other materials or new devices that are appearing on the educational market. The basic textbook, and in more recent years, the accompanying workbook have been standard materials for many years in American schools. The record of achievement of our students has not been a totally successful one. The teacher must select his instructional materials with an open mind and realize the possibility of there being better materials and better devices than he has used thus far.

The teacher's responsibility. With the multiplication of instructional materials available to our modern schools, some new departments and some new positions have been developed in the school system. There are schools that have given overall responsibility for materials to a director of a resource center. Other professional persons coordinate and supervise the purchase and use of audio-visual materials. Notwithstanding the professional assistance that is becoming available in increasingly more schools in the United States, the teacher must make the ultimate decision about what materials will be used in a particular course. Of course, there will be many instances when groups of teachers responsible for the same subject will want to make a decision together, for there may be reasons that justify the use of the same materials in the several sections of the same course.

To choose wisely, the teacher must have professional preparation of the highest degree. The teacher must have a high level of professional taste. We know, for example, that long before the successful interior decorator comes to the task of selecting fabrics and furniture for a particular room in a particular house, he has had training and experience with a wide range of interiors. His tastes have been developed to the point where his choices reflect an excellence in combining color and items of furniture that is pleasing to his client. So, too, before coming to the task of selecting appropriate materials, the teacher has had thorough preparation. The teacher, first of all, has had comprehensive study of the subject matter with which he now deals. A teacher of bookkeeping would not choose an instructional media which simplified the subject to the point of being inaccurate; a secretarial studies teacher, who knows the range of vocabulary that the top-flight secretary must possess, would not select materials for an advanced class when those materials deal only with the most commonly used words.

Second, the teacher thoroughly understands how learning takes place and the nature of experiences that students must have if the learning is to be meaningful. If the teacher feels, for example, that there must be considerable reinforcement of new learning, he will not choose a book that provides nothing more than a mere introduction to the material.

Third, the teacher must know the materials that are available. He must know the sources for keeping informed. He must know the places where he can expect to get useful reviews and evaluations of new materials. His professional magazines are an excellent source for information on new materials and devices; catalogues of publishing companies, brochures from institutes that represent many American industries, publications of large corporations are other possible sources. Periodicals such as *Audiovisual Instruction* and *Educational Screen and Audiovisual Guide* are two of several in the field that the teacher will find enlightening and useful in learning about the newest devices for teaching and in becoming aware of the multidimensional problem of choosing materials.

CRITERIA FOR SELECTION. While it would be possible to identify a long list of criteria for use in selecting materials, only five will be listed here. These are considered basic.

Criterion 1: *The material reflects sound scholarship and retains the vitality of the original ideas*. Possibly, this criterion is somewhat obvious. We see evidence of its awareness, however, in far too few places. Books and other materials that cite original documents, that indicate the unresolved areas in the field of scholarship, that identify conflicting points of view will not only tend to be more interesting to students, but will also give them more of the richness of the subject which they are studying. The social studies teacher who has students reading original documents in order to learn why the founding fathers of the town made certain decisions adds a special excitement to a class session. How much more interesting such materials will be to students than a general discussion in a textbook about early laws on the records of municipalities.

Criterion 2: *The material covers the topic or topics as intensively and extensively as the teacher feels is appropriate for the class*. Often materials which are available for use in our classrooms fail to provide sufficient detail to make meaningful a general statement. For example, in a high school textbook on salesmanship there was a paragraph devoted to the need to make a "good first impression." However, there was no explanation whatsoever of what might lead to a "good first impression." The student would gain no idea of how he could make such an impression when he attempted to sell a product.

We have heard a great deal in recent years about the need to develop an understanding of basic concepts. The teacher must review the material available to determine if there are sufficient examples and explanations to give students a full awareness of the basic concepts that are deemed important for a full knowledge of the subject matter.

Criterion 3: *The total material selected for the course fulfills the objectives for the course.* This criterion assumes that first the teacher has not only developed general objectives for his course, but he has made each of his general objectives sufficiently concrete so that he is able to make wise choices of materials.

For example, the teacher using the *Curriculum Guide for Business Education* for the Public Schools of Kansas City, Missouri, accepts the general objective "To develop an understanding of an appreciation for our capitalistic economic system." He finds a specific listing of business concepts related to this objective which includes:

1. Mercantilism gave way to capitalism.
2. Capitalism holds that individuals should have several kinds of economic freedom.
3. The hope for profit motivates production.
4. Business produces goods and services in the form in which they can be used and makes them available at a place where they can be used, and at a time when they can be used.[1]

Now, such a specificity of what concepts are to be included gives the teacher a guide in the selection of the materials. There is not to be implied here that the teacher selects wholeheartedly the objectives as outlined by someone else, but for purposes of illustration here, we might assume that our teacher has participated in the development of the material in the *Guide* and finds it appropriate for his students.

The teacher, then, comes to the task of selection with a list of fully meaningful objectives – ones that are unambiguous and appropriate. He is able, therefore, to base judgment of materials on a highly rational analysis.

Criterion 4: *The material selected is organized in a manner that enhances the development considered central for the course.* The teacher must not only understand the content that is appropriate for his course, but he must also have a full understanding of how the learning can best take place. Is the sequence of presentation psychologically sound? Is there sufficient reinforcement of the new learning? Does the material encourage thinking and the development of problem solving ability?

The teacher needs to understand what students will need as they learn. Bruner discusses aids to learning that provide vicarious experiences, that help students to grasp the underlying structure of a phenomenon, and that help students to automatize the learning.[2] The business teacher may find this categorization valuable as he determines the materials he will use. For example, a film that shows students how workers harvest coffee in Brazil can provide a valuable

---

[1] *Kansas City Public Schools, Curriculum Guide for Business Education, Secondary Bulletin No. 145 (Duplicated publication of Board of Education, Kansas City, Missouri Public Schools, 1964), pp. 179-183.*

[2] *Jerome Bruner, "Aids to Teaching," The Process of Learning (Vintage Books, 1963), pp. 81-92.*

vicarious experience of how people in another country earn a living. An experiment with textiles in a consumer economics class might enhance the learning of the composition of textiles and, thereby, lead to a far more meaningful understanding of the processes involved in the production of a particular textile. The use of programmed materials for students who are having difficulty reaching the next goal (or for those who have quickly mastered the goals thus far set) can provide for the reinforcement or the automatization of new skills.

The wide range of understandings, skills, attitudes, and appreciations that often are implicit in the objectives which the teacher sets means that the teacher must be fully cognizant of this criterion.

Criterion 5: *The total material selected for a given course reflects an awareness of the range of individual differences that will be present in the given class.* A teacher's commitment to a commonly accepted responsibility to make provisions for individual differences in his class is tacitly reflected in the materials he chooses. Are there sufficient materials for the talented student who may be able to go far beyond the typical student in the class? Are there sufficient materials for the slower student who must have the material presented several times, but possibly in different ways, in order to fully grasp its meaning? Are there materials for the student who develops an intense interest in a particular topic and wishes to probe in more detail? Are there materials appropriate for the student who finds it difficult to accept the point of view of the teacher's presentation?

The teacher who chooses wisely will not be leading students down a one-way road (and maybe one that is too narrow) for he will have overheads, bypaths, and sideroads to lead students in other directions, momentarily, so that they come back to the main stream of the course with an enrichment and an understanding that will be sustained long after the course is concluded.

THE IMPORTANCE OF SELECTION. There is far more vitality in the classroom where thought and attention have gone into every aspect of what takes place there. Indifference to the selection of materials can diminish this vitality seriously. As the teacher makes plans for a class, he must strive to select the best materials for optimum contribution to learning. He will use as few materials as are necessary for the quality of learning he strives to introduce to students. Only through experience and careful appraisal of his choices will he be able to judge his success — not only his success as a teacher but the success of his students as well.

REPORT CARD TIME

Neville Pearson

Periodically across the nation students receive reports on their school work. The tests have been given, scores averaged, and the grades assigned. Some will be in the average range. A few will make the honor roll.

Suppose there were an Audiovisual Instructional Materials Center Report Card for you on your work and program. How would you rate? Would you be on the honor roll, or might the record indicate that you had failed and would have to do the job all over again without having moved ahead with a bigger and better A-V media and materials utilization program?

Here are some questions on which an evaluation — a report card — might be based. If you can answer yes to most of the questions below, chances are that you could be a candidate for the A-V honor roll.

BASIC A-V SKILLS PERFORMANCE

Do you like your position?

Are you enthusiastic about your job?

Do you demonstrate creative leadership which results in better teaching and helps the teacher and the student?

Have you sold your administration on the importance of the audiovisual position?

What significant innovations or changes have you contributed to your school or effected with your faculty during the past school year?

Are you qualified for your position in terms of certification standards?

Are you allotted time to do your job? (Check state recommendations.)

What types of assistance are you allowed:

> Professional?
> Clerical?
> Technical?
> Student (part time)?

SUPERVISORY RESPONSIBILITY

Are you director of the media program for the entire school district?

Do you participate in curriculum planning?

Are you responsible for preparation and administration on the IMC budget?

Do you prepare proposals for federal funds?

Reprinted with permission from: Pearson, Neville, "Report Card Time," AUDIOVISUAL JOURNAL, Vol. 2, No. 5, May, 1968.

Do you administer federal funds granted to media programs?
Do you direct media research studies?
Do you help plan new building construction or remodeling?
Do you prepare in-service training programs? How many? How often? How effective are they?
How do you measure their contribution to your school system's objectives?

PROFESSIONAL DEVELOPMENT

Are you a member of professional organizations corresponding to your job assignment:

> Audiovisual Coordinators of Minnesota? (AVCAM)
> Department of Audiovisual Instruction?
> Minnesota School Library Association?
> American School Library Association?
> American Library Association?

Have you participated during the past year in:

> AV Institute?
> AVCAM meeting?
> DAVI national meeting?
> Regional AV meetings?
> MSLA meetings?
> ASLA meetings?
> ALA meetings?

Have you been active in AVCAM, DAVI, MSLA, ASLA?
Have you crossed over and joined or attended meetings of other professional groups?
Have you written and published articles during the past school year in a journal or periodical in the AV field? The library field? Other educational fields?
Do you read periodicals and publications regularly in the area of both A-V and library?
Have you started course work which will result in your certification as an audiovisual director? As a librarian?

MANAGERIAL MECHANICS

Does your equipment meet or exceed state recommendations?
Where do you exceed suggested state standards?
Do you have graphic production equipment? Do you have adequate space for production?
What AV materials have you produced locally:

> 16mm films?
> 8mm films?
> 35mm films?

Filmstrips or slides?

Transparencies (Total production — not just printing prepared masters)?

Audio tapes (Total production — not just recording from records or radio)?

Video tapes (Total production for instructional purposes)?

Do you have an IMC?

Does it really function with all materials available to all staff and all students in various modes of educational application?

Do you have a film library? (How large?)

Do you have a library of stored sounds? Does your center have listening stations?

How accessible to students are your AV materials?

Are all students instructed in the operation of equipment?

May students check out equipment and materials for use at home?

Have students been given an opportunity to produce tapes, transparencies, slides, motion pictures, or other such materials?

OPERATIONAL FACILITIES

Are all classrooms equipped for presentation of projected materials?

Is the AV center/IMC adequate in size to function effectively and efficiently?

Has your school allowed for the possible addition of TV, computer-assisted instruction, dial access sound or picture systems?

MATERIALS UTILIZATION

Do teachers use effectively the resources available to them?

Do teachers have the opportunity to rent materials from circulating libraries other than those within their local school system?

Do teachers participate in the selection of AV materials?

Do teachers have easy access to materials in your center?

Do students have access to class materials for individual viewing?

Do students have an opportunity to order materials which can help their individual interests or needs?

PUBLIC RELATIONS

Does the community know how instructional technology is being used in your school system?

Have you sold the community on experimental use of new materials?

*   *   *

Let us hope that more and more schools will find a place on the audiovisual honor roll.

SELECTED BIBLIOGRAPHY OF READINGS
OF THE IMC

Ahlers, Eleanor E. and Morrison, Perry D., "The Materials Center at the School District Level," LIBRARY TRENDS, vol. 16, no. 4, April, 1968, p. 446.

Alexander, Elenora, "The IMS Merger," LIBRARY JOURNAL, October 15, 1964, pp. 115-117.

_____,"Audio Center for the College of San Mateo," AMERICAN SCHOOL AND UNIVERSITY, July, 1964, p. 27.

Backin, Samuel, ed., "Higher Education: Some Newer Developments," McGraw Hill, 1965.

Buehler, Donald G., "How to Help Your Teachers Use the New Media," THE NATIONS SCHOOLS, July, 1962, p. 41.

Burget, Robert H., "Instructional Materials Center – Innovation, Motivation, Cooperation," SCHOLASTIC TEACHER, February 3, 1967.

Cleaves, Paul D., "Coordinated AV: Weymouth Instructional Materials Center," GRADE TEACHER, June, 1964, pp. 11-19, 64-75.

Conference on Training of Library Technical Assistants, "Library Technology in California Junior Colleges," Communication Service Corporation, Washington, D.C., 1968.

Congreve, Willard J., "Learning Center . . . Catalyst for Change?" EDUCATIONAL LEADERSHIP, January, 1964, p. 211.

Dane, Chase, "The School Library as an Instructional Materials Center," PEABODY JOURNAL OF EDUCATION, September, 1963, pp. 81-85.

Davis, Harold S., "Instructional Materials Center: An Annotated Bibliography," Educational Research Council of Greater Cleveland, Cleveland, Ohio, 1967.

Davis, John A., "What About the Media Administrator?" PEABODY JOURNAL OF EDUCATION, vol. 43 no. 4, January, 1966, p. 238.

Ely, Donald P., ed., "Functions of Personnel Within the Field," AV COMMUNICATION REVIEW, January-February, 1963, pp. 27-30.

Gardner, Dwayne E., "Educational Specifications for the School Library," ALA BULLETIN, February, 1964.

Gaver, Mary V. and Jones, Milbrey L., "Secondary Library Services: A Search for Essentials," TEACHERS COLLEGE RECORD, Columbia University, December, 1966, pp. 200-210.

Gerlach, Vernon S., "The Professional Education of the Media Specialist," AV COMMUNICATION REVIEW, Summer, 1966, pp. 185-201.

Grazier, Margaret Hayes, "What Happens in the School Library," ALA BULLETIN, February, 1964.

Grouix Harry J., "An Elementary Library Is Not Enough," MICHIGAN EDUCATION JOURNAL, February, 1963, p. 454.

Hall, Sedley D., "The Instructional Materials Center," THE ELEMENTARY SCHOOL JOURNAL, January, 1964, p. 210.

Harcleroad, Fred F., "The Education of the AV Communication Specialist," AV COMMUNICATION REVIEW, September-October, 1960, pp. 7-17.

Harding, Robert G., "You, Too, Can Have Distinctive AV Dispatches," AUDIO-VISUAL INSTRUCTION, March, 1963, p. 152.

Hartsell, Horace C., "The Teacher and the Instructional Materials Center," SCHOLASTIC TEACHER, February 3, 1967, p. 13.

Helms, Annie Lou, "The Creative Elementary School Library as a Materials Center," WILSON LIBRARY BULLETIN, October, 1962, p. 161.

Henne, Frances, "Standards for School Library Services at the District Level," LIBRARY TRENDS, vol. 16, no. 4, April, 1968, p. 502.

_____,"The Cost of Audio-Visual Instruction," SCHOOL MANAGEMENT, June, 1966, pp. 111-120.

Johnson, Frances Kennon and Bomar, Cora Paul, "Planning School Library Quarters," ALA BULLETIN, February, 1964.

Johnson, Frances Kennon and Bomar, Cora Paul, editors, "Case Studies in School Library Planning," ALA BULLETIN, February, 1964.

Johnson, Marvin R. A., "The High School Library — A Service and A Place," THE HIGH SCHOOL JOURNAL, November, 1966, pp. 91-95.

Johnson, Marvin R. A., "How the Architect Works," ALA BULLETIN, February, 1964.

Jones, R. C., "Multicampus Instructional Resources," JUNIOR COLLEGE JOURNAL, March, 1966.

Kelley, Gaylen B., "A Study of Teachers' Attitudes Toward Audiovisual Materials," EDUCATIONAL SCREEN AND AUDIOVISUAL GUIDE, March, 1960, p. 119.

Knade, Oscar, "A Library Is To Serve," ELEMENTARY ENGLISH, March, 1964, p. 289.

Konick, Marcus and Jenkins, Benjamin, "The Regional Instructional Materials Center In Pennsylvania," AUDIOVISUAL INSTRUCTION, September, 1966, pp. 554-557.

_____ , "AV Center Brings 'Pacemaker' Award to Penfield Schools," NEW YORK STATE EDUCATION, November, 1964, p. 15.

Michigan State Department of Public Instruction,"Planning the Instructional Materials Center for Elementary and Secondary Schools," Bulletin No. 422, Lansing: the Department, 1958.

Michigan State Department of Public Instruction, "Staffing the Instructional Materials Center in Elementary and Secondary Schools," Bulletin No. 427, Lansing: the Department, 1960.

Nelson, Ervin N., "Establishing and Operating the Audio-Visual Library," SCHOOL BOARD JOURNAL, April, 1963, p. 22.

Pearson, Neville P., "Instant Transparencies," EDUCATIONAL SCREEN AND AUDIOVISUAL GUIDE, March, 1961, p. 127.

Posner, A. N., "The Instructional Materials Center As A Means For Constructive Use Of Teachers' Talents," CALIFORNIA JOURNAL OF SECONDARY EDUCATION, April, 1960, pp. 250-251.

Preston, Ellinor G., "The Librarian Sees His Role in the Materials Center," EDUCATIONAL LEADERSHIP, January, 1964, p. 214.

Reed, Paul C., "Aids Is Obsolete: an editorial," EDUCATIONAL SCREEN AND AUDIOVISUAL GUIDE, November, 1963, p. 615.

Reid, Chandos, "The Instructional Materials Center — A Service Center for Teachers," THE HIGH SCHOOL JOURNAL, November, 1960, pp. 59-65.

Schofield, Edward T., "Materials Integration: Philosophy of the Future?" AUDIOVISUAL INSTRUCTION, February, 1962, p. 102.

Shores, Louis, "The Library Junior College," JUNIOR COLLEGE JOURNAL, March, 1966, vol. 36, no. 6, p. 6.

Shores, Louis, "If I Were President (of a Junior College)," MINNESOTA JUNIOR COLLEGE FACULTY ASSOCIATION Convention, Minneapolis, April, 26, 1968.

Snider, Robert C., "The Communications Specialist in the 1960's," AUDIO-VISUAL INSTRUCTION, February, 1962, pp. 96-99.

Solomon, Albert E., "AV- Outdated?" AUDIOVISUAL INSTRUCTION, April, 1963, p. 282.

Tanzman, Jack, "Multi-district Communication," SCHOOL MANAGEMENT, August, 1963, p. 63.

Witt, Paul W. F., "High School Libraries as Instructional Materials Centers," THE BULLETIN OF THE NATIONAL ASSOCIATION OF SECONDARY SCHOOL PRINCIPALS, November, 1959, pp. 112-118.

AUTHOR INDEX

JOURNAL INDEX